EVERYMAN, I will go with thee,

and be thy guide,

In thy most need to go by thy side

⋇ DANIEL DEFOE (FOE) ⋇

Born in St Giles about 1660. Joined Monmouth's army, 1685; William III's, 1688.
Employed in the Glass Duty Office, 1695–9.
Worked as journalist, pamphleteer, poet and
novelist. Toured Britain as government
agent. Died in 1731.

DANIEL DEFOE

A Tour Through the Whole Island of Great Britain

Introductions by
G. D. H. COLE
and
D. C. BROWNING

IN TWO VOLUMES
VOLUME ONE

DENT: LONDON
EVERYMAN'S LIBRARY
DUTTON: NEW YORK

© *Introduction to 'The Tour Through Scotland',*
J. M. Dent & Sons Ltd, 1962
All rights reserved
Made in Great Britain
at the
Aldine Press · Letchworth · Herts
for
J. M. DENT & SONS LTD
Aldine House · Bedford Street · London
First published in Everyman's Library 1928
Revised edition, with 'The Tour Through Scotland', 1962

NO. *820*

PREFATORY NOTE

To the Everyman edition of Defoe's *Tour Through England and Wales* there has now been added the section on Scotland, thus providing in two volumes the entire *Tour Through the Whole Island of Great Britain* published in 1724–6. The Scottish part is in some ways even more interesting than the rest, both because of the lack of other data about eighteenth-century Scotland and because of the critical period it covers in the relations of the two countries. Defoe's tour, which draws upon material gathered in the early years of the century, gives a full and well-informed account of conditions in Britain before and after the Union of the Parliaments in 1707.

A separate introduction has been provided for the new section, giving some account of the historical background and of Defoe's unique part in it, and a completely new index has been compiled for the entire work.

D. C. B.

1962.

INTRODUCTION TO THE TOUR
THROUGH ENGLAND AND WALES

BETWEEN the civil commotions of the seventeenth century and the great changes, political and economic, of the eventful years after Watt's steam engine and the French and American Revolutions lies a tract of time, well known to students of politics and literature, but for the economic historian still largely uncharted and unexplored. Economic histories, until the last few years, have been apt to deal fully with the days of Queen Elizabeth and then, after a half-hearted sally into the seventeenth century, to take a deep breath and leap straight to the Industrial Revolution. The "antecedents" of that revolution are, indeed, described; and we are told a good deal about the "Mercantile System" and the State's ways of regulating trade and commerce, and also a good deal about the so-called "Domestic System" in the textile industries. A famous passage from Defoe's *Tour*, which I am seeking to introduce to the modern reader, is often quoted, and hardly less often misunderstood, when the "Domestic System" is being described. We are told of Cromwell's Navigation Act, and, very hazily, of Walpole's economic reforms. The East India Company and the newly created Bank of England loom large in the background. But the picture of economic and social England in the Augustan Age is left woefully incomplete and more than a little misleading even in the best of the text-books. In all of them, there is too much about Mercantilism and the "Domestic System," and too little about the social and economic structure of the British community in this dawning time of the modern age.

Slowly, indeed, this defect is being put right. Historians who quarrel about the effects of the Industrial Revolution and its repercussions upon the working people are compelled to go back in search of evidence for the support of their several opinions. Mrs. George's scholarly *London Life in the Eighteenth Century* has been used by partisans as a counterblast to the alleged radical romanticism of the picture painted by Mr. and Mrs. Hammond in their books on the period of

vii

the Industrial Revolution. Was that period one of crushing severity, misfortune and degradation for the workers, or was it, on the contrary, one of chequered but indubitable economic and social advance? The question cannot be answered until we know what England in the late seventeenth and early eighteenth centuries was like; and, until quite recently, most of those who were active in the argument had hardly begun to know this.

Daniel Defoe's *Tour through the Whole Island of Great Britain*, though it makes no pretence of providing a detailed or accurate survey of the condition of the country, is by far the most graphic contemporary account of the state of economic and social affairs near the beginning of the eighteenth century. Read in conjunction with certain other books of its astonishingly industrious and versatile author—with his *Complete English Tradesman*, his *Plan of the English Commerce*, and his *Family Instructor*, for example—it does succeed in conveying an impression which no derivative history, however brilliant or scholarly, is ever likely to convey. For Defoe was, by temperament and way of life, extraordinarily well-fitted to paint the picture of that bustling time of economic and social transition in which he lived, and of which his own life was a remarkable manifestation. He wrote his *Tour*, indeed, in the guise of a popular guide-book; and as a guide-book it achieved a great success, passing through nine distinct editions between its first issue (1724–6) and 1778, and undergoing revision at the hands of several successive editors, of whom one was Samuel Richardson, the author of *Pamela* and of *Clarissa Harlowe*. These editors may have served their immediate purpose; but, from the standpoint of the modern reader they spoilt the book, and only Defoe's own edition, from which this reprint is made, will give him what he needs. For Defoe's book, though it served as a guide-book, was a good deal besides. He put into it not merely the usual descriptions of historic places and buildings, seats of the noblemen and gentlemen who were the unquestioned political rulers of the England of his day, picturesque scenes and anecdotes after the fashion of the times, and travellers' information of the approved sort, but also the things that interested him, and seemed to him significant of the great social transition he saw proceeding around him. So much did these latter things concern him that he was often perfunctory, and not seldom inaccurate, in providing the customary tourist's fare. In describing Oxford, for example, he annexed the Codrington Library to Magdalen instead of All Souls'; and slips of this sort are studded throughout the book. But this was because Oxford did not really interest him. He looked at England with the eye of a tradesman, appraising most things in the light of their contribution to the economics of the national life, and most people in accordance with their place in the economic rather than the social system. A gentleman's house interested him most when it was occupied by an upstart merchant or financier, a nobleman when he had married into trade. And so, while he might "mug up" his facts about the picturesque and the merely antiquarian out of some previous guide-book, and often get them wrong, he did not often make mistakes when he was describing what seemed to him really living and important.

Defoe's *Tour* is to be read, then, to-day above all for the light which it throws on the economic and social condition of England half a century or so before the coming of the Industrial Revolution. In the shadow of that great series of changes, the England that went before is apt to appear static and unchanging. The French Revolution in the realms of thought and government, the great inventions and the enclosure movement in the realm of economic life, so overshadow earlier developments as to hide their real significance. It is easy to fall into the belief that squirearchy was practically unchallenged before 1789, that agriculture and the "Domestic System" completely dominated economic life till the coming of Watt's steam engine and the great textile inventions, that the capitalist class was a product of steam and power-driven machinery, and that a proletariat was unknown until the advent of the "Factory System." Such beliefs can hardly survive a reading of Defoe's *Tour*. The England which he describes is, indeed, remote enough from the modern England of steam-power and joint-stock organisation; but it is even more remote from the half-primitive rural oligarchy which is often mistaken for a picture of the England of two centuries ago.

The England of Defoe's day was, doubtless, to a great extent static in a purely political sense. It had settled down to a period of stable government under a powerful landed aristocracy with a Hanoverian king. But this stability was very new, and the memory of the great troubles of the seventeenth century was fresh in men's minds. The Jacobites still seriously menaced it from the North; and the Union with Scotland, in the making of which Defoe played a not unimportant part, was but two decades old. The landed classes were firmly in the saddle; and some sort of toleration was beginning to be in fashion—sure sign of settling down. But the aristocracy could govern only on terms; and the chief condition of its power was that it should recognise the importance, and meet the needs, of the commercial interest. The men of substance in the business world were not yet making the claim to govern the country themselves. But they had no mind that it should be governed out of harmony with their views.

Everywhere in Defoe's book, the rapid rise of the mercantile classes confronts the reader as an outstanding social fact. London is rapidly ringing itself round with suburbs full of the substantial residences of successful tradesmen. One country seat after another is found to have passed into the possession of some great merchant, or to have been maintained by the foresight of its noble owner in marrying into trade. There are abundant signs of that salient characteristic of the English aristocracy of the eighteenth century—its success in absorbing and fusing its own interest with the upper strata of the commercial classes. This success has often been adduced in order to explain why, when France had a Revolution, Great Britain had only a constitutional and belated Reform.

The English political system was static in appearance, but in reality it was in process of constant adaptation. The rotten borough, owned by the "borough lord," was even on occasion a source of its power. For it enabled the merchant to buy his way into Parliament, and rise, by double purchase of seat and lands, into the charmed circle of the governing class. The French aristocracy closed itself to the new men, and was swept away: the English left the door open, and was able, not merely to avert revolution aud postpone reform, but even in large measure to hold its possessions and its prestige even when the inevitable reform came. Even after 1832, the English Parliament remained predominantly aristocratic. The events of the seventeenth century had saved the English aristocracy from exclusiveness, and had taught it to value power above exclusive privilege and ancestral prestige. It was already half commercialised in Defoe's day.

The trade and commerce of the early eighteenth century, on which the merchant class was rising swiftly to wealth and power, were of course widely different from the trade and

commerce of nineteenth-century England. For one thing, the
entire social configuration of the country was different. The
great centres of population were in the South and the Southern
Midlands: the North, though the wool industry was already
growing fast in the West Riding, the coal trade fully established round the Tyne, and Lancashire rising rapidly in
importance, was in comparison sparsely peopled. Save for
the widely spread provenance of the wool industry, manufacturers avoided, wherever possible, the interior of the
country, and gathered closely round the ports and navigable
rivers. Till the coming of the canals no other course was open.
The manufacturer who carried on his trade in the interior,
unless he served a purely local public, was sorely handicapped,
and found much ado in getting his wares to market. Defoe
comments, indeed, on the great progress made in the first
quarter of the eighteenth century in the construction of turnpike roads: but the turnpikes of his day were made for travellers
rather than for commodities, and served mainly the populous
residential areas of the South. The North and even the Midlands were still suffering under the handicap of roads which
the parishioners reluctantly maintained by throwing into the
quagmire a few hurdles, loose earth, and a cartload or two of
stones. Birmingham, for example, despite the enterprise of
its citizens, was held back all through the eighteenth century
by the inconvenience of its geographical situation.

We must learn, then, to see the map of England in a new
way in order to realise the effective shape of the country two
centuries ago. The mass of the people lived in the South. There
were the best agriculture, the most flourishing village life, the
main concentration of wealth and activity. There, too, were
the old-established centres of the wool industry in the Eastern
and South-Western Counties—the home of the "Domestic
System." The iron industry, though it was beginning to migrate
in search of fuel, was still vigorous in Sussex. Next to the merchants of London, the Bristol traders were still the foremost
in commerce, though Liverpool was growing fast, and Glasgow
was building up its trading connections with the American
colonies and the West Indies. All round the coast—but especially in the South—were studded little ports of vital significance
in the national life. For to these ports came, by road or river,
the merchandise of the interior, seeking ever the shortest route
to the sea, which afforded by far the cheapest and easiest means
of transport. Many of these little ports had their own commerce

with foreign lands; but most of them were chiefly occupied in carrying goods to the great ports of England itself — and above all to London. Coastwise shipping possessed an economic importance which it is hard to appreciate in a railway age.

London stood out pre-eminent. Again and again Defoe records, almost with awe, the overwhelming significance of the Metropolis in the life of the nation. Relatively to the rest of the country, London was even larger two centuries ago than it is to-day. And in it were concentrated a vastly greater share of the national wealth, and a far larger proportion of the national trade. Place after place, we are told, as Defoe journeys round the island, lives mainly by supplying the population of London with the means of life and luxury, or by ministering to London's demand for goods to send out into the markets of the world. London is by far the greatest consumer; and it is also an entrepôt centre of overwhelming importance in overseas commerce.

Overseas commerce itself looms large in Defoe's description. England was already a great exporter and importer of goods of many sorts. She specialised in the production of woollen goods designed to fit the needs and tastes of particular foreign markets. Her traders with the East Indies and the West Indies were already busy with their long and fertile rivalries and contentions. Defoe finds indeed ports that are silting up and falling into disuse. But this is not a sign of commercial decay, but itself an indication of the growth of commerce. The new merchant ships, tiny as they still were by more modern standards, were too big to get into the tinier ports of olden times. Trade was becoming concentrated as it developed; and the larger ports were busily providing better harbours to meet the expanding need.

Of the processes of production in industry Defoe as a rule tells his readers little, though there are, as we shall see, notable exceptions. In general, he is more interested in trade than in manufacture, in the buying and selling of goods than in their production. By far his best description of a productive industry is his famous account of the cloth manufacture in the West Riding; and even there he is far more concerned to tell us how the manufacturer gets his wares to market than how they are actually made. In this, he is the child of his time. Until the Industrial Revolution, the capitalist trader overshadowed the manufacturer, and far more fortunes were made by selling things than by directly undertaking their production. The "complete English tradesman"—by which he meant what we should now call "merchant" as well as shopkeeper—is the hero of Defoe's story.

Defoe is, indeed, the first great apologist of the English middle class. The man who appeals to him above all is one in the middle walk of life, with no frills or nonsense, engaged in making good by the useful art of trafficking in commodities of daily use. The small cloth manufacturers whom he describes in his account of the Yorkshire woollen industry were of this type. They were not, as some modern commentators seem to have imagined, simply skilled operatives working in their own houses under the "Domestic System." They were essentially small masters, capitalists in a small way, organising the business of production in workshops attached to their houses, employing weavers and other craftsmen to work for them in these workshops, as well as gathering the yarn spun for them by women and children in the surrounding cottages. Their homes were not labourers' cottages, but substantial, if small houses, and they were well enough to do to rank in the middle way of life. They had independent access to the market, and sold their wares to the merchants on equal terms. Of such men as these came the capitalists who, in a later generation, carried through the conversion of the Yorkshire industry to the factory system and to steam power. But in Defoe's day they were already small employers, as different as could be from the ordinary hand-loom weavers of the Eastern and Western Counties. It is precisely on the score of this difference that he so carefully describes them. They were types of the small bourgeoisie which seemed to him the backbone of England.

Very different is Defoe's account of the cloth industry in other parts. Sudbury, in Suffolk, an important manufacturing centre, is remarkable, he tells us, for nothing, "except for being very populous and very poor." Norwich is full of operatives working at their looms in the garrets of their homes: the Western Counties present the familiar contrast of rich clothiers and poor operatives working under the "Domestic System." The Yorkshire manufacture is described because it was the exception, and not the rule. The pushing small masters of the West Riding had already begun their successful competition with the old-established domestic manufactures of East and West. The new employer of the North was beating the capitalist merchant of the older centres by the superior economy of a workshop system that was the direct forerunner of the capitalist factory.

In short, Defoe depicts for us a society well adapted for the coming of the great changes of the next hundred years. In the seat of power was a governing class of landowners which had the foresight to recruit itself steadily out of the uppermost section of the trading community. Below these was an active, efficient and rapidly growing small middle class of lesser merchants, traders, shopkeepers and small industrial employers, full of confidence in itself and in its ability to take advantage of the rapidly expanding opportunities of amassing riches. This class consisted largely of Dissenters, and retained something of the Puritan tradition, especially in the intense individualism of its business outlook. It did not aspire to gentility, or to play a part in the exercise of political power; but it did mean to have freedom to develop its affairs in its own way, and it did mean to insist that the classes above it, linked to it in interest through the greater merchants and financiers, should govern in accordance with its desires. Defoe, himself a Dissenter and a political protagonist of the Dissenting interest, with direct experience as both trader and manufacturer—he had kept shop as a hosier and managed a tile factory—represents faithfully the political and economic outlook of this class. It is the class which a hundred years later took charge of the new force of steam, and formed the backbone of the middle-class demand for Radical Reform.

The England of 1724 is, then, very far from being adequately summed up as an agricultural country. Still, indeed, it fed itself; and agriculture was by far its most important means of life. But a large part of the population lived by trade and manufactures; and overseas commerce already counted for a great deal in the national life. The fact that by far the most important industry was the making of woollen goods served to prevent any sharp division between the agricultural and the industrial interest; for the raw material of the woollen industry was produced at home, and a good demand for wool sent up the landlords' rents. Hence, there was no such cleavage as occurred between the agriculturists and the cotton lords—whose raw material came from overseas—over the Corn Laws a century later. And the extent of industrialisation was further concealed by the prevalence in certain industries of the "Domestic System," which left many industrial workers scattered over the countryside, and still in close touch with the land. Many households in the eighteenth century subsisted partly by agriculture and partly on the proceeds of industrial work.

Inevitably, Defoe's *Tour* suggests a comparison with certain later books—not, indeed, with the picturesque tourists who were thick as flies as the eighteenth century advanced, but with Arthur Young and, above all, with Cobbett. Both Young and Cobbett were, however, interested mainly in the country-side, whereas Defoe hurries over the country to the nearest town or manufacturing village, pausing only to note here a picturesque beauty that must be recorded for guide-book reasons, and there a successful adoption in agriculture of commercial method, which interests him for its own sake. Cobbett and Young were essentially countrymen; but it is difficult to visualise Defoe except in a town. There is also this difference. Young and Cobbett both certainly went over every inch of the ground they described. Did Defoe? In all probability he did not. His book does not pretend to be a record of an actual journey, but a compilation of memories of journeys made over a considerable number of years. He probably describes some places which he never visited at all, and many others visited long before he wrote. But, even if he sometimes merely "cribbed" from previous guide-books, there is no doubt of the essential first-handness of his picture taken as a whole. He was for years employed by the Government as a sort of confidential agent, to spy out the land, and report the state of opinion in all parts of the country. In this capacity and in others, he journeyed far and wide, and un-doubtedly visited most of the areas which he describes, many of them on a number of separate occasions. Of course, every-one knows him for one of the world's greatest liars, with a peculiar art for making fictitious narrative sound like truth —as in the *Journal of the Plague Year*, the *Memoirs of a Cavalier*, and many others of his books. He would have been able, doubtless, to write a most plausible description of the Whole Island of Great Britain without ever stirring out of his lodgings in London. But in fact, we know, he did stir out of them a great deal; and for the most part, in his *Tour*, he did not need to draw on his faculty of invention, because he really knew the facts. It should be added that economic information is the one sort of information that Defoe seldom or never invents. He knew too much about it, and it interested him too much, to make it a suitable subject for promiscuous

lying. The reader need not suspect, because he finds out
Defoe in a dozen antiquarian inaccuracies, that his facts
about his own day and its business doings are equally un-
reliable. On these, where he can be checked from other sources,
he usually comes out right.

It is a remarkable fact that between 1778, when the Ninth
Edition appeared, and 1927, when I edited for Mr. Peter
Davies a large and beautiful reprint of the first edition (I can
say this safely, because the credit for its beauty belongs to
Mr. Davies and not to me), no new issue appeared. The book
was often quoted by historians; but commonly the same few
passages were quoted over and over again. Two small reprints,
each of a single short section, were indeed included by Professor Henry Morley in Cassell's National Library; but that
was all. As a guide-book, the *Tour*, despite frequent botchings,
inevitably went out of date; and meanwhile Defoe's text had
been so overlaid with insertions, and so damaged by omissions
as to lose its original quality. It is here presented as he
wrote it.

The *Tour* belongs to the last period of Defoe's life, which
is also by far the best of his career as a writer. Between 1719
and 1724, when the first volume appeared, he had published
*Robinson Crusoe, Memoirs of a Cavalier, Captain Singleton,
Moll Flanders, A Journal of the Plague Year, Colonel Jacque*
and *Roxana*—not to mention a host of minor writings—truly
an astonishing literary output for a period of little over five
years. From 1724 to 1728 he was occupied mainly with the
Tour, the *Complete English Tradesman*, the *Plan of the English
Commerce*, and other writings bearing directly on economic
and social questions. He died in 1731, about seventy years old.

G .D. H. COLE.

1928.

INTRODUCTION TO THE TOUR
THROUGH SCOTLAND

DEFOE'S account of his journeys in Scotland is in some ways the most interesting part of his *Tour Through the Whole Island of Great Britain*, because it deals with a little-known region. The most remote parts of England were sufficiently well known in the early eighteenth century, but Scotland up till that time was largely a *terra incognita*, and was even supposed by some Europeans to be a separate island. There had, of course, been earlier travellers in Scotland. In the fourteenth century Jean Froissart spent six months there, and wrote about it with picturesque garrulity. In the fifteenth Aeneas Silvius, later to become Pope, paid it a visit, and left a short account of the people. Ben Jonson travelled to Scotland in 1618, pursued by the scoffs of friends who thought him much too corpulent for such a journey; and a few weeks behind him came his humble acquaintance, John Taylor the Water-Poet, who entitled his narrative *The Penniless Pilgrimage* because he had undertaken to do the journey on foot like a modern hiker, and without a coin in his pocket. In 1655 Thomas Tucker was sent by Cromwell to make a commercial survey, with a view to the union which the Protector planned but did not live to bring about; and around the end of the century intelligent accounts of the country were published by two clergymen, James Brome and Thomas Morer, the latter being chaplain to a Scottish regiment.

The unique value of Defoe's work is due partly to the very important political developments of his time, partly to his own exceptional gifts and opportunities. As *A Journey Through Scotland* the work was first published in 1723, just sixteen years after the Union of the Parliaments of England and Scotland, and it embodies the results of investigations carried out during years that were among the most eventful in the history of Great Britain. Although the two kingdoms had been united a century earlier, when James VI of Scotland became also James I of England, the relation between them was still one of mutual suspicion, and there was no certainty that even the union of the Crowns would continue when the Stuart line came to an end. The Scots blamed the English for the Darien fiasco, and resented being debarred from English trading privileges, while the English were always on the watch for a revival of the old alliance between Scots and French. The Union was not popular in Scotland, where there was general apprehension that the smaller country would be absorbed in the larger one and its interests neglected. Both before and after the Act was passed in 1707 it was felt by many Scots that they had the worst of the bargain. The Treaty was at best a matter of practical expedience, with England trading commercial advantages for political safeguards.

In this most critical period Defoe played a dual role. He was sent to Edinburgh in 1706 as an agent of the English Government to find out the temper of the Scottish people and collect information useful for the direction of English policy; and at the same time he was to use his influence to persuade the Scottish public that the Union would be to their advantage. All this he was to do in the guise of a private individual, carefully concealing the fact that he was an official emissary of the English Secretary of State. Defoe adopted various "cover stories," posing now as a trader, now as a moneyed Englishman planning to invest in Scottish enterprises, while he was in reality a sort of combined propagandist and secret service agent. But it would be quite unfair to picture him as a spy in a hostile country. He had carried out the same task of gathering information in England, and he himself was quite sincerely convinced that the Union was in Scotland's best interests. It is because of his genuine sympathy with the Scots that his account of the country and people is so valuable.

In his own introduction to the narrative of the tour Defoe sets out his aims with admirable frankness. He promises to give a true picture of the Scots of his time, without either prejudice or flattery, giving the people due praise when they merit it, but not glossing over those failings that show them to lag behind the English in progress. Defoe was in fact extremely fair minded, and was as much alive to the defects of his own countrymen as to the good qualities of other nations. To the former he had borne witness in his lampoon *The True-born Englishman*, which pokes fun, somewhat in the manner of

W. S. Gilbert, at English complacency; and in 1706, the year before the Union, he published *Caledonia*, a poetic tribute to Scotland and its people. It is not a good poem; it is tedious and rambling, and weighed down with a profusion of elaborate footnotes to explain its classical and historical allusions. But it is complimentary throughout, and represents a sincere effort to propound a solution, through better methods and management, for Scotland's problem of poverty. Its main message is crystallised in the lines:

> Thus blest with art, enriched with heads and hands,
> Producing seas, and more productive lands;
> The climate sound, the people prompt and strong,
> Why is her happiness delayed so long?

For the part of inquiring traveller Defoe was ideally fitted. The fame and popularity of *Robinson Crusoe* has led him to be styled the father of the novel. But he was in an even truer sense the father of journalism. He had all the qualities of the successful journalist—power of close observation, facility in clear and vivid description, fluency in argumentative writing, and an unflagging energy which enabled him to pursue his objective through the most arduous obstacles and under the most difficult conditions. Above all, he had the gift of forming useful contacts and getting people to talk about themselves and their affairs. In one respect, however, he had the defects of his age; he had no appreciation of nature in her wilder aspects. The grandeur of Scottish scenery was wasted on him, even as it was half a century later on Dr Johnson, who regarded a towering peak as merely "a considerable protuberance." It was not until Walter Scott's time that the magnificence of Scottish mountain and loch began to be appreciated by the visiting tourist. The eighteenth century liked its landscape tamed and planned.

The actual itinerary of the tour must not be taken too literally, for Defoe was drawing on information obtained in the course of several visits, and indeed it is obvious at times that he had to go back on his tracks to describe alternative routes. Much of his space is given up to noting the houses and estates of the Scottish nobility, to whom he pays the compliment: "None in Europe better deserve the name of gentlemen." He praises the magnificence of such seats as Hamilton Palace and Drumlanrig, and when writing of Dunfermline observes that "the kings of Scotland had more fine palaces than most princes in Europe." Among the towns his first tribute is of course to Edinburgh, and he declares that its High Street "is perhaps the largest, longest, and finest street, for buildings and number of inhabitants, not in Britain only, but in the world." Its reputation for dirtiness he attributes to "the scarcity of convenient water and the crowded nature of the city." Glasgow, on the other hand, he considers "the cleanest and beautifullest and best built city in Britain, London excepted."

With the Scottish people in general, with their deep religious feelings, Defoe was the more readily in sympathy because he was himself a Dissenter, and had been educated for the Presbyterian ministry and pilloried for his religious pamphlets. In Scotland he attended an open-air congregation where the preacher went on for seven hours with a half-hour break for refreshments. He commends the Scots' strict observance of the Sabbath, and is at pains to point out that in Scotland it is the Episcopalians who must be styled Dissenters. He also pays tribute to Scottish hospitality. After his survey of the Lowlands he had some misgivings about travelling in the Highlands, where clan feuds and general lawlessness were not uncommon, but "cheerfully passed the Tay, trusting very much to that natural known civility which the Scots, in the remote parts, always show to strangers." More than once he speaks of the bravery of Scottish soldiers, and when commenting on their defeat at Dunbar he declares: "We must always blush when we pretend to say the Scots ever wanted courage in the field, let the cause, or the time, or the government be what, when, and how they will."

Throughout the work Defoe is extremely matter-of-fact and sensible. He gives practical suggestions about farming and forestry, in both of which Scottish methods were old-fashioned and inefficient. He recommends the cutting of a canal from the Forth to the Clyde. Above all, he is fully alive to the problems and results of the Union, of which, indeed, he published a valuable history in 1709. He foresees at once the tremendous benefit that will accrue to Glasgow from unrestricted trade with the American colonies. Glasgow being in the west is at a great advantage over southern English ports, because its ships "are oftentimes at the capes of Virginia before the London ships get clear of the Channel," and can save as much as a month on the round voyage. He foreshadows the tobacco trade which made Glasgow's "tobacco lords" of later decades so famous. Scottish wool trade, he admits, suffers from competition with the English product, of whose supreme economic importance in those days the Woolsack in the House of Lords still reminds us. But there is no reason, he argues, why Scottish methods should not be improved so that Scottish wool could command wider markets. Other benefits of the Union are obvious. The danger of crippling and expensive wars will be averted, and the burden of defence will fall on England, while taxes will be lighter and overseas trade more profitable. It is a well-reasoned and well-informed review of the most controversial issue of the time.

D. C. BROWNING.

1962.

SELECT BIBLIOGRAPHY

1691: *A New Discovery of an Old Intrigue* (verse).

1697: *Character of Dr Samuel Annesley* (verse).

1698: *An Essay upon Projects*; *An Enquiry into the Occasional Conformity of Dissenters*.

1700: *The Pacificator* (verse); *The Two Great Questions Considered*.

1701: *The True-born Englishman* (verse); *Legion's Memorial to the House of Commons*.

1702: *The Mock Mourners* (verse); *Reformation of Manners* (verse); *A New Test of the Church of England's Loyalty*; *The Shortest Way with the Dissenters*.

1703: *Ode to the Athenian Society* (verse); *An Enquiry into Asgill's General Translation*; *More Reformation* (verse); *A Hymn to the Pillory*.

1704: *The Storm*; *A Layman's Sermon on the Late Storm*; *An Elegy on the Author of the True-born Englishman*; *A Hymn to Victory*; *Giving Alms no Charity*.

1705: *The Consolidator or Memoirs of Sundry Transactions from the World in the Moon*; *The Experiment or The Shortest Way with the Dissenters Exemplified*; *The Double Welcome* (verse); *The Dyet of Poland* (verse).

1706: *A True Relation of the Apparition of one Mrs Veal*; *A Sermon on the Filling-up of Dr Burgess's Meeting-house*; *Jure Divino* (verse); *Caledonia* (verse).

1709: *History of the Union of Great Britain*.

1710: *An Essay on Public Credit*; *An Essay upon Loans*.

1712: *The Present State of Parties in Great Britain*.

1713: *A General History of Trade*.

1715: *An Appeal to Honour and Justice*; *The Family Instructor*; *History of the Wars of Charles XII*; *A Hymn to the Mob*.

1717: *Memoirs of the Church of Scotland*; *The Life and Death of Count Patkul*.

1718: *Memoirs of the Duke of Shrewsbury*; *Memoirs of Daniel Williams*; *The Family Instructor*, part ii.

1719: *The Life and Strange Surprising Adventures of Robinson Crusoe, of York, Mariner*; *The Farther Adventures of Robinson Crusoe*; *The Dumb Philosopher or Great Britain's Wonder* (Dickory Cronke); *The King of Pirates* (Captain Avery); *Life of Baron de Goertz*.

1720: *The Life and Adventures of Duncan Campbell*; *Memoirs of a Cavalier*; *The Life, Adventures, and Piracies of the Famous Captain Singleton*; *Serious Reflections during the Life and Surprising Adventures of Robinson Crusoe*; *The Supernatural Philosopher or The Mysteries of Magick*; Translation of du Fresnoy's *Compleat Art of Painting* (verse).

1722: *The Fortunes and Misfortunes of Moll Flanders*; *A Journal of the Plague Year*; *Due Preparations for the Plague*; *The Life of Dominique Cartouche*; *The History of Colonel Jacque*; *Religious Courtship*.

1723: *The Highland Rogue* (Rob Roy); *History of Peter the Great*.

1724: *The Fortunate Mistress* (Roxana); *Life of John Sheppard*; *The Robberies, Escapes, etc., of John Sheppard*; *The Great Law of Subordination or The Insolence and Unsufferable Behaviour of Servants in England*; *A Tour Thro' the Whole Island of Great Britain*, 3 vols. (1724–6).

1725: *A New Voyage round the World*; *Account of Jonathan Wild*; *Account of John Gow*; *Everybody's Business is Nobody's Business* (on servants); *The Complete English Tradesman*, part i.

1726: *The Friendly Demon*; *Mere Nature Delineated* (Peter the Wild Boy); *The Political History of the Devil*; *An Essay upon Literature*; *A System of Magic*; *The Protestant Monastery*; *The History of Discoveries* (1726–7)

1727: *Parochial Tyranny*; *Conjugal Lewdness*, and with new title, *A Treatise on the Use and Abuse of the Marriage Bed*; *The Complete English tradesman*, part ii; *A New Family Instructor*; *History and Reality of Apparitions*, and with new title (1728), *The Secrets of the Invisible World Disclosed*.

1728: *A New Family Instructor*; *Augusta Triumphans or The Way to make London the most Flourishing City in the Universe*; *A Plan of the English Commerce*; *Second Thoughts are Best* (on street robberies); *Street Robberies Considered*.

1729: *A Humble Proposal to the People of England for the Increase of Trade, etc.*; Preface to R. Dodsley's poem *Servitude*.

1731: *An Efficient Scheme for preventing Street Robberies*.

Besides the above-mentioned publications a large number of further tracts on politics, church matters, etc., are extant. Of Defoe's journalistic enterprises the most important was the *Review*, which he conducted from 1704 to 1713, writing nearly all of it himself.

The best collected edition of Defoe's works is the *Novels and Selected Writings*, published at Oxford, 1927–8, in fourteen volumes.

BIOGRAPHY. *Life of Defoe*, by George Chalmers, 1785; *Memories of the Life and Times of Daniel Defoe*, by Walter Wilson, 3 vols., 1830; *Life and Times of Daniel Defoe*, by Willian Chadwick, 1859; *Daniel Defoe: his Life and recently discovered Writings*, by William Lee, 1869; *Defoe* (English Men of Letters), by William Minto, 1879; *Life of Daniel Defoe*, by Thomas Wright, 1894; *Daniel Defoe: how to know him*, by W. P. Trent, 1916; *Defoe et ses romans*, by Paul Dottin, 1924; *Defoe*, by James Sutherland, 1937; *The Incredible Defoe*, by William Freeman, 1950; *Daniel Defoe, a Study in Conflict*, by Brian Fitzgerald, 1954; *Daniel Defoe, a Citizen of the Modern World*, by J. R. Moore, 1958.

CONTENTS

VOLUME ONE

THE AUTHOR'S PREFACE TO
THE FIRST VOLUME

If this work is not both pleasant and profitable to the reader, the author most freely and openly declares the fault must be in his performance, and it cannot be any deficiency in the subject.

As the work it self is a description of the most flourishing and opulent country in the world, so there is a flowing variety of materials; all the particulars are fruitful of instructing and diverting objects.

If novelty pleases, here is the present state of the country describ'd, the improvement, as well in culture, as in commerce, the encrease of people, and employment for them: Also here you have an account of the encrease of buildings, as well in great cities and towns, as in the new seats and dwellings of the nobility and gentry; also the encrease of wealth, in many eminent particulars.

If antiquity takes with you, tho' the looking back into remote things is studiously avoided, yet it is not wholly omitted, nor any useful observations neglected; the learned writers on the subject of antiquity in Great Britain have so well discharg'd themselves, that we can never over-value their labours, yet there are daily farther discoveries made, which give future ages, room, perhaps not to mend, yet at least to add to what has been already done.

In travelling thro' England, a luxuriance of objects presents it self to our view: Where-ever we come, and which way soever we look, we see something new, something significant, something well worth the travellers stay, and the writer's care; nor is any check to our design, or obstruction to its acceptance in the world, to say the like has been done already, or to pane-gyrick upon the labours and value of those authors who have gone before, in this work: A compleat account of Great Britain will be the work of many years, I might say ages, and may employ many hands: Whoever has travell'd Great Britain before us, and whatever they have written, tho' they may have had a harvest, yet they have always, either by necessity, ignorance or negligence pass'd over so much, that others may come and glean after them by large handfuls.

Nor cou'd it be otherwise, had the diligence and capacities of all who have gone before been greater than they are; for the face of things so often alters, and the situation of affairs in this great British Empire gives such new turns, even to nature it self, that there is matter of new observation every day presented to the traveller's eye.

The fate of things gives a new face to things, produces changes in low life, and innumerable incidents; plants and supplants families, raises and sinks towns, removes manufactures, and trades; great towns decay, and small towns rise; new towns, new palaces, new seats are built every day; great rivers and good harbours dry up, and grow useless; again, new ports are open'd, brooks are made rivers, small rivers navigable, ports and harbours are made where none were before, and the like.

Several towns, which antiquity speaks of as considerable, are now lost and swallow'd up by the sea, as Dunwich in Suffolk for one; and others, which antiquity knew nothing of, are now grown considerable: In a word, new matter offers to new observation, and they who write next, may perhaps find as much room for enlarging upon us, as we do upon those that have gone before.

The author says, that indeed he might have given his pen a loose here, to have complain'd how much the conduct of the people diminishes the reputation of the island, on many modern occasions, and so we could have made his historical account a satyr upon the country, as well as upon the people; but they are ill friends to England, who strive to write a history of her nudities, and expose, much less recommend her wicked part to posterity; he has rather endeavour'd to do her justice in those things which recommend her, and humbly to move a reformation of those, which he thinks do not; In this he thinks he shall best pay the debt of a just and native writer, who, in regard to the reader, should conceal nothing which ought to be known, and in regard to his country, expose nothing which ought to be conceal'd.

A description of the country is the business here, not discanting upon the errors of the people; and yet, without boasting, we may venture to say, we are at least upon a level with the best of our neighbours, perhaps above them in morals, whatever we are in their pride; but let that stand as it does, till times mend; 'tis not, I say, the present business.

The observations here made, as they principally regard the present state of things, so, as near as can be, they are adapted to the present taste of the times: The situation of things is given not as they have been, but as they are; the improvements in the soil, the product of the earth, the labour of the poor, the improvement in manufactures, in merchandizes, in navigation, all respects the present time, not the time past.

In every county something of the people is said, as well as of the place, of their customs, speech, employments, the product of their labour, and the manner of their living, the circumstances as well as situation of the towns, their trade and government; of the rarities of art, or nature; the rivers, of the inland, and river navigation; also of the lakes and medicinal springs, not forgetting the general dependance of the whole country upon the city of London, as well for the consumption of its produce, as the circulation of its trade.

The preparations for this work have been suitable to the author's earnest concern for its usefulness; seventeen very large circuits, or journeys have been taken thro' divers parts separately, and three general tours over almost the whole English part of the island; in all which the author has not been wanting to treasure up just remarks upon particular places and things, so that he is very little in debt to other mens labours, and gives but very few accounts of things, but what he has been an eye-witness of himself.

Besides these several journeys in England, he has also lived some time in Scotland, and has travell'd critically over great part of it; he has viewed the north part of England, and the south part of Scotland five several times over; all which is hinted here, to let the readers know what reason they will have to be satisfy'd with the authority of the relation, and that the accounts here given are not the produce of a cursory view, or rais'd upon the borrow'd lights of other observers.

It must be acknowledged, that some foreigners, who have pretended to travel into England, and to give account of things when they come home, have treated us after a very indifferent manner: As they viewed us with envy, so they have made their account rather equal to what they wish'd we should be, than to what we are; and wrote as if they were afraid the country they wrote to should be in love with us, and come away to live among us: In short, speaking of England, they have, like the

Israelitish spies, carried abroad a very ill report of the land: Seignior Gratiano a Spaniard, is one of those; he has given such a scandalous account of England in Spanish, as made a wiser man than himself, say, That if the history of England written by Augustin Gratiano had been written in the days of Philip II. and he had believ'd it to be true, he would never have thought it worth his while to fit out such an Armada for the conquest of it; but that it appear'd by King Philip's making that unfortunate attempt, that he was certainly better acquainted with it, than Gratiano.

It is worth no man's while to examine and confute foreign authors, whose errors are their ignorance. Our business is to give just ideas of our country to our readers, by which foreigners may be rightly inform'd, if they please to judge impartially; if any man will not be inform'd, we must write on that blindness, let him be ignorant.

But after all that has been said by others, or can be said here, no description of Great Britain can be, what we call a finished account, as no cloaths can be made to fit a growing child; no picture carry the likeness of a living face; the size of one, and the countenance of the other always altering with time: so no account of a kingdom thus daily altering its countenance, can be perfect.

Even while the sheets are in the press, new beauties appear in several places, and almost to every part we are oblig'd to add appendixes, and supplemental accounts of fine houses, new undertakings, buildings, &c. and thus posterity will be continually adding; every age will find an encrease of glory. And may it do so, till Great Britain as much exceeds the finest country in Europe, as that country now fancies they exceed her.

A TOUR
IN CIRCUITS, THROUGH
THE ISLAND OF GREAT BRITAIN

LETTER I

CONTAINING A DESCRIPTION OF THE SEA-COASTS OF THE COUNTIES OF ESSEX, SUFFOLK, NORFOLK, ETC., AS ALSO OF PART OF CAMBRIDGE-SHIRE

I BEGAN my travels, where I purpose to end them, viz. at the city of London, and therefore my account of the city itself will come last, that is to say, at the latter end of my southern progress; and as in the course of this journey I shall have many occasions to call it a circuit, if not a circle, so I chose to give it the title of circuits, in the plural, because I do not pretend to have travelled it all in one journey, but in many, and some of them many times over; the better to inform my self of every thing I could find worth taking notice of.

I hope it will appear that I am not the less, but the more capable of giving a full account of things, by how much the more deliberation I have taken in the view of them, and by how much the oftner I have had opportunity to see them.

I set out, the 3d of April, 1722, going first eastward, and took what I think, I may very honestly call a circuit in the very letter of it; for I went down by the coast of the Thames thro' the marshes or hundreds, on the south-side of the county of Essex, till I came to Malden, Colchester, and Harwich, thence continuing on the coast of Suffolk to Yarmouth; thence round by the edge of the sea, on the north and west-side of Norfolk, to Lynn, Wisbich, and the Wash; thence back again on the north-side of Suffolk and Essex, to the west, ending it in Middlesex, near the place where I began it, reserving the middle or center of the several counties to some little excursions, which I made by themselves.

Passing Bow-Bridge, where the county of Essex begins, the

first observation I made was, That all the villages which may be called the neighbourhood of the city of London on this, as well as on the other sides thereof, which I shall speak to in their order; I say, all those villages are increased in buildings to a strange degree, within the compass of about 20 or 30 years past at the most.

The village of Stratford, the first in this county from London, is not only increased, but, I believe, more than doubled in that time; every vacancy filled up with new houses, and two little towns or hamlets, as they may be called, on the forest side of the town, entirely new, namely, Mary-land-Point, and the Gravel-Pits, one facing the road to Woodford, and Epping, and the other facing the road to Illford: And as for the hither part, it is almost joined to Bow, in spite of rivers, canals, marshy-grounds, &c. Nor is this increase of building the case only, in this and all the other villages round London; but the increase of the value and rent of the houses formerly standing, has, in that compass of years above-mentioned, advanced to a very great degree, and I may venture to say at least a fifth part; some think a third part, above what they were before.

This is indeed most visible, speaking of Stratford in Essex; but it is the same thing in proportion in other villages adjacent, especially on the forest-side; as at Low-Layton, Layton-stone, Walthamstow, Woodford, Wansted, and the towns of West-Ham, Plaistow, Upton, &c. In all which places, or near them, (as the inhabitants say) above a thousand new foundations have been erected, besides old houses repaired, all since the Revolution: And this is not to be forgotten too, that this increase is, generally speaking, of handsom large houses, from 20l. a year to 60l. very few under 20l. a year; being chiefly for the habitations of the richest citizens, such as either are able to keep two houses, one in the country, and one in the city; or for such citizens as being rich, and having left off trade, live altogether in these neighbouring villages, for the pleasure and health of the latter part of their days.

The truth of this may at least appear, in that they tell me there are no less than two hundred coaches kept by the inhabitants within the circumference of these few villages named above, besides such as are kept by accidental lodgers.

This increase of the inhabitants, and the cause of it, I shall inlarge upon when I come to speak of the like in the counties of Middlesex, Surrey, &c. Where it is the same, only in a much greater degree: But this I must take notice of here, that this increase causes those villages to be much pleasanter and more sociable than formerly, for now people go to them, not for retirement into the country, but for good company; of which, that I may speak to the ladies as well as other authors do, there are in these villages, nay, in all, three or four excepted, excellent conversation, and a great deal of it, and that without the mixture of assemblées, gaming houses, and publick foundations of vice and debauchery; and particularly I find none of those incentives kept up on this side the country.

Mr. Camden, and his learned continuator, Bishop Gibson, have ransacked this country for its antiquities, and have left little unsearched; and, as it is not my present design to say much of what has been said already, I shall touch very lightly where two such excellent antiquaries have gone before me; except it be to add what may have been since discovered, which as to these parts is only this; That there seems to be lately found out, in the bottom of the marshes, (generally called Hackney-Marsh, and beginning near about the place now called the Wyck), between Old-Ford and the said Wyck, the remains of a great stone causeway, which, as it is supposed, was the highway, or great road from London into Essex, and the same, which goes now over the great bridge between Bow and Stratford.

That the great road lay this way, and that the great causeway landed again just over the river, where now the Temple-Mills stand, and passed by Sir Tho. Hickes's house at Ruckolls, all this is not doubted; and that it was one of those famous highways made by the Romans, there is undoubted proof, by the several marks of Roman work, and by Roman coins, and other antiquities found there, some of which are said to be deposited in the hands of the Revd. Mr. Strype, vicar of the parish of Low-Layton.

From hence the great road passed up to Layton-stone, a place by some known, now as much, by the sign of the Green-Man, formerly a lodge upon the edge of the forest; and crossing by Wansted House, formerly the dwelling of Sir Josiah Child, now of his son the Lord Castlemain, (of which, hereafter) went over the same river which we now pass at Ilford; and passing that part of the great forest which we now call Henault Forest, came into that which is now the great road, a little on this side the Whalebone, a place on the road so called, because a rib-bone of a great whale, which was taken in the river of Thames the same year that Oliver Cromwel died, 1658, was fixed there for a monument of that monstrous creature, it being at first about eight-and twenty foot long.

According to my first intention of effectually viewing the sea-coast of these three counties, I went from Stratford to Barking, a large market-town, but chiefly inhabited by fishermen, whose smacks ride in the Thames, at the mouth of their river, from whence their fish is sent up to London to the market at Billingsgate, by small boats, of which I shall speak by itself in my description of London.

One thing I cannot omit in the mention of these Barking fisher-smacks, viz. That one of those fishermen, a very substantial and experienced man, convinced me, that all the pretences to bringing fish alive to London market from the North Seas, and other remote places on the coast of Great Britain, by the new-built sloops called fish-pools, have not been able to do any thing, but what their fishing-smacks are able on the same occasion to perform. These fishing-smacks are very useful vessels to the publick upon many occasions; as particularly, in time of war they are used as press-smacks, running to all the northern and western coasts to pick up seamen to mann the navy, when any expedition is at hand that requires a sudden equipment: At other times, being excellent sailors, they are tenders to particular men of war; and on an expedition they have been made use of as machines, for the blowing up fortified ports and havens; as at Calais, St. Maloes, and other places.

This parish of Barking is very large; and by the improvement of lands taken in, out of the Thames, and out of the river which runs by the town, the tithes, as the townsmen assured me, are worth above 600*l.* per annum, including small tithes. Note, This parish has two or three chapels of ease, viz. one at Ilford, and one on the side of Henault Forest, called New Chapel.

Sir Tho. Fanshaw, of an antient Roman Catholick family, has a very good estate in this parish: A little beyond the town, on the road to Dagenham, stood a great house, antient, and now almost fallen down, where tradition says the Gunpowder Treason Plot was at first contriv'd, and that all the first consultations about it were held there.

This side of the county is rather rich in land, than in inhabitants, occasioned chiefly by the unhealthiness of the air; for these low marsh grounds, which, with all the south-side of the county, have been saved out of the River Thames, and out of the sea, where the river is wide enough to be call'd so, begin here, or rather begin at West-Ham, by Stratford, and continue to extend themselves. From hence eastward, growing wider and wider, till we come beyond Tilbury, when the flat country lyes six, seven, or eight miles broad, and is justly said to be both unhealthy, and unpleasant.

However the lands are rich, and, as is observable, it is very good farming in the marshes, because the landlords let good penny-worths, for it being a place where every body cannot live, those that venture it, will have encouragement, and indeed it is but reasonable they should.

Several little observations I made in this part of the county of Essex.

1. We saw passing from Barking to Dagenham, The famous breach, made by an inundation of the Thames, which was so great, as that it laid near 5000 acres of land under water, but which after near ten years lying under water, and being several times blown up has been at last effectually stopped by the application of Captain Perry; the gentleman, who for several year. had been employed, in the Czar of Muscovy's works, at Veronitza, on the River Don. This breach appeared now effectually made up, and they assured us, that the new work, where the breach was, is by much esteemed the strongest of all the sea walls in that level.

2. It was observable that great part of the lands in these levels, especially those on this side East Tilbury, are held by the farmers, cow-keepers, and grasing butchers who live in and near London, and that they are generally stocked (all the winter half year) with large fat sheep, (viz.) Lincolnshire and Leicestershire wethers, which they buy in Smithfield in September and October, when the Lincolnshire and Leicestershire grasiers sell off their stock, and are kept here till Christmas, or Candlemas, or thereabouts, and tho' they are not made at all fatter here, than they were when bought in, yet the farmer, or butcher finds very good advantage in it, by the difference of the price of mutton between Michaelmas, when 'tis cheapest, and Candlemas when 'tis dearest; this is what the butchers value themselves upon, then they tell us at the market, that it is right marsh-mutton.

3. In the bottom of these marshes, and close to the edge of the rivers stands the strong fortress of Tilbury, called Tilbury Fort, which may justly be looked upon, as the key of the river of Thames, and consequently the key of the city of London:

It is a regular fortification, the design of it, was a pentagon,
but the water bastion as it would have been call'd, was never
built; the plan was laid out by Sir Martin Beckman, chief
engineer to King Charles II. who also designed the works at
Sheerness. The esplanade of the fort is very large, and the
bastions, the largest of any in England, the foundation is
laid so deep, and piles under that, driven down two on end
of one another, so far, till they were assur'd they were below
the channel of the river, and that the piles, which were shod
with iron, entered into the solid chalk rock adjoyning to, or
reaching from the chalk-hills on the other side. These bastions
settled considerably at first, as did also part of the curtain, the
great quantity of earth that was brought to fill them up,
necessarily, requiring to be made solid by time; but they are
now firm as the rocks of chalk which they came from, and the
filling up one of these bastions, as I have been told by good
hands, cost the Government 6000*l.* being filled with chalk-
rubbish fetched from the chalk-pits at North-Fleet, just above
Gravesend.

The works to the land side are compleat; the bastions are
faced with brick. There is a double ditch, or moat, the inner-
most part of which is 180 foot broad, there is a good counterscarp, and a covered way marked out, with ravelins, and
tenailles, but they are not raised a second time after their
first settling.

On the land side there are also two small redoubts of brick,
but of very little strength, for the chief strength of this fort
on the land side consists in this, that they are able to lay the
whole level under water, and so to make it impossible for an
enemy to make any approaches to the fort that way.

On the side next the river, there is a very strong curtain,
with a noble gate called the water-gate in the middle, and that
ditch is pallisadoed. At the place where the water-bastion
was designed to be built, and which by the plan should run
wholly out into the river, so to flank the two curtains on each
side; I say, in the place where it should have been, stands a
high tower, which they tell us was built in Queen Elizabeth's
time, and was called the Block-house; the side next the water
is vacant.

Before this curtain above and below the said vacancy, is
a platform in the place of a counterscarp, on which are planted

106 pieces of cannon, generally all of them carrying from 24 to 46 pound ball; a battery, so terrible, as well imports the consequence of that place: Besides which, there are smaller pieces planted between, and the bastions and curtain also are planted with guns, so that they must be bold fellows who will venture in the biggest ships the world has heard of, to pass such a battery, if the men appointed to serve the guns, do their duty like stout fellows, as becomes them.

The present government of this important place is under the prudent administration of the Right Honourable the Lord Newbrugh.

From hence, there is nothing for many miles together remarkable, but a continued level of unhealthy marshes, called, the Three Hundreds, till we come before Leigh, and to the mouth of the River Chelmer, and Black-water. These rivers united make a large firth, or inlet of the sea, which by Mr. Camden is called *Idumanum Fluvium*; but by our fishermen and seamen, who use it as a port, 'tis called Malden-Water.

In this inlet of the sea is Osey or Osyth Island, commonly called Oosy Island, so well known by our London men of pleasure, for the infinite number of wild-fowl, that is to say, duck, mallard, teal and widgeon, of which there are such vast flights, that they tell us the island, namely the creek, seems covered with them, at certain times of the year, and they go from London on purpose for the pleasure of shooting; and indeed often come home very well loaden with game. But it must be remembred too, that those gentlemen who are such lovers of the sport, and go so far for it, often return with an Essex ague on their backs, which they find a heavier load than the fowls they have shot.

'Tis on this shoar, and near this creek, that the greatest quantity of fresh fish is caught, which supplies not this country only, but London markets also: On the shoar beginning a little below Candy Island, or rather below Leigh Road, there lies a great shoal or sand called the Black Tayl, which runs out near three leagues into the sea due east; at the end of it, stands a pole or mast, set up by the Trinity-House men of London, whose business is, to lay buoys, and set up sea marks for the direction of the sailors; this is called Shoo-Bacon, from the point of land where this sand begins, which is call'd Shooberry-Ness, and that from the town of Shooberry, which stands by it. From this sand, and on the edge of Shooberry, before it, or south-west of it, all along, to the mouth of Colchester Water, the shoar is full of shoals and sands, with some deep channels between; all which are so full of fish, that not only the Barking fishing-smacks come hither to fish, but the whole shoar is full of small fisher-boats in very great numbers, belonging to the villages and towns on the coast, who come in every tide with what they take; and selling the smaller fish in the country, send the best and largest away upon horses, which go night and day to London market.

N.B. I am the more particular in my remark on this place, because in the course of my travels the reader will meet with the like in almost every place of note through the whole island, where it will be seen how this whole kingdom, as well the people, as the land, and even the sea, in every part of it, are employ'd to furnish something, and I may add, the best of every thing, to supply the city of London with provisions; I mean by provisions, corn, flesh, fish, butter, cheese, salt, fewel, timber, &c. and cloths also; with every thing necessary for building, and furniture for their own use, or for trades; of all which in their order.

On this shoar also are taken the best and nicest, tho' not the largest oysters in England; the spot from whence they have their common appellation is a little bank called Woelfleet, scarce to be called an island, in the mouth of the River Crouch, now called Crooksea Water; but the chief place where the said oysters are now had, is from Wyvenhoo and the shoars adjacent whither they are brought by the fishermen, who take them at the mouth of, that they call, Colchester Water, and about the sand they call the Spits, and carry them up to Wyvenhoo, where they are laid in beds or pits on the shoar to feed, as they call it; and then being barrelled up, and carried to Colchester, which is but three miles off, they are sent to London by land, and are, from thence, called Colchester oysters.

The chief sort of other fish which they carry from this part of the shoar to London, are soals, which they take sometimes exceeding large, and yield a very good price at London market: Also sometimes midling turbet, with whitings, codling, and large flounders; the small fish as above, they sell in the country.

In the several creeks and openings, as above, on this shoar, there are also other islands, but of no particular note, except Mersey, which lies in the middle of the two openings, between

Malden Water and Colchester Water; being of the most difficult access, so that 'tis thought a thousand men well provided, might keep possession of it against a great force, whether by land or sea; on this account, and because if possessed by an enemy, it would shut up all the navigation and fishery on that side: The Government formerly built a fort on the south-east point of it: And generally in case of Dutch war, there is a strong body of troops kept there to defend it.

At this place may be said to end what we call the Hundreds of Essex; that is to say, the three hundreds or divisions, which include the marshy country, viz. Barnstaple Hundred, Rochford Hundred, and Dengy Hundred.

I have one remark more, before I leave this damp part of the world, and which I cannot omit on the womens account; namely, that I took notice of a strange decay of the sex here; insomuch, that all along this county it was very frequent to meet with men that had had from five or six, to fourteen or fifteen wives; nay, and some more; and I was inform'd that in the marshes on the other side the river over-against Candy Island, there was a farmer, who was then living with the five and twentieth wife, and that his son who was but about 35 years old, had already had about fourteen; indeed this part of the story, I only had by report, tho' from good hands too; but the other is well known, and easie to be inquired in to, about Fobbing, Curringham, Thundersly, Benfleet, Prittlewell, Wakering, Great Stambridge, Cricksea, Burnham, Dengy, and other towns of the like situation: The reason, as a merry fellow told me, who said he had had about a dozen and half of wives, (tho' I found afterwards he fibb'd a little) was this; That they being bred in the marshes themselves, and season'd to the place, did pretty well with it; but that they always went up into the hilly country, or to speak their own language into the uplands for a wife: That when they took the young lasses out of the wholesome and fresh air, they were healthy, fresh and clear, and well; but when they came out of their native air into the marshes among the fogs and damps, there they presently chang'd their complexion, got an ague or two, and seldom held it above half a year, or a year at most; and then, said he, we go to the uplands again, and fetch another; so that marrying of wives was reckon'd a kind of good farm to them: It is true, the fellow told this in a kind of drollery, and mirth; but the fact, for all that, is certainly true; and that they have abundance of wives by that very means: Nor is it less true, that the inhabitants in these places do not hold it out, as in other countries, and as first you seldom meet with very antient people among the poor, as in other places we do, so, take it one with another, not one half of the inhabitants are natives of the place; but such as from other countries, or in other parts of this county settle here for the advantage of good farms; for which I appeal to any impartial enquiry, having myself examin'd into it critically in several places.

From the marshes, and low grounds, being not able to travel without many windings, and indentures, by reason of the creeks, and waters, I came up to the town of Malden, a noted market town situate at the conflux or joyning of two principal rivers in this county, the Chelm or Chelmer, and the Blackwater, and where they enter into the sea. The channel, as I have noted, is call'd by the sailors Malden-Water, and is navigable up to the town, where, by that means, is a great trade for carrying corn by water to London; the county of Essex being (especially on all that side) a great corn country.

When I have said this, I think I have done Malden justice, and said all of it that there is to be said, unless I should run into the old story of its antiquity, and tell you it was a Roman colony in the time of Vespasian, and that it was call'd Camolodunum. How the Britons under Queen Boadicia, in revenge for the Romans ill usage of her, for indeed they used her majesty ill; they stripp'd her naked, and whipped her publickly thro' their streets for some affront she had given them; I say, how for this, she rais'd the Britons round the country, overpowered, and cut in peices the Tenth Legion, killed above eighty thousand Romans, and destroyed the colony; but was afterwards overthrown again in a great battle, and sixty thousand Britons slain. I say, unless I should enter into this story, I have nothing more to say of Malden, and as for that story, it is so fully related by Mr. Camden, in his history of the Romans in Britain, at the beginning of his *Britannia*, that I need only refer the reader to it, and go on with my journey.

Being obliged to come thus far into the uplands, as above, I made it my road to pass thro' Witham, a pleasant well situated market-town, in which, and in its neighbourhood, there are as many gentlemen of good fortunes, and families, as I believe can be met with in so narrow a compass in any of the three counties, of which I make this circuit.

In the town of Witham dwells the Lord Pasely, eldest son of the Earl of Abercorne of Ireland, (a branch of the noble family of Hamilton, in Scotland:) His Lordship has a small, but a neat well built new house, and is finishing his gardens in such a manner, as few in that part of England will exceed them.

Nearer Chelmsford, hard by Boreham, lives the Lord Viscount Barrington, who tho' not born to the title, or estate, or name which he now possesses, had the honour to be twice made heir to the estates of gentlemen, not at all related to him, at least one of them, as is very much to his honour mention'd in his patent of creation. His name was Shute, his uncle a linnen draper in London, and serv'd sheriff of the said city, in very troublesome times. He chang'd the name of Shute, for that of Barrington, by an Act of Parliament, obtain'd for that purpose, and had the dignity of a baron of the kingdom of Ireland conferr'd on him by the favour of King GEORGE. His lordship is a Dissenter, and seems to love retirement. He was a Member of Parliament for the town of Berwick upon Tweed.

On the other side of Witham, at Fauburn, an antient mansion house, built by the Romans, lives Mr. Bullock, whose father married the daughter of that eminent citizen, Sir Josiah Child of Wansted, by whom she had three sons, the eldest enjoys the estate, which is considerable.

It is observable, that in this part of the country, there are several very considerable estates purchas'd, and now enjoy'd by citizens of London, merchants and tradesmen, as Mr. Western an iron merchant, near Kelvedon, Mr. Cresnor, a wholesale grocer, who was, a little before he died, nam'd for sheriff at Earls Coln, Mr. Olemus, a merchant at Braintree, Mr. Westcomb, near Malden, Sir Thomas Webster at Copthall, near Waltham, and several others.

I mention this, to observe how the present encrease of wealth in the city of London, spreads it self into the country, and plants families and fortunes, who in another age will equal the families of the antient gentry, who perhaps were bought out. I shall take notice of this in a general head, and when I have run thro' all the counties, collect a list of the families of citizens and tradesmen thus established in the several counties, especially round London.

The product of all this part of the country is corn, as that of the marshy feeding grounds mention'd above, is grass, where their chief business is breeding of calves, which I need not say are the best and fattest, and the largest veal in England, if not in the world; and as an instance, I eat part of a veal or calf, fed by the late Sir Josiah Child at Wansted, the loyn of which weigh'd above 30*l.* and the flesh exceeding white and fat.

From hence I went on to Colchester: The story of Kill Dane, which is told of the town of Kelvedon, three miles from Witham, namely, That this is the place where the massacre of the Danes was begun by the women, and that therefore it was call'd Kill-Dane. I say of it, as we generally say of improbable news, it wants confirmation. The true name of the town is Kelvedon, and has been so for many hundred years. Neither does Mr. Camden, or any other writer I meet with worth naming, insist on this piece of empty tradition, the town is commonly called Keldon.

COLCHESTER is an antient Corporation; the town is large, very populous; the streets fair and beautiful; and tho' it may not be said to be finely built, yet there are abundance of very good and well-built houses in it: It still mourns, in the ruins of a civil war; during which, or rather after the heat of the war was over, it suffer'd a severe siege; which, the garrison making a resolute defence, was turn'd into a blockade, in which the garrison and inhabitants also, suffered the utmost extremity of hunger, and were at last oblig'd to surrender at discretion, when their two chief officers, Sir Charles Lucas, and Sir George Lisle, were shot to death under the castle-wall. The inhabitants had a tradition, that no grass would grow upon the spot where the blood of those two gallant gentlemen was spilt; and they shew'd the place bare of grass for many years, but whether for this reason, I will not affirm; the story is now dropp'd, and the grass, I suppose, grows there as in other places.

However, the batter'd walls, the breaches in the turrets, and the ruin'd churches still remain, except that the church of St. Mary's (where they had the royal fort) is rebuilt; but the steeple, which was two thirds batter'd down, because the besieged had a large culverine upon it, that did much execution, remains still in that condition.

There is another church which bears the marks of those times, namely, on the south-side of the town, in the way to the Hithe, of which more hereafter.

The lines of contravallation, with the forts built by the besiegers, and which surrounded the whole town, remain very visible in many places; but the chief of them are demolish'd.

The River Coln, which passes through this town, compasses it on the north and east-sides, and serv'd in those times for a compleat defence on those sides. They have three bridges over it, one called North-Bridge, at the north gate, by which the road leads into Suffolk; one call'd East-Bridge, at the foot of the High Street, over which lies the road to Harwich, and one at the Hithe, as above.

The river is navigable within three miles of the town for ships of large burthen; a little lower it may receive even a royal navy: And up to that part called the Hithe, close to the houses, it is navigable for hoys and small barks. This Hithe is a long street, passing from west to east, on the south-side of the town; at the west-end of it, there is a small inter-mission of the buildings, but not much; and towards the river it is very populous; (it may be call'd the Wapping of Colchester;) there is one church in that part of the town, a large key by the river, and a good custom-house.

The town may be said chiefly to subsist by the trade of making bays, which is known over most of the trading parts of Europe, by the name of Colchester bays, tho' indeed all the towns round carry on the same trade, namely, Kelvedon, Wittham, Coggshall, Braintree, Bocking, &c. and the whole county, large as it is, may be said to be employ'd, and in part maintain'd, by the spinning of wool for the bay trade of Col-chester, and its adjacent towns. The account of the siege, anno 1648, with a DIARY of the most remarkable passages, are as follows, which I had from so good a hand, as that I have no reason to question its being a true relation.

A DIARY

OR, AN ACCOUNT OF THE

SIEGE AND BLOCKADE OF COLCHESTER
AN. 1648

On the 4th of June, we were alarm'd in the town of Colchester, that the Lord Goring, the Lord Capel, and a body of 2000 of the Loyal Party, who had been in arms in Kent, having left a great body of an army in possession of Rochester Bridge, where they resolv'd to fight the Lord Fairfax, and the Parliament army; had given the said General Fairfax the slip, and having pass'd the Thames at Greenwich, were come to Stratford, and were advancing this way: Upon which news, Sir Charles Lucas, Sir George Lisle, Col. Cook, and several gentlemen of the Loyal army, and all that had commissions from the king, with a gallant appearance of gentlemen voluntiers, drew together from all parts of the country, to join with them.

The 8th, we were further informed, that they were advanc'd to Chelmsford, to New Hall House, and to Witham; and the 9th, some of the horse arriv'd in the town, taking possession of the gates, and having ingeneers with them, told us, that General Goring had resolv'd to make this town his head quarters, and would cause it to be well fortified; they also caused the drums to beat for voluntiers; and a good number of the poor bay-weavers, and such-like people, wanting employment, listed: So that they compleated Sir Charles Lucas's regiment, which was but thin, to near 800 men.

On the 10th we had news, that the Lord Fairfax having beaten the Royalists at Maidstone, and re-taken Rochester, had pass'd the Thames at Gravesend, tho' with great difficulty, and with some loss, and was come to Horndon on the Hill, in order to gain Colchester before the Royalists; but that hearing Sir Charles Lucas had prevented him, had order'd his rendezvous at Billerecay, and intended to possess the pass at Malden on the 11th, where Sir Thomas Honnywood, with the county Trained Bands, was to be the same day.

18

The same evening the Lord Goring, with all his forces, making about 5600 men, horse and foot, came to Colchester, and encamping without the suburbs, under command of the cannon of St. Mary's Fort, made disposition to fight the Parliament forces, if they came up.

The 12th, the Lord Goring came into Colchester, viewed the fort in St. Mary's churchyard, order'd more cannon to be planted upon it; posted two regiments in the suburbs without the Head-Gate; let the town know he would take them into his majesty's protection; and that he would fight the enemy in that situation. The same evening, the Lord Fairfax, with a strong party of 1000 horse, came to Lexden, at two small miles distance, expecting the rest of his army there, the same night.

The Lord Goring brought in prisoners the same day, Sir William Masham, and several other gentlemen of the county, who were secured under a strong guard; which the Parliament hearing, order'd twenty prisoners of the Royal Party to be singl'd out, declaring, that they should be used in the same manner as the Lord Goring used Sir William Masham, and the gentlemen prisoners with him.

On the 13th, early in the morning, our spies brought intelligence, that the Lord Fairfax, all his forces being come up to him, was making dispositions for a march, resolving to attack the Royalists in their camp: Upon which, the Lord Goring drew all his forces together resolving to fight. The ingineers had offer'd the night before to entrench his camp and to draw a line round it in one night's time; but his lordship declined it; and now there was no time for it: Whereupon the general, Lord Goring, drew up his army in order of battle, on both sides the road, the horse in the open fields on the wings; the foot were drawn up, one regiment in the road; one regiment on each side, and two regiments for reserve in the suburb, just at the entrance of the town, with a regiment of voluntiers, advanc'd as a forlorn hope, and a regiment of horse at the Head-Gate, ready to support the reserve, as occasion should require.

About nine in the morning we heard the enemy's drums beat a march, and in half an hour more their first troops appeared on the higher grounds towards Lexden; immediately the cannon from St. Mary's fir'd upon them, and put some troops of horse into confusion, doing great execution; which, they not being able to shun it, made them quicken their pace, to fall on, when our cannon were oblig'd to cease firing, least we should hurt our own troops, as well as the enemy: Soon after, their foot appeared, and our cannon saluted them in like manner, and killed them a great many men.

Their first line of foot was led up by Col. Barkstead, and consisted of three regiments of foot, making about 1700 men, and these charged our regiment in the lane, commanded by Sir George Lisle, and Sir William Campion: They fell on with great fury, and were receiv'd with as much gallantry, and three times repulsed; nor could they break in here, tho' the Lord Fairfax sent fresh men to support them, till the Royalists horse, oppressed with numbers on the left, were obliged to retire, and at last, to come full gallop into the street, and so on into the town: Nay, still the foot stood firm, and the voluntiers, being all gentlemen, kept their ground with the greatest resolution: But the left wing being routed, as above, Sir William Campion was oblig'd to make a front to the left; and lining the hedge with his musqueteers, made a stand with a body of pikes against the enemy's horse, and prevented them entering the lane. Here that gallant gentleman was kill'd with a carabine shot; and after a very gallant resistance, the horse on the right being also over-power'd, the word was given to retreat; which however was done in such good order, the regiments of reserve standing drawn up at the end of the street, ready to receive the enemy's horse upon the points of their pikes, that the royal troops came on in the openings between the regiments, and entered the town with very little loss, and in very good order.

By this, however, those regiments of reserve, were brought, at last, to sustain the efforts of the enemy's whole army, till being overpower'd by numbers, they were put into disorder, and forced to get into the town in the best manner they could; by which means near 200 men were kill'd or made prisoners.

Encouraged by this success, the enemy push'd on, supposing they should enter the town pelmel with the rest; nor did the Royalists hinder them, but let good part of Barksteads own regiment enter the Head Gate; but then sallying from St. Mary's with a choice body of foot on their left, and the horse rallying in the High-street, and charging them again in the front, they were driven back quite into the street of the suburb, and most of those that had so rashly enter'd, were cut in pieces.

Thus they were repulsed at the south entrance into the town; and tho' they attempted to storm three times after that with great resolution, yet they were as often beaten back, and that with great havock of their men; and the cannon from the fort all the while did execution upon those who stood drawn up to support them: So that at last seeing no good to be done, they retreated, having small joy of their pretended victory.

They lost in this action Colonel Needham, who commanded a regiment call'd the Tower Guards, and who fought very desperately; Capt. Cox, an old experienc'd horse officer, and several other officers of note, with a great many private men, tho' as they had the field, they concealed their number, giving out, that they lost but an hundred, when we were assured, they lost near a thousand men besides the wounded.

They took some of our men prisoners, occasion'd by the regiment of Colonel Farr, and two more, sustaining the shock of their whole army, to secure the retreat of the main body, as above.

The 14th, the Lord Fairfax finding he was not able to carry the town by storm, without the formality of a siege, took his head quarters at Lexden, and sent to London, and to Suffolk for more forces; also he order'd the Trained Bands to be raised, and posted on the roads, to prevent succours; notwithstanding which, divers gentlemen, with some assistance of men and arms, found means to get into the town.

The very same night they began to break ground; and particularly, to raise a fort between Colchester and Lexden, to cover the generals quarter from the salleys from the town; for the Royalists having a good body of horse, gave them no rest, but scour'd the fields every day, falling on all that were found stragling from their posts, and by this means kill'd a great many.

The 17th, Sir Charles Lucas having been out with 1200 horse, and detatching parties toward the sea-side, and towards Harwich, they brought in a very great quantity of provisions, and abundance of sheep and black cattle, sufficient for the supply of the town for a considerable time; and had not the Suffolk forces advanced over Cataway Bridge to prevent it, a larger supply had been brought in that way; for now it appeared plainly, that the Lord Fairfax finding the garrison strong and resolute, and that he was not in a condition to reduce them by force, at least without the loss of much blood, had resolved to turn his siege into a blockade, and reduce them by hunger; their troops being also wanted to oppose several other parties, who had, in several parts of the kingdom, taken arms for the king's cause.

This same day General Fairfax sent in a trumpet, to propose

exchanging prisoners, which the Lord Goring rejected, expecting a reinforcement of troops, which were actually coming to him, and were to be at Linton in Cambridge-shire as the next day.

The same day two ships brought in a quantity of corn and provisions, and 56 men from the shore of Kent with several gentlemen, who all landed, and came up to the town, and the greatest part of the corn was with the utmost application unloaded the same night into some hoys, which brought it up to the Hithe, being apprehensive of the Parliaments ships which lay at Harwich, who having intelligence of the said ships, came the next day into the mouth of the river, and took the said two ships, and what corn was left in them. The besieg'd sent out a party to help the ships, but having no boats they could not assist them.

18. Sir Charles Lucas sent an answer about exchange of prisoners, accepting the conditions offer'd, but the Parliaments general returned that he would not treat with Sir Charles, for that he Sir Charles being his prisoner upon his parole of honour, and having appear'd in arms contrary to the rules of war, had forfeited his honour and faith, and was not capable of command or trust in martial affairs: To this Sir Charles sent back an answer, and his excuse for his breach of his parole, but it was not accepted, nor would the Lord Fairfax enter upon any treaty with him.

Upon this second message, Sir William Masham, and the Parliament committee and other gentlemen, who were prisoners in the town, sent a message in writing under their hands to the Lord Fairfax, intreating him to enter into a treaty for peace; but the Lord Fairfax returned, he could take no notice of their request, as supposing it forced from them under restraint; but, that, if the Lord Goring desir'd peace, he might write to the Parliament, and he would cause his messenger to have a safe conduct to carry his letter: There was a paper sent enclosed in this paper, sign'd Capel, Norwich, Charles Lucas, but to that the general would return no answer, because it was sign'd by Sir Charles, for the reason above.

All this while, the Lord Goring, finding the enemy strengthning themselves, gave order for fortifying the town, and drawing lines in several places, to secure the entrance, as particularly without the east bridge, and without the north-gate and bridge, and to plant more cannon upon the works: To which end, some great guns were brought in from some ships at Wevenhoe.

The same day, our men sally'd out in three places, and

attack'd the besiegers, first at their fort, call'd Essex; then at their new works, on the south of the town; a third party sallying at the east bridge, brought in some booty from the Suffolk troops, having killed several of their straglers on the Harwich road: They also took a lieutenant of horse prisoner, and brought him into the town.

19. This day we had the unwelcome news, that our friends at Linton were defeated by the enemy, and Major Muschamp, a loyal gentleman, kill'd.

The same night, our men gave the enemy alarm at their new Essex Fort, and thereby drew them out as if they would fight, till they brought them within reach of the cannon of St. Mary's, and then our men retiring, the great guns let fly among them, and made them run: Our men shouted after them; several of them were kill'd on this occasion, one shot having kill'd three horsemen in our sight.

20. We now found the enemy in order to a perfect blockade, resolv'd to draw a line of circumvallation round the town; having receiv'd a train of forty pieces of heavy cannon from the Tower of London.

This day the Parliament sent a messenger to their prisoners, to know how they far'd, and how they were used; who return'd word, that they far'd indifferent well, and were very civilly used, but that provisions were scarce, and therefore dear.

This day a party of horse with 300 foot, sally'd out, and marched as far as the fort on the Isle of Mersey, which they made a shew of attacking, to keep in the garrison; mean while the rest took a good number of cattle from the country, which they brought safe into the town, with five waggons loaden with corn: This was the last they could bring in that way, the lines being soon finished on that side.

This day the Lord Fairfax sent in a trumpet to the Earl of Norwich, and the Lord Goring, offering honourable conditions to them all; allowing all the gentlemen their lives and arms, exemption from plunder; and passes, if they desir'd to go beyond sea; and all the private men pardon, and leave to go peaceably to their own dwellings; but the Lord Goring and the rest of the gentlemen rejected it, and laughed at them: Upon which the Lord Fairfax made proclamation, that his men should give the private soldiers in Colchester free leave to pass through their camp, and go where they pleased without molestation, only leaving their arms, but that the gentlemen should have no quarter: This was a great loss to the Royalists, for now the men foreseeing the great hardships they were like to suffer, began to slip away, and the Lord Goreing was obliged to forbid any to desert on pain of present death, and to keep parties of horse continually patrolling to prevent them; notwithstanding which, many got away.

21. The town desir'd the Lord Goreing to give them leave to send a message to Lord Fairfax, to desire they might have liberty to carry on their trade and sell their bays and says, which Lord Goreing granted; but the enemy's general return'd, that they should have consider'd that before they let the Royalists into the town: That to desire a free trade from a town besieg'd, was never heard of, or at least, was such a motion, as was never yet granted: That however, he would give the baymakers leave to bring their bays and says, and other goods, once a week, or oftener, if they desire it, to Lexden Heath, where they should have a free market, and might sell them or carry them back again, if not sold, as they found occasion.

22. The beseig'd sally'd out in the night with a strong party, and disturb'd the enemy in their works, and partly ruin'd one of their forts, call'd Ewer's Fort, where the besiegers were laying a bridge over the River Coln; Also they sally'd again at East-Bridge, and faced the Suffolk troops, who were now declared enemies, these brought in six and fifty good bullocks, and some cows, and they took and kill'd several of the enemy.

23. The besiegers began to fire with their cannon from Essex Fort, and from Barksted's Fort, which was built upon the Malden road, and finding that the besieged had a party in Sir Harbottle Grimston's house, call'd, The Fryery, they fir'd at it with their cannon, and batter'd it almost down, and then the soldiers set it on fire.

This day upon the townsmen's treaty for the freedom of the bay trade, the Lord Fairfax sent a second offer of conditions to the besieg'd, being, the same as before, only excepting Lord Goring, Lord Capel, Sir George Lisle, and Sir Charles Lucas.

This day we had news in the town, that the Suffolk forces were advanc'd to assist the besiegers and that they began a fort call'd Fort Suffolk, on the north side of the town, to shut up the Suffolk road towards Stratford. This day the besieg'd sally'd out at North-Bridge, attack'd the out-guards of the Suffolk men on Mile-End Heath, and drove them into their fort in the woods.

This day Lord Fairfax sent a trumpet, complaining of chew'd

and poison'd bullets being shot from the town, and threatning
to give no quarter if that practice was allow'd; but Lord Goring
return'd answer, with a protestation, that no such thing was
done by his order or consent.

24th. They fir'd hard from their cannon against St. Mary's
steeple, on which was planted a large culverin, which annoy'd
them even in the general's head quarters at Lexden. One of
the best gunners the garrison had, was kill'd with a cannon
bullet. This night the besieg'd sally'd towards Audly, on the
Suffolk road, and brought in some cattle.

25. Lord Capell sent a trumpet to the Parliament-General,
but the rogue ran away, and came not back, nor sent any
answer; whether they receiv'd his message or not, was not known.

26. This day having finish'd their new bridge, a party of
their troops pass'd that bridge, and took post on the hill over-
against Mile-End Church, where they built a fort, call'd Fother-
gall's Fort, and another on the east side of the road, call'd
Rainsbro's Fort, so that the town was entirely shut in, on that
side, and the Royalists had no place free but over East Bridge,
which was afterwards cut off by the enemy's bringing their line
from the Hithe within the river to the Stone Causeway leading
to the east bridge.

July 1. From the 26th to the 1st, the besiegers continu'd
finishing their works, and by the 2d the whole town was shut
in; at which the besiegers gave a general salvo from their
cannon at all their forts; but the besieged gave them a return,
for they sally'd out in the night, attack'd Barkstead's Fort,
scarce finish'd, with such fury, that they twice enter'd the
work sword in hand, kill'd most part of the defendant's, and
spoil'd part of the forts cast up; but fresh forces coming up,
they retir'd with little loss, bringing eight prisoners, and having
slain, as they reported, above 100.

On the second, Lord Fairfax offer'd exchange for Sir William
Masham in particular, and afterwards for other prisoners, but
the Lord Goring refus'd.

5. The besieged sally'd with two regiments, supported by
some horse, at midnight; They were commanded by Sir George
Lisle; They fell on with such fury, that the enemy were put
into confusion, their works at East-Bridge ruin'd, and two
pieces of cannon taken, Lieutenant Col. Sambrook, and several
other officers, were kill'd, and our men retir'd into the town,
bringing the captain, two lieutenants, and about 50 men with
them prisoners into the town; but having no horse, we could

not bring off the cannon, but they spik'd them, and made them unfit for service.

From this time to the 11th, the besieged, sally'd almost every night, being encourag'd by their successes, and they constantly cut off some of the enemy, but not without loss also on their own side.

About this time we receiv'd by a spy, the bad news of defeating the king's friends almost in all parts of England, and particularly several parties which had good wishes to our gentlemen, and intended to relieve them.

Our batteries from St. Mary's Fort and Steeple, and from the North-Bridge, greatly annoy'd them, and kill'd most of their gunners and fire-men. One of the messengers who brought news to Lord Fairfax of the defeat of one of the parties in Kent, and the taking of Weymer Castle, slip'd into the town, and brought a letter to the Lord Goring, and listed in the regiment of the Lord Capel's horse.

14. The besiegers attack'd and took the Hithe Church, with a small work the besieged had there, but the defenders retir'd in time; some were taken prisoners in the church, but not in the fort: Sir Charles Lucas's house was attack'd by a great body of the besiegers; the besieged defended themselves with good resolution for some time, but a hand-grenado thrown in by the assailants, having fir'd the magazine, the house was blown up, and most of the gallant defenders buried in the ruines. This was a great blow to the Royalists, for it was a very strong pass, and always well guarded.

15. The Lord Fairfax sent offers of honourable conditions to the soldiers of the garrison, if they would surrender, or quit the service, upon which the Lords Goring and Capel, and Sir Charles Lucas, returned an answer signed by their hands, that it was not honourable or agreeable to the usage of war, to offer conditions separately to the soldiers, exclusive of their officers, and therefore civilly desir'd his lordship to send no more such messages or proposals, or if he did, that he would not take it ill if they hang'd up the messenger.

This evening all the gentlemen voluntiers, with all the horse of the garrison, with Sir Charles Lucas, Sir George Lisle, and Sir Bernard Gascoign at the head of them, resolved to break through the enemy, and forcing a pass to advance into Suffolk by Nayland Bridge; to this purpose, they pass'd the river near Middle-Mill; but their guides having mislead them, the enemy took the alarm; upon which their guides, and some pioneers which they had with them, to open the hedges, and level the banks, for their passing to Boxted, all run away; so the horse were obliged to retreat; the enemy pretended to pursue, but thinking they had retreated by the North Bridge, they miss'd them; upon which being enraged, they fir'd the suburbs without the bridge, and burn'd them quite down.

18. Some of the horse attempted to escape the same way; and had the whole body been there as before, they had effected it; but there being but two troops, they were obliged to retire. Now the town began to be greatly distress'd, provisions failing; and the town's people, which were numerous, being very uneasy, and no way of breaking through being found practicable, the gentlemen would have joined in any attempt wherein they might die gallantly with their swords in their hands, but nothing presented; they often sally'd and cut off many of the enemy, but their numbers were continually supplied, and the besieged diminished; their horse also sunk and became unfit for service, having very little hay, and no corn; and at length they were forced to kill them for food; so that they began to be in a very miserable condition, and the soldiers deserted every day in great numbers, not being able to bear the want of food, as being almost starved with hunger.

22. The Ld. Fairfax offered again an exchange of prisoners, but the Lord Goring rejected it, because they refused conditions to the chief gentlemen of the garrison.

During this time, two troops of the Royal Horse sallied out in the night, resolving to break out or die: The first rode up full gallop to the enemy's horse-guards on the side of Malden Road, and exchanged their pistols with the advanced troops, and wheeling, made as if they would retire to the town; but finding they were not immediately pursued, they wheeled about to the right, and passing another guard at a distance, without being perfectly discovered, they went clean off, and passing towards Tiptree Heath, and having good guides, they made their escape towards Cambridge-shire, in which length of way they found means to disperse without being attack'd, and went every man his own way as fate directed; nor did we hear that many of them were taken: They were led, as we are informed, by Sir Bernard Gascoigne.

Upon these attempts of the Horse to break out, the enemy built a small fort in the meadow right against the ford, in the river, at the Middle Mill, and once set that mill on fire, but it was extinguished without much damage; however the fort prevented any more attempts that way.

23. The Parliament General sent in a trumpet, to propose again the exchange of prisoners, offering the Lord Capel's son for one, and Mr. Ashburnham, for Sir William Masham; but the Lord Capel, Lord Goring, and the rest of the loyal gentlemen rejected it; and Lord Capel in particular sent the Lord Fairfax word, it was inhuman to surprize his son, who was not in arms, and offer him to insult a father's affection, but that he might murther his son if he pleased, he would leave his blood to be revenged as Heaven should give opportunity; and the Lord Goring sent word, that as they had reduced the king's servants to eat horse-flesh, the prisoners should feed as they fed.

The enemy sent again to complain of the Royalists shooting poison'd bullets, and sent two affidavits of it made by two deserters, swearing it was done by the Lord Norwich's direction: The generals in the town returned under all their hands, that they never gave any such command or direction; that they disown'd the practice; and that the fellows who swore it were perjured before in running from their colours, and the service of their king, and ought not to be credited again: But they added, that for shooting rough-cast slugs they must excuse them, as things stood with them at that time.

About this time a porter in a soldier's habit got through the enemy's leaguer, and passing their out-guards in the dark, got into the town, and brought letters from London, assuring the Royalists, that there were so many strong parties up in arms for the king, and in so many places, that they would be very suddenly reliev'd: This they caus'd to be read to the soldiers to encourage them; and particularly it related to the rising of the Earl of Holland, and the Duke of Buckingham, who with 500 Horse were gotten together in arms about Kingston in Surrey; but we had notice in a few days after, that they were defeated, and the Earl of Holland taken, who was afterwards beheaded.

26. The enemy now began to batter the walls, and especially on the west-side, from St. Mary's towards the North Gate; and we were assured they intended a storm; on which the ingeniers were directed to make entrenchments behind the walls where the breaches should be made, that in case of a storm, they might meet with a warm reception: Upon this, they gave over the design of storming. The Lord Goring finding that the enemy had set the suburbs on fire right against the Hithe, ordered the remaining houses, which were empty of inhabitants, from whence their musketeers fir'd against the town, to be burn'd also.

31. A body of foot sally'd out at midnight, to discover what the enemy were doing at a place where they thought a new fort raiseing; they fell in among the workmen, and put them to flight, cut in pieces several of the guard, and brought in the officer who commanded them prisoner.

Aug. 2. The town was now in a miserable condition, the soldiers searched and rifled the houses of the inhabitants for victuals; they had liv'd on horse-flesh several weeks, and most of that also was lean as carrion, which not being well salted bred worms; and this want of diet made the soldiers sickly, and many died of fluxes, yet they boldly rejected all offers of surrender, unless with safety to their officers: However, several hundreds got out, and either pass'd the enemy's guards, or surrender'd to them, and took passes.

Aug. 7. The town's people became very uneasy to the soldiers, and the mayor of the town, with the aldermen, waited upon the general, desiring leave to send to the Lord Fairfax, for leave to all the inhabitants to come out of the town, that they might not perish; to which the Lord Goring consented; but the Lord Fairfax refused them.

12. The rabble got together in a vast crowd about the Lord Goring's quarters, clamouring for a surrender, and they did this every evening, bringing women and children, who lay howling and crying on the ground for bread; the soldiers beat off the men, but the women and children would not stir, bidding the soldiers kill them, saying they had rather be shot than be starv'd.

16. The general mov'd by the cries and distress of the poor inhabitants, sent out a trumpet to the Parliament General, demanding leave to send to the prince, who was with a fleet of 19 men of war in the mouth of the Thames, offering to surrender, if they were not reliev'd in 20 days. The Lord Fairfax refused it, and sent them word, he would be in the town in person, and visit them in less than 20 days, intimating that they were preparing for a storm. Some tart messages and answers were exchanged on this occasion. The Lord Goring sent word, they were willing, in compassion to the poor town's people, and to save that effusion of blood, to surrender upon honourable terms, but that as for the storming them, which was threaten'd, they might come on when they thought fit, for that they (the Royalists) were ready for them. This held to the 19.

20. The Lord Fairfax return'd, what he said, was his last answer, and should be the last offer of mercy: The conditions

offered were, That upon a peaceable surrender, all soldiers and officers under the degree of a captain, in commission, should have their lives, be exempted from plunder, and have passes to go to their respective dwellings: All the captains and superior officers, with all the lords and gentlemen, as well in commission as voluntiers, to surrender prisoners at discretion, only that they should not be plundered by the soldiers.

21. The generals rejected those offers; and when the people came about them again for bread, set open one of the gates, and bid them go out to the enemy, which a great many did willingly; upon which the Lord Goring ordered all the rest that came about his door, to be turn'd out after them: But when the people came to the Lord Fairfax's camp, the out-guards were order'd to fire at them, and drive them all back again to the gate; which the Lord Goring seeing, he order'd them to be receiv'd in again. And now, altho' the generals and soldiers also, were resolute to die with their swords in their hands, rather than yield, and had maturely resolv'd to abide a storm; yet the mayor and aldermen having petitioned them, as well as the inhabitants, being wearied with the importunities of the distressed people, and pitying the deplorable condition they were reduced to, they agreed to enter upon a treaty, and accordingly, sent out some officers to the Lord Fairfax, the Parliament General, to treat; and with them was sent two gentlemen of the prisoners upon their parole to return.

Upon the return of the said messengers with the Lord Fairfax's terms, the Lord Goring, &c. sent out a letter, declaring they would die with their swords in their hands, rather than yield without quarter for life, and sent a paper of articles, on which they were willing to surrender: But in the very interim of this treaty, news came, that the Scots army under Duke Hamilton, which was enter'd into Lancashire, and was joyn'd by the Royalists in that county, making 21000 men, were entirely defeated. After this, the Ld. Fairfax would not grant any abatement of articles, viz. To have all above lieutenants surrender at mercy.

Upon this, the Lord Goring and the general refused to submit again, and proposed a general sally, and to break through or die, but found upon preparing for it, that the soldiers, who had their lives offered them, declined it, fearing the gentlemen would escape, and they should be left to the mercy of the Parliament soldiers; and that upon this they began to mutiny, and talk of surrendering the town, and their officers too. Things being brought to this pass, the lords and general laid aside that design, and found themselves oblig'd to submit: And so the town was surrendered the 28th of August, 1648, upon conditions, as follows,

The lords and gentlemen all prisoners at mercy.

The common soldiers had passes to go home to their several dwellings, but without arms, and on oath not to serve against the Parliament.

The town to be preserv'd from pillage, paying 14000*l*. ready money.

The same day a Council of War being call'd about the prisoners of war, it was resolv'd, That the lords should be left to the disposal of the Parliament. That Sir Charles Lucas, Sir George Lisle, and Sir Marmaduke Gascoign, should be shot to death, and the other officers prisoners, to remain in custody till farther order.

The two first of the three gentlemen were shot to death, and the third respited.

Thus ended the Siege of COLCHESTER.

N.B. Notwithstanding the number killed in the siege, and dead of the flux, and other distempers, occasioned by bad diet, which were very many, and notwithstanding the number which deserted and escap'd in the time of their hardships, yet there remained at the time of the surrender,

Earl of Norw. (Goring)	69 Ensigns
Lord Capell.	183 Serj. and corpor.
Lord Loughbro'	3067 Private soldiers
11 Knights	65 Servants to the lords
9 Colonels	and general officers and
8 Lieut. Colonels	gentlemen.
9 Majors	
30 Captains	
72 Lieutenants	3513. in all.

The town of Colchester has been suppos'd to contain about 40000 people, including the out-villages which are within its liberty, of which there are a great many, the liberty of the town being of a great extent: One sad testimony of the town being so populous is, that they bury'd upwards of 5259 people in the Plague Year, 1665. But the town was severely visited indeed, even more in proportion than any of its neighbours, or than the city of London.

The government of the town is by a mayor, high steward, a recorder, or his deputy, eleven aldermen, a chamberlain, a town-clerk, assistants, and eighteen common-council-men. Their high-steward (this year, 1722.) is Sir Isaac Rebow, a gentleman of a good family and known character, who has generally, for above 30 years, been one of their representatives in Parliament: He has a very good house at the entrance in at the South, or head gate of the town, where he has had the honour, several times, to lodge and entertain the late King William, of glorious memory, in his returning from Holland, by way of Harwich to London. Their recorder is Earl Cowper, who has been twice lord high-chancellor of England: But his lordship not residing in those parts, has put in for his deputy, —— Price, Esq; Barrister at Law, and who dwells in the town. There are in Colchester eight churches, besides those which are damag'd, and five meeting-houses, whereof two for Quakers; besides a Dutch church and a French church.

Public edifices are,

1. Bay-Hall, an ancient society kept up for ascertaining the manufactures of bays; which are, or ought to be, all brought to this hall, to be viewed and sealed according to their goodness, by the masters; and to this practice has been owing the great reputation of the Colchester bays in foreign markets; where to open the side of a bale and shew the seal, has been enough to give the buyer a character of the value of the goods without any farther search; and so far as they abate the integrity and exactness of their method, which, I am told, of late is much omitted; I say, so far, that reputation will certainly abate in the markets they go to, which are principally in Portugal and Italy. This corporation is govern'd by a particular set of men who are call'd Governors of the Dutch Bay Hall. And in the same building is the Dutch church.

2. The Guild Hall of the town, called by them the Moot Hall; to which is annex'd the town goal.

3. The Work-house, being lately enlarg'd, and to which belongs a corporation, or a body of the inhabitants, consisting of sixty persons incorporated by Act of Parliament anno 1698, for taking care of the poor: They are incorporated by the name and title of The Governor, Deputy Governor, Assistants, and Guardians, of the Poor of the Town of Colchester. They are in number eight and forty; to whom are added the mayor and

aldermen for the time being, who are always guardians by the same Charter: These make the number of sixty, as above.

There is also a grammar free-school, with a good allowance to the master, who is chosen by the town.

4. The Castle of Colchester is now become only a monument shewing the antiquity of the place, it being built as the walls of the town also are, with Roman bricks; and the Roman coins dug up here, and ploughed up in the fields adjoining, confirm it. The inhabitants boast much, that Helena, the mother of Constantine the Great, first Christian Emperor of the Romans, was born there; and it may be so for ought we know; I only observe what Mr. Camden says of the castle of Colchester, viz.

"In the middle of this city stands a castle ready to fall with age." [1]

Tho' this castle has stood an hundred and twenty years from the time Mr. Camden wrote that account, and it is not fallen yet; nor will another hundred and twenty years, I believe, make it look one jot the older: And it was observable, that in the late siege of this town, a cannon shot, which the besiegers made at this old castle, were so far from making it fall, that they made little or no impression upon it; for which reason, it seems, and because the garrison made no great use of it against the besiegers, they fir'd no more at it.

There are two CHARITY SCHOOLS set up here, and carried on by a generous subscription, with very good success.

The title of Colchester is in the family of Earl Rivers; and the eldest son of that family, is called Lord Colchester; tho', as I understand, the title is not settled by the creation, to the eldest son, till he enjoys the title of Earl with it; but that the other is by the courtesy of England; however this I take *ad referendum.*

From Colchester, I took another step down to the coast, the land running out a great way into the sea, south, and S.E. makes that promontory of land called the Nase, and well known to sea-men, using the northern trade. Here one sees a sea open as an ocean, without any opposite shore, tho' it be no more than the mouth of the Thames. This point call'd the Nase, and the N.E. point of Kent, near Margate, call'd the North Foreland, making (what they call) the mouth of the river, and the port of London, tho' it be here above 60 miles over.

[1] Camd., *Brit. Fol.* 353.

At Walton, under the Nase, they find on the shoar, copperas-stone in great quantities; and there are several large works call'd Copperas Houses, where they make it with great expence.

On this promontory is a new sea mark, erected by the Trinity-House men, and at the publick expence, being a round brick tower, near 80 foot high. The sea gains so much upon the land here, by the continual winds at S.W. that within the memory of some of the inhabitants there, they have lost above 30 acres of land in one place.

From hence we go back into the country about four miles, because of the creeks which lie between; and then turning east again, come to Harwich, on the utmost eastern point of this large country.

Harwich is a town so well known, and so perfectly describ'd by many writers, I need say little of it: 'Tis strong by situation, and may be made more so by art. But 'tis many years since the Government of England have had any occasion to fortify towns to the landward; 'tis enough that the harbour or road, which is one of the best and securest in England, is cover'd at the entrance by a strong fort, and a battery of guns to the sea-ward, just as at Tilbury, and which sufficiently defend the mouth of the river: And there is a particular felicity in this fortification, viz. That tho' the entrance or opening of the river into the sea, is very wide, especially at high-water, at least two miles, if not three over; yet the channel, which is deep, and in which the ships must keep and come to the harbour, is narrow, and lies only on the side of the fort; so that all the ships which come in, or go out, must come close under the guns of the fort; that is to say, under the command of their shot.

The fort is on the Suffolk side of the bay, or entrance, but stands so far into the sea upon the point of a sand or shoal, which runs out toward the Essex side, as it were, laps over the mouth of that haven like a blind to it; and our surveyors of the country affirm it to be in the county of Essex. The making this place, which was formerly no other than a sand in the sea, solid enough for the foundation of so good a fortification, has not been done but by many years labour, often repairs, and an infinite expence of money, but 'tis now so firm, that nothing of storms and high tides, or such things, as make the sea dangerous to these kind of works, can affect it.

The harbour is of a vast extent; for, as two rivers empty themselves here, viz, Stour from Mainingtree, and the Orwel from Ipswich, the channels of both are large and deep, and safe

for all weathers; so where they joyn they make a large bay or
road, able to receive the biggest ships, and the greatest number
that ever the world saw together; I mean, ships of war. In the
old Dutch War, great use has been made of this harbour; and
I have known that there has been 100 sail of men of war and
their attendants, and between three and four hundred sail of
collier ships, all in this harbour at a time, and yet none of them
crowding, or riding in danger of one another.

Harwich is known for being the port where the packet-boats
between England and Holland, go out and come in: The inhabitants are far from being fam'd for good usage to strangers,
but on the contrary, are blamed for being extravagant in their
reckonings, in the publick houses, which has not a little
encourag'd the setting up of sloops, which they now call passage-
boats, to Holland, to go directly from the river of Thames;
this, tho' it may be something the longer passage, yet as they
are said to be more obliging to passengers, and more reasonable
in the expence, and as some say also the vessels are better
sea-boats, has been the reason why so many passengers do
not go or come by the way of Harwich, as formerly were wont
to do; insomuch, that the stage-coaches, between this place
and London, which ordinarily went twice or three times a
week, are now entirely laid down, and the passengers are left
to hire coaches on purpose, take post-horses, or hire horses
to Colchester, as they find most convenient.

The account of a petrifying quality in the earth here, tho'
some will have it to be in the water of a spring hard by, is very
strange: They boast that their town is wall'd, and their streets
pav'd with clay, and yet, that one is as strong, and the other
as clean as those that are built or pav'd with stone: The fact is
indeed true, for there is a sort of clay in the cliff, between the
town and the beacon-hill adjoining, which when it falls down
into the sea, where it is beaten with the waves and the weather,
turns gradually into stone: but the chief reason assign'd, is
from the water of a certain spring or well, which rising in the
said cliff, runs down into the sea among those pieces of clay,
and petrifies them as it runs, and the force of the sea often
stirring, and perhaps, turning the lumps of clay, when storms
of wind may give force enough to the water, causes them to
harden every where alike; otherwise those which were not quite
sunk in the water of the spring, would be petrify'd but in part.
These stones are gathered up to pave the streets, and build
the houses, and are indeed very hard: 'Tis also remarkable,

that some of them taken up before they are thoroughly petrify'd, will, upon breaking them, appear to be hard as a stone without, and soft as clay in the middle; whereas others, that have layn a due time, shall be thorough stone to the center, and as exceeding hard within, as without: The same spring is said to turn wood into iron: But this I take to be no more or less than the quality, which as I mention'd of the shoar at the Ness, is found to be in much of the stone, all along this shoar, (viz.) Of the copperas kind; and 'tis certain, that the copperas stone (so call'd) is found in all that cliff, and even where the water of this spring has run; and I presume, that those who call the harden'd pieces of wood, which they take out of this well by the name of iron, never try'd the quality of it with the fire or hammer; if they had, perhaps they would have given some other account of it.

On the promontory of land, which they call Beacon-Hill, and which lies beyond, or behind the town, towards the sea, there is a light-house, to give the ships directions in their sailing by, as well as their coming into the harbour in the night. I shall take notice of these again all together, when I come to speak of the Society of Trinity House, as they are called, by whom they are all directed upon this coast.

This town was erected into a marquisate, in honour of the truly glorious family of Schomberg, the eldest son of Duke Schomberg, who landed with King William, being stiled Marquis of Harwich; but that family (in England at least) being extinct, the title dies also.

Harwich is a town of hurry and business, not much of gaiety and pleasure; yet the inhabitants seem warm in their nests, and some of them are very wealthy: There are not many (if any) gentlemen or families of note, either in the town, or very near it. They send two members to Parliament; the present are, Sir Peter Parker, and Humphrey Parsons, Esq.

And now being at the extremity of the county of Essex, of which I have given you some view, as to that side next the sea only; I shall break off this part of my letter, by telling you, that I will take the towns which lie more towards the center of the county, in my return by the north and west part only, that I may give you a few hints of some towns which were near me in my rout this way, and of which being so well known, there is but little to say.

On the road from London to Colchester, before I came into it at Witham, lie four good market-towns at equal distance from one another; namely, Rumford, noted for two markets, (viz.) one for calves and hogs, the other for corn and other provisions; most, if not all, bought up for London market. At the farther end of the town, in the middle of a stately park, stood Guldy Hall, vulgarly Giddy Hall, an antient seat of one Coke, sometime Lord-Mayor of London, but forfeited, on some occasion, to the Crown: It is since pull'd down to the ground, and there now stands a noble stately fabrick or mansion-house, built upon the spot by Sir John Eyles, a wealthy merchant of London, and chosen sub-governor of the South-Sea Company, immediately after the ruin of the former sub-governor and directors, whose overthrow makes the history of these times famous.

Brent-Wood and Ingarstone, and even Chelmsford itself, have very little to be said of them, but that they are large thorough-fair towns, full of good inns, and chiefly maintained by the excessive multitude of carriers and passengers, which are constantly passing this way to London, with droves of cattle, provisions, and manufactures for London.

The last of these towns is indeed the county-town, where the county jayl is kept, and where the assizes are very often held; it stands on the conflux of two rivers, the Chelmer, whence the town is called, and the Cann.

At Lees, or Lee's Priory, as some call it, is to be seen an antient house, in the middle of a beautiful park, formerly the seat of the late Duke of Manchester, but since the death of the duke, it is sold to the Dutchess Dowager of Buckinghamshire; the present Duke of Manchester, retiring to his antient family seat at Kimbolton in Huntingdonshire, it being a much finer residence. His grace is lately married to a daughter of the Duke of Montague by a branch of the house of Marlborough.

Four market-towns fill up the rest of this part of the country; Dunmow, Braintre, Thaxted, and Coggshall; all noted for the manufacture of bays, as above, and for very little else, except I shall make the ladies laugh, at the famous old story of the Flitch of Bacon at Dunmow, which is this:

One Robert Fitz-Walter, a powerful baron in this county, in the time of Hen. III. on some merry occasion, which is not preserv'd in the rest of the story, instituted a custom in the priory here; That whatever married man did not repent of his being marry'd, or quarrel, or differ and dispute with his wife, within a year and a day after his marriage, and would swear to the truth of it, kneeling upon two hard pointed stones in the church yard, which stones he caus'd to be set up in the priory church-yard, for that purpose: The prior and convent, and as many of the town as would, to be present: such person should have a flitch of bacon.

I do not remember to have read, that any one ever came to demand it; nor do the people of the place pretend to say, of their own knowledge, that they remember any that did so; a long time ago several did demand it, as they say, but they know not who; neither is there any record of it; nor do they tell us, if it were now to be demanded, who is obliged to deliver the flitch of bacon, the priory being dissolved and gone.

The forest of Epping and Henalt, spreads a great part of this country still: I shall speak again of the former in my return from this circuit. Formerly, ('tis thought) these two forests took up all the west and south part of the county; but particularly we are assur'd, that it reach'd to the River Chelmer, and into Dengy Hundred; and from thence again west to Epping and Waltham, where it continues to be a forest still.

Probably this forest of Epping has been a wild or forest ever since this island was inhabited, and may shew us, in some parts of it, where enclosures and tillage has not broken in upon it, what the face of this island was before the Romans time; that is to say, before their landing in Britain.

The constitution of this forest is best seen, I mean, as to the antiquity of it, by the merry grant of it from Edward the Confessor, before the Norman Conquest to Randolph Peperking, one of his favourites, who was after called Peverell, and whose name remains still in several villages in this county; as particularly that of Hatfield Peverell, in the road from Chelmsford to Witham, which is suppos'd to be originally a park, which they call'd a field in those days; and Hartfield may be as much as to say a park for deer; for the stags were in those days called harts; so that this was neither more nor less than Randolph Peperking's Hartfield; that is to say, Ralph Peverell's deer-park.

N.B. This Ralph Randolph, or Ralph Peverell (call him as you please) had, it seems, a most beautiful lady to his wife, who was daughter of Ingelrick, one of Edward the Confessor's noblemen: He had two sons by her, William Peverell, a fam'd soldier, and Lord or Governor of Dover Castle; which he surrender'd to William the Conqueror, after the Battle of Sussex; and Pain Peverell, his youngest, who was Lord of Cambridge: When the eldest son delivered up the castle, the lady his mother, above nam'd, who was the celebrated beauty of the age, was it seems there; and the Conqueror fell in love with her, and whether by force, or by consent, took her away, and she became his mistress, or what else you please to call it: By her he had a son, who was call'd William, after the Conqueror's Christian name, but retain'd the name of Peverell, and was afterwards created by the Conqueror, Lord of Nottingham.

This lady afterwards, as is supposed, by way of penance, for her yielding to the Conqueror, founded a nunnery at the village of Hatfield-Peverell, mentioned above, and there she lies buried in the chapel of it, which is now the parish-church, where her memory is preserv'd by a tomb-stone under one of the windows.

Thus we have several towns, where any antient parks have been plac'd, call'd by the name of Hatfield on that very account.

As Hatfield Broad Oak in this county, Bishop's Hatfield in Hertfordshire, and several others.

But I return to King Edward's merry way, as I call it, of granting this forest to this Ralph Peperking, which I find in the antient records, in the very words it was pass'd in, as follows: Take my explanations with it, for the sake of those that are not us'd to the antient English.

The GRANT *in Old English*	*The Explanation in Modern English*
I Che EDWARD Koning, Have given of my forrest the kepen of the Hundred of Chelmer and Dancing,	I EDWARD the King, Have made Ranger of my forest of Chelmsford Hundred, and Deering Hundred,
To RANDOLPH PEPERKING, And to his kindling,	Ralph Peverell, for him and his heirs for ever;
With heorte and hind, doe and bocke,	With both the red and fallow deer,
Hare and fox, cat and brock, Wild fowle with his flock;	Hare and fox, otter and badger; Wild fowl of all sorts,
Patrich, pheasant hen, and pheasant cock,	Partridges and pheasants,
With green and wild stub and stock,	Timber and underwood, roots and tops:
To kepen and to yemen with all her might, Both by day, and eke by night;	With power to preserve the forest, And watch it against deer stealers and others:
And hounds for to hold, Good and swift, and bold:	With a right to keep hounds of all sorts,
Four greyhound, and six raches, For hare and fox, and wild cattes,	Four grey-hounds, and six terriers, Harriers and fox-hounds, and other hounds.
And therefore Iche made him my book;	And to this end I have registered this my Grant, in the Crown rolls or books;
Witness the Bishop of Wolston, And book ylrede many on,	To which the bishop has set his hand as a witness for any one to read;

And Sweyne of Essex, our brother,	Also signed by the king's brother (or, as some think, the Chancellor Sweyn, then Earl or Count of Essex)
And taken him many other	He might call such other witnesses to sign as he thought fit.
And our steward Howelin, That by-sought me for him.	Also the king's high steward was a witness, at whose request this Grant was obtained of the king.

There are many gentlemen's seats on this side the county, and a great assemblee set up at New-Hall, near this town, much resorted to by the neighbouring gentry. I shall next proceed to the county of Suffolk, as my first design directed me to do.

From HARWICH therefore, having a mind to view the harbour, I sent my horses round by Maningtree, where there is a timber bridge over the Stour, called Cataway Bridge, and took a boat up the River Orwell, for Ipswich; a traveller will hardly understand me, especially a seaman, when I speak of the River Stour and the River Orwell at Harwich, for they know them by no other names than those of Maningtre-Water, and Ipswich-Water; so while I am on salt water, I must speak as those who use the sea may understand me, and when I am up in the country among the in-land towns again, I shall call them out of their names no more.

It is twelve miles from Harwich up the water to Ipswich: Before I come to the town, I must say something of it, because speaking of the river requires it: In former times, that is to say, since the writer of this remembers the place very well, and particularly just before the late Dutch Wars, Ipswich was a town of very good business; particularly it was the greatest town in England for large colliers or coal-ships, employed between New Castle and London: Also they built the biggest ships and the best, for the said fetching of coals of any that were employ'd in that trade: They built also there so prodigious strong, that it was an ordinary thing for an Ipswich collier, if no disaster happen'd to him, to reign (as seamen call it) forty or fifty years, and more.

In the town of Ipswich the masters of these ships generally dwelt, and there were, as they then told me, above a hundred sail of them, belonging to the town at one time, the least of which carried fifteen-score, as they compute it, that is, 300 chaldron of coals; this was about the year 1668 (when I first knew the place). This made the town be at that time so populous, for those masters, as they had good ships at sea, so they had large families, who liv'd plentifully, and in very good houses in the town, and several streets were chiefly inhabited by such.

The loss or decay of this trade, accounts for the present pretended decay of the town of Ipswich, of which I shall speak more presently: The ships wore out, the masters died off, the trade took a new turn; Dutch flyboats taken in the war, and made free ships by Act of Parliament, thrust themselves into the coal-trade for the interest of the captors, such as the Yarmouth and London merchants, and others; and the Ipswich men dropt gradually out of it, being discouraged by those Dutch flyboats: These Dutch vessels which cost nothing but the caption, were bought cheap, carried great burthens, and the Ipswich building fell off for want of price, and so the trade decay'd, and the town with it; I believe this will be own'd for the true beginning of their decay, if I must allow it to be call'd a decay.

But to return to my passage up the river. In the winter time those great collier-ships, abovemention'd, are always laid up, as they call it: That is to say, the coal trade abates at London, the citizens are generally furnish'd, their stores taken in, and the demand is over; so that the great ships, the northern seas and coast being also dangerous, the nights long, and the voyage hazardous, go to sea no more, but lie by, the ships are unrigg'd, the sails, &c. carry'd a shore, the top-masts struck, and they ride moor'd in the river, under the advantages and security of sound ground, and a high woody shore, where they lie as safe as in a wet dock; and it was a very agreeable sight to see, perhaps two hundred sail of ships, of all sizes lye in that posture every winter: All this while, which was usually from Michaelmas to Lady Day, The masters liv'd calm and secure with their families in Ipswich; and enjoying plentifully, what in the summer they got laboriously at sea, and this made the town of Ipswich very populous in the winter; for as the masters, so most of the men, especially their mates, boatswains, carpenters, &c. were of the same place, and liv'd in their proportions, just as the masters did; so that in the winter there might be perhaps a thousand men in the town more than in the summer, and perhaps a greater number.

To justify what I advance here, that this town was formerly very full of people, I ask leave to refer to the account of Mr. Camden, and what it was in his time, his words are these.

"Ipswich has a commodious harbour, has been fortified with a

ditch and rampart, has a great trade, and is very populous; being
adorned with fourteen churches, and large private buildings."

This confirms what I have mentioned of the former state of
this town; but the present state is my proper work; I therefore
return to my voyage up the river.

The sight of these ships thus laid up in the river, as I have
said, was very agreeable to me in my passage from Harwich,
about five and thirty years before the present journey; and
it was in its proportion equally melancholly to hear, that there
were now scarce 40 sail of good colliers that belong'd to the
whole town.

In a creek in this river call'd Lavington-Creek we saw at
low water, such shoals, or hills rather, of muscles that great
boats might have loaded with them, and no miss have been
made of them. Near this creek Sir Samuel Barnadiston had
a very fine seat, as also a decoy for wild ducks, and a very
noble estate; but it is divided into many branches since the
death of the antient possessor; but I proceed to the town,
which is the first in the county of Suffolk of any note this way.

Ipswich is seated, at the distance of 12 miles from Harwich,
upon the edge of the river, which taking a short turn to the
west, the town forms, there, a kind of semi-circle, or half moon
upon the bank of the river: It is very remarkable, that tho'
ships of 500 tun may upon a spring tide come up very near
this town, and many ships of that burthen have been built
there; yet the river is not navigable any farther than the town
itself, or but very little; no not for the smallest boats, nor does
the tide, which rises sometimes 13 or 14 foot, and gives them
24 foot water very near the town, flow much farther up the river
than the town, or not so much as to make it worth speaking of.

He took little notice of the town, or at least of that part of
Ipswich, who published in his wild observations on it, that
ships of 200 [1] tun are built there: I affirm, that I have seen a
ship of 400 tun launch'd at the building-yard, close to the
town; and I appeal to the Ipswich colliers (those few that
remain) belonging to this town, if several of them carrying
seventeen score of coals, which must be upward of 400 tun,
have not formerly been built here; but superficial observers,
must be superficial writers, if they write at all; and to this day,
at John's Ness, within a mile and half of the town it self, ships
of any burthen may be built and launched even at neap tides.

[1] Familiar Letters, vol. x., p. 9.

I am much mistaken too, if since the Revolution, some very good ships have not been built at this town, and particularly the *Melford* or *Milford*-gally, a ship of 40 guns; as the *Greyhound* frigate, a man of war of 36 to 40 guns, was at John's Ness. But what is this towards lessening the town of Ipswich, any more than it would be to say, they do not build men of war, or East-India ships, or ships of 500 tun burthen, at St. Catherines, or at Battle-Bridge in the Thames? when we know that a mile or two lower, (viz.) at Radcliffe, Limehouse, or Deptford, they build ships of 1000 tun, and might build first-rate men of war too, if there was occasion; and the like might be done in this river of Ipswich, within about two or three miles of the town; so that it would not be at all an out-of-the-way speaking to say, such a ship was built at Ipswich, any more than it is to say, as they do, that the *Royal Prince*, the great ship lately built for the South-Sea Company, was London built, because she was built at Lime-house.

And why then is not Ipswich capable of building and receiving the greatest ships in the navy, seeing they may be built and brought up again loaden, within a mile and half of the town?

But the neighbourhood of London, which sucks the vitals of trade in this island to itself, is the chief reason of any decay of business in this place; and I shall in the course of these observations, hint at it, where many good sea-ports and large towns, tho' farther off than Ipswich, and as well fitted for commerce, are yet swallow'd up by the immense indraft of trade to the city of London; and more decay'd beyond all comparison, than Ipswich is suppos'd to be; as Southampton, Weymouth, Dartmouth, and several others which I shall speak to in their order: And if it be otherwise at this time, with some other towns, which are lately encreas'd in trade and navigation, wealth, and people, while their neighbours decay, it is because they have some particular trade or accident to trade, which is a kind of nostrum to them, inseparable to the place, and which fixes there by the nature of the thing; as the herring-fishery to Yarmouth; the coal trade to New-Castle; the Leeds cloathing-trade; the export of butter and lead, and the great corn trade for Holland, is to Hull; the Virginia and West-India trade at Liverpool, the Irish trade at Bristol, and the like; Thus the war has brought a flux of business and people, and consequently of wealth, to several places, as well as to Portsmouth, Chatham, Plymouth, Falmouth, and others; and were any wars like those, to continue 20 years with the Dutch, or any nation whose fleets lay that way, as the Dutch do, it would be the like perhaps at Ipswich in a few years, and at other places on the same coast.

But at this present time an occasion offers to speak in favour of this port; namely, the Greenland fishery, lately propos'd to be carry'd on by the South-Sea Company: On which account I may freely advance this, without any compliment to the town of Ipswich, no place in Britain, is equally qualified like Ipswich; whether we respect the cheapness of building and fitting out their ships and shalloups; also furnishing, victualling, and providing them with all kind of stores; convenience for laying up the ships after the voyage; room for erecting their magazines, ware-houses, roap-walks, cooperage, &c. on the easiest terms; and especially for the noisome cookery, which attends the boiling their blubber, which may be on this river, (as it ought to be) remote from any places of resort; Then their nearness to the market for the oil when 'tis made, and, which above all, ought to be the chief thing considered in that trade, the easiness of their putting out to sea when they begin their voyage, in which the same wind that carries them from the mouth of the haven, is fair to the very seas of Greenland.

I could say much more to this point, if it were needful, and in few words could easily prove, that Ipswich must have the preference of all the port towns of Britain, for being the best center of the Greenland trade, if ever that trade fall into the management of such a people as perfectly understand, and have a due honest regard to its being managed with the best husbandry, and to the prosperity of the undertaking in general: But whether we shall ever arrive at so happy a time, as to recover so useful a trade to our country, which our ancestors had the honour to be the first undertakers of, and which has been lost only thro' the indolence of others, and the encreasing vigilance of our neighbours, that is not my business here to dispute.

What I have said, is only to let the world see, what improvement this town and port is capable of; I cannot think, but that Providence, which made nothing in vain, cannot have reserv'd so useful, so convenient a port to lie vacant in the world, but that the time will some time or other come (especially considering the improving temper of the present age) when some peculiar beneficial business may be found out, to make the port of Ipswich as useful to the world, and the town as flourishing, as nature has made it proper and capable to be.

As for the town, it is true, it is but thinly inhabited, in

SUFFOLK

comparison of the extent of it; but to say, there are hardly any people to be seen there, is far from being true in fact; and whoever thinks fit to look into the churches and meeting-houses on a Sunday, or other publick days, will find there are very great numbers of people there: Or if he thinks fit to view the market, and see how the large shambles, call'd Cardinal Wolsey's Butchery, are furnish'd with meat, and the rest of the market stock'd with other provisions, must acknowledge that it is not for a few people that all those things are provided: A person very curious, and on whose veracity I think I may depend, going thro' the market in this town, told me, that he reckon'd upwards of 600 country people on horseback and on foot, with baskets and other carriage, who had all of them brought something or other to town to sell, besides the butchers, and what came in carts and waggons.

It happen'd to be my lot to be once at this town, at the time when a very fine new ship, which was built there, for some merchants of London, was to be launched; and if I may give my guess at the numbers of people which appeared on the shore, in the houses, and on the river, I believe I am much within compass, if I say there were 20,000 people to see it; but this is only a guess, or they might come a great way to see the sight, or the town may be declin'd farther since that: But a view of the town is one of the surest rules for a gross estimate.

It is true, here is no settled manufacture: the French refugees, when they first came over to England, began a little to take to this place; and some merchants attempted to set up a linnen manufacture in their favour; but it has not met with so much success as was expected, and at present I find very little of it. The poor people are however employ'd, as they are all over these counties, in spinning wool for other towns where manufactures are settled.

The country round Ipswich, as are all the counties so near the coast, is applied chiefly to corn, of which a very great quantity is continually shipped off for London; and sometimes they load corn here for Holland, especially if the market abroad is encouraging. They have 12 parish-churches in this town, with three or four meetings; but there are not so many Quakers here as at Colchester, and no Anabaptists, or Anti-pœdo Baptists, that I could hear of, at least there is no meeting-house of that denomination: There is one meeting-house for the Presbyterians, one for the Independants, and one for the Quakers; the first is as large and as fine a building of that kind as most on this side of England, and the inside the best finished of any I have seen, London not excepted; that for the Independants is a handsome new-built building, but not so gay or so large as the other.

There is a great deal of very good company in this town; and tho' there are not so many of the gentry here as at Bury, yet there are more here than in any other town in the county; and I observ'd particularly, that the company you meet with here, are generally persons well informed of the world, and who have something very solid and entertaining in their society: This may happen, perhaps, by their frequent conversing with those who have been abroad, and by their having a remnant of gentlemen and masters of ships among them, who have seen more of the world than the people of an inland town are likely to have seen. I take this town to be one of the most agreeable places in England, for families who have liv'd well, but may have suffered in our late calamities of stocks and bubbles, to retreat to, where they may live within their own compass; and several things indeed recommend it to such;

1. Good houses, at very easie rents.

2. An airy, clean, and well govern'd town.

3. Very agreeable and improving company almost of every kind.

4. A wonderful plenty of all manner of provisions, whether flesh or fish, and very good of the kind.

5. Those provisions very cheap; so that a family may live cheaper here, than in any town in England of its bigness, within such a small distance from London.

6. Easie passage to London, either by land or water, the coach going through to London in a day.

The Lord Viscount Hereford, has a very fine seat and park in this town; the house indeed is old built, but very commodious; 'tis call'd Christ-Church, having been as 'tis said, a priory, or religious house in former times: The green and park is a great addition to the pleasantness of this town, the inhabitants being allowed to divert themselves there with walking, bowling, &c.

The large spire steeple, which formerly stood upon that they call the Tower-Church, was blown down by a great storm of wind many years ago, and in its fall did much damage to the church.

The government of this town is by two bailiffs, as at Yarmouth:

Mr. Camden says they are chosen out of twelve burgesses called Portmen, and two justices out of twenty-four more. There has been lately a very great struggle between the two parties for the choice of these two magistrates, which had this amicable conclusion, namely, that they chose one of either side; so that neither party having the victory, 'tis to be hoped it may be a means to allay the heats and un-neighbourly feuds, which such things breed in towns so large as this is. They send two members to Parliament, whereof those at this time, are Sir William Thompson, Recorder of London, and Colonel Negus, deputy-master of the horse to the king.

There are some things very curious to be seen here, however some superficial writers have been ignorant of them. Dr. Beeston, an eminent physician, began, a few years ago, a physick garden adjoining to his house in this town; and as he is particularly curious, and as I was told exquisitely skill'd in botanick knowledge, so he has been not only very diligent, but successful too, in making a collection of rare and exotick plants, such as are scarce to be equall'd in England.

One Mr. White, a surgeon, resides also in this town; But before I speak of this gentleman, I must observe, that I say nothing from personal knowledge; Tho' if I did, I have too good an opinion of his sense to believe he would be pleased with being flattered, or complimented in print: But I must be true to matter of fact; This gentleman has begun a collection, or chamber of rarities, and with good success too. I acknowledge I had not the opportunity of seeing them; But I was told there are some things very curious in it, as particularly a sea-horse carefully preserv'd, and perfect in all its parts; two Roman urns full of ashes of human bodies, and supposed to be above 1700 years old; besides a great many valuable medals, and antient coins. My friend who gave me this account, and of whom I think I may say he speaks without byass, mentions this gentleman, Mr. White, with some warmth, as a very valuable person in his particular employ, of a surgeon, I only repeat his words; "Mr. White," says he, "to whom the whole town and country are greatly indebted and obliged to pray for his life, is our most skilful surgeon." These I say are his own words, and I add nothing to them but this, that 'tis happy for a town to have such a surgeon, as it is for a surgeon to have such a character.

The country round Ipswich, as if qualify'd on purpose to accommodate the town for building of ships, is an inexhaustable store-house of timber, of which now their trade of building ships is abated, they send very great quantities to the king's building-yards at Chatham, which by water is so little a way, that they often run to it from the mouth of the river at Harwich in one tide.

From Ipswich I took a turn into the country to Hadley, principally to satisfy my curiosity, and see the place where that famous martyr, and pattern of charity and religious zeal in Queen Mary's time, Dr. Rowland Taylor, was put to death; the inhabitants, who have a wonderful veneration for his memory, shew the very place where the stake which he was bound to, was set up, and they have put a stone upon it, which no body will remove; but it is a more lasting monument to him that he lives in the hearts of the people; I say more lasting than a tomb of marble would be, for the memory of that good man will certainly never be out of the poor peoples minds, as long as this island shall retain the Protestant religion among them; how long that may be, as things are going, and if the detestable conspiracy of the Papists now on foot, should succeed, I will not pretend to say.

A little to the left is Sudbury, which stands upon the River Stour, mentioned above; a river which parts the counties of Suffolk and Essex, and which is within these few years made navigable to this town, tho' the navigation does not (it seems) answer the charge, at least not to advantage.

I know nothing for which this town is remarkable, except for being very populous and very poor. They have a great manufacture of says and perpetuana's; and multitudes of poor people are employ'd in working them; but the number of the poor is almost ready to eat up the rich: However this town sends two members to Parliament, tho' it is under no form of government particularly to itself, other than as a village, the head magistrate whereof is a constable.

Near adjoining to it, is a village call'd Long-Melfort, and a very long one it is, from which I suppose it had that addition to its name; it is full of very good houses, and, as they told me, is richer, and has more wealthy masters of the manufacture in it than in Sudbury itself.

Here and in the neighbourhood, are some antient families of good note; particularly here is a fine dwelling, the antient seat of the Cordells, whereof Sir William Cordell was Master of the Rolls in the time of Queen Elizabeth; but the family is now extinct; the last heir, Sir John Cordell, being killed by a fall from his horse, died unmarry'd, leaving three sisters co-heiresses to a very noble estate most of which, if not all, is now center'd in the only surviving sister, and with her in marriage is given to Mr. Firebrass, eldest son of Sir Basil Firebrass, formerly a flourishing merchant in London, but reduc'd by many disasters. His family now rises by the good fortune of his son, who proves to be a gentleman of very agreeable parts, and well esteemed in the country.

From this part of the country I return'd north-west by Lenham, to visit St. Edmund's Bury, a town of which other writers have talk'd very largely, and perhaps a little too much: It is a town fam'd for its pleasant situation and wholsome air, the Montpelier of Suffolk, and perhaps of England; this must be attributed to the skill of the monks of those times, who chose so beautiful a situation for the seat of their retirement; and who built here the greatest and in its time, the most flourishing monastery in all these parts of England, I mean the monastery of St. Edmund the Martyr: It was, if we believe antiquity, a house of pleasure in more antient times; or to speak more properly, a Court of some of the Saxon or East-Angle kings; and, as Mr. Camden says, was even then call'd a royal village; tho' it much better merits that name now; it being the town of all this part of England, in proportion to its bigness, most thronged with gentry, people of the best fashion, and the most polite conversation: This beauty and healthiness of its situation, was no doubt the occasion which drew the clergy to settle here, for they always chose the best places in the country to build in, either for richness of soil, or for health and pleasure in the situation of their religious houses.

For the like reason, I doubt not, they translated the bones of the martyr'd King St. Edmund, to this place; for it is a vulgar error to say he was murther'd here; his martyrdom, it is plain was at Hoxon or Henilsdon, near Harlston, on the Waveney, in the farthest northern verge of the county; but Segebert, King of the East Angles, had built a religious house in this pleasant rich part of the country; and as the monks began to taste the pleasure of the place, they procur'd the body of this saint to be remov'd hither, which soon encreas'd the wealth and revenues of their house, by the zeal of that day, in going on pilgrimage to the shrine of the blessed St. Edmund.

We read however, that after this, the Danes under King Sweno, over-running this part of the country, destroyed this

monastery and burnt it to the ground, with the church and
town; but see the turn religion gives to things in the world;
His son King Canutus, at first a pagan and a tyrant, and the
most cruel ravager of all that crew, coming to turn Christian;
and being touch'd in conscience for the soul of his father, in
having robb'd God and His holy martyr St. Edmund, sacri-
legiously destroying the church, and plundering the monastery;
I say, touch'd with remorse, and, as the monks pretend terrify'd
with a vision of St. Edmund appearing to him, he rebuilt the
house, the church, and the town also, and very much added
to the wealth of the abbot and his fraternity, offering his crown
at the feet of St. Edmund, giving the house to the monks, town
and all; so that they were absolute lords of the town, and
govern'd it by their steward for many ages. He also gave them
a great many good lordships, which they enjoy'd till the general
suppression of abbies, in the time of Henry VIII.

But I am neither writing the history, or searching the
antiquity, of the abbey, or town, my business is the present
state of the place.

The abbey is demolish'd; its ruins are all that is to be seen
of its glory: Out of the old building, two very beautiful churches
are built, and serve the two parishes, into which the town is
divided, and they stand both in one church-yard. Here it was,
in the path-way between these two churches, that a tragical
and almost unheard of act of barbarity was committed, which
made the place less pleasant for some time, than it us'd to be,
when Arundel Coke, Esq; a Barrister at Law, of very antient
family, attempted, with the assistance of a barbarous assassin,
to murther in cold blood, and in the arms of hospitality, Edward
Crisp, Esq; his brother-in-law, leading him out from his own
house, where he had invited him, his wife and children, to
supper: I say, leading him out in the night, on pretence of going
to see some friend that was known to them both; but in this
church-yard, giving a signal to the assassin he had hir'd, he
attack'd him with a hedge bill, and cut him, as one might say,
almost in pieces; and when they did not doubt of his being dead,
they left him: His head and face was so mangled, that it may be
said to be next to a miracle that he was not quite killed: Yet so
Providence directed for the exemplary punishment of the
assassins, that the gentleman recover'd to detect them, who,
(tho' he out-lived the assault) were both executed as they
deserv'd, and Mr. Crisp is yet alive. They were condemned on the
statute for defacing and dismembring, called the Coventry Act.

But this accident does not at all lessen the pleasure and agreeable delightful shew of the town of Bury; it is crouded with nobility and gentry, and all sorts of the most agreeable company; and as the company invites, so there is the appearance of pleasure upon the very situation; and they that live at Bury, are supposed to live there for the sake of it.

The Lord Jermin, afterwards Lord Dover, and since his lordship's decease, Sir Robert Davers, enjoy'd the most delicious seat of Rushbrook, near this town.

The present Members of Parliament for this place are, Jermyn Davers, and James Reynolds, Esquires.

Mr. Harvey, afterwards created Lord Harvey, by King William, and since that, made Earl of Bristol by King George, liv'd many years in this town, leaving a noble and pleasantly situated house in Lincolnshire, for the more agreeable living on a spot so compleatly qualified for a life of delight as this of Bury.

The Duke of Grafton, now Lord Lieutenant of Ireland, has also a stately house at Euston, near this town, which he enjoys in right of his mother, daughter to the Earl of Arlington, one of the chief ministers of State in the reign of King Charles II. and who made the second letter in the word C A B A L; a word form'd by that famous satirerist Andrew Marvell, to represent the five heads of the politicks of that time, as the word SMECTYMNUS was on a former occasion.

I shall believe nothing so scandalous of the ladies of this town and the county round it, as a late writer [1] insinuates: That the ladies round the country appear mighty gay and agreeable at the time of the fair in this town, I acknowledge; one hardly sees such a show in any part of the world; but to suggest they come hither as to a market, is so coarse a jest that the gentlemen that wait on them hither, (for they rarely come but in good company) ought to resent and correct him for it.

It is true, Bury-Fair, like Bartholomew-Fair, is a fair for diversion, more than for trade; and it may be a fair for toys and for trinkets, which the ladies may think fit to lay out some of their money in, as they see occasion. But to judge from thence, that the knights daughters of Norfolk, Cambridge-shire, and Suffolk, that is to say, for it cannot be understood any otherwise, the daughters of all the gentry of the three counties, come

---

[1] *Familiar Letters*, Vol. 1, p. 7. He says, An infinite number of knights daughters from Norfolk, Cambridge, and Suffolk, come here to market; intimating that they come to be bought, or to buy.

hither to be pick'd up, is a way of speaking I never before heard
any author have the assurance to make use of in print.

The assemblèe he justly commends for the bright appearance
of the beauties; but with a sting in the tayl of this compliment, where he says, They seldom end without some considerable
match or intrigue; and yet he owns, that during the fair, these
assemblèes are held every night. Now that these fine ladies
go intriguing every night, and that too after the comedy is
done, which is after the fair and raffling is over for the day;
so that it must be very late: This is a terrible character for the
ladies of Bury, and intimates in short, that most of them are
whores, which is a horrid abuse upon the whole country.

Now, tho' I like not the assemblèes at all, and shall in another
place give them something of their due; yet having the opportunity to see the fair at Bury, and to see that there were indeed
abundance of the finest ladies, or as fine as any in Britain, yet
I must own, the number of the ladies at the comedy, or at the
assemblèe, is no way equal to the number that are seen in the
town, much less are they equal to the whole body of the ladies
in the three counties, and I must also add, that tho' it is far
from true, that all that appear at the assemblèe, are there for
matches or intrigues, yet I will venture to say, that they are
not the worst of the ladies who stay away; neither are they the
fewest in number, or the meanest in beauty, but just the contrary; and I do not at all doubt, but that the scandalous liberty
some take at those assemblèes, will in time bring them out of
credit with the virtuous part of the sex here, as it has done
already in Kent and other places; and that those ladies who
most value their reputation, will be seen less there than they
have been; for tho' the institution of them has been innocent
and virtuous, the ill use of them, and the scandalous behaviour
of some people at them, will in time arm virtue against them,
and they will be lay'd down as they have been set up, without
much satisfaction.

But the beauty of this town consists in the number of gentry
who dwell in and near it, the polite conversation among them;
the affluence and plenty they live in; the sweet air they breathe
in, and the pleasant country they have to go abroad in.

Here is no manufacturing in this town, or but very little,
except spinning; the chief trade of the place depending upon
the gentry who live there, or near it, and who cannot fail to
cause trade enough by the expence of their families and
equipages, among the people of a county town. They have

but a very small river, or rather but a very small branch of a small river, at this town, which runs from hence to Milden-Hall, on the edge of the Fens. However, the town and gentlemen about, have been at the charge, or have so encourag'd the engineer who was at the charge, that they have made this river navigable to the said Milden-Hall, from whence there is a navigable dyke, call'd Milden-Hall Dreyn, which goes into the River Ouse, and so to Lynn; so that all their coal and wine, iron, lead, and other heavy goods, are brought by water from Lynn, or from London, by the way of Lynn, to the great ease of the tradesmen.

This town is famous for two great events, one was that in the year 1447, in the 25th year of Henry the VIth, a Parliament was held here.

The other was, That at the meeting of this Parliament, the great Humphry, Duke of Glocester, regent of the kingdom, during the absence of King Henry the Vth, and the minority of Henry the VIth, and to his last hour, the safeguard of the whole nation, and darling of the people, was basely murthered here; by whose death, the gate was opened to that dreadful war between the Houses of Lancaster and York, which ended in the confusion of that very race, who are supposed to have contrived that murther.

From St. Edmund's Bury I returned by Stow-Market and Needham, to Ipswich, that I might keep as near the coast as was proper to my design'd circuit or journey; and from Ipswich, to visit the sea again, I went to Woodbridge, and from thence to Orford, on the sea-side.

Woodbridge has nothing remarkable, but that it is a considerable market for butter and corn to be exported to London; for now begins that part which is ordinarily called High-Suffolk; which being a rich soil, is for a long tract of ground, wholly employed in dayries; and again famous for the best butter, and perhaps the worst cheese, in England: The butter is barrelled, or often pickled up in small casks, and sold, not in London only, but I have known a firkin of Suffolk butter sent to the West-Indies, and brought back to England again, and has been perfectly good and sweet, as at first.

The port for the shipping off their Suffolk butter is chiefly Woodbridge, which for that reason is full of corn-factors, and butter-factors, some of whom are very considerable merchants.

From hence turning down to the shore, we see Orford Ness, a noted point of land for the guide of the colliers and coasters, and a good shelter for them to ride under, when a strong north-east wind blows and makes a foul shore on the coast.

South of the Ness is Orford Haven, being the mouth of two little rivers meeting together; 'tis a very good harbour for small vessels, but not capable of receiving a ship of burthen.

Orford was once a good town, but is decay'd, and as it stands on the land-side of the river, the sea daily throws up more land to it, and falls off itself from it, as if it was resolved to disown the place, and that it should be a sea port no longer.

A little farther lies Albro', as thriving, tho' without a port, as the other is decaying, with a good river in the front of it.

There are some gentlemen's seats up farther from the sea, but very few upon the coast.

From Albro' to Dunwich, there are no towns of note; even this town seems to be in danger of being swallowed up; for fame reports, that once they had fifty churches in the town; I saw but one left, and that not half full of people.

This town is a testimony of the decay of publick things, things of the most durable nature; and as the old poet expresses it,

> By numerous examples we may see,
> That towns and cities die, as well as we.

The ruins of Carthage, or the great city of Jerusalem, or of antient Rome, are not at all wonderful to me; the ruins of Nineveh, which are so entirely sunk, as that 'tis doubtful where the city stood; the ruins of Babylon, or the great Persepolis, and many capital cities, which time and the change of monarchies have overthrown; these, I say, are not at all wonderful, because being the capitals of great and flourishing kingdoms, where those kingdoms were overthrown, the capital cities necessarily fell with them; But for a private town, a sea-port, and a town of commerce, to decay, as it were of itself (for we never read of Dunwich being plundered, or ruin'd, by any disaster, at least not of late years); this I must confess, seems owing to nothing but to the fate of things, by which we see that towns, kings, countries, families, and persons, have all their elevation, their medium, their declination, and even their destruction in the womb of time, and the course of nature. It is true, this town is manifestly decayed by the invasion of the waters, and as other towns seem sufferers by the sea, or the tide withdrawing from their ports, such as Orford just now named; Winchelsea in Kent, and the like: So this town is, as it were, eaten up by the sea, as above; and the still encroaching ocean seems to threaten it with a fatal immersion in a few years more.

Yet Dunwich, however ruin'd, retains some share of trade, as particularly for the shipping off butter, cheese, and corn, which is so great a business in this county, and it employs a great many people and ships also; and this port lies right against the particular part of the county for butter, as Framlingham, Halsted, &c. Also a very great quantity of corn is bought up hereabout for the London market; for I shall still touch that point, how all the counties in England contribute something towards the subsistence of the great city of London, of which the butter here is a very considerable article; as also coarse cheese, which I mention'd before, us'd chiefly for the king's ships.

Hereabouts they begin to talk of herrings, and the fishery; and we find in the antient records, that this town, which was then equal to a large city; paid, among other tribute to the Government, 50000 of herrings. Here also, and at Swole, or Southole, the next sea-port, they cure sprats in the same manner as they do herrings at Yarmouth; that is to say, speaking in their own language, they make red sprats; or to speak good English, they make sprats red.

It is remarkable, that this town is now so much washed away by the sea, that what little trade they have, is carry'd on by Walderswick, a little town near Swole, the vessels coming in there, because the ruines of Dunwich make the shore there unsafe and uneasie to the boats; from whence the northern coasting seamen a rude verse of their own using, and I suppose of their own making; as follows,

> Swoul and Dunwich, and Walderswick,
> All go in at one lousie creek.

This lousie creek, in short, is a little river at Swoul, which our late famous atlas-maker calls a good harbour for ships, and rendezvous of the royal navy; but that by the bye; the author it seems knew no better.

From Dunwich, we came to Southwold, the town above-named; this is a small port-town upon the coast, at the mouth of a little river call'd the Blith: I found no business the people here were employ'd in, but the fishery, as above, for herrings and sprats; which they cure by the help of smoak, as they do at Yarmouth.

There is but one church in this town, but it is a very large one and well-built, as most of the churches in this county are, and of impenetrable flint; indeed there is no occasion for its being so large, for staying there one Sabbath-Day, I was surprized to see an extraordinary large church, capable of receiving five or six thousand people, and but twenty-seven in it besides the parson and the clerk; but at the same time the meeting-house of the Dissenters was full to the very doors, having, as I guess'd from 6 to 800 people in it.

This town is made famous for a very great engagement at sea, in the year 1672, between the English and Dutch fleets, in the bay opposite to the town; in which, not to be partial to ourselves, the English fleet was worsted; and the brave Montague Earl of Sandwich, admiral under the Duke of York, lost his life: The ship *Royal Prince*, carrying 100 guns, in which he was, and which was under him, commanded by Sir Edward Spragg, was burnt, and several other ships lost, and about 600 seamen; part of those kill'd in the fight, were, as I was told, brought on shore here and buried in the church-yard of this town, as others also were at Ipswich.

At this town in particular, and so at all the towns on this coast, from Orford-Ness to Yarmouth, is the ordinary place where our summer friends the swallows, first land when they come to visit us; and here they may be said to embark for their return, when they go back into warmer climates; and, as I think the following remark, tho' of so trifling a circumstance, may be both instructing, as well as diverting, it may be very proper in this place. The case is this; I was some years before at this place, at the latter end of the year (viz.) about the beginning of October, and lodging in a house that looked into the church-yard, I observ'd in the evening an unusual multitude of birds sitting on the leads of the church; curiosity led me to go nearer to see what they were, and I found they were all swallows; that there was such an infinite number that they cover'd the whole roof of the church, and of several houses near, and perhaps might, of more houses which I did not see; this led me to enquire of a grave gentleman whom I saw near me, what the meaning was of such a prodigious multitude of swallows sitting there; O SIR, says he, turning towards the sea, you may see the reason, the wind is off sea. I did not seem fully informed by that expression; so he goes on: I perceive, sir, says he, you are a stranger to it; you must then understand first, that this is the season of the year when the swallows, their food here failing, begin to leave us, and return to the country, where-ever it be, from whence I suppose they came; and this being the nearest to the coast of Holland, they come here to embark; this he said smiling a little; and now, sir, says he, the weather being too calm, or the wind contrary, they are waiting for a gale, for they are all wind-bound.

This was more evident to me, when in the morning I found the wind had come about to the north-west in the night, and there was not one swallow to be seen, of near a million, which I believe was there the night before.

How those creatures know that this part of the island of Great-Britain is the way to their home, or the way that they are to go; that this very point is the nearest cut over, or even that the nearest cut is best for them, that we must leave to the naturalists to determin, who insist upon it, that brutes cannot think.

Certain it is, that the swallows neither come hither for warm weather, nor retire from cold, the thing is of quite another nature; they, like the shoals of fish in the sea, pursue their prey; they are a voracious creature, they feed flying; their food is found in the air, viz. the insects; of which in our summer evenings, in damp and moist places, the air is full; they come hither in the summer, because our air is fuller of fogs and damps than in other countries, and for that reason, feeds great quantities of insects; if the air be hot and dry, the gnats die of themselves, and even the swallows will be found famish'd for want, and fall down dead out of the air, their food being taken from them: In like manner, when cold weather comes in, the insects all die, and then of necessity, the swallows quit us, and follow their food where-ever they go; this they do in the manner I have mention'd above; for sometimes they are seen to go off in vast flights like a cloud; And sometimes again, when the wind grows fair, they go away a few and a few, as they come, not staying at all upon the coast.

Note, This passing and re-passing of the swallows, is observ'd no where so much, that I have heard of, or in but few other places, except on this eastern coast; namely, from above Harwich to the east point of Norfolk, call'd Winterton Ness, north; which is all right against Holland; we know nothing of them any farther north, the passage of the sea being, as I suppose, too broad from Flambro' Head, and the shoar of Holderness in Yorkshire, &c.

I find very little remarkable on this side of Suffolk, but what is on the sea shore as above; the inland country is that which they properly call High-Suffolk, and is full of rich feeding-grounds and large farms, mostly employ'd in dayries for making the Suffolk butter and cheese, of which I have spoken already: Among these rich grounds stand some market-towns, tho' not of very considerable note; such as Framlingham, where was once a royal castle, to which Queen Mary retir'd, when the Northumberland faction, in behalf of the Lady Jane, endeavour'd to supplant her; and it was this part of Suffolk where the Gospellers, as they were then called, prefer'd their loyalty to their religion, and complimented the popish line at expence of their share of the Reformation; but they paid dear for it, and their successors have learn'd better politicks since.

In these parts are also several good market-towns, some in this county, and some in the other, as Becles, Bungay, Harlston, &c. all on the edge of the River Waveney, which parts here the counties of Suffolk and Norfolk: And here in a bye-place, and out of common remark, lies the antient town of Hoxon, famous for being the place where St. Edmund was martyr'd, for whom so many cells and shrines have been set up, and monasteries built; and in honour of whom, the famous monastery of St. Edmund's Bury above-mentioned, was founded, which most people erroneously think was the place where the said murther was committed.

Besides the towns mention'd above, there are Halesworth, Saxmundham, Debenham, Aye, or Eye, all standing in this eastern side of Suffolk; in which, as I have said, the whole country is employ'd in dayries, or in feeding of cattle.

This part of England is also remarkable for being the first where the feeding and fattening of cattle, both sheep as well as black cattle with turnips, was first practis'd in England, which is made a very great part of the improvement of their lands to this day; and from whence the practice is spread over most of the east and south parts of England, to the great enriching of the farmers, and encrease of fat cattle: And tho' some have objected against the goodness of the flesh thus fed with turnips, and have fansied it would taste of the root; yet upon experience 'tis found, that at market there is no difference nor can they that buy, single out one joynt of mutton from another by the taste: So that the complaint which our nice palates at first made, begins to cease of itself; and a very great quantity of beef, and mutton also, is brought every year, and every week

to London, from this side of England, and much more than was
formerly known to be fed there.

I can't omit, however little it may seem, that this county of
Suffolk is particularly famous for furnishing the city of London
and all the counties round, with turkeys; and that 'tis thought,
there are more turkeys bred in this county, and the part of
Norfolk that adjoins to it, than in all the rest of England,
especially for sale; tho' this may be reckon'd, as I say above,
but a trifling thing to take notice of in these remarks; yet, as
I have hinted, that I shall observe, how London is in general
supplied with all its provisions from the whole body of the
nation, and how every part of the island is engaged in some
degree or other of that supply; On this account I could not
omit it; nor will it be found so inconsiderable an article as some
may imagin, if this be true which I receiv'd an account of from
a person living on the place, (viz.) That they have counted
300 droves of turkeys (for they drive them all in droves on
foot) pass in one season over Stratford-Bridge on the River
Stour, which parts Suffolk from Essex, about six miles from
Colchester on the road from Ipswich to London. These droves,
as they say, generally contain from three hundred to a thousand
each drove; so that one may suppose them to contain 500
one with another, which is 150000 in all; and yet this is one
of the least passages, the numbers which travel by New
Market-Heath, and the open country and the forest, and
also the numbers that come by Sudbury and Clare, being
many more.

For the further supplies of the markets of London with
poultry, of which these countries particularly abound: They
have within these few years found it practicable to make the
geese travel on foot too, as well as the turkeys; and a prodigious number are brought up to London in droves from the
farthest parts of Norfolk; even from the fenn-country, about
Lynn, Downham, Wisbich, and the Washes; as also from all
the east-side of Norfolk and Suffolk, of whom 'tis very frequent
now to meet droves, with a thousand, sometimes two thousand
in a drove: They begin to drive them generally in August, by
which time the harvest is almost over, and the geese may feed
in the stubbles as they go. Thus they hold on to the end of
October, when the roads begin to be too stiff and deep for their
broad feet and short leggs to march in.

Besides these methods of driving these creatures on foot,
they have of late also invented a new method of carriage, being

carts form'd on purpose, with four stories or stages, to put the creatures in one above another, by which invention one cart will carry a very great number; and for the smoother going, they drive with two horses a-breast, like a coach, so quartering the road for the ease of the gentry that thus ride; changing horses they travel night and day; so that they bring the fowls 70, 80, or 100 miles in two days and one night: The horses in this new-fashion'd voiture go two a-breast, as above, but no perch below as in a coach, but they are fasten'd together by a piece of wood lying cross-wise upon their necks, by which they are kept even and together, and the driver sits on the top of the cart, like as in the publick carriages for the army, &c.

In this manner they hurry away the creatures alive, and infinite numbers are thus carried to London every year. This method is also particular for the carrying young turkeys, or turkey-poults in their season, which are valuable, and yield a good price at market; as also for live chickens in the dear seasons; of all which a very great number are brought in this manner to London, and more prodigiously out of this country than any other part of England, which is the reason of my speaking of it here.

In this part, which we call High-Suffolk, there are not so many families of gentry or nobility plac'd, as in the other side of the country: But 'tis observ'd that tho' their seats are not so frequent here, their estates are; and the pleasure of West Suffolk is much of it supported by the wealth of High-Suffolk; for the richness of the lands, and application of the people to all kinds of improvement, is scarce credible; also the farmers are so very considerable, and their farms and dayries so large, that 'tis very frequent for a farmer to have a thousand pounds stock upon his farm in cows only.

NORFOLK

From High-Suffolk, I pass'd the Waveney into Norfolk, near Schole-Inn; in my passage I saw at Redgrave, (the seat of the family) a most exquisite monument of Sir John Holt, Knight, late lord chief justice of the King's-Bench, several years, and one of the most eminent lawyers of his time. One of the heirs of the family is now building a fine seat about a mile on the south-side of Ipswich, near the road.

The epitaph, or inscription on this monument, is as follows.

M. S.

D. JOHANNIS HOLT, Equitis Aur
Totius Angliæ in Banco Regis
per 21 Annos continuos
Capitalis Justitiarii
Gulielmo Regi Annæq; Reginæ
Consiliarii perpetui:
Libertatis ac Legum Anglicorum
Assertoris, Vindicis, Custodis,
Vigilis Acris & Intrepidi,
Rolandus Frater Vnicus & Hæres
Optime de se Merito
posuit,
Die Martis Vᵗᵒ. 1709 Sublatus est
ex Oculis nostris
Natus 30 Decembris, Anno 1642.

When we come into Norfolk, we see a face of diligence spread over the whole country; the vast manufactures carry'd on (in chief) by the Norwich weavers, employs all the country round in spinning yarn for them; besides many thousand packs of yarn which they receive from other countries, even from as far as Yorkshire, and Westmoreland, of which I shall speak in its place.

This side of Norfolk is very populous, and throng'd with great and spacious market-towns, more and larger than any other part of England so far from London, except Devonshire, and the West-riding of Yorkshire; for example, between the frontiers of Suffolk and the city of Norwich on this side, which is not above 22 miles in breadth, are the following market-towns, viz.

Thetford,	Hingham,	Harleston,
Dis,	West Deerham,	E. Deerham,
Harling,	Attleboro',	Watton,
Bucknam,	Windham,	Loddon, &c.

Most of these towns are very populous and large; but that which is most remarkable is, that the whole country round them is so interspers'd with villages, and those villages so large, and so full of people, that they are equal to market-towns in other counties; in a word, they render this eastern part of Norfolk exceeding full of inhabitants.

An eminent weaver of Norwich, gave me a scheme of their trade on this occasion, by which, calculating from the number of looms at that time employ'd in the city of Norwich only, besides those employ'd in other towns in the same county, he made it appear very plain, that there were 120000 people employ'd in the woollen and silk and wool manufactures of that city only, not that the people all lived in the city, tho' Norwich is a very large and populous city too: But I say, they were employ'd for spinning the yarn used for such goods as were all made in that city. This account is curious enough, and very exact, but it is too long for the compass of this work.

This shews the wonderful extent of the Norwich manufacture, or stuff-weaving trade, by which so many thousands of families are maintained. Their trade indeed felt a very sensible decay, and the cries of the poor began to be very loud, when the wearing of painted callicoes was grown to such an height in England, as was seen about two or three years ago; but an Act of Parliament having been obtained, tho' not without great struggle, in the years 1720, and 1721, for prohibiting the use and wearing of callico's, the stuff trade reviv'd incredibly; and as I pass'd this part of the country in the year 1723, the manufacturers assured me, that there was not in all the eastern and middle part of Norfolk, any hand, unemploy'd, if they would work; and that the very children after four or five years of age, could every one earn their own bread. But I return to speak of the villages and towns in the rest of the county; I shall come to the city of Norwich by itself.

This throng of villages continues thro' all the east part of the county, which is of the greatest extent, and where the manufacture is chiefly carry'd on: If any part of it be waste and thin of inhabitants, it is the west part, drawing a line from about Brand, or Brandon, south, to Walsingham, north. This part of the country indeed is full of open plains, and somewhat sandy and barren, and feeds great flocks of good sheep: But put it all together, the county of Norfolk has the most people in the least tract of land of any county in England, except about London, and Exon, and the West-Riding of Yorkshire, as above.

Add to this, that there is no single county in England, except as above, that can boast of three towns so populous, so rich, and so famous for trade and navigation, as in this county: By these three towns, I mean the city of Norwich, the towns of Yarmouth and Lynn; besides, that it has several other sea-ports of very good trade, as Wisbich, Wells, Burnham, Clye, &c.

NORWICH is the capital of all the county, and the center of

all the trade and manufactures which I have just mention'd; an antient, large, rich, and populous city: If a stranger was only to ride thro' or view the city of Norwich for a day, he would have much more reason to think there was a town without inhabitants, than there is really to say so of Ipswich; but on the contrary, if he was to view the city, either on a Sabbath-day, or on any publick occasion, he would wonder where all the people could dwell, the multitude is so great: But the case is this; the inhabitants being all busie at their manufactures, dwell in their garrets at their looms, and in their combing-shops, so they call them, twisting-mills, and other work-houses; almost all the works they are employ'd in, being done within doors. There are in this city thirty-two parishes besides the cathedral, and a great many meeting-houses of Dissenters of all denominations. The publick edifices are chiefly the castle, antient and decayed, and now for many years past made use of for a jayl. The Duke of Norfolk's house was formerly kept well, and the gardens preserved for the pleasure and diversion of the citizens, but since feeling too sensibly the sinking circumstances of that once glorious family, who were the first peers and hereditary earl-marshals of England.

The walls of this city are reckon'd three miles in circumference, taking in more ground than the city of London; but much of that ground lying open in pasture-fields and gardens; nor does it seem to be, like some antient places, a decayed declining town, and that the walls mark out its antient dimensions; for we do not see room to suppose that it was ever larger or more populous than it is now: But the walls seem to be placed, as if they expected that the city would in time encrease sufficiently to fill them up with buildings.

The cathedral of this city is a fine fabrick, and the spire-steeple very high and beautiful; it is not antient, the bishop's see having been first at Thetford; from whence it was not translated hither till the twelfth century; yet the church has so many antiquities in it, that our late great scholar and physician, Sir Tho. Brown, thought it worth his while to write a whole book to collect the monuments and inscrpitions in this church, to which I refer the reader.

The River Yare runs through this city, and is navigable thus far without the help of any art, (that is to say, without locks or stops) and being encreas'd by other waters, passes afterwarde thro' a long tract of the richest meadows, and the largest, taks them all together, that are any where in England, lying for thirty miles in length, from this city to Yarmouth, including the return of the said meadows on the bank of the Waveney south, and on the River Thyrn, north.

Here is one thing indeed strange in itself, and more so, in that history seems to be quite ignorant of the occasion of it. The River Waveney is a considerable river, and of a deep and full channel, navigable for large barges as high as Beccles; it runs for a course of about fifty miles, between the two counties of Suffolk and Norfolk, as a boundary to both; and pushing on, tho' with a gentle stream, towards the sea, no one would doubt, but, that when they see the river growing broader and deeper, and going directly towards the sea, even to the edge of the beach; that is to say, within a mile of the main ocean; no stranger, I say, but would expect to see its entrance into the sea at that place, and a noble harbour for ships at the mouth of it; when on a sudden, the land rising high by the sea-side, crosses the head of the river, like a dam, checks the whole course of it, and it returns, bending its course west, for two miles, or thereabouts; and then turning north, thro' another long course of meadows (joining to those just now mention'd) seeks out the River Yare, that it may join its water with her's, and find their way to the sea together.

Some of our historians tell a long fabulous story of this river's being once open, and a famous harbour for ships belonging to the town of Leostof adjoining; But that the town of Yarmouth envying the prosperity of the said town of Leostof, made war upon them; and that after many bloody battles, as well by sea as by land, they came at last to a decisive action at sea with their respective fleets, and the victory fell to the Yarmouth men, the Leostof fleet being overthrown and utterly destroyed; and that upon this victory, the Yarmouth men either actually did stop up the mouth of the said river, or oblig'd the vanquish'd Leostof men to do it themselves, and bound them never to attempt to open it again.

I believe my share of this story, and I recommend no more of it to the reader; adding, that I see no authority for the relation, neither do the relators agree either in the time of it, or in the particulars of the fact; that is to say, in whose reign, or under what government all this happened; in what year, and the like: So I satisfy my self with transcribing the matter of fact, and then leave it as I find it.

In this vast tract of meadows are fed a prodigious number of black cattle, which are said to be fed up for the fattest beef, tho' not the largest in England; and the quantity is so great, as that they not only supply the city of Norwich, the town of Yarmouth, and county adjacent, but send great quantities of them weekly in all the winter season, to London.

And this in particular is worthy remark, That the gross of all the Scots cattle which come yearly into England, are brought hither, being brought to a small village lying north of the city of Norwich, call'd St. Faiths, where the Norfolk grasiers go and buy them.

These Scots runts, so they call them, coming out of the cold and barren mountains of the Highlands in Scotland, feed so eagerly on the rich pasture in these marshes, that they thrive in an unusual manner, and grow monstrously fat; and the beef is so delicious for taste, that the inhabitants prefer 'em to the English cattle, which are much larger and fairer to look at, and they may very well do so: Some have told me, and I believe with good judgment, that there are above 40,000 of these Scots cattle fed in this country every year, and most of them in the said marshes between Norwich, Beccles, and Yarmouth.

YARMOUTH is an antient town, much older than Norwich; and at present, tho' not standing on so much ground, yet better built; much more compleat; for number of inhabitants, not much inferior; and for wealth, trade, and advantage of its situation, infinitely superior to Norwich.

It is plac'd on a peninsula between the River Yare and the sea; the two last lying parallel to one another, and the town in the middle: The river lies on the west-side of the town, and being grown very large and deep, by a conflux of all the rivers on this side the county, forms the haven; and the town facing to the west also, and open to the river, makes the finest key in England, if not in Europe, not inferior even to that of Marseilles itself.

The ships ride here so close, and as it were, keeping up one another, with their head-fasts on shore, that for half a mile together, they go cross the stream with their bolsprits over the land, their bowes, or heads, touching the very wharf; so that one may walk from ship to ship as on a floating bridge, all along by the shore-side: The key reaching from the draw-bridge almost to the south-gate, is so spacious and wide, that in some places 'tis near one hundred yards from the houses to the wharf. In this pleasant and agreeable range of houses are some very magnificent buildings, and among the rest, the custom-house and town-hall, and some merchants houses, which look like little palaces, rather than the dwelling-houses of private men.

The greatest defect of this beautiful town, seems to be, that tho' it is very rich and encreasing in wealth and trade, and consequently in people, there is not room to enlarge the town by building; which would be certainly done much more than it is, but that the river on the land-side prescribes them, except at the north end without the gate; and even there the land is not very agreeable: But had they had a larger space within the gates, there would before now, have been many spacious streets of noble fine buildings erected, as we see is done in some other thriving towns in England, as at Liverpool, Manchester, Bristol, Frome, &c.

The key and the harbour of this town during the fishing-fair, as they call it, which is every Michaelmas, one sees the land cover'd with people, and the river with barks and boats, busy day and night, landing and carrying off the herrings, which they catch here in such prodigious quantities, that it is incredible. I happen'd to be there during their fishing-fair, when I told, in one tide, one hundred and ten barks and fishing vessels coming up the river, all loaden with herrings, and all taken the night before; and this was besides what was brought on shore on the Dean, (that is the seaside of the town) by open boats, which they call cobles,[1] and which often bring in two or three last [2] of fish at a time. The barks [3] often bring in ten last a piece.

This fishing-fair begins on Michaelmas Day, and lasts all the month of October, by which time the herrings draw off to sea, shoot their spawn, and are no more fit for the merchants business; at least not those that are taken thereabouts.

The quantity of herrings that are catch'd in this season are diversly accounted for; some have said, that the towns of Yarmouth and Leostof only, have taken forty thousand last in a season: I will not venture to confirm that report; but this I have heard the merchants themselves say, (viz.) That they

---

[1] The cobles are open boats, which come from the north, from Scarbro', Whitby, &c., and come to Yarmouth to let themselves out to fish for the merchants during the fair-time.

[2] Note, a last is ten barrels, each barrel containing a thousand herrings.

[3] The barks come from the coast of Kent and Sussex, as from Foulkston, Dover, and Rye in Kent, and from Brithelmston in Sussex, and let themselves out to fish for the merchants during the said fair, as the cobles do from the north.

have cur'd, that is to say, hang'd and dry'd in the smoak 40,000 barrels of merchantable redherrings in one season, which is in itself (tho' far short of the other) yet a very considerable article; and it is to be added, that this is besides all the herrings consum'd in the country towns of both those populous counties, for thirty miles from the sea, whither very great quantities are carry'd every tide during the whole season.

But this is only one branch of the great trade carry'd on in this town; Another part of this commerce, is in the exporting these herrings after they are cur'd; and for this their merchants have a great trade to Genoa, Leghorn, Naples, Messina, and Venice; as also to Spain and Portugal, also exporting with their herring very great quantities of worsted stuffs, and stuffs made of silk and worsted; camblets, &c. the manufactures of the neighbouring city of Norwich, and the places adjacent.

Besides this, they carry on a very considerable trade with Holland, whose opposite neighbours they are; and a vast quantity of woollen manufactures they export to the Dutch every year. Also they have a fishing trade to the north-seas for white fish, which from the place are called the North-Sea cod.

They have also a considerable trade to Norway, and to the Baltick, from whence they bring back deals, and fir-timber, oaken plank, baulks, sparrs, oars, pitch, tar, hemp, flax, spruce canvas, and sail-cloth; with all manner of naval stores, which they generally have a consumption for in their own port, where they build a very great number of ships every year, besides re-fitting and repairing the old.

Add to this the coal trade between Newcastle and the river of Thames, in which they are so improv'd of late years, that they have now a greater share of it than any other town in England; and have quite work'd the Ipswich men out of it, who had formerly the chief share of the colliery in their hands.

For the carrying on all these trades, they must have a very great number of ships, either of their own, or employ'd by them; and it may in some measure be judg'd of by this, That in the year 1697, I had an account from the town register, that there was then 1123 sail of ships using the sea, and belong'd to the town, besides such ships as the merchants of Yarmouth might be concern'd in, and be part-owners of, belonging to any other ports.

To all this I must add, without compliment to the town, or to the people, that the merchants, and even the generality of traders of Yarmouth, have a very good reputation in trade,

as well abroad as at home, for men of fair and honourable
dealing, punctual and just in their performing their engage-
ments, and in discharging commissions; and their seamen, as
well masters as mariners, are justly esteem'd among the ablest
and most expert navigators in England.

This town however populous and large, was ever contained
in one parish, and had but one church; but within these two
years they have built another very fine church, near the south-
end of the town. The old church is dedicated to St. Nicholas,
and was built by that famous Bishop of Norwich, Will. Herbert,
who flourished in the reign of William II, and Hen. I. William
of Malmsbury calls him *Vir pecuniosus*; he might have called him
Vir Pecuniosissimus, considering the times he lived in, and the
works of charity and munificence, which he has left as witnesses
of his immense riches; for he built the cathedral church; the
priory for sixty monks; the bishop's palace, and the parish-
church of St. Leonard, all in Norwich; this great church at
Yarmouth, the church of St. Margaret at Lynn, and of St. Mary
at Elmham. He remov'd the episcopal see from Thetford to
Norwich, and instituted the Cluniack Monks at Thetford, and
gave them, or built them a house. This old church, is very
large, and has a high spire, which is a useful sea-mark.

Here is one of the finest market-places, and the best serv'd
with provisions, in England, London excepted, and the inhabitants are so multiplied in a few years, that they seem to want
room in their town, rather than people to fill it, as I have
observ'd above.

The streets are all exactly strait from north to south, with
lanes or alleys, which they call rows, crossing them in strait
lines also from east to west; so that it is the most regular
built town in England, and seems to have been built all at once;
Or, that the dimensions of the houses, and extent of the streets,
were laid out by consent.

They have particular privileges in this town, and a jurisdiction by which they can try, condemn, and execute in especial
cases, without waiting for a warrant from above; and this they
exerted once very smartly, in executing a captain of one of the
king's ships of war in the reign of King Charles II, for a murther
committed in the street, the circumstance of which did indeed
call for justice; but some thought they would not have ventur'd
to exert their power as they did; however, I never heard that
the government resented it, or blamed them for it.

It is also a very well govern'd town; and I have no where in England observed the Sabbath-Day so exactly kept, or the breach so continually punished as in this place, which I name to their honour.

Among all these regularities, it is no wonder if we do not find abundance of revelling, or that there is little encouragement to assemblies, plays, and gaming-meetings at Yarmouth, as in some other places; and yet I do not see that the ladies here come behind any of the neighbouring counties, either in beauty, breeding, or behaviour; to which may be added too, not at all to their disadvantage, that they generally go beyond them in fortunes.

From Yarmouth I resolv'd to pursue my first design, (viz.) To view the sea-side on this coast, which is particularly famous for being one of the most dangerous and most fatal to the sailors in all England, I may say in all Britain; and the more so, because of the great number of ships which are continually going and coming this way, in their passage between London and all the northern coasts of Great-Britain. Matters of antiquity are not my enquiry, but principally observations on the present state of things, and if possible, to give such accounts of things worthy of recording, as have never been observed before; and this leads me the more directly to mention the commerce and the navigation when I come to towns upon the coast, as what few writers have yet medled with.

The reason of the dangers of this particular coast, are found in the situation of the county, and in the course of ships sailing this way, which I shall describe as well as I can, thus; the shoar from the mouth of the river of Thames to Yarmouth Road, lies in a strait line from S.S.E. to N.N.W. the land being on the W. or larboard side.

From Winterton Ness, which is the utmost northerly point of land in the county of Norfolk, and about four miles beyond Yarmouth, the shoar falls off for near sixty miles to the west, as far as Lynn and Boston, till the shoar of Lincolnshire tends north again for about sixty miles more, as far as the Humber, whence the coast of Yorkshire, or Holderness, which is the East Riding, shoots out again into the sea, to the Spurn, and to Flambro' Head, as far east almost as the shoar of Norfolk had given back at Winterton, making a very deep gulph or bay, between those two points of Winterton and the Spurn Head; so that the ships going north, are oblig'd to stretch away to sea from Winterton Ness, and leaving the sight of land in that deep bay which I have mention'd, that reaches to Lynn, and the shoar of Lincolnshire, they go, I say, N. or still N.N.W. to meet the shoar of Holderness, which I said runs out into the sea again at the Spurn; This they leave also and the first land they make, or desire to make, is called as above, Flambro' Head; so that Winterton Ness and Flambro' Head, are the two extremes of this course, there is, as I said, the Spurn Head indeed between; but as it lies too far in towards the Humber, they keep out to the north to avoid coming near it.

In like manner the ships which come from the north, leave the shoar at Flambro' Head, and stretch away S.S.E. for Yarmouth Roads; and the first land they make is Winterton Ness (as above). Now, the danger of the place is this; If the ships coming from the north are taken with a hard gale of wind from the S.E. or from any point between N.E. and S.E. so that they cannot, as the seamen call it, weather Winterton Ness, they are thereby kept in within that deep bay; and if the wind blows hard, are often in danger of running on shoar upon the rocks about Cromer, on the north coast of Norfolk, or stranding upon the flat shoar between Cromer and Wells; all the relief they have, is good ground tackle to ride it out, which is very hard to do there, the sea coming very high upon them; Or if they cannot ride it out then, to run into the bottom of the great bay I mention'd, to Lynn or Boston, which is a very difficult and desperate push: So that sometimes in this distress whole fleets have been lost here all together.

The like is the danger to ships going northward, if after passing by Winterton they are taken short with a north-east wind, and cannot put back into the Roads, which very often happens, then they are driven upon the same coast, and embay'd just as the latter. The danger on the north part of this bay is not the same, because if ships going or coming should be taken short on this side Flambro', there is the River Humber open to them, and several good roads to have recourse to, as Burlington Bay, Grimsby Road, and the Spurn Head, and others, where they ride under shelter.

The dangers of this place being thus consider'd, 'tis no wonder, that upon the shoar beyond Yarmouth, there are no less than four light-houses kept flaming every night, besides the lights at Castor, north of the town, and at Goulston S, all which are to direct the sailors to keep a good offing, in case of bad weather, and to prevent their running into Cromer Bay, which the seamen call the Devils Throat.

As I went by land from Yarmouth northward, along the shoar towards Cromer aforesaid, and was not then fully master of the reason of these things, I was surpris'd to see, in all the way from Winterton, that the farmers, and country people had scarce a barn, or a shed, or a stable; nay, not the pales of their yards, and gardens, not a hogstye, not a necessary-house, but what was built of old planks, beams, wales and timbers, &c. the wrecks of ships, and ruins of mariners and merchants' fortunes; and in some places were whole yards fill'd, and piled up very high with the same stuff laid up, as I suppos'd to sell for the like building purposes, as there should be occasion.

About the year 1692, (I think it was that year) there was a melancholy example of what I have said of this place; a fleet of 200 sail of light colliers (so they call the ships bound northward empty to fetch coals from Newcastle to London) went out of Yarmouth Roads with a fair wind, to pursue their voyage, and were taken short with a storm of wind at N.E, after they were past Winterton Ness, a few leagues; some of them, whose masters were a little more wary than the rest, or perhaps, who made a better judgment of things, or who were not so far out as the rest, tack'd, and put back in time, and got safe into the roads; but the rest pushing on, in hopes to keep out to sea, and weather it, were by the violence of the storm driven back, when they were too far embay'd to weather Winterton Ness, as above; and so were forc'd to run west, every one shifting for themselves, as well as they could; some run away for Lyn Deeps but few of them, (the night being so dark) cou'd find their way in there; some but very few rid it out, at a distance; the rest being above 140 sail were all driven on shore, and dash'd to pieces, and very few of the people on board were sav'd: At the very same unhappy juncture, a fleet of loaden ships were coming from the north, and being just crossing the same bay, were forcibly driven into it, not able to weather the Ness, and so were involv'd in the same ruin as the light fleet was; also some coasting vessels loaden with corn from Lyn, and Wells, and bound for Holland, were with the same unhappy luck just come out, to begin their voyage, and some of them lay at anchor; these also met with the same misfortune, so that in the whole, above 200 sail of ships, and above a thousand people perished in the disaster of that one miserable night, very few escaping.

Cromer is a market town close to the shoar of this dangerous coast, I know nothing it is famous for (besides it's being thus

the terror of the sailors) except good lobsters, which are taken
on that coast in great numbers, and carryed to Norwich, and in
such quantities sometimes too, as to be convey'd by sea to
London.

Farther within the land, and between this place and Norwich,
are several good market towns, and innumerable villages, all
diligently applying to the woollen manufacture, and the country
is exceeding fruitful and fertil, as well in corn as in pastures;
particularly, (which was very pleasant to see) the phesants were
in such great plenty, as to be seen in the stubbles like cocks
and hens; a testimony tho' (by the way) that the county had
more tradesmen than gentlemen in it; indeed this part is so
entirely given up to industry, that what with the seafaring men
on the one side, and the manufactures on the other, we saw no
idle hands here, but every man busie on the main affair of
life, that is to say, getting money: Some of the principal of
these towns are Alsham, North Walsham, South Walsham,
Wursted, Caston, Reepham, Holt, Saxthorp, St. Faith's,
Blikling, and many others. Near the last Sir John Hobart, of
an antient family in this county, has a noble seat, but old
built. This is that St. Faiths, where the drovers bring their
black cattle to sell to the Norfolk graziers, as is observ'd above.

From Cromer, we ride on the strand or open shoar to Weyburn
Hope, the shoar so flat that in some places the tide ebbs out
near two miles: From Weyburn west lyes Clye, where there are
large salt-works, and very good salt made, which is sold all
over the county, and some times sent to Holland, and to the
Baltick: From Clye, we go to Masham, and to Wells, all towns
on the coast, in each whereof there is a very considerable trade
cary'd on with Holland for corn, which that part of the county
is very full of: I say nothing of the great trade driven here
from Holland, back again to England, because I take it to be a
trade carryed on with much less honesty than advantage;
especially while the clandestine trade, or the art of smuggling
was so much in practice; what it is now, is not to my present
purpose.

Near this town lye the Seven Burnhams, as they are call'd,
that is to say seven small towns, all call'd by the same name,
and each employ'd in the same trade of carrying corn to
Holland, and bringing back —— &c.

From hence we turn to the S.W. to Castle-Rising, an old
decay'd burrough town with perhaps not ten families in it,
which yet (to the scandal of our prescription right) sends two

members to the British Parliament, being as many as the city of Norwich it self, or any town in the kingdom, London excepted can do.

On our left we see Walsingham, an antient town, famous for the old ruins of a monastery of note there, and the shrine of our Lady, as noted as that of St. Thomas-a-Becket at Canterbury, and for little else.

Near this place are the seats of the two ally'd families of the Lord Viscount Townsend, and Robert Walpole, Esq; the latter at this time one of the lords commissioners of the Treasury, and minister of state, and the former one of the principal secretaries of state to King GEORGE, of which again.

From hence we went to Lyn, another rich and populous thriving port-town. It stands on more ground than the town of Yarmouth, and has I think more parishes, yet I cannot allow that it has more people than Yarmouth, if so many. It is a beautiful well built, and well situated town, at the mouth of the River Ouse, and has this particular attending it, which gives it a vast advantage in trade; namely, that there is the greatest extent of inland navigation here, of any port in England, London excepted. The reason whereof is this, that there are more navigable rivers empty themselves here into the sea, including the Washes which are branches of the same port, than at any one mouth of waters in England, except the Thames and the Humber. By these navigable rivers the merchants of Lynn supply about six counties wholly, and three counties in part, with their goods, especially wine and coals, (viz.) By the Little Ouse, they send their goods to Brandon, and Thetford, by the Lake to Mildenhall, Barton-Mills, and St. Edmunds-Bury; by the river Grant to Cambridge, by the Great Ouse it self to Ely, to St. Ives, to St. Neots, to Barford-Bridge, and to Bedford; by the River Nyne, to Peterboro'; by the dreyns and washes to Wysbich, to Spalding, Market-Deeping, and Stamford; besides the several counties, into which these goods are carryed by land carriage, from the places where the navigation of those rivers ends; which has given rise to this observation on the town of Lynn, that they bring in more coals, than any sea-port between London and Newcastle; and import more wines than any port in England, except London and Bristol; their trade to Norway, and to the Baltick Sea is also great in proportion, and of late years they have extended their trade farther to the southward.

Here are more gentry, and consequently is more gayety in

this town than in Yarmouth, or even in Norwich it self; the place abounding in very good company.

The situation of this town renders it capable of being made very strong, and in the late wars it was so; a line of fortification being drawn round it at a distance from the walls; the ruins, or rather remains of which works appear very fair to this day; nor would it be a hard matter to restore the bastions, with the ravelins and counterscarp, upon any sudden emergency, to a good state of defence; and that in a little time, a sufficient number of workmen being employed, especially because they are able to fill all their ditches with water from the sea, in such a manner as that it cannot be drawn off.

There is, in the market-place of this town, a very fine statue of King William on horseback, erected at the charge of the town. The Owse is mighty large and deep, close to the very town itself, and ships of good burthen may come up to the key; but there is no bridge, the stream being too strong, and the bottom moorish and unsound: Nor for the same reason is the anchorage computed the best in the world; but there are good roads farther down.

They pass over here in boats into the fenn-country, and over the famous washes into Lincolnshire, but the passage is very dangerous and uneasy, and where passengers often miscarry and are lost; but then it is usually on their venturing at improper times, and without the guides, which if they would be persuaded not to do, they would very rarely fail of going or coming safe.

From Lynn, I bent my course to Downham, where is an ugly wooden bridge over the Ouse; from whence we pass'd the fenn country to Wisbich, but saw nothing that way to tempt our curiosity but deep roads, innumerable dreyns and dykes of water, all navigable, and a rich soil, the land bearing a vast quantity of good hemp; but a base unwholsom air; so we came back to Ely, whose cathedral, standing in a level flat country, is seen far and wide; and of which town, when the minster, so they call it, is describ'd, every thing remarkable is said that there is room to say; and of the minster this is the most remarkable thing that I could hear, namely, that some of it is so antient, totters so much with every gust of wind, looks so like a decay, and seems so near it, that when ever it does fall, all that 'tis likely will be thought strange in it, will be, that it did not fall a hundred years sooner.

From hence we came over the Ouse, and in a few miles to Newmarket: In our way near Snaybell we saw a noble seat of the late Admiral Russel, now Earl of Orford, a name made famous by the glorious victory obtain'd under his command over the French fleet, and the burning their ships at La Hogue; a victory equal in glory to, and infinitely more glorious to the English nation in particular, than that at Blenheim, and above all more to the particular advantage of the Confederacy, because it so broke the heart of the naval power of France, that they have not fully recover'd it to this day: But of this victory it must be said, it was owing to the haughty, rash, and insolent orders given by the King of France to his admiral, (viz.) To fight the Confederate fleet wherever he found them, without leaving room for him to use due caution if he found them too strong; which pride of France was doubtless a fate upon them, and gave a cheap victory to the Confederates; the French coming down rashly, and with the most impolitick bravery, with about five and forty sail to attack between seventy and eighty sail; by which means they met their ruin; whereas, had their own fleet been join'd, it might have cost more blood to have master'd them, if it had been done at all.

The situation of this house is low, and on the edge of the fenn-country, but the building is very fine, the avenues noble, and the gardens perfectly finished; the apartments also are rich; and I see nothing wanting but a family and heirs, to sustain the glory and inheritance of the illustrious ancestor, who rais'd it, *sed caret pedibus*, these are wanting.

Being come to Newmarket in the month of October, I had the opportunity to see the horse-races; and a great concourse of the nobility and gentry, as well from London as from all parts of England; but they were all so intent, so eager, so busy upon the sharping part of the sport, their wagers and bets, that to me they seem'd just as so many horse-coursers in Smithfield, descending (the greatest of them) from their high dignity and quality, to picking one another's pockets, and biting one another as much as possible, and that with such eagerness, as that it might be said they acted without respect to faith, honour, or good manners.

There was Mr. Frampton, the oldest, and as some say, the cunningest jockey in England, one day he lost 1000 guineas, the next he won two thousand; and so alternately he made as light of throwing away five hundred or one thousand pounds at a time, as other men do of their pocket-money, and as perfectly calm, cheerful, and unconcern'd, when he had lost one thousand pounds, as when he had won it. On the other

side, there was Sir R—— Fagg, of Sussex, of whom fame says
he has the most in him and the least to shew for it, relating to
jockeyship, of any man there; yet he often carry'd the prize;
his horses, they said, were all cheats, how honest soever their
master was; for he scarce ever produc'd a horse but he look'd
like what he was not, and was what no body cou'd expect him
to be: If he was as light as the wind, and could fly like a meteor,
he was sure to look as clumsie, and as dirty, and as much like
a cart-horse as all the cunning of his master and the grooms
could make him; and just in this manner he bit some of the
greatest gamesters in the field.

I was so sick of the jockeying part, that I left the crowd
about the posts, and pleased my self with observing the horses;
how the creatures yielded to all the arts and managements of
their masters; how they took their airings in sport, and play'd
with the daily heats which they ran over the course before the
grand day; but how! as knowing the difference equally with
their riders, would they exert their utmost strength at the
time of the race itself; and that to such an extremity, that one
or two of them died in the stable when they came to be rubb'd
after the first heat.

Here I fansy'd myself in the Circus Maximus at Rome, seeing
the antient games, and the racings of the chariots and horsemen; and in this warmth of my imagination I pleas'd and
diverted myself more and in a more noble manner, than I could
possibly do in the crowds of gentlemen at the weighing and
starting posts, and at their coming in; or at their meetings at
the coffee-houses and gaming-tables after the races were over,
where there was little or nothing to be seen, but what was the
subject of just reproach to them, and reproof from every wise
man that look'd upon them. *N.B.* Pray take it with you as you
go, you see no ladies at New-Market, except a few of the neighbouring gentlemen's families who come in their coaches on any
particular day to see a race and so go home again directly.

As I was pleasing myself with what was to be seen here, I went
in the intervals of the sport to see the fine seats of the gentlemen
in the neighbouring county, for this part of Suffolk, being an
open champain country, and a healthy air, is form'd for pleasure,
and all kinds of country diversions; nature, as it were, inviting
the gentlemen to visit her, where she was fully prepar'd to receive
them; in conformity to which kind summons they came; for
the country is, as it were, cover'd with fine palaces of the
nobility, and pleasant seats of the gentlemen.

The Earl of Orford's house I have mention'd already, the next is Euston Hall, the seat of the Duke of Grafton; it lies in the open country towards the side of Norfolk, not far from Thetford; a place capable of all that is pleasant and delightful in nature, and improv'd by art to every extreme that Nature is able to produce.

From thence I went to Rushbrook, formerly the seat of the noble family of Jermyns, lately Lord Dover, and now of the house of Davers. Here Nature, for the time I was there, droopt, and veil'd all the beauties of which she once boasted; the family being in tears, and the house shut up; Sir Robert Davers, the head thereof, and knight of the shire for the county of Suffolk, and who had married the eldest daughter of the late Lord Dover, being just dead, and the corpse lying there in its funeral form of ceremony, not yet buried; yet all look'd lovely in their sorrow, and a numerous issue promising and grown up, intimated that the family of Davers would still flourish, and that the beauties of Rushbrook, the mansion of the family, were not form'd with so much art in vain, or to die with the present possessor.

After this we saw Brently, the seat of the Earl of Dysert, and the antient palace of my Lord Cornwallis, with several others of exquisite situation, and adorn'd with the beauties both of art and nature; so that I think, any traveller from abroad, who would desire to see how the English gentry live, and what pleasures they enjoy, should come into Suffolk and Cambridgeshire, and take but a light circuit among the country seats of the gentlemen on this side only, and they would be soon convinc'd, that not France, no not Italy itself, can out-do them, in proportion to the climate they lived in.

I had still the county of Cambridge to visit, to compleat this tour of the eastern part of England, and of that I come now to speak.

We enter Cambridgeshire out of Suffolk with all the advantage in the world; the county beginning upon those pleasant and agreeable plains call'd New Market-Heath, where passing the Devil's Ditch, which has nothing worth notice but its name, and that but fabulous too, from the hills call'd Gogmagog, we see a rich and pleasant vale westward, cover'd with corn-fields, gentlemen's seats, villages, and at a distance, to crown all the rest, that antient and truly famous town and university of Cambridge; capital of the county, and receiving its name from, if not as some say, giving name to it; for if it be true—that the town takes its name of Cambridge from its bridge over the River Cam; then certainly the shire or county, upon the division of England into counties, had its name from the town, and Cambridgeshire signifies no more or less than the county of which Cambridge is the capital town.

As my business is not to lay out the geographical situation of places, I say nothing of the buttings and boundings of this county: It lies on the edge of the great level, call'd by the people here the fenn-country; and great part, if not all, the Isle of Ely, lies in this county and Norfolk: The rest of Cambridgeshire is almost wholly a corn country; and of that corn five parts in six of all they sow, is barly, which is generally sold to Ware and Royston, and other great malting-towns in Hertfordshire, and is the fund from whence that vast quantity of malt, call'd Hertfordshire malt is made, which is esteem'd the best in England. As Essex, Suffolk, and Norfolk, are taken up in manufacturing, and fam'd for industry, this county has no manufacture at all; nor are the poor, except the husband-men, fam'd for any thing so much as idleness and sloth, to their scandal be it spoken; what the reason of it is, I know not.

It is scarce possible to talk of anything in Cambridgeshire but Cambridge itself; whether it be that the county has so little worth speaking of in it, or that the town has so much, that I leave to others; however, as I am making modern observations, not writing history, I shall look into the county as well as into the colleges, for what I have to say.

As I said, I first had a view of Cambridge from Gogmagog Hills: I am to add, that there appears on the mountain that goes by this name, an antient camp, or fortification, that lies on the top of the hill, with a double or rather treble rampart and ditch, which most of our writers say was neither Roman nor Saxon, but British: I am to add, that King James II. caused a spacious stable to be built in the area of this camp, for his running-horses, and made old Mr. Frampton, whom I mention'd above, master or inspector of them: The stables remain still there, tho' they are not often made use of. As we descended westward, we saw the fenn country on our right, almost all cover'd with water like a sea, the Michaelmas rains having been very great that year, they had sent down great floods of water from the upland countries, and those fenns being, as may be very properly said, the sink of no less than thirteen counties; that is to say, that all the water, or most part of the water of thirteen counties, falls into them, they are often thus

overflow'd. The rivers which thus empty themselves into these
fenns, and which thus carry off the water, are the Cam or
Grant, the Great Ouse, and Little Ouse, the Nene, the Welland,
and the river which runs from Bury to Milden-Hall; the counties
which these rivers drain, as above, are as follows,

Lincoln,	Warwick,	Norfolk,
*Cambridge,	Oxford,	Suffolk,
*Huntingdon,	Leicester,	Essex.
*Bedford,	*Northampton,	
Buckingham,	*Rutland,	

N. Those mark'd with (*) empty all their waters this way,
the rest but in part.

In a word, all the water of the middle part of England which
does not run into the Thames or the Trent, comes down into
these fenns.

In these fenns are abundance of those admirable pieces of
art call'd duckoys; that is to say, Places so adapted for the
harbour and shelter of wild-fowl, and then furnish'd with a
breed of those they call decoy-ducks, who are taught to allure
and entice their kind to the places they belong to, that it is
incredible what quantities of wild-fowl of all sorts, duck, mallard,
teal, widgeon, &c. they take in those duckoys every week,
during the season; it may indeed be guess'd at a little by this,
that there is a duckoy not far from Ely, which pays to the
landlord, Sir Tho. Hare 500*l.* a year rent, besides the charge of
maintaining a great number of servants for the management;
and from which duckoy alone they assured me at St. Ives, (a
town on the Ouse, where the fowl they took was always brought
to be sent to London;) that they generally sent up three thousand
couple a week.

There are more of these about Peterbro' who send the fowl
up twice a week in waggon loads at a time, whose waggons
before the late Act of Parliament to regulate carriers, I have
seen drawn by ten, and twelve horses a piece, they were loaden
so heavy.

As these fenns appear cover'd with water, so I observ'd too,
that they generally at this latter part of the year appear also
cover'd with foggs, so that when the Downs and higher grounds
of the adjacent country were gilded by the beams of the sun,
the Isle of Ely look'd as if wrapp'd up in blankets, and nothing
to be seen, but now and then, the lanthorn or cupola of Ely
Minster.

*D 820

One could hardly see this from the hills and not pity the many thousands of families that were bound to or confin'd in those foggs, and had no other breath to draw than what must be mix'd with those vapours, and that steam which so universally overspread the country: But notwithstanding this, the people, especially those that are used to it, live unconcern'd, and as healthy as other folks, except now and then an ague, which they make light of, and there are great numbers of very antient people among them.

I now draw near to Cambridge, to which I fansy I look as if I was afraid to come, having made so many circumlocutions beforehand; but I must yet make another digression before I enter the town; (for in my way, and as I came in from New Market, about the beginning of September;) I cannot omit, that I came necessarily through Sturbridge Fair, which was then in its height.

If it is a diversion worthy a book to treat of trifles, such as the gayety of Bury Fair, it cannot be very unpleasant, especially to the trading part of the world, to say something of this fair, which is not only the greatest in the whole nation, but in the world; nor, if I may believe those who have seen them all, is the fair at Leipsick in Saxony, the mart at Frankfort on the Main, or the fairs at Neuremberg, or Augsburg, any way to compare to this fair at Sturbridge.

It is kept in a large corn-field, near Casterton, extending from the side of the River Cam, towards the road, for about half a mile square.

If the husbandmen who rent the land, do not get their corn off before a certain day in August, the fair-keepers may trample it under foot and spoil it to build their booths, or tents; for all the fair is kept in tents, and booths: On the other hand, to ballance that severity, if the fair-keepers have not done their business of the fair, and remov'd and clear'd the field by another certain day in September, the plowmen may come in again, with plow and cart, and overthrow all and trample it into the dirt; and as for the filth, dung, straw, &c. necessarily left by the fair-keepers, the quantity of which is very great, it is the farmers fees, and makes them full amends for the trampling, riding, and carting upon, and hardening the ground.

It is impossible to describe all the parts and circumstances of this fair exactly; the shops are placed in rows like streets, whereof one is call'd Cheapside; and here, as in several other streets, are all sorts of trades, who sell by retale, and who come principally from London with their goods; scarce any trades are omitted, goldsmiths, toyshops, brasiers, turners, milleners, haberdashers, hatters, mercers, drapers, pewtrers, china-warehouses, and in a word all trades that can be named in London; with coffee-houses, taverns, brandy-shops, and eating-houses, innumerable, and all in tents, and booths, as above.

This great street reaches from the road, which as I said goes from Cambridge to New-Market, turning short out of it to the right towards the river, and holds in a line near half a mile quite down to the river-side: In another street parallel with the road are like rows of booths, but larger, and more intermingled with wholesale dealers, and one side, passing out of this last street to the left hand, is a formal great square, form'd by the largest booths, built in that form, and which they call the Duddery; whence the name is deriv'd, and what its significa-tion is, I could never yet learn, tho' I made all possible search into it. The area of this square is about 80 to a 100 yards, where the dealers have room before every booth to take down, and open their packs, and to bring in waggons to load and unload.

This place is separated, and peculiar to the wholesale dealers in the woollen manufacture. Here the Booths, or tents, are of a vast extent, have different apartments, and the quantities of goods they bring are so great, that the insides of them look like another Blackwell-Hall, being as vast ware-houses pil'd up with goods to the top. In this Duddery, as I have been inform'd, there have been sold one hundred thousand pounds worth of woollen manufactures in less than a week's time, besides the prodigious trade carry'd on here, by wholesale-men, from London, and all parts of England, who transact their business wholly in their pocket-books, and meeting their chapmen from all parts, make up their accounts, receive money chiefly in bills, and take orders: These they say exceed by far the sales of goods actually brought to the fair, and deliver'd in kind; it being frequent for the London wholesale men to carry back orders from their dealers for ten thousand pounds worth of goods a man, and some much more. This especially respects those people, who deal in heavy goods, as wholesale grocers, salters, brasiers, iron-merchants, wine-merchants, and the like; but does not exclude the dealers in woollen manufactures, and especially in mercery goods of all sorts, the dealers in which generally manage their business in this manner.

Here are clothiers from Hallifax, Leeds, Wakefield and Huthersfield in Yorkshire, and from Rochdale, Bury, &c. in

Lancashire, with vast quantities of Yorkshire cloths, kerseyes, pennistons, cottons, &c. with all sorts of Manchester ware, fustians, and things made of cotton wool; of which the quantity is so great, that they told me there were near a thousand horse-packs of such goods from that side of the country, and these took up a side and half of the Duddery at least; also a part of a street of booths were taken up with upholsterer's ware, such as tickings, sackings, Kidderminster stuffs, blankets rugs, quilts, &c.

In the Duddery I saw one ware-house, or booth, with six apartments in it, all belonging to a dealer in Norwich stuffs only, and who they said had there above twenty thousand pounds value, in those goods, and no other.

Western goods had their share here also, and several booths were fill'd as full with serges, du-roys, druggets, shalloons, cantaloons, Devonshire kersies, &c. from Exeter, Taunton, Bristol, and other parts west, and some from London also.

But all this is still outdone, at least in show, by two articles, which are the peculiars of this fair, and do not begin till the other part of the fair, that is to say for the woollen manufacture, begins to draw to a close: These are the WOOLL, and the HOPS, as for the hops, there is scarce any price fix'd for hops in England, till they know how they sell at Sturbridge Fair; the quantity that appears in the fair is indeed prodigious, and they, as it were, possess a large part of the field on which the fair is kept, to themselves; they are brought directly from Chelmsford in Essex, from Canterbury and Maidstone in Kent, and from Farnham in Surrey, besides what are brought from London, the growth of those, and other places.

Enquiring why this fair should be thus, of all other places in England, the center of that trade; and so great a quantity of so bulky a commodity be carryed thither so far: I was answer'd by one thoroughly acquainted with that matter thus: The hops, said he, for this part of England, grow principally in the two counties of Surrey and Kent, with an exception only to the town of Chelmsford in Essex, and there are very few planted any where else.

There are indeed in the west of England some quantities growing; as at Wilton, near Salisbury; at Hereford and Broomsgrove, near Wales, and the like; but the quantity is inconsiderable, and the places remote, so that none of them come to London.

As to the north of England they formerly used but few hops

there, their drink being chiefly pale smooth ale, which requir'd no hops, and consequently they planted no hops in all that part of England, north of Trent; nor did I ever see one acre of hop-ground planted beyond Trent, in my observations; but as for some years past, they not only brew great quantities of beer in the north; but also use hops in the brewing their ale much more than they did before; so they all come south of Trent to buy their hops; and here being vast quantities bought, 'tis great part of their back carriage into Yorkshire, and North-amptonshire, Derbyshire, Lancashire, and all those counties; nay, of late, since the Union, even to Scotland it self; for I must not omit here also to mention, that the river Grant, or Cam, which runs close by the N.W. side of the fair in its way from Cambridge to Ely, is navigable, and that by this means, all heavy goods are brought even to the fair-field, by water carriage from London, and other parts; first to the port of Lynn, and then in barges up the Ouse, from the Ouse into the Cam, and so, as I say, to the very edge of the fair.

In like manner great quantities of heavy goods, and the hops among the rest, are sent from the fair to Lynn by water, and shipped there for the Humber, to Hull, York, &c. and for New-Castle upon Tyne, and by New-Castle, even to Scotland itself. Now as there is still no planting of hops in the north, tho' a great consumption, and the consumption increasing daily, this, says my friend, is one reason why at Sturbridge Fair there is so great a demand for the hops: he added, that besides this, there were very few hops, if any worth naming, growing in all the counties even on this side Trent, which were above forty miles from London; those counties depending on Sturbridge Fair for their supply, so the counties of Suffolk, Norfolk, Cambridge, Huntingdon, Northampton, Lincoln, Leicester, Rutland, and even to Stafford, Warwick and Worcestershire, bought most if not all of their hops at Sturbridge Fair.

These are the reasons why so great a quantity of hops are seen at this fair, as that it is incredible, considering too, how remote from this fair the growth of them is, as above.

This is likewise a testimony of the prodigious resort of the trading people of all parts of England to this fair; the quantity of hops that have been sold at one of these fairs is diversly reported, and some affirm it to be so great, that I dare not copy after them; but without doubt it is a surprising account, especially in a cheap year.

The next article brought hither, is wool, and this of several sorts, but principally fleece wool, out of Lincolnshire, where the longest staple is found; the sheep of those countries being of the largest breed.

The buyers of this wool, are chiefly indeed the manufacturers of Norfolk and Suffolk, and Essex, and it is a prodigious quantity they buy.

Here I saw what I have not observ'd in any other country of England, namely, a pocket of wool. This seems to be first call'd so in mockery, this pocket being so big, that it loads a whole waggon, and reaches beyond the most extream parts of it, hanging over both before, and behind, and these ordinarily weigh a ton or 25 hundred weight of wool, all in one bag.

The quantity of wool only, which has been sold at this place at one fair, has been said to amount to fifty or sixty thousand pounds in value, some say a great deal more.

By these articles a stranger may make some guess, at the immense trade carry'd on at this place; what prodigious quantities of goods are bought, and sold here, and what a confluence of people are seen here from all parts of England.

I might go on here to speak of several other sorts of English manufactures, which are brought hither to be sold; as all sorts of wrought iron, and brass ware from Birmingham; edg'd tools, knives, &c. from Sheffield; glass ware, and stockings, from Nottingham, and Leicester; and an infinite throng of other things of smaller value, every morning.

To attend this fair, and the prodigious conflux of people, which come to it, there are sometimes no less than fifty hackney coaches, which come from London, and ply night and morning to carry the people to and from Cambridge; for there the gross of the people lodge; nay, which is still more strange, there are wherries brought from London on waggons to plye upon the little river Cam, and to row people up and down from the town, and from the fair as occasion presents.

It is not to be wondered at, if the town of Cambridge cannot receive, or entertain the numbers of people that come to this fair; not Cambridge only, but all the towns round are full; nay, the very barns, and stables are turn'd into inns, and made as fit as they can to lodge the meaner sort of people: As for the people in the fair, they all universally eat, drink, and sleep in their booths, and tents; and the said booths are so inter-mingled with taverns, coffee-houses, drinking-houses, eating-houses, cooks-shops, &c. and all in tents too; and so many butchers, and higglers from all the neighbouring counties come into the fair every morning, with beef, mutton, fowls, butter, bread, cheese, eggs, and such things; and go with them from tent to tent, from door to door, that there's no want of any provisions of any kind, either dress'd, or undress'd.

In a word, the fair is like a well fortify'd city, and there is the least disorder and confusion (I believe) that can be seen any where, with so great a concourse of people.

Towards the latter end of the fair, and when the great hurry of wholesale business begins to be over, the gentry come in, from all parts of the county round; and tho' they come for their diversion; yet 'tis not a little money they lay out; which generally falls to the share of the retailers, such as toy-shops, goldsmiths, brasiers, ironmongers, turners, milleners, mercers, &c. and some loose coins, they reserve for the puppet-shows, drolls, rope-dancers, and such like; of which there is no want, though not considerable like the rest: The last day of the fair is the horse-fair where the whole is clos'd with both horse and foot-races, to divert the meaner sort of people only, for nothing considerable is offer'd of that kind: Thus ends the whole fair and in less than a week more there is scarce any sign left that there has been such a thing there: except by the heaps of dung and straw; and other rubbish which is left behind, trod into the earth, and which is as good as a summer's fallow for dunging to the land; and as I have said above, pays the husbandmen well for the use of it.

I should have mention'd, that here is a court of justice always open, and held every day in a shed built on purpose in the fair; this is for keeping the peace, and deciding controversies in matters deriving from the business of the fair: The magistrates of the town of Cambridge are judges in this court, as being in their jurisdiction, or they holding it by special priviledge: Here they determine matters in a summary way, as is practis'd in those we call Pye-Powder Courts in other places, or as a court of conscience; and they have a final authority without appeal.

I come now to the town, and university of Cambridge; I say the town and university, for tho' they are blended together in the situation, and the colleges, halls, and houses for literature are promiscuously scatter'd up and down among the other parts, and some even among the meanest of the other buildings; as Magdalen College over the bridge, is in particular; yet they are all encorporated together, by the name of the university, and are govern'd apart, and distinct from the town, which they are so intermix'd with.

As their authority is distinct from the town, so are their priviledges, customs, and government; they choose representatives, or Members of Parliament for themselves, and the town does the like for themselves, also apart.

The town is govern'd by a mayor, and aldermen. The university by a chancellor, and vice-chancellor, &c. Tho' their dwellings are mix'd, and seem a little confus'd, their authority is not so; in some cases the vice-chancellor may concern himself in the town, as in searching houses for the scholars at improper hours, removing scandalous women, and the like.

But as the colleges are many, and the gentlemen entertain'd in them are a very great number, the trade of the town very much depends upon them, and the tradesmen may justly be said to get their bread by the colleges; and this is the surest hold the university may be said to have of the townsmen and by which they secure the dependence of the town upon them, and consequently their submission.

I remember some years ago a brewer, who being very rich and popular in the town, and one of their magistrates, had in several things so much oppos'd the university, and insulted their vice-chancellor, or other heads of houses, that in short the university having no other way to exert themselves, and show their resentment, they made a by-law or order among themselves, that for the future they would not trade with him; and that none of the colleges, halls, &c. would take any more beer of him; and what follow'd? The man indeed brav'd it out a while, but when he found he cou'd not obtain a revocation of the order, he was fain to leave off his brewhouse, and if I remember right, quitted the town.

Thus I say, interest gives them authority; and there are abundance of reasons why the town shou'd not disoblige the university, as there are some also on the other hand, why the university shou'd not differ to any extremity with the town; nor, such is their prudence, do they let any disputes between them run up to any extremities, if they can avoid it. As for society; to any man who is a lover of learning, or of learn'd men, here is the most agreeable under heaven; nor is there any want of mirth and good company of other kinds: But 'tis to the honour of the university to say, that the governors so well understand their office, and the governed their duty, that here is very little encouragement given to those seminaries of crime the assemblies, which are so much boasted of in other places.

Again, as dancing, gaming, intriguing, are the three principal articles which recommend those assemblies; and that generally the time for carrying on affairs of this kind, is the night, and sometimes all night; a time as unseasonable as scandalous; add to this, that the orders of the university admit no such excesses: I therefore say, as this is the case, 'tis to the honour of the whole body of the university, that no encouragement is given to them here.

As to the antiquity of the university in this town, the originals and founders of the several colleges, their revenues, laws, government and governors, they are so effectually and so largely treated by other authors, and are so foreign to the familiar design of these letters, that I refer my readers to Mr. Camden's *Britannia*, and the author of the *Antiquities of Cambridge*, and other such learned writers, by whom they may be fully informed.

The present vice-chancellor is Dr. Snape, formerly master of Eaton School near Windsor; and famous for his dispute with and evident advantage over the late Bishop of Bangor, in the time of his government; the dispute between the university and the master of Trinity College has been brought to a head, so as to employ the pens of the learned on both sides; but at last prosecuted in a judicial way, so as to deprive Dr. Bently of all his dignities and offices in the university; but the Dr. flying to the royal protection, the university is under a writ of mandamus, to shew cause why they do not restore the doctor again, to which it seems they demur, and that demur has not, that we hear, been argued, at least when these sheets were sent to the press; what will be the issue time must shew.

From Cambridge the road lies north-west, on the edge of the fenns, to Huntingdon, where it joins the Great North-Road; on this side, 'tis all an agreeable corn country, as above; adorn'd with several seats of gentlemen, but the chief is the noble house, seat, or mansion of Wimple, or Wimple-Hall, formerly built at a vast expence, by the late Earl of Radnor; adorn'd with all the natural beauties of situation; and to which was added all the most exquisite contrivances which the best heads cou'd invent to make it artificially as well as naturally pleasant.

However, the fate of the Radnor family so directing, it was bought, with the whole estate about it, by the late Duke of Newcastle; in a partition of whose immense estate, it fell to the Right Honourable the Lord Harley, (son and heir apparent of the present Earl of Oxford and Mortimer) in right of the Lady Harriot Cavendish, only daughter of the said Duke of Newcastle, who is married to his lordship, and brought him this estate, and many other, sufficient to denominate her the richest heiress in Great-Britain.

Here his lordship resides, and has already so recommended himself to this country, as to be by a great majority chosen knight of the shire for the county of Cambridge.

From Cambridge, my design obliging me, and the direct road, in part concurring, I came back thro' the west part of the county of Essex, and at Saffron Walden I saw the ruins of the once largest and most magnificent pile in all this part of England, (viz.) Audley End; built by, and decaying with the noble Dukes and Earls of Suffolk.

A little north of this part of the country rises the River Stour, which for a course of fifty miles or more, parts the two counties of Suffolk and Essex; passing thro' or near Haveril, Clare, Cavendish, Halsted, Sudbury, Buers, Nayland, Stretford, Dedham, Manningtree, and into the sea at Harwich; assisting by its waters to make one of the best harbours for shipping that is in Great-Britain; I mean Orwell Haven, or Harwich, of which I have spoken largely already.

As we came on this side we saw at a distance Braintree and Bocking, two towns, large, rich and populous, and made so originally by the bay trade, of which I have spoken at large at Colchester, and which flourishes still among them.

The manour of Braintree I found descended by purchase, to the name of Olmeus, the son of a London merchant of the same name; making good what I had observ'd before, of the great number of such who have purchas'd estates in this county.

Near this town is Felsted, a small place, but noted for a free-school, of an antient foundation; for many years under the mastership of the late reverend Mr. Lydiat, and brought by him to the meridian of its reputation: 'Tis now supplied, and that very worthily, by the reverend Mr. Hutchins.

Near to this is the priory of Lees, a delicious seat of the late Dukes of Manchester, but sold by the present duke to the Dutchess Dowager of Bucks; his grace the Duke of Manchester removing to his yet finer seat of Kimbolton in Northamptonshire, the antient mansion of the family. From hence keeping the London road I came to Chelmsford, mention'd before, and Ingerstone, five miles west, which I mention again; because in the parish-church of this town are to be seen the antient monuments of the noble family of Petre; whose seat, and a large estate, lie in the neighbourhood; and whose whole family, by a constant series of beneficent actions to the poor, and bounty upon all charitable occasions, have gain'd an affectionate esteem thro' all that part of the country, such as no prejudice of religion could wear out, or perhaps ever may; and I must confess, I think, need not; for good and great actions command our respect, let the opinions of the persons be otherwise what they will.

From hence we cross'd the country to the great forest, called Epping Forest, reaching almost to London. The country on that side of Essex is called the Roodings, I suppose because there are no less than ten towns almost together, called by the name of Roding, and is famous for good land, good malt, and dirty roads; the latter indeed in the winter are scarce passable for horse or man. In the midst of this we see Chipping Onger, Hatfield Broad-Oak, Epping, and many forest-towns, fam'd, as I have said, for husbandry and good malt; but of no other note. On the south-side of the county is Waltham-Abbey; the ruins of the abbey remain; and tho' antiquity is not my proper business, I cou'd not but observe, that King Harold, slain in the great battle in Sussex against William the Conqueror, lies buried here; his body being begg'd by his mother, the Conqueror allow'd it to be carried hither; but no monument was, as I can find, built for him, only a flat grave-stone, on which was engraven, *Harold Infælix*.

From hence I came over the forest again, that is to say, over the lower or western part of it, where it is spangled with fine villages, and these villages fill'd with fine seats, most of them built by the citizens of London, as I observed before; but the lustre of them seems to be entirely swallow'd up in the magnificent palace of the Lord Castlemain, whose father, Sir Josiah Child, as it were, prepar'd it in his life for the design of his son, tho' altogether unforeseen; by adding to the advantage of its situation innumerable rows of trees, planted in curious order for avenues and visto's, to the house, all leading up to the place where the old house stood, as to a center.

In the place adjoining, his lordship, while he was yet Sir Richard Child only, and some years before he began the foundation of his new house, laid out the most delicious as well as most spacious pieces of ground for gardens that is to be seen in all this part of England. The green-house is an excellent building fit to entertain a prince; 'tis furnish'd with stoves and artificial places for heat from an apartment, in which is a bagnio, and other conveniences, which render it both useful and pleasant; and these gardens have been so the just admiration of the world, that it has been the general diversion of the citizens to go out to see them, till the crowds grew too great, and his lordship was oblig'd to restrain his servants from shewing them, except on one or two days in a week only.

The house is built since these gardens have been finish'd: The building is all of Portland stone in the front, which makes it look extremely glorious and magnificent at a distance; it being the particular property of that stone, except in the streets of London, where it is tainted and ting'd with the smoak of the city, to grow whiter and whiter the longer it stands in the open air.

As the front of the house opens to a long row of trees, reaching to the great road at Leighton Stone; so the back-face, or front, if that be proper, respects the gardens, and with an easy descent lands you upon the terras, from whence is a most beautiful prospect to the river, which is all form'd into canals and openings, to answer the views from above, and beyond the river, the walks and wildernesses go on to such a distance, and in such a manner up the hill, as they before went down, that the sight is lost in the woods adjoining, and it looks all like one planted garden as far as the eye can see.

I shall cover as much as possible the melancholy part of a story, which touches too sensibly, many, if not most of the great and flourishing families in England: Pity and matter of grief is it to think that families, by estate, able to appear in such a glorious posture as this, should ever be vulnerable by so mean a disaster as that of stock-jobbing: But the general infatuation of the day is a plea for it; so that men are not now blamed on that account: South-Sea was a general possession; and if my Lord Castlemain was wounded by that arrow shot in the dark, 'twas a misfortune: But 'tis so much a happiness, that it was not a mortal wound, as it was to some men, who once seem'd as much out of the reach of it; and that blow, be it what it will, is not remember'd for joy of the escape; for we see this noble family, by prudence and management rise out of all that cloud, if it may be allow'd such a name, and shining in the same full lustre as before.

This cannot be said of some other families in this county, whose fine parks and new-built palaces are fallen under forfeitures and alienations by the misfortunes of the times, and by the ruin of their masters fortunes in that South-Sea Deluge.

But I desire to throw a veil over these things, as they come in my way; 'tis enough that we write upon them as was written upon King Harold's tomb at Waltham-Abbey, INFÆLIX, and let all the rest sleep among things that are the fittest to be forgotten.

From my Lord Castlemain's house, and the rest of the fine dwellings on that side of the forest, for there are several very good houses at Wanstead, only that they seem all swallow'd up in the lustre of his lordship's palace; I say, from thence I went south, towards the great road over that part of the forest call'd the Flatts, where we see a very beautiful, but retired and rural seat of Mr. Lethulier's, eldest son of the late Sir John Lethulier, of Lusum in Kent, of whose family I shall speak when I come on that side.

By this turn I came necessarily on to Stratford, where I set out: And thus having finished my first circuit, I conclude my first letter; and am,

SIR,

Your most humble,

And obedient servant.

APPENDIX TO LETTER I

Whoever travels, as I do, over England, and writes the account of his observations, will, as I noted before, always leave something, altering or undertaking, by such a growing, improving nation as this; or something to discover in a nation, where so much is hid, sufficient to employ the pens of those that come after him, or to add, by way of Appendix to what he has already observ'd.

This is my case, with respect to the particulars which follow: 1. Since these sheets were in the press, a noble palace of Mr. Walpole's, at present first commissioner of the treasury, privy-counsellor, &c. to King George, is, as it were, risen out of the ruins of the ancient seat of the family of Walpole, at Houghton, about 8 miles distant from Lynn, and on the north coast of Norfolk, near the sea.

As the house is not yet finished, and when I pass'd by it, was but newly design'd; it cannot be expected that I should be able to give a particular description of what it will be: I can do little more than mention, that it appears already to be exceeding magnificent, and suitable to the genius of the great founder.

But a friend of mine, who lives in that county, has sent me the following lines, which, as he says, are to be plac'd upon the building; whether on the frize of the cornish, or over the portico, or on what part of the building, of that I am not as yet certain: The inscription is as follows, viz.

H. M. P.

Fundamen ut essem Domus
In Agro Natali Extruendæ,
Robertus ille Walpole
Quem nulla nesciet Posteritas:
           Faxit Deus.

Postquam Maturus Annis Dominus.
Diu Lætatus fuerit absoluta
Incolumem tueantur Incolumes.
Ad Summam omnium Diem
Et nati matorum et qui nascentur ab illis,
           Hic me Posuit.

A second thing proper to be added here, by way of Appendix, relates to what I have mention'd of the Port of London, being bounded by the Naze on the Essex shore, and the North Foreland on the Kentish shore, which some people, guided by the present usage of the custom-house, may pretend is not so, to answer such objectors. The true state of that case stands thus.

I. The clause taken from the Act of Parliament establishing the extent of the Port of London, and publish'd, in some of the books of rates, is this:

To prevent all future differences and disputes touching the extent and limits of the Port of London, the said port is declared to extend, and be accounted, from the promentary, or point, call'd the North Foreland, in the Isle of Thanet, and from thence northward in a right line to the point call'd the NAZE, beyond the Gunfleet, upon the coast of Essex; and so continued westward throughout the river Thames, and the several channels, streams and rivers falling into it, to London-Bridge; saving the usual and known rights, liberties and privileges of the ports of Sandwich, and Ipswich, and either of them, and the known members thereof, and of the customers, comptrolers, searchers, and their deputies, of and within the said ports of Sandwich and Ipswich, and the several creeks, harbours and havens to them, or either of them, respectively belonging, within the counties of Kent and Essex.

II. Notwithstanding what is above written, the Port of London, as in use since the said Order, is understood to reach no farther than Gravesend in Kent, and Tilbury Point in Essex; and the ports of Rochester, Milton and Feversham, belong to the port of Sandwich.

In like manner the ports of Harwich, Colchester, Wevenhoe, Malden, Leigh, &c. are said to be members of the port of Ipswich.

This observation may suffice for what is needful to be said upon the same subject, when I may come to speak of the port of Sandwich, and its members, and their privileges, with respect to Rochester, Milton, Feversham, &c. in my circuit thro' the county of Kent.

LETTER II

SIR,—As in my first journey I went over the eastern counties of ENGLAND, viz. ESSEX, SUFFOLK, NORFOLK, and CAMBRIDGE, and took my course on that side the river Thames, to view the sea-coasts, harbours, &c. so being now to traverse the southern counties, I begin with the other side of the Thames, and shall surround the sea-coast of KENT, as I did that of NORFOLK and SUFFOLK, and perhaps it is as fruitful of instructing and diverting observations as any of the other.

I took boat at Tower-Wharf, sending my horses round by land to meet me at Greenwich, that I might begin my journey at the beginning of the county, and here I had the advantage of making my first step into the county of Kent, at a place which is the most delightful spot of ground in Great-Britain; pleasant by situation, those pleasures encreas'd by art, and all made compleatly agreeable by the accident of fine buildings, the continual passing of fleets of ships up and down the most beautiful river in Europe; the best air, best prospect, and the best conversation in England.

The Royal Hospital for Seamen, though not yet finished; the park, the queen's house, the Observatory on the hill, commonly call'd Flamstead-House, are all things so well known, they need no particular description.

The ground, part of this hospital now stands upon, and is to stand upon, is the same on which formerly stood the royal palace of our kings. Here Henry VIII. held his royal feasts with justs and tournaments, and the ground which was call'd the Tilt-yard, is the spot on which the easternmost wing of the hospital is built; the park, (for it was even then a park also) was enlarg'd, wall'd about, and planted with beautiful rows, or walks of trees by King Charles II. soon after the Restoration; and the design or plan of a royal palace was then lay'd out, one wing of which was finished and covered in a most magnificent manner, and makes now the first wing of the hospital as you come

94

to it from London: The building is regular, the lower part a strong Dorick, the middle part a most beautiful Corinthian, with an Attick above all, to compleat the height; the front to the water-side is extreamly magnificent and graceful; embellish'd with rich carv'd work and fine devices, such as will hardly be outdone in this, or any age for beauty or art.

They must be very ignorant of our English affairs, who have publish'd very lately that Queen Elizabeth built the royal palace of Greenwich; whereas it is evident, that it was the palace of King Henry VIII. her father, before she was born; and this is prov'd beyond contradiction by this particular circumstance, that her majesty was born in this very palace which she is there said to have built.

But the beauty of Greenwich is owing to the lustre of its inhabitants, where there is a kind of collection of gentlemen, rather than citizens, and of persons of quality and fashion, different from most, if not all, the villages in this part of England.

Here several of the most active and useful gentlemen of the late armies, after having grown old in the service of their country, and cover'd with the honours of the field, are retired to enjoy the remainder of their time, and reflect with pleasure upon the dangers they have gone thro', and the faithful services they have perform'd both abroad and at home.

Several generals, and several of the inferior officers, I say, having thus chosen this calm retreat, live here in as much honour and delight as this world can give.

Other gentlemen still in service, as in the navy ordnance, docks, yards, &c. as well while in business, as after laying down their employments, have here planted themselves, insomuch, that the town of Greenwich begins to out-swell its bounds, and extends itself not only on this side the park to the top of the heath, by the way call'd Crum-Hill, but now stretches out on the east-side, where Sir John Vanburg has built a house castlewise, and where in a little time 'tis probable, several streets of like buildings will be erected, to the enlarging and beautifying the town, and encreasing the inhabitants; who, as I have said, are already the chief beauty and ornament of the place: We are told also that leave will be obtained to build a new church on that side; the parish church, tho' new rebuilt, and very large and beautiful, not being sufficient to receive the inhabitants, much less will it be so, if the buildings go on to encrease, as they have done, and as they now seem to do.

The river of Thames is here very broad, and the channel

deep, and the water at some very high spring-tides is salt; but in ordinary tides, is very sweet and fresh, especially at the tide of ebb.

The country behind Greenwich adds to the pleasure of the place: Black-Heath, both for beauty of situation, and an excellent air, is not out-done by any spot of ground so near the river and so near land in England.

On the east-side stands an hospital very particular for its foundation or design, tho' thro' the misfortunes of the times, the generous design of the founder has been much straiten'd, and in great part, defeated.

It was built by Sir John Morden a Turkey merchant of London, but who liv'd in a great house at the going off from the heath, a little south of the hospital on the road to Eltham; his first design, as I had it from his own mouth the year before he began to build, was to make apartments for forty decay'd merchants, to whom he resolv'd to allow 40l. per annum, each; with coals, a gown, (and servants to look after their apartments) and many other conveniences so as to make their lives as comfortable as possible, and that, as they had liv'd like gentlemen, they might dye so.

Sir John Morden and his lady lye bury'd in a vault in the chancel of the chapel of this hospital: The chapel is a very neat building facing the entrance into the court; the lodgings for the merchants, are on either side; two apartments in each stair case, with cellars for their conveniences, coals, beer, &c. and each apartment consists of a bed-chamber, and a study, or large closet, for their retreat, and to divert themselves in with books, &c.

They have a publick kitchen, a hall to dine in, and over the hall is a large room for the trustees (who manage the whole) to meet in; there is also a very good apartment for the chaplain, whose sallery is 50l. a year; there are also dwellings for the cooks, buttlers, porter, the women and other servants, and reasonable salaries allow'd them: And behind the chapel is a handsome burying ground wall'd in; there are also very good gardens; In a word, it is the noblest foundation, and most considerable single piece of charity that has been erected in England since Sutton's Hospital in London: I call it single, because it has been built and endow'd by one single hand; the situation is very pleasant, and the air very healthy and good.

There is erected over the gate, since Sir John's death, his statue in stone, set up by his lady, and since her death, her

own is set up near it, by the trustees, she having been a benefactress to the foundation many ways since his decease.

There is a velvet pall given, by her ladyship in particular,
to be laid up in the chapel for the use of the gentlemen; as also
a large quantity of communion-plate; and the chaplain is
oblig'd to read prayers twice every day, viz. at eleven a clock,
and at three; at which all the pensioners are oblig'd to attend.

On the other side of the heath, north, is Charleton, a village
famous, or rather infamous for the yearly collected rabble of
mad-people, at Horn-Fair; the rudeness of which I cannot but
think, is such as ought to be suppress'd, and indeed in a civiliz'd
well govern'd nation, it may well be said to be unsufferable.
The mob indeed at that time take all kinds of liberties, and the
women are especially impudent for that day; as if it was a
day that justify'd the giving themselves a loose to all manner
of indecency and immodesty, without any reproach, or without
suffering the censure which such behaviour would deserve at
another time.

The introduction of this rude assembly, or the occasion of
it, I can meet with very little account of, in antiquity; and
I rather recommend it to the publick justice to be suppress'd,
as a nusance and offence to all sober people, than to spend any
time to enquire into its original.

There are some very good houses lately built in this town,
and abating the rabble and hurry of the 19th of October, as
above, 'tis indeed a very pleasant village; standing on the top
of a high hill, yet shelter'd on one side by Shooter's-Hill, which
is much higher, and on the other side, over-looking the marshes
and the river Thames, on which it has a very agreeable prospect
from London almost to Gravesend.

Thro' this town lies the road to Woolwich, a town on the bank
of the same river, wholly taken up by, and in a manner rais'd
from, the yards, and publick works, erected there for the publick
service; here, when the business of the royal navy encreased,
and Queen Elizabeth built larger and greater ships of war than
were usually employ'd before, new docks, and launches were
erected, and places prepared for the building and repairing
ships of the largest size; because, as here was a greater depth
of water and a freer chanel, than at Deptford, (where the chief
yard in the river of Thames was before) so there was less hazard
in the great ships going up and down; the croud of merchant-

ships at Deptford, being always such, as that it could not be so safe to come up thither, as to put in at Woolwich.

At this dock the *Royal-Sovereign* was built, once the largest ship in the whole royal navy, and in particular esteem'd, for so large a ship, the best sailor in the world. Here also was rebuilt the *Royal Prince*, now call'd the *Queen*, a first rate, carrying a hundred guns, and several others: Close under the south-shore from the west-end of Woolwich, the Thames is very deep, and the men of war lye there moor'd, and as we call it, laid up; their topmasts, and all their small rigging taken down and laid in ware-houses; this reaches as high as the point over-against Bow-River and is call'd Bugby's-Hole.

The docks, yards, and all the buildings belonging to it, are encompassed with a high wall, and are exceeding spacious and convenient; and are also prodigious full of all manner of stores of timber, plank, masts, pitch, tar, and all manner of naval provisions to such a degree, as is scarce to be calculated.

Besides the building-yards, here is a large rope-walk where the biggest cables are made for the men of war; and on the east or lower part of the town is the gun-yard, or place set a part for the great guns belonging to the ships, commonly call'd the Park, or the Gun-Park; where is a prodigious quantity of all manner of ordnance-stores, such as are fit for sea-service, that is to say, cannon of all sorts for the ships of war, every ship's guns by themselves; heavy cannon for batteries, and mortars of all sorts and sizes; insomuch, that, as I was inform'd, here has been sometimes laid up at one time between seven and eight thousand pieces of ordnance, besides mortars and shells without number.

Here also is the house where the firemen and engineers prepare their fireworks, charge bombs, carcasses, and grenades for the publick service, in time of war; and here (if I remember right, it was in the time of a Dutch war) by mischance, the fire in the lab'ratory took hold of some combustibles, which spreading fir'd first a bomb or shell, and the bursting of that shell blew up all the works with such a terrible blast and noise, as shook and shatter'd the whole town of Woolwich almost in pieces, and terrify'd the people to the last degree, but kill'd no person as I heard of, except about eleven men who were in or near the fireworking house, where it first took hold.

In this park, close on the south bank of the river, a large battery of forty pieces of heavy cannon was rais'd, to have saluted the Dutch, if they had thought fit to have ventur'd up

the river in 1667, as was given out they would when they burnt
our ships at Chatham; and large furnaces and forges were
erected to have furnish'd the gunners with red hot bullets for
that service; but the Dutch had no design that way and did their
business with far less hazard, and as much to our disgrace in
another place.

Here is usually a guardship riding, especially in time of
service; also here is a large hulk made of the carcass of an old
man of war, sufficiently large for setting the masts of the
biggest ships in the navy. The Thames is here at high water
near a mile over, and the water salt upon the flood; and as
the chanel lyes strait east and west for about three miles, the
tide runs very strong; 'tis entirely free from shoals and sands,
and has seven or eight fathom water, so that the biggest ships,
and a great many of them, might ride here with safety even at
low water.

From this town there is little remarkable upon the river,
till we come to Gravesend, the whole shore being low, and
spread with marshes and unhealthy grounds, except with small
intervals, where the land bends inward as at Erith, Greenwhich,
North-Fleet, &c. in which places the chalk hills come close to
the river, and from thence the city of London, the adjacent
countries, and even Holland and Flanders, are supply'd with
lime, for their building, or chalk to make lime, and for other uses.

From these chalky cliffs on the river side, the rubbish of the
chalk, which crumbles away when they dig the larger chalk for
lime, or (as we might call it) the chips of the chalk, and which
they must be at the charge of removing to be out of their way,
is bought and fetch'd away by lighters and hoys, and carry'd
to all the ports and creeks in the opposite county of Essex, and
even to Suffolk and Norfolk, and sold there to the country
farmers to lay upon their land, and that in prodigious quantities;
and so is it valued by the farmers of those countries, that they
not only give from two shillings and six pence, to four shillings
a load for it, according to the distance the place is from the
said chalk-cliff, but they fetch it by land-carriage ten miles,
nay fifteen miles, up into the country.

This is the practice in all the creeks and rivers in Essex, even
to Malden, Colchester, the Nase, and into Harwich Harbour up
to Maningtree, and to Ipswich; as also in Suffolk, to Albro,
Orford, Dunwich, Swold, and as high as Yarmouth in Norfolk.

Thus the barren soil of Kent, for such the chalky grounds
are esteem'd, make the Essex lands rich and fruitful, and the

mixture of earth forms a composition, which out of two barren
extreams, makes one prolifick medium; the strong clay of
Essex and Suffolk is made fruitful by the soft meliorating melting
chalk of Kent, which fattens and enriches it.

On the back-side of these marshy grounds in Kent at a small
distance, lies the road from London to Dover, and on that
highway, or near it, several good towns; for example, Eltham,
formerly a royal palace when the Court was kept at Greenwich;
and Queen Elizabeth, who (as before) was born at Greenwich,
was often carry'd, as they say, to Eltham by her nurses to suck
in the wholesome air of that agreeable place; but at present
there are few or no signs of the old palace to be seen.

It is now a pleasant town, very handsomely built, full of
good houses, and many families of rich citizens inhabit here:
(As I observ'd of the villages adjacent to London in other
counties) So it is here, they bring a great deal of good company
with them: Also abundance of ladies of very good fortunes
dwell here, and one sees at the church such an appearance of
the sex, as is surprising; but 'tis complain'd of that the youths
of these families where those beauties grow, are so generally
or almost universally bred abroad, either in Turkey, Italy, or
Spain, as merchants, or in the army or court as gentlemen;
that for the ladies to live at Eltham, is, as it were, to live recluse
and out of sight; since to be kept where the gentlemen do not
come, is all one as to be kept where they cannot come. This
they say threatens Eltham with a fatal turn, unless the scene
alters in a few years, and they tell us, that all the ladies will
abandon the place.

In the neighbourhood of this place at LVSVM, Sir John
Lethulier, a Turkey merchant, liv'd for many years, and to a
great age, and has establish'd his family in the separate houses
of three or four several sons, to all which he has left plentiful
estates in this country, but especially in Essex, where his eldest
son has a very noble seat, and estate near Barking.

From this side of the country all pleasant and gay, we go
over Shooter's Hill, where the face of the world seems quite
alter'd; for here we have but a chalky soil, and indifferently
fruitful, far from rich; much overgrown with wood, especially
coppice-wood, which is cut for faggots and bavins, and sent
up by water to London. Here they make those faggots which
the wood-mongers call ostrey wood, and here in particular
those small light bavins which are used in taverns in London

to light their faggots, and are call'd in the taverns a brush, the woodmen call them pimps; 'tis incredible what vast quantities of these are lay'd up at Woolwich, Erith, and Dartford; but since the taverns in London are come to make coal fires in their upper rooms, that cheat of a trade declines; and tho' that article would seem to be trifling in it self, 'tis not trifling to observe what an alteration it makes in the value of those woods in Kent, and how many more of them than usual are yearly stubb'd up, and the land made fit for the plow.

As I passed, I saw Gravesend from the hills, but having been often in the town, I know enough to be able to say, that there is nothing considerable in it; except first that it is the town where the great ferry (as they call it) is kept up between London and East-Kent, it is hardly credible what numbers of people pass here every tide, as well by night as by day, between this town and London: Almost all the people of East-Kent, when they go for London, go no farther by land than this town; and then for six-pence in the tilt-boat, or one shilling in a small boat or wherry, are carry'd to London by water.

About 25 years ago one of these tilt-boats was cast away, occasion'd by the desperate obstinacy and rudeness of the steersman or master, as they call him, who would tack again and stand over upon a wind, in the reach call'd Long-Reach, contrary to the advice and intreaties not of the passengers only but of his own rowers, who told him it blew a storm and she would founder; but he call'd them fools, bid the wind blow-devil, (a rude sailor's proverb) the more wind the better boat, till coming into the chanel where the sea ran very high, he took in a wave, or a sea, as they call it, which run her down, and founder'd her, as was foretold; and himself and three and fifty passengers were all drown'd, only about five escaping by swimming.

The other thing for which this town is worth notice, is, that all the ships which go to sea from London, take, as we say, their departure from hence; for here all outward-bound ships must stop, come to an anchor, and suffer what they call a second clearing, (viz.) here a searcher of the customs comes on board, looks over all the coquets or entries of the cargo, and may, if he pleases, rummage the whole loading, to see if there are no more goods than are enter'd; which however they seldom do, tho' they forget not to take a compliment for their civility, and besides being well treated on board, have generally three or five guns fir'd in honour to them when they go off.

The method of causing all ships to stop here before they go, is worth observing, and is as follows:

When a merchant-ship comes down from London, (if they have the tide of ebb under foot, or a fresh gale of wind from the west, so that they have, what they call fresh-way, and the ships come down apace) they generally hand some of their sails, haul up a fore-sail or main-sail, or lower the fore-top sail; so to slaken her way, as soon as they come to the Old Man's Head; when they open the reach, which they call Gravesend Reach, which begins about a mile and half above the town, they do the like, to signify that they intend to bring too, as the sailors call it, and come to an anchor.

As soon as they come among the ships that are riding in the road, (as there are always a great many) the centinel at the block-house, as they call it, on Gravesend side fires his musquet, which is to tell the pilot he must bring too; if he comes on, as soon as the ship passes broad side with the block-house, the centinel fires again, which is as much as to say, Why don't you bring too? if he drives a little farther, he fires a third time, and the language of that is, Bring too immediately, and let go your anchor, or we will make you.

If the ship continues to drive down, and does not let go her anchor, the gunner of the fort is fetch'd, and he fires a piece of cannon tho' without ball; and that is still a threat, tho' with some patience, and is to say, Will you come to an anchor or won't you? If he still ventures to go on, by which he gives them to understand he intends to run for it; then the gunner fires again, and with a shot, and that shot is a signal to the fortress over the river, (viz.) Tilbury Fort, (which I describ'd in my account of Essex) and they immediately let fly at the ship from the guns on the east bastion and after from all the guns they can bring to bear upon her; it is very seldom that a ship will venture their shot, because they can reach her all the way unto the Hope, and round the Hope-Point almost to Hole-Haven.

Yet I happen'd once to be upon the shore just by Tilbury-Fort, when a ship ventur'd to run off in spight of all those fireings; and it being just at the first shoot of the ebb, and when a great fleet of light colliers and other ships were under sail too; by that time, the ship escaping came round the Hope-Point, she was so hid among the other ships, that the gunners on the bastion hardly knew who to shoot at; upon which they mann'd out several boats with soldiers, in hopes to overtake her or to make signals to some men of war at the Nore, to man out their boats, and stop her, but she laugh'd at them all; for as it blew a fresh gale of wind at south-west, and a tide of ebb strong under her foot, she went three foot for their one, and by that time the boats got down to Hole Haven, the ship was beyond the Nore, and as it grew dark, they soon lost sight of her, nor could they ever hear to this day what ship it was, or on what account she ventur'd to run such a risque.

Another time I was with some merchants in a large yatch, bound to France; they had a great quantity of block-tin on board, and other goods, which had not been enter'd at the custom-house; and the master or captain told us, he did not doubt but he would pass by Gravesend without coming to an anchor; he lay, when this thought came into his head, at an anchor in Gray's Reach just above the Old Man's Head, mention'd above, which is a point or head of land on the Essex shore, which makes the bottom of Gray's Reach and the upper end of Gravesend Reach: He observ'd that the mornings were likely to be exceeding foggy; particularly on the morning next after his resolution of trying there was so thick a fog, that it was scarce possible to see from the main-mast to the bow-sprit, even of a hoy; it being high water, he resolv'd to weigh and drive, as he call'd it, and so he did: When he came among the other ships and over against the town, his greatest danger was running foul of them, to prevent which he kept a man lying on his belly at the bow-sprit end, to look out, and so, tho' not without some danger too, he went clear: As for Gravesend or Tilbury-Fort, they could see no more of us than they could of London-Bridge; and we drove in this fog undiscern'd by the forts of the custom-house men, as low as Hole-Haven, and went afterwards clear away to Caen in Normandy without being visited.

But such attempts as these, are what would very hardly be brought to pass again now, nor is the risque worth any body's running if the value be considerable that may be lost; and therefore one may venture to say, that all the ships which go out of the river from London, are first clear'd here, even the empty colliers and coasters go on shore, and give an account who they are, and take a signal from the customs-house office, and pay six-pence, and then pass on: As for ships coming in, they all go by here without any notice taken of them, unless it be to put waiters on board them, if they are not supply'd before.

From Gravesend we see nothing remarkable on the road but GAD'S-HILL, a noted place for robbing of sea-men after they have receiv'd their pay at Chatham. Here it was that famous robbery was commited in the year 1676 or thereabouts; it was about four a clock in the morning when a gentleman was robb'd by one Nicks on a bay mare, just on the declining part of the hill, on the west-side, for he swore to the spot and to the man; Mr. Nicks who robb'd him, came away to Gravesend, immediately ferry'd over, and, as he said, was stopp'd by the difficulty of the boat, and of the passage, near an hour; which was a great discouragement to him, but was a kind of bait to his horse: From thence he rode cross the county of Essex, thro' Tilbury, Hornden, and Bilerecay to Chelmsford: Here he stopp'd about half an hour to refresh his horse, and gave him some balls; from thence to Braintre, Bocking, Wethersfield; then over the downs to Cambridge, and from thence keeping still the cross roads, he went by Fenny Stanton to Godmanchester, and Huntington, where he baited himself and his mare about an hour; and, as he said himself, slept about half an hour, then holding on the North Road, and keeping a full larger gallop most of the way, he came to York the same afternoon, put off his boots and riding cloaths, and went dress'd as if he had been an inhabitant of the place, not a traveller, to the bowling-green, where, among other gentlemen, was the lord mayor of the city; he singling out his lordship, study'd to do something particular that the mayor might remember him by, and accordingly lays some odd bett with him concerning the bowls then running, which should cause the mayor to remember it the more particularly; and then takes occasion to ask his lordship what a clock it was; who, pulling out his watch, told him the hour, which was a quarter before, or a quarter after eight at night.

Some other circumstances, it seems, he carefully brought into their discourse, which should make the lord mayor remember the day of the month exactly, as well as the hour of the day.

Upon a prosecution which happen'd afterwards for this robbery, the whole merit of the case turn'd upon this single point: The person robb'd swore as above to the man, to the place, and to the time, in which the fact was committed: Namely, that he was robb'd on Gad's-Hill in Kent, on such a day, and at such a time of the day, and on such a part of the hill, and that the prisoner at the bar was the man that robb'd him: Nicks, the prisoner, deny'd the fact, call'd several persons to his reputation, alledg'd that he was as far off as Yorkshire at that time, and that particularly the day whereon the prosecutor swore he was robb'd, he was at bowles on the publick green in the city of York; and to support this, he produced the Lord Mayor of York to testify that he was so, and that the mayor acted so and so with him there as above.

This was so positive, and so well attested, that the jury acquitted him on a bare supposition, that it was impossible the man could be at two places so remote on one and the same day. There are more particulars related of this story, such as I do not take upon me to affirm; namely, That King Charles II. prevailed on him on assurance of pardon, and that he should not be brought into any farther trouble about it, to confess the truth to him privately, and that he own'd to his majesty that he commited the robbery, and how he rode the journey after it, and that upon this the king gave him the name or title of Swift Nicks, instead of Nicks; but these things, I say, I do not relate as certain: I return to the business in hand.

From Gad's-Hill we come to Rochester Bridge, the largest, highest, and the strongest built of all the bridges in England, except London-Bridge; some indeed say, the bridge of Newcastle upon Tyne, exceeds all the bridges in England for strength; and it is indeed very firm and wide, and has a street of houses upon it like London-Bridge, and a gate in the middle as large as a little castle, of which in its place; but then it is neither so high nor so long as this bridge at Rochester.

Rochester, Stroud, and Chatham, are three distinct places, but contiguous, except the interval of the river between the two first, and a very small marsh or vacancy between Rochester and Chatham.

There's little remarkable in Rochester, except the ruins of a very old castle, and an antient but not extraordinary cathedral; but the river, and its appendices are the most considerable of the kind in the world. This being the chief arsenal of the royal navy of Great-Britain. The buildings here are indeed like the ships themselves, surprisingly large, and in their several kinds beautiful: The ware-houses, or rather streets of ware-houses, and store-houses for laying up the naval treasure are the largest in dimension, and the most in number, that are any where to be seen in the world: The rope-walk for making cables, and the forges for anchors and other iron-work, bear a proportion to the rest; as also the wet-dock for keeping masts, and yards of the greatest size, where they lye sunk in the water to preserve them, the boat-yard, the anchor yard; all like the whole, monstrously great and extensive, and are not easily describ'd.

We come next to the stores themselves, for which all this provision is made; and first, to begin with the ships that are laid up there: The sails, the rigging, the ammunition, guns, great and small-shot, small-arms, swords, cutlasses, half pikes, with all the other furniture belonging to the ships that ride at their moorings in the river Medway: These take up one part of the place, having separate buildings, and store-houses appropriated to them, where the furniture of every ship lies in particular ware-houses by themselves, and may be taken out on the most hasty occasion without confusion, fire excepted.

N.B. The powder is generally carry'd away to particular magazines to avoid disaster.

Besides these, there are store-houses for laying up the furniture, and stores for ships; but which are not appropriated, or do not belong (as it is express'd by the officers) to any particular ship; but lye ready to be delivered out for the furnishing other ships to be built, or for repairing and supplying the ships already there, as occasion may require.

For this purpose there are separate and respective magazines of pitch, tarr, hemp, flax, tow, rosin, oyl, tallow; also of sail cloth, canvas, anchors, cables, standing and running rigging, ready fitted, and cordage not fitted; with all kinds of ship-chandlery necessaries, such as blocks, tackles, runners, &c. with the cooks, boatswains, and gunners stores, and also anchors of all sizes, grapnells, chains, bolts, and spikes, wrought and unwrought iron, cast-iron work, such as potts, caldrons, furnaces, &c. also boats, spare-masts and yards; with a great quantity of lead and nails, and other necessaries, (too many to be enumerated) whose store looks as if it were inexhaustible.

To observe these things deliberately, one wou'd almost wonder what ships they were, and where they should be found, which cou'd either for building, or repairing, fiting, or refiting, call for such a quantity of all those things; but when, on the other hand, one sees the ships, and considers their dimension, and consequently the dimension of all things which belong to them; how large, how strong every thing must be; how much of the materials must go to the making every thing proportionable to the occasion, the wonder would change its prospect, and one would be as much amaz'd to think how and where they should be supply'd.

The particular government of these yards, as they are call'd, is very remarkable, the commissioners, clerks, accomptants, &c. within doors, the store-keepers, yard-keepers, dock-keepers, watchmen, and all other officers without doors, with the sub-ordination of all officers one to another respectively, as their degree and offices require, is admirable. The watchmen are set duly every night at stated and certain places, within the several yards, with every one a bell over his head, which they ring or toll every hour, giving so many strokes as the hour reckons, and then one taking it from another through every part of the yard, and of all the yards, makes the watching part be perform'd in a very exact and regular manner. In the river there is a guard-boat, which, as the main guard in a garrison, goes the grand-rounds at certain times, to see that every centinel does his duty on board the ships; these go by every ship in the river, and see that the people on board are at their post: If the ship does not challenge, that is to say, If the man plac'd to look out does not call, Who comes there? the guard-boat boards them immediately, to examine who is deficient in their duty.

They told us an odd story of a guard-boat which having not been challeng'd by the person who ought to have been walking on the forecastle of the ship, boarded them on the bow, and as the boat's crew was entering the ship by the fore-chains they found a man fallen over board, but the lap of his coat catching in a block, was drawn so hard in by the running of the rope in the block, that it held the man fast; but he was fallen so low, that his head and arms hung in the water, and he was almost drown'd: However it seems he was not quite dead; so that catching hold of him, and pulling him out of the water, they saved his life: But they added, as the main part of the story, that the man could never give any account of his disaster, or how he came to fall over-board, only said that it must be the Devil that threw him over-board, for nothing else could do it. How true this passage may be, I do not undertake to enter upon the debate of.

The expedition that has been sometimes used here in fitting out men of war, is very great, and as the workmen relate it, 'tis indeed incredible; particularly, they told us, That the *Royal Sovereign*, a first rate of 106 guns, was riding at her moorings, entirely unrigg'd, and nothing but her three masts standing, as is usual when a ship is lay'd up, and that she was completely rigg'd, all her masts up, her yards put too, her sails bent, anchors and cables on board, and the ship sailed down to Black-Stakes in three days, Sir Cloudesly Shovell being then her captain.

I do not vouch the thing, but when I consider, first, that every thing lay ready in her store-houses, and wanted nothing but to be fetch'd out and carry'd on board; a thousand or fifteen hundred men to be employ'd in it and more if they were wanted; and every man, knowing his business perfectly well, boats, carriages, pullies, tacklers, cranes, and hulk all ready, I do not know, but it might be done in one day if it was try'd; certain it is, the dexterity of the English sailors in those things is not to be match'd by the world.

The building-yards, docks, timber-yard, deal-yard, mast-yard, gun-yard, rope-walks; and all the other yards and places, set apart for the works belonging to the navy, are like a well ordered city; and tho' you see the whole place as it were in the utmost hurry, yet you see no confusion, every man knows his own business; the master builders appoint the working, or converting, as they call it, of every piece of timber; and give to the other head workmen, or foremen their moulds for the squaring and cutting out of every piece, and placing it in its proper byrth (so they call it) in the ship that is in building, and every hand is busy in pursuing those directions, and so in all the other works.

It is about sixteen or eighteen miles from Rochester Bridge to Sheerness Fort by water on the river Medway, of this it is about fourteen miles to Black-Stakes, the channel is so deep all the way, the banks soft, and the reaches of the river so short, that in a word, 'tis the safest and best harbour in the world; and we saw two ships of eighty guns, each riding a float at low water within musquet-shot of Rochester Bridge. The ships ride as in a mill-pond, or a wet-dock, except that being moor'd at the chains, they swing up and down with the tide; but as there is room enough, so they are moor'd in such manner, that they cannot swing foul of one another; 'tis as safe (I say) as in a wet-dock, nor did I ever hear of any accident that befel any of the king's ships here, I mean by storms and weather; except in that dreadful tempest in 1703, when one ship, (viz.) the *Royal Catherine* was driven on shoar, and receiving some damage sunk, and the ship also being old, could not be weigh'd again; but this was such a storm as never was known before, and 'tis hoped the like may never be known again.

There are two castles on the shore of this river, the one at Upnore, where there is a good platform of guns, and which guards two reaches of the river, and is supposed to defend all the ships which ride above, between that and the bridge; also on the other shore is Gillingham Castle, form'd for the same purpose, and well furnish'd with guns which command the river, besides which there is a fort or platform of guns at a place call'd the swamp and another at Cockham Wood. But all these are added, or at least additions made to them, since the time that the Dutch made that memorable attempt upon the royal navy in this river (viz.) on the 22d of June, in the year 1667; for at that time all was left unguarded, and as it were, secure; there were but four guns that could be used at Upnore, and scarce so many at Gillingham, the carriages being rotten and broke; and in a word, every thing concurring to invite the enemy. There were about twelve guns at the Isle of Shepey, where since, Sheerness Fort is built; but the Dutch soon beat them from those guns, and made the place too hot for them, dismounting also most of the guns, after which they went boldly up to Black-Stakes with their whole squadron; and after that seven of their biggest men of war went up as high as Upnore, where they did what mischief they could, and went away again, carrying off the *Royal Charles*, a first rate ship of 100 guns, and burning the *London*, and several others, besides the damaging most of the ships which were within their reach; and all things consider'd, it was a victory, that they went away without ruining all the rest of the navy that was in that river.

But as this is a dull story in it self, so it is none of my present business farther than to introduce what follows; namely, That this allarm gave England such a sense of the consequence of the river Medway, and of the docks and yards at Chatham, and of the danger the royal navy lay exposed to there, that all these doors which were open then, are lock'd up and sufficiently barr'd since that time; and 'tis not now in the power of any nation under heaven, no, tho' they should be masters at sea, unless they were masters at land too at the same time, to give us such another affront; for besides all the castles, lines of guns, and platforms on each side the river Medway, as we go up, as above; there is now a royal fort built at the point of the Isle of Shepey, call'd Sheerness, which guards that entrance into the river: This is a regular, and so compleat a fortification, and has such a line of heavy cannon commanding the mouth of the river, that no man of war, or fleet of men of war, would attempt to pass by as the Dutch did; or at least cou'd not effect it without hazard of being torn to pieces by those batteries.

SHEERNESS is not only a fortress, but a kind of town, with several streets in it, and inhabitants of several sorts; but chiefly such whose business obliges them to reside here: The officers of the ordnance have here apartments, and an office, they being often oblig'd to be here many days together; especially in time of war, when the rendezvous of the fleet is at the Nore, to see to the furnishing every ship with military stores as need requires, and to cheque the officers of the ships in their demands of those stores, and the like.

Here is also a yard for building ships, with a dock; the reason of which, is to repair any ship speedily that may meet with any accident, either riding at the Nore, or in any service at sea near the river. But then 'tis to be observ'd, that those are but fifth and sixth rate ships, small frigats, yatches, and such vessels; at biggest, nothing above a fourth rate can come in here. The *Sheerness* galley, as I am told, was built here, and had her name on that occasion. This yard is a late thing also, and built many years since the fort.

This fort commands only the entrance into the Medway, or that branch of the Medway, properly, which they call West-Swale: The East-Swale, not navigable by ships of force, goes in by the town of Queenborough, passes east, makes the Isle of Shepey, parting it on the south side, and opens to the sea, near Feversham, and Swale-Cliff, and is therefore of small consequence. As for the expression of a certain author, that Sheerness divides the mouth of the two rivers, Thames and Medway, 'tis not said for want of ignorance, and cannot be true in fact; the mouth of the Medway opening into the Thames, and the mouth of the Thames, not being within twenty miles of it, (viz.) from the Nase and North-Foreland.

At the south-west point of the Isle of Shepey, where the East-Swale parts from the West, and passes on, as above, stands a town memorable for nothing, but that which is rather a dishonour to our country than otherwise: Namely, Queenborough, a miserable, dirty, decay'd, poor, pitiful, fishing town; yet vested with corporation priviledges, has a mayor, aldermen, &c. and his worship the mayor has his mace carry'd before him to church, and attended in as much state and ceremony as the mayor of a town twenty times as good: I remember when I was there, Mr. Mayor was a butcher, and brought us a shoulder of mutton to our inn himself in person, which we bespoke for our dinner, and afterwards he sat down and drank a bottle of wine with us.

But that which is still worse, and which I meant in what I said before, is, that this town sends two burgesses to Parliament, as many as the borough of Southwark, or the city of Westminster: Tho' it may be presumed all the inhabitants are not possess'd of estates answerable to the rent of one good house in either of those places I last mentioned: The chief business of this town, as I could understand, consists in ale-houses, and oyster-catchers.

Here we took boat, and went up the East-Swale to a town, which lies, as it were hid, in the country, and among the creeks; for 'tis out of the way, and almost out of sight, as well by water as by land, I mean Milton; it lyes up so many creeks and windings of the water, that nobody sees it by water, but they who go on purpose out of the way to it; and as to the road, it lyes also about a mile on the left-hand of the great road, as we pass thro' Sittingbourn, so that no body sees it on that side neither, unless they go on purpose out of the road to it; and yet it is a large town, has a considerable market, and especially for corn, and fruit and provisions, which they send to London by water.

From hence following the coast, and the great road together, for they are still within view of one another, we come to Feversham, a large populous, and as some say, a rich town: Tho' here is no particular remarkable trade, either for manufacture or navigation; the principal business we found among them, was fishing for oysters, which the Dutch fetch hence in such extraordinary quantities, that when I was there, we found twelve large Dutch hoys and doggers lying there to load oysters; and some times, as they told us, there are many more: This is greatly to the advantage of the place, as it employs abundance of men and boats in drudging for the oysters, which they catch in great plenty, in the mouth of the East-Swale; which, as I said above, enters in this part of the country into the sea, and opens very wide.

It was at the mouth of this Swale, namely, at Shell-Ness, so call'd from the abundance of oyster-shells always lying there, that the smack in which the late King James II. was embark'd for his escape into France, ran on shoar, and being boarded by the fishermen, the king was taken prisoner; and I must mention it to the reproach of the people of Feversham, let the conduct of that unfortunate prince be what it will, that the fishermen and rabble can never be excus'd, who treated the king, even after they were told who he was, with the utmost indecency, using his majesty; (for he was then their sovereign, even in the acknowledged sense of his enemies) I say, using him with such indignity in his person, such insolence in their behaviour, and giving him such opprobrious and abusive language, and searching him in the rudest and most indecent manner, and indeed

*E 820

rifling him; that the king himself said, he was never more apprehensive of his life than at that time. He was afterwards carry'd by them up to the town, where he was not much better treated for some time, till some neighbouring gentlemen in the county came in, who understood their duty better, by whom he was at least preserv'd from farther violence, till coaches and a guard came from London, by the Prince of Orange's order, to bring him with safety and freedom to London; where he was at least for the present much better received, as in the history of those times is to be seen.

While I was near this town some years ago, a most surprising accident happen'd, namely, the blowing up of a powder-mill, which stood upon the river, close to the town; the blast was not only frightful, but it shatter'd the whole town, broke the windows, blew down chimneys, and gable-ends not a few; also several people were kill'd at the powder-house it self, tho' not any, as I remember, in the town: but what was most remarkable in it all, was, that the eldest son of the master of the powder-mill, a youth of about fifteen years of age, who was not in the mill, or near it, when it blew up; but in a boat upon the river, rowing cross for his diversion, was kill'd by a piece of the building of the mill, which blew up into the air by the force of the powder, and fell down upon him in the boat: I know nothing else this town is remarkable for, except the most notorious smuggling trade, carry'd on partly by the assistance of the Dutch, in their oyster-boats, and partly by other arts, in which they say, the people hereabouts are arriv'd to such a proficiency, that they are grown monstrous rich by that wicked trade; nay, even the owling trade (so they call the clandestine exporting of wool) has seem'd to be transposed from Rumney Marsh to this coast, and a great deal of it had been carry'd on between the mouth of the East-Swale and the North-Foreland.

As to the landing goods here from Holland and France, such as wine and brandy from the latter, and pepper, tea, coffee, callicoes, tobacco, and such goods, (the duties of which being very high in England, had first been drawn back by debentures) that black trade has not only been carry'd on here, as I was informed, but on both sides the river, on the Essex as well as the Kentish shores, of which I shall speak again in its place.

From this East Swale, and particularly from these last three towns, Queenborough, Milton, and Feversham, the fish-market at Billingsgate is supply'd with several sorts of fish; but particularly with the best and largest oysters, such as they call

stewing oysters: which are generally call'd also Milton Oysters;
some of which are exceeding large, as also with a very great
quantity of others of a lesser size, as they are from the Essex
side, with a smaller and greener sort, call'd Wallfleot; so that
the whole city of London is chiefly supplied with oysters from
this part of the Thames.

From hence also are sent by water to London very great
quantities of fruit; that is to say, apples and cherries; which
are produc'd in this county, more than in any county in England,
especially cherries; and this leads me to cross the hills from
Milton to Maidstone, a town on the river Medway, about ten
miles distant.

This is a considerable town, very populous, and the inhabitants generally wealthy; 'tis the county town, and the river
Medway is navigable to it by large hoys, of fifty to sixty tuns
burthen, the tide flowing quite up to the town; round this
town are the largest cherry orchards, and the most of them that
are in any part of England; and the gross of the quantity of
cherries, and the best of them which supply the whole city of
London come from hence, and are therefore call'd Kentish
cherries.

Here likewise, and in the country adjacent, are great quantities of hops planted, and this is call'd the Mother of Hop
Grounds in England; being the first place in England where
hops were planted in any quantity, and long before any were
planted at Canterbury, tho' that be now supposed to be the
chief place in England, as shall be observ'd in its place: These
were the hops, I suppose, which were planted at the beginning
of the Reformation, and which gave occasion to that old distich:

> Hops, Reformation, bays, and beer,
> Came into England all in a year.

Maidstone is eminent for the plenty of provisions, and richness of lands in the country all round it, and for the best market
in the county, not Rochester, no not Canterbury excepted.

From this town, and the neighbouring parts, London is
supplied with more particulars than from any single market
town in England, which I mention in pursuance of my first
resolution of observing, how every part of England furnishes
something to the city of London.

1. From the wild of Kent, which begins but about six miles
off, and particularly from that part which lyes this way; they
bring the large Kentish bullocks, fam'd for being generally all

red, and with their horns crooked inward, the two points standing one directly against the other, they are counted the largest breed in England.

2. From the same country are brought great quantities of the largest timber for supply of the king's yards at Chattham, and often to London; most of which comes by land carriage to Maidstone.

3. From the country adjoining to Maidstone also, is a very great quantity of corn brought up to London, besides hops and cherries, as above.

4. Also a kind of paving stone, about eight to ten inches square, so durable that it scarce ever wears out; 'tis used to pave court-yards, and passages to gentlemens houses, being the same the Royal Exchange at London is pav'd with, which has never yet wanted the least repair.

5. Also fine white sand for the glass-houses, esteem'd the best in England for melting into flint-glass, and looking glass-plates; and for the stationer's use also, vulgarly call'd writing-sand.

6. Also very great quantities of fruit, such as Kentish pipins, runetts, &c. which come up as the cherries do, whole hoy-loads at a time to the wharf, call'd the Three Cranes, in London; which is the greatest pipin market perhaps in the world.

At Maidstone you begin to converse with gentlemen, and persons of rank of both sexes, and some of quality: All that side of the county which I have mentioned already, as it is marshy, and unhealthy, by its situation among the waters; so it is embarass'd with business, and inhabited chiefly by men of business, such as ship-builders, fisher-men, seafaring-men, and husband-men, or such as depend upon them, and very few families of note are found among them. But as soon as we come down Boxley Hill from Rochester, or Hollingbourn-Hill, from Milton, and descend from the poor chalky downs, and deep foggy marshes, to the wholesome rich soil, the well wooded, and well water'd plain on the banks of the Medway, we find the country every where spangl'd with populous villages, and delicious seats of the nobility and gentry; and especially on the north-side of the river, beginning at Aylesford, on the Medway, and looking east towards the sea: This Aylesford was formerly the seat of Sir John Banks, and since descended, by his daughter, to Heneage Lord Finch, brother to the Earl of Nottingham, and created Earl of Aylesford, which estate he came to in right of his said lady: the country this way, I say, is full of gentlemens houses, reckoning from this Aylesford, below Maidstone, on the Medway to Eastwell, near Ashford, the seat of the Earl of Winchelsea; another noble family of the name of Finch also; tho' not nearly ally'd to the Nottingham house.

Among these are the antient families of Fane, Colepeper, Deerham, Honywood, Wotton, Roberts, Hales, and others, with some good families extinct and gone, whose names however remain in memory.

This neighbourhood of persons of figure and quality, makes Maidstone a very agreeable place to live in, and where a man of letters, and of manners, will always find suitable society, both to divert and improve himself; so that here is, what is not often found, namely, a town of very great business and trade, and yet full of gentry, of mirth, and of good company.

It is to be recorded here for the honour of the gentry in this part of England; that tho' they are as sociable and entertaining as any people are, or can be desir'd to be, and as much fam'd for good manners, and good humour; yet the new mode of forming assemblies so much, and so fatally now in vogue, in other parts of England, could never prevail here; and that tho' there was an attempt made by some loose persons, and the gentlemen, and ladies, did for a little while appear there; yet they generally dislik'd the practice, soon declin'd to give their company, as to a thing scandalous, and so it drop'd of course.

There is not much manufacturing in this county; what is left, is chiefly at Canterbury, and in this town of Maidstone, and the neighbourhood; the manufacture of this town is principally in thread, that is to say, linnen thread, which they make to pretty good perfection, tho' not extraordinary fine. At Cranbrook, Tenterden, Goudhurst, and other villages thereabout, which are also in the neighbourhood of this part, on the other side the Medway, there was once a very considerable cloathing trade carry'd on, and the yeomen of Kent, of which so much has been fam'd, were generally the inhabitants on that side, and who were much enrich'd by that clothing trade; but that trade is now quite decay'd, and scarce ten clothiers left in all the county.

These clothiers and farmers, and the remains of them, upon the general elections of members of parliament for the county, show themselves still there, being ordinarily 14 or 1500 freeholders brought from this side of the county; and who for the plainness of their appearance, are call'd the gray coats of Kent;

but are so considerable, that who ever they vote for is always sure to carry it, and therefore the gentlemen are very careful to preserve their interest among them.

This town of Maidstone is a peculiar of the Archbishoprick of Canterbury, and the Archbishop for the time being, is the proper incumbent, or parson of the parish, and puts in a curate to officiate for him. Here is the county gaol also, and generally the assizes, and always the elections are held here: Here was a hot action in the time of the Civil Wars, between a party of gentlemen who took arms for the king, and who being defeated here, march'd boldly towards London, as if they had intended to go directly thither; but turn'd short, and to their enemies surprise, unexpectedly cross'd the Thames, and joining some Essex gentlemen of the same party, went to Colchester, where they suffered a furious siege and blockade; and defended the town to the last extremity, as you have seen in my account of that place.

In prosecution of my journey east, I went from hence to Canterbury; of which town and its antiquities so much has been said, and so accurately, that I need do no more than mention it by recapitulation; for, as I have said, the antiquities, and histories of particular places is not my business here, so much as the present state of them. However I observe here.

1. That the first Christian bishop, if not the first Christian preacher, that ever came to England, (for I know not what to say to the story of Joseph of Arimathea, and his holy thorn at Glassenbury) landed in this country, and settled in this place; I mean St. Augustin, sent over by Gregory, Bishop of Rome. This Gregory it seems was a true primitive Christian Bishop of Rome; not such as since are called so; long before they assum'd the title of popes, or that usurp'd honour of Universal Bishop.

2. That, seven Bishops of Canterbury, from St. Augustine, inclusive of himself, lye bury'd here in one vault.

3. That Thomas Becket, or Thomas a Becket, as some call him, arch-bishop of this see, and several arch-bishops before him, plagued, insulted, and tyranniz'd over the Kings of England, their soveraigns, in an unsufferable manner.

4. That the first of these, having made himself intolerable to King Henry II, by his obstinacy, pride and rebellion, was here murther'd by the connivance, and as some say, by the express order of the king, and that they shew his blood upon the pavement to this day.

5. That he was afterwards canoniz'd, and his shrine made the greatest idol of the world; and they show the stone-steps ascending to his shrine, worn away to a slope, by the knees of the pilgrims, and ignorant people who came thither to pray to him, and to desire him to pray for them.

6. That the bodies of King Henry IV and of Edward the Black Prince are buried here, and the magnificent effigies of the latter very curiously carv'd and engrav'd, lyes on his tomb, or monument; also that King Stephen should have lain here, but on some scruple of the monks, the corpse was stopt short on the road, and was afterwards buried at Feversham, about seven miles off. What the monks objected, or whether they had no money offered them, is not recorded with the rest of the story.

7. That the immense wealth offer'd by votaries, and pilgrims, for several ages to the altar, or shrine of this mock saint, Thomas Becket, was such, that Erasmus Roterdamus, who was in the repository and saw it, relates of it, That the whole place glitter'd and shone with gold and diamonds.

8. That all this immense treasure, with the lands and revenues of the whole monastery were seiz'd upon, and taken away by King Henry VIII, at the general suppression of religious houses, except such as are annex'd to the Dean and Chapter, and to the revenue of the arch-bishoprick, which are not large.

The church is a noble pile of building indeed, and looks venerable and majestick at a distance, as well as when we come nearer to it. The old monastery of all, with the church there, dedicated to St. Augustine, and in the porch of which St. Augustine himself, with the six bishops above mention'd lye buried, stands at, or rather stood at a distance, and the ruins of it shew the place sufficiently; what remains of the old buildings about Christ-Church, or the cathedral, are principally the cloyster, and the bishop's palace, which however is rather to be call'd a building raised from the old house, than a part of it.

Under the church is a large Protestant French church, given first by Queen Elizabeth to the Walloons, who fled hither from the persecution of the Duke D'Alva, and the King of France; and whose number has been since very much encreased by the particular cruelty of Louis XIV.

The close or circumvallation, where the houses of the prebendaries, and other persons belonging to the cathedral stand, is very spacious and fair, and a great many very good houses are built in it, and some with good gardens; where those gentlemen live at large, and among whom a very good neighbourhood is kept up; as for the town, its antiquity seems to be its greatest beauty: The houses are truly antient, and the many ruins of churches, chapels, oratories, and smaller cells of religious people, makes the place look like a general ruin a little recover'd.

The city will scarce bear being call'd populous, were it not for two or three thousand French Protestants, which, including men, women and children, they say there are in it, and yet they tell me the number of these decreases daily.

The employment of those refugees was chiefly broad silk weaving; but that trade was so decay'd before the first Act for Prohibiting the Wearing of East India Silks pass'd, that there were not twenty broad looms left in the city, of near three hundred, that had formerly been there; upon the passing that Act, the trade reviv'd again and the number of master workmen encreased, and the masters encreased; and the masters which were there before, encreasing their works also, the town fill'd again, and a great many looms were employ'd; but after this by the encroaching of the printed callicoes, chints, &c. and the prevailing of the smuggling trade as above, the silk trade decay'd a second time. But now the use and wear of printed callicoes and chints, being by Act of Parliament severely prohibited, 'tis expected the silk trade at Canterbury will revive a third time, and the inhabitants promise themselves much from it.

But the great wealth and encrease of the city of Canterbury, is from the surprizing encrease of the hop-grounds all round the place; it is within the memory of many of the inhabitants now living, and that none of the oldest neither, that there was not an acre of ground planted with hops in the whole neighbourhood, or so few as not to be worth naming; whereas I was assured that there are at this time near six thousand acres of ground so planted, within a very few miles of the city; I do not vouch the number, and I confess it seems incredible, but I deliver it as I receiv'd it.

It is observ'd that the ground round this city proves more particularly fruitful for the growth of hops than of any other production, which was not at first known; but which, upon its being discover'd, set all the world, speaking in the language of a neighbourhood, a digging up their grounds and planting; so that now they may say without boasting, there is at Canterbury the greatest plantation of hops in the whole island.

The river Stour was made navigable to this city, by virtue

of an Act of Parliament in the reign of King Henry VIII, but the person who undertook it, not meeting with encouragement, and failing in the carrying it on, the locks and sluices are all run to decay, and the citizens are oblig'd to fetch all their heavy goods, either from Fordwich, three miles off, or from Whitstable seven miles off; the latter they chuse for such heavy goods as come from London; as oyl, wine, grocery, &c. because 'tis the less hazard by sea; but as for coals, deals, &c. they come by way of Sandwich, and are brought up the river to Fordwich, as above.

In the neighbourhood of this city are some antient families, as Sir Tho. Hales, the Lord Strangford, Sir Henry Oxenden, and several others, the two former Roman; also Sir George Rook, famous for his services at sea against the French; the last of which was in the Streights, where the French fleet was commanded by the Count de Tourville, Admiral of France; where both sides fought with such equal gallantry, and resolution, and the strength of the fleets were so equal, tho' the French the most in number of the two, that neither seem'd to seek a second engagement; and of which the following lines were made by some of the merry wits of that time.

> The great Tourville Sir George did beat,
>   The great Sir George beat him;
> But if they chance again to meet,
>   George will his jacket trim:
> They both did fight, they both did beat,
>   They both did run away;
> They both did strive again to meet,
>   The clean contrary way.

The shore from Whitstable, and the East-Swale, affords nothing remarkable but sea-marks, and small towns on the coast, till we come to Margate and the North Foreland; the town of Margate is eminent for nothing that I know of, but for King William's frequently landing here in his returns from Holland, and for shipping a vast quantity of corn for London Market, most, if not all of it, the product of the Isle of Thanet, in which it stands.

On the north-east point of this land, is the promontory, or head-land which I have often mentioned, call'd the North Foreland; which, by a line drawn due north to the Nase in Essex, about six miles short of Harwich, makes the mouth of the river of Thames, and the Port of London: As soon as any vessels pass this Foreland from London, they are properly said to be in the open sea; if to the north, they enter the German

Ocean, if to the south, the Chanel, as 'tis call'd, that is the narrow seas between England and France; and all the towns or harbours before we come this length, whether on the Kentish or Essex shoar, are call'd members of the Port of London.

From this point westward, the first town of note is Ramsgate, a small port, the inhabitants are mighty fond of having us call it Roman's-Gate; pretending that the Romans under Julius Cæsar made their first attempt to land here, when he was driven back by a storm; but soon return'd, and coming on shore, with a good body of troops beat back the Britains, and fortify'd his camp, just at the entrance of the creek, where the town now stands; all which may be true for ought any one knows, but is not to be prov'd, either by them or any one else; and is of so little concern to us, that it matters nothing whether here or at Deal, where others pretend it was.

It was from this town of Ramsgate, that a fellow of gigantick strength, tho' not of extraordinary stature, came abroad in the world, and was call'd the English Sampson, and who suffer'd men to fasten the strongest horse they could find to a rope, and the rope round his loins, sitting on the ground, with his feet strait out against a post, and no horse could stir him; several other proofs of an incredible strength he gave before the king, and abundance of the nobility at Kensington, which no other man could equal; but his history was very short, for in about a year he disappear'd, and we heard no more of him since.

Sandwich is the next town, lying in the bottom of a bay, at the mouth of the river Stour, an old, decay'd, poor, miserable town, of which when I have said that it is an antient town, one of the Cinque Ports, and sends two members to Parliament; I have said all that I think can be worth any bodies reading of the town of Sandwich.

From hence to Deal is about —— miles. This place is famous for the road for shipping, so well known all over the trading world, by the name of the Downs, and where almost all ships which arrive from foreign parts for London, or go from London to foreign parts, and who pass the Channel, generally stop; the homeward-bound to dispatch letters, send their merchants and owners the good news of their arrival, and set their passengers on shoar, and the like; and the outward-bound to receive their last orders, letters, and farewells from owners, and friends, take in fresh provisions, &c.

Sometimes, and when the wind presents fair, ships do come

in here, and pass thro' at once, without coming to an anchor;
for they are not oblig'd to stop, but for their own convenience:
This place would be a very wild and dangerous road for ships,
were it nor for the South Foreland, a head of land, forming the
east point of the Kentish shoar; and is called, the South, as its
situation respects the North Foreland; and which breaks the
sea off, which would otherwise come rowling up from the west,
this and a flat, or the bank of sands, which for three leagues
together, and at about a league, or league and half distance
run parallel with the shore, and are dry at low water, these
two I say, break all the force of the sea, on the east and south,
and south-west; so that the Downs is counted a very good road.

And yet on some particular winds, and especially, if they
over-blow, the Downs proves a very wild road; ships are driven
from their anchors, and often run on shoar, or are forced on the
said sands, or into Sandwich-Bay, or Ramsgate-Peer, as above,
in great distress; this is particularly when the wind blows hard
at S.E. or at E. by N. or E.N.E. and some other points; and
terrible havock has been made in the Downs at such times.

But the most unhappy account that can be given of any
disaster in the Downs, is in the time of that terrible tempest,
which we call by way of distinction, the Great Storm, being on
27th of November 1703, unhappy in particular; for that there
chanced just at that time to be a great part of the royal navy
under Sir Cloudesly Shovel, just come into the Downs, in their
way to Chatham, to be laid up.

Five of the biggest ships had the good hap to push thro' the
Downs the day before, finding the wind then blow very hard,
and were come to an anchor at the Gunfleet; and had they had
but one fair day more, they had been all safe at the Nore, or
in the river Medway at Blackstakes.

There remain'd in the Downs about twelve sail when this
terrible blast began, at which time England may be said to have
received the greatest loss that ever happen'd to the royal
navy at one time; either by weather, by enemies, or by any
accident whatsoever; the short account of it, as they shewed
it me in the town, I mean of what happened in the Downs,
is as follows.

The *Northumberland*, a third rate, carrying 70 guns, and
353 men; the *Restoration*, a second rate, carrying 76 guns, and
386 men; the *Sterling-Castle*, a second rate, carrying 80 guns,
and 400 men, but had but 349 men on board; and the *Mary*,
a third rate, of 64 guns, having 273 men on board; these were

all lost, with all their men, high and low; except only one man out of the *Mary*, and 70 men out of the *Sterling-Castle*, who were taken up by boats from Deal.

All this was besides the loss of merchants ships, which was exceeding great, not here only, but in almost all the ports in the south, and west of England; and also in Ireland, which I shall have occasion to mention again in another place.

From hence we pass over a pleasant champain country, with the sea, and the coast of France, clear in your view; and by the very gates of the antient castle (to the town) of Dover: As we go, we pass by Deal Castle, and Sandown Castle, two small works, of no strength by land, and not of much use by sea; but however maintain'd by the government for the ordinary services of salutes, and protecting small vessels, which can lye safe under their cannon from picaroons, privateers, &c. in time of war.

Neither Dover nor its castle has any thing of note to be said of them, but what is in common with their neighbours; the castle is old, useless, decay'd, and serves for little; but to give the title and honour of government to men of quality, with a salary, and sometimes to those that want one.

The town is one of the Cinque Ports, sends members to Parliament, who are call'd barons, and has it self an ill repair'd, dangerous, and good for little harbour and peir, very chargeable and little worth: The packets for France go off here, as also those for Nieuport, with the mails for Flanders, and all those ships which carry freights from New-York to Holland, and from Virginia to Holland, come generally hither, and unlade their goods, enter them with, and show them to the custom-house officers, pay the duties, and then enter them again by certificate, reload them, and draw back the duty by debenture, and so they go away for Holland.

In the time of the late war with France, here was a large victualling-office kept for the use of the navy, and a commissioner appointed to manage it, as there was also at Chatham, Portsmouth, and other places; but this is now unemploy'd: The Duke of Queensberry in Scotland, who was lord commissioner to the Parliament there, at the time of making the Union, was after the said Union created Duke of Dover, which title is possess'd now by his son.

From this place the coast affords nothing of note; but some other small Cinque-Ports, such as Hith and Rumney, and Rye; and as we pass to them Folkstone, eminent chiefly for a multitude of fishing-boats belonging to it, which are one part of the year employ'd in catching mackarel for the city of London: The Folkstone men catch them, and the London and Barking mackarel-smacks, of which I have spoken at large in Essex, come down and buy them, and fly up to market with them, with such a cloud of canvas, and up so high that one would wonder their small boats cou'd bear it and should not overset: About Michaelmas these Folkstone barks, among others from Shoreham, Brighthelmston and Rye, go away to Yarmouth, and Leostoff, on the coast of Suffolk and Norfolk, to the fishing-fair, and catch herrings for the merchants there, of which I have spoken at large in my discourse on that subject.

As I rode along this coast, I perceiv'd several dragoons riding, officers, and others arm'd and on horseback, riding always about as if they were huntsmen beating up their game; upon inquiry I found their diligence was employ'd in quest of the owlers, as they call them, and sometimes they catch some of them; but when I came to enquire farther, I found too, that often times these are attack'd in the night, with such numbers, that they dare not resist, or if they do, they are wounded and beaten, and sometimes kill'd; and at other times are oblig'd, as it were, to stand still, and see the wool carry'd off before their faces, not daring to meddle; and the boats taking it in from the very horses backs, go immediately off, and are on the coast of France, before any notice can be given of them, while the other are as nimble to return with their horses to their haunts and retreats, where they are not easily found out.

But I find so many of these desperate fellows are of late taken up, by the courage and vigilance of the soldiers, that the knots are very much broken, and the owling-trade much abated, at least on that side; the French also finding means to be supply'd from Ireland with much less hazard, and at very little more expence.

From Rumney-Marsh the shoar extends it self a great way into the sea, and makes that point of land, call'd Dengey-Ness; between this point of land and Beachy, it was that the French in the height of their naval glory took the English and Dutch fleets at some disadvantage, offering them battle, when the French were so superior in number, that it was not consistent with humane prudence to venture an engagement, the French being ninety two ships of the line of battle, and the English and Dutch, put together, not sixty sail; the French ships also generally bigger: yet such was the eagerness of both the English and Dutch seamen, and commanders, that it was not without infinite murmurings, that Admiral Herbert stood away, and call'd off the Dutch, who had the van, from engaging; the English it seems believ'd themselves so superiour to the French when they came to lye broad-side and broad-side, yard-arm and yard-arm, as the seamen call it in an engagement, that they would admit of no excuse for not fighting; tho' according to all the rules of war, no admiral could justify hazarding the royal navy on such terms; and especially the circumstances of the time then considered, for the king was in Ireland, and King James ready in France, if the English and Dutch fleets had received a blow, to have embark'd with an army for England, which perhaps would have hazarded the whole Revolution; so that wise men afterwards, and as I have been told the king himself upon a full hearing justify'd the conduct of Admiral Herbert, and afterwards created him Earl of Torrington.

Here, or rather a little farther, we saw the bones of one of the Dutch men of war, which was burnt and stranded by the French in that action; the towns of Rye, Winchelsea, and Hastings, have little in them to deserve more than a bare mention; Rye would flourish again, if her harbour, which was once able to receive the royal navy, cou'd be restor'd; but as it is, the bar is so loaded with sand cast up by the sea, that ships of 200 tun chuse to ride it out under Dengey or Beachy, tho' with the greatest danger, rather than to run the hazard of going into Rye for shelter: It is true there is now an Act of Parliament pass'd for the restoring this port to its former state, when a man of war of 70 guns might have safely gone in; but 'tis very doubtful, whether it will be effectual to the main end or no, after so long a time.

Indeed our merchants ships are often put to great extremity hereabout, for there is not one safe place for them to run into, between Portsmouth and the Downs; whereas in former days, Rye-Bay was an asylum, a safe harbour, where they could go boldly in, and ride safe in all weathers, and then go to sea again at pleasure.

From a little beyond Hastings to Bourn, we ride upon the sands in a straight line for eighteen miles, all upon the coast of Sussex, passing by Pemsey, or Pevensey Haven, and the mouth of the river, which cometh from Battle, without so much as knowing that there was a river, the tide being out, and all the water of the ordinary chanel of the river sinking away in the sands: This is that famous strand where William the

Norman landed with his whole army; and near to which, namely, at the town of Battle abovenamed, which is about nine miles off, he fought that memorable fight with Harold, then King of England; in which the fate of this nation was determined, and where victory gave the crown to the Conqueror and his race, of the particulars of all which, our histories are full; this town of Battle is remarkable for little now, but for making the finest gun-powder, and the best perhaps in Europe. Near this town of Battle, they show us a hill with a beacon upon it, which since the beacon was set up, indeed has been call'd Beacon Hill, as is usual in such cases; but was before that call'd Standard-Hill, being the place where William the Conqueror set up his great standard of defiance, the day before the great battle with Harold and the English.

From the beginning of Rumney Marsh, that is to say, at Sandgate, or Sandfoot Castle near Hith, to this place, the country is a rich fertile soil, full of feeding grounds, and where an infinite number of large sheep are fed every year, and sent up to London market; these Rumney Marsh sheep, are counted rather larger than the Leicester-shire and Lincolnshire sheep, of which so much is said elsewhere.

Besides the vast quantity of sheep as above, abundance of large bullocks are fed in this part of the country; and especially those they call stall'd oxen, that is, house fed, and kept within the farmers sheds or yards, all the latter season, where they are fed for the winter market. This I noted, because these oxen are generally the largest beef in England.

From hence it was that, turning north, and traversing the deep, dirty, but rich part of these two counties, I had the curiosity to see the great foundaries, or iron-works, which are in this county, and where they are carry'd on at such a prodigious expence of wood, that even in a country almost all over-run with timber, they begin to complain of the consuming it for those furnaces, and leaving the next age to want timber for building their navies: I must own however, that I found that complaint perfectly groundless, the three counties of Kent, Sussex, and Hampshire, (all which lye contiguous to one another) being one inexhaustible store-house of timber never to be destroy'd, but by a general conflagration, and able at this time to supply timber to rebuild all the royal navies in Europe, if they were all to be destroy'd, and set about the building them together.

After I had fatigued my self in passing this deep and heavy

part of the country, I thought it would not be foreign to my design, if I refresh'd my self with a view of Tunbridge-Wells, which were not then above twelve miles out of my way.

When I came to the wells, which were five miles nearer to me than the town, supposing me then at Battle to the southward of them; I found a great deal of good company there, and that which was more particular, was, that it happen'd to be at the time when his Royal Highness the Prince of Wales was there with abundance of the nobility, and gentry of the country, who to honour the prince's coming, or satisfy their own curiosity, throng'd to that place; so that at first I found it very difficult to get a lodging.

The prince appear'd upon the walks, went into the raffling shops, and to every publick place, saw every thing, and let every body see him, and went away, with the Duke of Dorset, and other of his attendance for Portsmouth; so in two or three days, things return'd all to their antient chanel, and Tunbridge was just what it used to be.

The ladies that appear here, are indeed the glory of the place; the coming to the Wells to drink the water is a meer matter of custom; some drink, more do not, and few drink physically: But company and diversion is in short the main business of the place; and those people who have nothing to do any where else, seem to be the only people who have any thing to do at Tunbridge.

After the appearance is over at the Wells, (where the ladies are all undress'd) and at the chapel, the company go home; and as if it was another species of people, or a collection from another place, you are surpriz'd to see the walks covered with ladies compleatly dress'd and gay to profusion; where rich cloths, jewels, and beauty not to be set out by (but infinitely above) ornament, dazzles the eyes from one end of the range to the other.

Here you have all the liberty of conversation in the world, and any thing that looks like a gentleman, has an address agreeable, and behaves with decency and good manners, may single out whom he pleases, that does not appear engag'd, and may talk, rally, be merry, and say any decent thing to them; but all this makes no acquaintance, nor is it taken so, or understood to mean so; if a gentleman desires to be more intimate, and enter into any acquaintance particular, he must do it by proper application, not by ordinary meeting on the walks, for the ladies will ask no gentleman there, to go off the walk, or invite any one to their lodgings, except it be a sort of ladies of whom I am not now speaking.

As for gaming, sharping, intrieguing; as also fops, fools, beaus, and the like, Tunbridge is as full of these, as can be desired, and it takes off much of the diversion of those persons of honour and virtue, who go there to be innocently recreated: However a man of character, and good behaviour cannot be there any time, but he may single out such company as may be suitable to him, and with whom he may be as merry as heart can wish.

The air here is excellent good, the country healthful, and the provisions of all sorts very reasonable: Particularly, they are supply'd with excellent fish, and that of almost all sorts, from Rye, and other towns on the sea-coast; and I saw a turbut of near 20l. weight sold there for 3s.: In the season of mackarel, they have them here from Hastings, within three hours of their being taken out of the sea, and the difference which that makes in their goodness, I need not mention.

They have likewise here abundance of wild-fowl, of the best sorts; such as pheasant, partridge, woodcock, snipe, quails, also duck, mallard, teal, &c. particularly they have from the South-Downs, the bird call'd a wheatear, or as we may call them, the English ortolans, the most delicious taste for a creature of one mouthful, for 'tis little more, that can be imagin'd; but these are very dear at Tunbridge, they are much cheaper at Seaford, Lewis, and that side of the country.

In a word, Tunbridge wants nothing that can add to the felicities of life, or that can make a man or woman compleatly happy, always provided they have money; for without money a man is no-body at Tunbridge, any more than at any other place; and when any man finds his pockets low, he has nothing left to think of, but to be gone, for he will have no diversion in staying there any longer.

And yet Tunbridge also is a place in which a lady however virtuous, yet for want of good conduct may as soon shipwreck her character as in any part of England; and where, when she has once injur'd her reputation, 'tis as hard to restore it; nay, some say no lady ever recover'd her character at Tunbridge, if she first wounded it there: But this is to be added too, that a lady very seldom suffers that way at Tunbridge, without some apparent folly of her own; for that they do not seem so apt to make havock of one another's reputation here, by tattle and slander, as I think they do in some other places in the world;

particularly at Epsome, Hampstead, and such like places; which I take to be, because the company who frequent Tunbridge, seem to be a degree or two above the society of those other places, and therefore are not so very apt, either to meddle with other peoples affairs, or to censure if they do; both which are the properties of that more gossiping part of the world.

In this I shall be much misunderstood, if it is thought I mean the ladies only, for I must own I look just the other way; and if I may be allow'd to use my own sex so coursly, it is really among them that the ladies characters first, and oftnest receive unjust wounds; and I must confess the malice, the reflections, the busy meddling, the censuring, the tatling from place to place, and the making havock of the characters of innocent women, is found among the men gossips more than among their own sex, and at the coffee-houses more than at the tea-table; then among the women themselves, what is to be found of it there, is more among the chamber-maids, than among their mistresses; slander is a meanness below persons of honour and quality, and to do injustice to the ladies, especially, is a degree below those who have any share of breeding and sense: On this account you may observe, 'tis more practis'd among the citizens than among the gentry, and in country towns and villages, more than in the city, and so on, till you come to the meer *canail*, the common mobb of the street, and there, no reputation, no character can shine without having dirt thrown upon it every day: But this is a digression.

I left Tunbridge, for the same reason that I give, why others should leave it, when they are in my condition; namely, that I found my money almost gone; and tho' I had bills of credit to supply my self in the course of my intended journey; yet I had none there; so I came away, or as they call it there, I retir'd; and came to Lewes, through the deepest, dirtiest, but many ways the richest, and most profitable country in all that part of England.

The timber I saw here was prodigious, as well in quantity as in bigness, and seem'd in some places to be suffer'd to grow, only because it was so far off of any navigation, that it was not worth cutting down and carrying away; in dry summers, indeed, a great deal is carry'd away to Maidstone, and other places on the Medway; and sometimes I have seen one tree on a carriage, which they call there a tug, drawn by two and twenty oxen, and even then, 'tis carry'd so little a way, and then thrown down, and left for other tugs to take up and carry on, that

sometimes 'tis two or three year before it gets to Chatham;
for if once the rains come in, it stirs no more that year, and
sometimes a whole summer is not dry enough to make the
roads passable: Here I had a sight, which indeed I never saw
in any other part of England: Namely, that going to church
at a country village, not far from Lewis, I saw an ancient lady,
and a lady of very good quality, I assure you, drawn to church
in her coach with six oxen; nor was it done in frolic or humour,
but meer necessity, the way being so stiff and deep, that no
horses could go in it.

Lewis is a fine pleasant town, well built, agreeably scituated
in the middle of an open champaign country, and on the edge
of the South Downs, the pleasantest, and most delightful of
their kind in the nation; it lies on the bank of a little wholsome
fresh river, within twelve miles of the sea; but that which adds
to the character of this town, is, that both the town and the
country adjacent, is full of gentlemen of good families and
fortunes, of which the Pelhams may be named with the first,
whose chief was by King William made a baron, and whose
eldest son succeeding to the greatest part of the estate of that
English Crassus, the late Duke of Newcastle, has since brought
the title and honour of Newcastle to the house of Pelham.
Here are also the antient families of Gage, Shelly, &c. formerly
Roman, but now Protestant, with many others.

From this town, following still the range of the South Downs,
west; we ride in view of the sea, and on a fine carpet ground,
for about twelve miles to Bright Helmston, commonly call'd
Bredhemston, a poor fishing town, old built, and on the very
edge of the sea: Here again, as I mention'd at Folkstone
and Dover, the fisher-men having large barks go away to
Yarmouth, on the coast of Norfolk, to the fishing fair there,
and hire themselves for the season to catch herrings for
the merchants; and they tell us, that these make a very good
business of it.

The sea is very unkind to this town, and has by its continual
encroachments, so gain'd upon them, that in a little time more
they might reasonably expect it would eat up the whole town,
above 100 houses having been devoured by the water in a few
years past; they are now obliged to get a brief granted them, to
beg money all over England, to raise banks against the water;
the expence of which, the brief expresly says, will be eight
thousand pounds; which if one were to look on the town, would
seem to be more than all the houses in it are worth.

From hence, still keeping the coast close on the left, we come to Shoreham, a sea-faring town, and chiefly inhabited by ship-carpenters, ship-chandlers, and all the several trades depending upon the building and fitting up of ships, which is their chief business; and they are fam'd for neat building, and for building good sea-boats; that is to say, ships that are wholesome in the sea, and good sailors; but for strong building, they do not come up to Yarmouth, Ipswich, and the north.

The builders of ships seemed to plant here, chiefly because of the exceeding quantity and cheapness of timber in the country behind them; being the same wooded country I mentioned above, which still continues thro' this county and the next also: The river this town stands upon, tho' not navigable for large vessels, yet serves them to bring down this large timber in floats from Bramber, Stenning, and the country adjacent; which is as it were all covered with timber.

Here in the compass of about six miles are three burrough towns, sending members to Parliament, (viz.) Shoreham, Bramber, and Stenning: and Shoreham, Stenning are tolerable little market-towns; but Bramber (a little ruin of an old castle excepted) hardly deserves the name of a town, having not above fifteen or sixteen families in it, and of them not many above asking you an alms as you ride by; the chiefest house in the town is a tavern, and here, as I have been told, the vintner, or ale-house-keeper rather, for he hardly deserv'd the name of a vintner, boasted, that upon an election, just then over, he had made 300*l.* of one pipe of canary.

This is the second town in this county, where the elections have been so scandalously mercenary; and of whom it is said, there was in one king's reign more money spent at elections, than all the lands in the parishes were worth, at twenty years purchase; the other town I mean is Winchelsea, a town, if it deserves the name of a town, which is rather the skeleton of an ancient city than a real town, where the antient gates stand near three miles from one another over the fields, and where the ruins are so bury'd, that they have made good corn fields of the streets, and the plow goes over the foundations, nay, over the first floors of the houses, and where nothing of a town but the destruction of it seems to remain; yet at one election for this town the strife was such between Sir John Banks, father-in-law to the Earl of Aylesford, and Colonel Draper, a neighbouring gentleman, that I was told in the country the latter spent 11000*l.* at one election, and yet lost it too; what the other spent who opposed him, may be guest at, seeing he that spent most was always sure to carry it in those days.

Bramber is the very exemplification of this, with this difference only, namely, that at the former they have given it over, at the latter it seems to be rather worse than ever.

Near Steyning, the famous Sir John Fagg had a noble antient seat, now possess'd with a vast estate by his grandson, Sir Robert Fagg; but I mention the antient gentleman on this occasion, that being entertained at his house, in the year 1697, he show'd me in his park four bullocks of his own breeding, and of his own feeding, of so prodigious a size, and so excessively overgrown by fat, that I never saw any thing like them; and the bullock which Sir Edward Blacket, in Yorkshire, near Rippon, fed, and caused to be shew'd about for a sight at Newcastle upon Tyne, was not any way equal to the least of them, nor had it so much flesh on it by near twenty stone a quarter.

While I continu'd at Sir John's, some London butchers came down to see them, and in my hearing offer'd Sir John six and twenty pound a head for them, but he refused it; and when I mov'd him afterward to take the money, he said No, he was resolv'd to have them to Smithfield himself, that he might say he had the four biggest bullocks in England at market.

He continued positive, and did go up to Smithfield-Market with them; but whether it was that they sunk a little in the driving, or that the butchers play'd a little upon him, I cannot tell; but he was obliged to sell them for twenty five pound a head when he came there: I knew one of the butchers that bought them, and on a particular occasion enquir'd of him what they weigh'd when kill'd, and he assur'd me that they weigh'd eighty stone a quarter, when kill'd and cut-out; which is so incredible, that if I had not been well assur'd of the truth of it, I should not have ventur'd thus to have recorded it: But by this may be judg'd something of the largeness of the cattle in the Wild of Kent and Sussex, for it is all the same, of which I mention'd something before, and for this reason I tell the story.

From hence we come to Arundel, a decay'd town also; but standing near the mouth of a good river, call'd Arun, which signifies, says Mr. Cambden, the swift, tho' the river it self is not such a rapid current as merits that name; at least it did not seem to be so to me.

The principal advantage to the country from this river, is the shipping of great quantities of large timber here; which is carry'd up the Thames to Woolwich and Deptford, and up the Medway to Chatham; as also westward to Portsmouth, and even to Plymouth, to the new dock there, that is to say, it goes to all the king's yards, where the business of the navy is carry'd on: The timber shipped off here is esteem'd the best, as it is also the largest that is brought by sea from any part of England; also great quantities of knee timber is had here, which is valuable in its kind above the strait timber, being not only necessary, but scarce, I mean that which is very large.

This river, and the old decay'd, once famous castle at Arundel, which are still belonging to the family of Howards, Earls of Arundel, a branch of the Norfolk family, is all that is remarkable here; except it be that in this river are catch'd the best mullets, and the largest in England, a fish very good in it self, and much valued by the gentry round, and often sent up to London.

From hence to the city of Chichester are twelve miles, and the most pleasant beautiful country in England, whether we go by the hill, that is the Downs, or by the plain, (viz.) the enclosed country. To the north of Arundel, and at the bottom of the hills, and consequently in the Wild, is the town of Petworth, a large handsome country market-town, and very populous, and as it stands upon an ascent, and is dry and healthy, it is full of gentlemens families, and good well built houses both in the town and neighbourhood; but the beauty of Petworth, is the antient seat of the old family of Peircy, Earls of Northumberland, now extinct; whose daughter, the sole heiress of all his vast estates, marry'd the present Duke of Somerset; of the noble and antient family of Seymour, and among other noble seats brought his grace this of Petworth.

The duke pull'd down the antient house, and on the same spot has built from the ground, one of the finest piles of building, and the best model'd houses then in Britain: It has had the misfortune to be once almost demolish'd by fire, but the damage is fully repair'd; but another disaster to the family can never be repaired, which has happen'd to it, even while these sheets were writing; namely, the death of the dutchess, who dy'd in November 1722, and lies buried in the burying place of the family of Seymor, Dukes of Somerset, in the cathedral church of Salisbury.

Her Grace was happy in a numerous issue, as well as in a noble estate; and besides two sons and one daughter, which lye bury'd with her, has left one son and —— daughters still living. I shall have occasion to mention the Northumberland estates again, when I come to speak of the other fine seats, which the duke enjoys in right of his late dutchess, and the many old castles which were formerly part of that Northumberland estate.

The duke's house at Petworth, is certainly a compleat building in it self, and the apartments are very noble, well contriv'd, and richly furnish'd; but it cannot be said, that the situation of the house is equally design'd, or with equal judgment as the rest; the avenues to the front want space, the house stands as it were with its elbow to the town, its front has no visto answerable, and the west front look'd not to the parks or fine gardens, but to the old stables.

To rectify this, when it was too late to order it any other way, the duke was oblig'd to pull down those noble buildings; I mean the mews, or stables, the finest of their kind in all the south of England, and equal to some noblemens whole houses, and yet even the demolishing the pile has done no more than open'd a prospect over the country, whereas had the house been set on the rising ground, on the side of the park, over against the north wing of the house, and a little more to the westward, the front had been south to the town, the back front to the parks, which were capable of fountains, canals, vistos, and all the most exquisite pieces of art, that sets out the finest gardens, whereas all now lyes on one angle, or opposite to one wing of the house. But with all these disadvantages, the house it self is a noble pile of building, and by far the finest in all this part of Britain.

From Petworth west, the country is a little less woody than the Wild, and there begin to show their heads above the trees, a great many fine seats of the nobility and gentlemen of the country, as the Duke of Richmond's seat at Goodwood, near Chichester. (This family also is in tears, at the writing these sheets, for the death of her grace the dutchess, who dyed the beginning of the month of December, and is bury'd in Westminster Abbey; and here the year closing, I think 'tis very remarkable, that this year 1722, no less than five dukes and two dutchesses are dead (viz.) the Dukes of Bucks, Bolton, Rutland, Manchester, and Marlborough, and the Dutchesses of Somerset and Richmond; besides earls (viz.) the Earl of Sunderland, of Stamford, Exeter, and others; and since the above was written, and sent to the press, the Duke of Richmond himself is also dead.) The seats of the late Earl of Tankerville, and the Earl of Scarborough, the antient house of the Lord Montacute at Midhurst, an antient family of the sirname of Brown, the eldest branch of the house: These and a great many more lying so near together, make the country hereabout much more sociable and pleasant than the rest of the woody country, call'd The Wild, of which I have made mention so often; and yet I cannot say much for the city of Chichester, in which, if six or seven good families were removed, there would not be much conversation, except what is to be found among the canons, and dignitaries of the cathedral.

The cathedral here is not the finest in England, but is far from being the most ordinary: The spire is a piece of excellent workmanship, but it received such a shock about —— years ago, that it was next to miraculous, that the whole steeple did not fall down; which in short, if it had, would almost have demolish'd the whole church.

It was a fire-ball, if we take it from the inhabitants, or, to speak in the language of nature, the lightning broke upon the steeple, and such was the irresistible force of it, that it drove several great stones out of the steeple, and carry'd them clear off, not from the roof of the church only, but of the adjacent houses also, and they were found at a prodigious distance from the steeple, so that they must have been shot out of the places where they stood in the steeple, as if they had been shot out of a cannon, or blown out of a mine: One of these stones of at least a ton weight, by estimation, was blown over the south side, or row of houses in the West-Street, and fell on the ground in the street at a gentleman's door, on the other side of the way; and another of them almost as big was blown over both sides of the said West-Street, into the same gentleman's garden, at whose door the other stone lay, and no hurt was done by either of them; whereas if either of those stones had fallen upon the strongest built house in the street, it would have dash'd it all to pieces, even to the foundation: This account of the two stones, I relate from a person of undoubted credit, who was an eye-witness, and saw them, but had not the curiosity to measure them, which he was very sorry for. The breach it made in the spire, tho' within about forty five foot of the top, was so large, that as the workmen said to me, a coach and six horses might have driven through it, and yet the steeple stood fast, and is now very substantially repair'd; withal, showing that it was before, an admirable sound and well finished piece of workmanship.

They have a story in this city, that when ever a bishop of that diocess is to dye, a heron comes and sits upon the pinnacle of the spire of the cathedral: This accordingly happen'd, about

—— when Dr. —— Williams was bishop: A butcher standing at his shop-door, in the South-Street, saw it, and ran in for his gun, and being a good marks-man shot the heron, and kill'd it, at which his mother was very angry with him, and said he had kill'd the bishop, and the next day news came to the town that Dr. Williams, the last bishop was dead; this is affirm'd by many people inhabitants of the place.

This city is not a place of much trade, nor is it very populous; but they are lately fallen into a very particular way of managing the corn trade here, which it is said turns very well to account; the country round it is very fruitful, and particularly in good wheat, and the farmers generally speaking, carry'd all their wheat to Farnham, to market, which is very near forty miles by land-carriage, and from some parts of the country more than forty miles.

But some money'd men of Chichester, Emsworth, and other places adjacent, have join'd their stocks together, built large granaries near the Crook, where the vessels come up, and here they buy and lay up all the corn which the country on that side can spare; and having good mills in the neighbourhood, they grind and dress the corn, and send it to London in the meal about by Long Sea, as they call it; nor now the war is over do they make the voyage so tedious as to do the meal any hurt, as at first in the time of war was sometimes the case for want of convoys.

It is true, this is a great lessening to Farnham Market, but that is of no consideration in the case; for, if the market at London is supply'd, the coming by sea from Chichester is every jot as much a publick good, as the encouraging of Farnham Market, which is of it self the greatest corn-market in England, London excepted. Notwithstanding all the decrease from this side of the country, this carrying of meal by sea met with so just an encouragement from hence, that it is now practised from several other places on this coast, even as far as Shampton.

From Chichester the road lying still west, passes in view of the Earl of Scarborough's fine seat at Stansted, a house seeming to be a retreat, being surrounded with thick woods, thro' which there are the most pleasant agreeable visto's cut, that are to be seen any where in England, particularly, because through the west opening, which is from the front of the house, they sit in the dining-room of the house, and see the town and harbour of Portsmouth, the ships at Spithead, and also at St. Helens; which when the royal navy happens to be there, as often happen'd during the late war, is a most glorious sight.

F 820

This house was fatal to Dr. Williams, mentioned above, Bishop of Chichester, who having been here to make a visit to the late Earl of Scarborough, was thrown out of his coach, or rather threw himself out, being frighted by the unruliness of his horses, and broke his leg in the fall, which, his lordship being in years, was mortal to him: He dy'd in a few days after.

From hence we descend gradually to Portsmouth, the largest fortification, beyond comparison, that we have in England, but it was not with any consideration, that the author before recited could say, it was the only regular fortification in England; especially the same writer owning afterwards that Shireness, Languardfort, and Tilbury, were all regular fortifications, as they really are.

The situation of this place is such, that it is chosen, as may well be said, for the best security to the navy above all the places in Britain; the entrance into the harbour is safe, but very narrow, guarded on both sides by terrible platforms of cannon, particularly on the Point; which is a suburb of Portsmouth properly so call'd, where there is a brick platform built with two tire of guns, one over another, and which can fire so in cover, that the gunners cannot be beaten from their guns, or their guns easily dismounted; the other is from the point of land on the side of Gosport, which they call Gilkicker, where also they have two batteries.

Before any ships attempt to enter this port by sea, they must also pass the cannon of the main platform of the garrison, and also another at South-Sea-Castle; so that it is next to impossible that any ships could match the force of all those cannon, and be able to force their way into the harbour; in which I speak the judgment of men well acquainted with such matters, as well as my own opinion, and of men whose opinion leads them to think the best of the force of naval batteries too; and who have talk'd of making no difficulty to force their way through the Thames, in the teeth of the line of guns at Tilbury; I say, they have talk'd of it, but it was but talk, as any one of judgment would imagin, that knew the works at Tilbury, of which I have spoken in its place: The reasons, however, which they give for the difference, have some force in them, as they relate to Portsmouth, tho' not as they relate to Tilbury; (viz.) That the mouth or entrance into Portsmouth is narrow, and may be lock'd up with booms, which before the ships could break, and while they were lying at them to break them away, they would be torn in pieces by the battery at the Point: (next) That the guns on the said battery at the Point at Portsmouth, are defended as above, with ambruziers, and the gunners stand cover'd, so that they cannot so soon be beaten from their guns, or their guns so soon dismounted by the warm quarter of a three deck ship, as at Tilbury, where all the gunners and guns too must stand open, both to small and great shot: Besides at Tilbury, while some of the ships lay battering the fort, others would pass behind them, close under the town, and if one or more received damage from the fort, the rest would pass in the cloud of smoke, and perhaps might compass their design, as is the case in all places, where the entrance is broad; whereas at Portsmouth, they would be batter'd within little more than pistol shot, and from both sides of the way; whereas at Tilbury there are very few guns on the Gravesend side of the river.

But to avoid comparing of strengths, or saying what may be done in one place, and not done in another; 'tis evident, in the opinion of all that I have met with, that the greatest fleet of ships that ever were in the hands of one nation at a time, would not pretend, if they had not an army also on shoar, to attack the whole work, to force their entrance into the harbour at Portsmouth.

As to the strength of the town by land, the works are very large and numerous, and besides the battery at the Point aforesaid, there is a large hornwork on the south-side, running out towards South-Sea Castle; there is also a good counterscarp, and double mote, with ravelins in the ditch, and double pallisadoes, and advanc'd works to cover the place from any approach, where it may be practicable: The strength of the town is also considerably augmented on the land-side, by the fortifications raised in King William's time about the docks and yards, which are now perfected, and those parts made a particular strength by themselves; and tho' they are indeed in some sense independent one of another, yet they cover and strengthen one another, so as that they cannot be separately attack'd on that side, while they are both in the same hands.

These docks and yards are now like a town by themselves, and are a kind of marine corporation, or a government of their own kind within themselves; there being particular large rows of dwellings, built at the publick charge, within the new works, for all the principal officers of the place; especially the commissioner, the agent of the victualling, and such as these; the tradesmen likewise have houses here, and many of the labourers are allow'd to live in the bounds as they can get lodging.

The town of Portsmouth, besides its being a fortification, is a well inhabited, thriving, prosperous corporation; and hath been greatly enrich'd of late by the fleet's having so often and so long lain there, as well as large fleets of merchant-men, as the whole navy during the late war; besides the constant fitting out of men here, and the often paying them at Portsmouth, has made a great confluence of people thither on their private business, with other things, which the attendance of those fleets hath requir'd: These things have not only been a great advantage to the town, but has really made the whole place rich, and the inhabitants of Portsmouth are quite another sort of people than they were a few years before the Revolution; this is what Mr. Cambden takes notice of, even so long ago as the reign of Queen Elizabeth; that "Portsmouth was populous in time of war, but not so in time of peace": but now the business of the navy is so much encreased, and so much of it always done here, that it may be said, there is as much to do at Portsmouth now in time of peace, as there was then in time of war, and more too.

There is also this note to be put upon the two great arsenals of England, Portsmouth, and Chatham; Namely, That they thrive by a war, as the war respects their situation (viz.) That when a war with France happens, or with Spain, then Portsmouth grows rich, and when a war with Holland, or any of the Powers of the north, then Chatham, and Woolwich, and Deptford are in request; but of this I shall speak again, when I come to speak of the like antithesis between Plymouth and the Humber, or Portsmouth and the Firth of Edinburgh.

The government of the place is by a mayor and aldermen, &c. as in other corporations, and the civil government is no more interrupted by the military, than if there was no garrison there, such is the good conduct of the governors, and such it has always been, since our soveraigns have ceas'd to encourage the soldiery to insult the civil magistrates: And we have very seldom had any complaint on either side, either of want of discipline among the soldiers, or want of prudence in the magistrates: The inhabitants indeed necessarily submit to such things as are the consequence of a garrison town, such as being examin'd at the gates, such as being obliged to keep garrison hours, and not be let out, or let in after nine a clock at night, and the like; but these are things no people will count a burthen, where they get their bread by the very situation of the place, as is the case here.

Since the encrease of business at this place, by the long continuance of the war, the confluence of people has been so great, and the town not admitting any enlargement for buildings, that a kind of a suburb, or rather a new town has been built on the healthy ground adjoining to the town, which is so well built, and seems to encrease so fast, that in time it threatens to outdo for numbers of inhabitants, and beauty of buildings, even the town it self; and particularly by being unconfin'd by the laws of the garrison, as above, and unencumbered with the corporation burthens, freedoms, town duties, services, and the like.

From Portsmouth west, the country lyes low and flat, and is full of creeks and inlets of the sea and rivers, all the way to Southampton, so that we ferry over three times in about eighteen miles; besides going over one bridge, namely, at Tichfield: The first of these ferries is that at Portsmouth it self, (viz.) cross the mouth of the harbour, from the Point abovemention'd to Gosport; from thence we ride to Tichfield, as above, where we pass the river Alre, which rises in the same county at Alresford, or near it, which is not above twenty two miles off; and yet it is a large river here, and makes a good road below, call'd Tichfield Bay: Thence at about four miles we pass another river at Busselton, narrow in breadth, but exceeding deep, and eminent for its being able to carry the biggest ships: Here is a building yard for ships of war, and in King William's time, two eighty gun ships were launch'd here. It seems the safety of the creek, and the plenty of timber in the country behind it, is the reason of building so much in this place.

From hence when we come opposite to Southampton, we pass another creek, being the mouth of the river Itchen which comes down from Winchester, and is both very broad and deep, and the ferry men having a very sorry boat, we found it dangerous enough passing it: On the other bank stands the antient town of Southampton, and on the other side of Southampton comes down another large river, entring Southampton Water by Red-Bridge; so that the town of Southampton stands upon a point running out into the sea, between two very fine rivers, both navigable, up some length into the country, and particularly useful for the bringing down timber out of one of the best wooded counties in Britain; for the river on the west side of the town in particular comes by the edge of the great forest, call'd New-Forest; here we saw a prodigious quantity of timber, of an uncommon size, vastly large, lying on the shoar of the river, for above two miles in length, which they told us was brought thither from the forest, and left there to be fetch'd by the builders at Portsmouth-Dock, as they had occasion for it.

In riding over the south part of Hampshire, I made this observation about that growth of timber, which I mention in supplement to what I said before concerning our timber being wasted and decay'd in England, (viz.) that notwithstanding the very great consumption of timber in King William's reign, by building or rebuilding almost the whole navy; and notwithstanding so many of the king's ships were built hereabouts, besides abundance of large merchant ships, which were about that time built at Southampton, at Redbridge, and at Bursleton, &c. yet I saw the gentlemens estates, within six, eight, or ten miles of Southampton, so over-grown with wood, and their woods so full of large full grown timber, that it seem'd as if they wanted sale for it, and that it was of little worth to them. In one estate at Hursely in particular near Winchester, the estate since bought by Mr. Cardonell, late manager for the Duke of Marlborough, and formerly belonging to Mr. Cromwell, grandson to Oliver Cromwell, the whole estate not above 800*l.* per ann. in rent, they might have cut twenty thousand pounds worth of timber down, and yet have left the woods in a thriving condition; in another estate between that and Petersfield, of about 1000*l.* per ann. they told me they could fell a thousand pounds a year in good large timber fit for building, for twenty years together, and do the woods no harm: Colonel Norton also, a known gentleman, whose seat at Southwick is within six miles of Portsmouth, and within three miles of the water carriage; this gentleman they told me had an immense quantity of timber, some growing within sight of the very docks in Portsmouth: Farther west it is the like, and as I rode through New-Forest, I cou'd see the antient oaks of many hundred years standing, perishing with their wither'd tops advanc'd up in the air, and grown white with age, and that could never yet get the favour to be cut down, and made serviceable to their country.

These in my opinion are no signs of the decay of our woods, or of the danger of our wanting timber in England; on the contrary, I take leave to mention it again, that if we were employ'd in England, by the rest of the world, to build a thousand sail of three deck ships, from 80 to 100 guns, it might be done to our infinite advantage, and without putting us in any danger of exhausting the nation of timber.

I shall give other hints of the like, when I come to speak of Hertfordshire, Buckinghamshire, Berkshire, and the counties which we call inland, where the timber is really of small value, for want of water carriage to carry it away; likewise again in the counties northward, bordering upon the Humber, and upon all the northern rivers, not to say a word of Ireland; which is still a store-house of timber, more inexhaustible if possible than England.

Southampton is a truly antient town, for 'tis in a manner dying with age; the decay of the trade is the real decay of the town; and all the business of moment that is transacted there, is the trade between us and the islands of Jersey and Guernsey, with a little of the wine trade, and much smuggling: The building of ships also is much stop'd of late; however, the town is large, has many people in it, a noble fair High-Street, a spacious key; and if its trade should revive, is able to entertain great numbers of people: There is a French church, and no inconsiderable congregation, which was a help to the town, and there are still some merchants who trade to Newfoundland, and to the Streights with fish; but for all other trade, it may be said of Southampton as of other towns, London has eaten it up. The situation of the town between two rivers was to its advantage formerly in point of strength, and the town was wall'd with a very strong wall, strengthen'd with a rampart, and a double ditch; but I don ot hear that they ever were put to make much use of them.

Whatever the fable of Bevis of Southampton, and the gyants in the woods thereabouts may be deriv'd from, I found the people mighty willing to have those things pass for true; and at the north gate of the town, the only entrance from the land side, they have the figures of two eminent champions, who might pass for gyants if they were alive now, but they can tell us very little of their history, but what is all fabulous like the rest, so I say no more of them.

I was now at the extent of my intended journey west, and thought of looking no farther this way for the present, so I came away north east, leaving Winchester a little on the left, and came into the Portsmouth road at Petersfield, a town eminent for little, but its being full of good inns, and standing in the middle of a country, still over-grown with a prodigious quantity of oak-timber. From hence we came to Alton, and in the road thither, began a little to taste the pleasure of the Western Downs, which reach from Winchester almost to Alton.

The Duke of Bolton has two very noble seats in this country, one between Alton and Alresford; and one at Basing, of which hereafter. Alton is a small market-town, of no note, neither is there any considerable manufacture in all this part of England; except a little drugget and shalloon making, which begins hereabouts, otherwise the whole counties of Kent, Sussex, Surrey, and Hampshire, are not employ'd in any considerable woollen manufacture; what there is, I have spoken of about Cranbrook in Kent, Guilford, and Farnham in Surrey, and a little in the north part of Barkshire, all which put together, is not equal to one ordinary manufacturing village in Essex or Norfolk.

From Alton we came to Farnham, of which I can only say, that it is a large populous market-town, the farthest that way in the county of Surrey, and without exception the greatest corn-market in England, London excepted; that is to say, particularly for wheat, of which so vast a quantity is brought every market-day to this market, that a gentleman told me, he once counted on a market-day eleven hundred teams of horse, all drawing waggons, or carts, loaden with wheat at this market; every team of which is supposed to bring what they call a load, that is to say, forty bushel of wheat to market; which is in the whole, four and forty thousand bushel; but I do not take upon me to affirm this relation, or to say whether it be a probable opinion or not; I know some have thought the quantity has been much more; but this also was, I suppose, before the people of Chichester and Emsworth on one side, and Southampton, Tichfield, and Redbridge on the other, took to the trade of sending their wheat in meal to London by sea, as is mentioned above,

At this town is a castle eminent for this, that it was built by a Bishop of Winchester; and tho' its antiquity is evident, as far back as King Stephen; yet it remains to the Bishops of Winchester to this day. Here the said Bishops of Winchester usually keep their ordinary residence, and tho' the county of Surrey, be generally speaking within the diocess, they may be truly said to reside in the middle of their ecclesiastical dominion. The Farnham people it seems, or some of the country folks, notwithstanding the liberality and bounty of the several bishops, who, if some people may be believ'd, have been very good benefactors to the town; I say, notwithstanding all this, have of late been very unkind to the bishop, in pulling down the pale of his park, and plundering it of the deer, killing, wounding, and disabling, even those they cou'd not carry away.

From Farnham, that I might take in the whole county of Surrey, I took the coach-road, over Bagshot-Heath, and that great forest, as 'tis call'd, of Windsor: Those that despise Scotland, and the north part of England, for being full of wast and barren land, may take a view of this part of Surrey, and look upon it as a foil to the beauty of the rest of England; or a mark of the just resentment shew'd by Heaven upon the Englishmen's pride; I mean the pride they shew in boasting of their country, its fruitfulness, pleasantness, richness, the fertility of the soil, &c. whereas here is a vast tract of land, some of it within seventeen or eighteen miles of the capital city; which is not only poor, but even quite steril, given up to barrenness, horrid and frightful to look on, not only good for little, but good for nothing; much of it is a sandy desert, and one may frequently be put in mind here of Arabia Deserta, where the winds raise the sands, so as to overwhelm whole caravans of travellers, cattle and people together; for in passing this heath, in a windy day, I was so far in danger of smothering with the clouds of sand, which were raised by the storm, that I cou'd neither keep it out of my mouth, nose or eyes; and when the wind was over, the sand appear'd spread over the adjacent fields of the forest some miles distant, so as that it ruins the very soil. This sand indeed is check'd by the heath, or heather, which grows in it, and which is the common product of barren land, even in the very Highlands of Scotland; but the ground is otherwise so poor and barren, that the product of it feeds no creatures, but some very small sheep, who feed chiefly on the said heather, and but very few of these, nor are there any villages, worth mentioning, and but few houses, or people for many miles far and wide; this desart lyes extended so much, that some say, there is not less than a hundred thousand acres of this barren land that lyes all together, reaching out every way in the three counties of Surrey, Hampshire and Berkshire; besides a great quantity of land, almost as bad as that between Godalming and Petersfield, on the road to Portsmouth, including some hills, call'd the Hind Head and others.

Thro' this desart, for I can call it no less, we come into the great western road, leading from London to Salisbury, Exeter, &c. and pass the Thames at Stanes; and here I could not but call to mind, upon viewing the beautiful prospect of the river, and of the meadows, on the banks of the river, on the left hand of the road, I say, I cou'd not but call to mind those two excellent lines of Sir John Denham, in his poem, call'd *Cooper's Hill*, viz.

> Tho' deep, yet clear, tho' gentle, yet not dull,
> Strong without rage, without o'erflowing full.

Here I remember'd that I had yet left the inland towns of the two counties of Kent and Sussex, and almost all the county of Surrey out of my account; and that having as it were taken a circuit round the coast only, I had a great many places worth viewing to give an account of; I therefore left Windsor, which was within my view, on one side of the river, and Hampton Court on the other, as being the subject of another letter; and resolv'd to finish my present view, in the order I had begun it; That is to say, to give an account of the whole country as I come on; that I may make no incongruous transitions from one remote part of England to another, at least as few as may be.

From Stanes therefore I turn'd S. and S.E. to Chertsey, another market-town, and where there is a bridge over the Thames: This town was made famous, by being the burial place of Henry VI. till his bones were after removed to Windsor by Henry VII. also by being the retreat of the incomparable Cowley, where he liv'd withdrawn from the hurries of the Court and town, and where he dy'd so much a recluse, as to be almost wholly taken up in country business, farming and husbandry, for his diversion, not for bread, according to the publick flight of his own fancy.

From this town wholly employ'd, either in malting, or in barges to carry it down the river to London; I went away south to Woking, a private country market-town, so out of all road, or thorough-fare, as we call it, that 'tis very little heard of in England; it claims however some honour, from its being once the residence of a royal branch of the family of Plantagenet, the old Countess of Richmond, mother to King Henry VII, who made her last retreat here, where the king her son built, or rather repair'd, an old royal house, on purpose for her residence, and where she ended her days in much honour and peace; the former part of her life having been sufficiently exposed to the storms and dangers of the times; especially under the tyranny and turbulent reign of the two precedent monarchs.

From hence we came to Guilford, a well known and considerable market-town: It has the name of being the county town, tho' it cannot properly be call'd so; neither the county gaol being here, or the assizes, any more than in common with other towns: But the election indeed for Parliament men for the county is always held here. The river which according to Mr. Camden is call'd the Wey, and which falls into the Thames at Oatlands, is made navigable to this town, which adds greatly to its trade; and by this navigation a very great quantity of timber is brought down to London, not from the neighbourhood of this town only, but even from the woody parts of Sussex and Hampshire above thirty miles from it, the country carriages bringing it hither in the summer by land: This navigation is also a mighty support to the great corn-market at Farnham, which I have mentioned so often: For as the meal-men and other dealers buy the corn at that market, much of it is brought to the mills on this river; which is not above seven miles distant, and being first ground and dress'd, is then sent down in the meal by barges to London; the expence of which is very small, as is practised on the other side of the Thames, for above fifty miles distance from London.

Here, as I observ'd in its place, is a small remainder of an old manufacture, that is to say, of the clothing trade, and it extends it self to Godalming, Haselmeer, and the vale country, on the side of the Holmwood; a place of which I shall speak on another occasion, quite to Darking: These cloths of a middling price, have formerly been in great repute, and then again were almost quite decay'd, but by the application and skill of the clothiers, maintain'd the credit of their make, and are encourag'd, and indeed revived in reputation of late years, when the clothiers of Cranbrook and Tenterden in Kent, whose goods are of the same kind, are almost sunk to nothing, as I have already observed.

This clothing trade, however small, is very assistant to the poor of this part of the country, where the lands, as I have noted, are but indifferent; except just above the great towns, and where abundance of the inhabitants are what we call cottagers, and live chiefly by the benefit of the large commons and heath ground, of which the quantity is so very great.

From this town of Guilford, the road to Farnham is very remarkable, for it runs along west from Guilford, upon the ridge of a high chalky hill, so narrow that the breadth of the road takes up the breadth of the hill, and the declivity begins on either hand, at the very hedge that bounds the highway, and is very steep, as well as very high; from this hill is a prospect either way, so far that 'tis surprising; and one sees to the north, or N.W. over the great black desart, call'd Bagshot-Heath, mentioned above, one way, and the other way south east into Sussex, almost to the South Downs, and west to an unbounded length, the horizon only restraining the eyes: This hill being all chalk, a traveller feels the effect of it in a hot summer's day, being scorch'd by the reflection of the sun from the chalk, so as to make the heat almost insupportable; and this I speak by my own experience: This hill reaches from Guilford town's end to within a mile and half of Farnham.

The hill, or the going up to it from Guilford rather, is call'd St. Katharine's-Hill, and at the top of the ascent from the town stands the gallows, which is so placed, respecting the town, that the towns people from the High-Street may sit at their shop doors, and see the criminals executed.

The great road from London to Chichester, and from London to Portsmouth, lying thro' this town; it is consequently a town very well furnish'd with inns for accommodation of travellers, as is Godalming, also the next town within three miles of it.

From Guilford there lies a cross-road, as it may be call'd, to London, not frequented by coaches or carriers, or the ordinary passengers to London; tho' 'tis by some reckon'd the nearest way, and is without question much the pleasanter road, if it is not the pleasantest in this part of England: (viz.) From this town to Letherhead, ten miles from Letherhead to London, over Banstead Downs fifteen miles, or if you please by Epsome seventeen miles; which, tho' it is call'd the farthest way, makes amends abundantly by the goodness of the way, and the advantage and pleasantness of the road.

The ten miles from Guilford to Leatherhead make one continued line of gentlemens houses, lying all, or most of them, on the west side of the road, and their parks, or gardens almost touching one another: Here are pleasantly seated several very considerable persons, as the posterity of Sir Tho. Bludworth, once Lord Mayor of London, a person famous for the implacable passion he put the people of London in, by one rash expression, at the time of the Great Fire: (viz.) "That it was nothing, and they might piss it out"; which was only spoken at the beginning of the fire, when neither Sir Thomas or the citizens themselves cou'd foresee the length it would go; and without any design to lessen their endeavours to quench it: But this they never forgot, or forgave to him, or his family after him; but fix'd the expression on him, as a mark of indelible reproach, even to this day: Among the other fine seats in this row, is that of Arthur Moor, Esq; at Fetcham, where no cost has been spar'd to make a most beautiful and delicious situation be beholden to art, and which is set out at an immense charge: Near to Guilford, at the village of Clendon, at the west end of this line of fine seats, is the antient mansion of the Onslow's: The father of the present lord, was Sir Richard Onslow, Baronet; several years one of the Lords Commissioners of the Treasury or Admiralty; and created Baron Onslow by King GEORGE.

The seat is old, and the estate is old too (but the latter is much the better for its age) for it has been many years in the family, as appears in Mr. Camden, and has gone on, encreasing from hand to hand. The late Lord Onslow improv'd and beautify'd both the house and the estate too very much. The house has several times been honour'd with the presence of both King William and King George; the former erected an annual race for a royal plate of 100 guineas, call'd the King's Gold Plate, to be run for every year, and the latter has been so good, as twice at least to honour the diversion with his presence.

At the like distance north from Guilford, and on the banks of the Wey, is a fine seat, every way as fit for the possession of a peer as is Clendon Park; and belonging to a branch of the same family, (viz.) to Denzil Onslow, Esq; uncle to the present Lord Onslow, younger brother to his father the first lord: This seat is call'd Pyrford, and is exceeding pleasant, especially for the most beautiful intermixture of wood, and water in the park, and gardens, and grounds adjoining; by which the possessor, whose genius lay wonderfully in improving lands, and making things more pleasant, brought Pyrford to such a perfection, as to be inferior to very few, if any, of the finest houses in Surrey; particularly in one thing, which is not found in all that part of England; namely, a duckoy, which adjoins to his park, and which makes the rest inimitably agreeable.

At the north east end of this range of fine seats, is Letherhead, a little thorough-fare town, with a stone-bridge over the river Mole; this river is called the Mole, from its remarkable sinking into the earth, at the foot of Box-Hill, near a village call'd Mickleham, and working its way under ground like a mole, rising again at or near this town of Leatherhead, where its wandering streams are united again, and form a pretty large river, as they were before, running together under Leatherhead Bridge, and from thence to Cobham, and so it pursues its course to the Thames, which it joins at Molesy, which takes its name to be sure from the name of the river Mole.

And here I cannot but take notice of an unaccountable error, which all the writers I have met with fall unwarily into, on account of this little river hiding itself in the earth, and finding its way under ground, from the foot of Beechworth, more properly Betsworth-Castle, near Box-Hill, and then rising again at Letherhead, as above; as if the water had at once ingulph'd itself in a chasm of the earth, or sunk in a whirlpit, as is said of the Caspian-Sea, which they say rises again in the Persian Gulph with the same violence that it ingulphs it self: 'Tis strange this error should prevail in this manner, and with men of learning too, and in a case so easily discover'd and so near. But thus it is, nor is it at all remote from the true design of this work, to undeceive the world in the false or mistaken accounts, which other men have given of things, especially when those mistakes are so demonstrably gross; and when the subject is significant too, as in this part now in hand: Mr. Camden expresses it thus: "The Mole," says he, "coming to White-Hill," (he should have said Box-Hill) "hides it self, or is rather swallow'd up at the foot of it; and for that reason the place is call'd Swallow, but after two miles it bubbles up, and rises again"; then he adds, (alluding to the river Guadiana in Castile) "that the inhabitants of this tract no less than the Spaniards may boast of having a bridge that feeds several flocks of sheep." Thus far Mr. Camden. The right reverend and learned editor of the Additions to Mr. Camden, makes it yet worse, speaking of Beechworth Castle, which is a mile before we come to Darking; and 'tis at the foot of this castle here, says his lordship, that the river Mole being nigh to the precipice of Box-Hill is swallow'd up.

Now 'tis something strange for me to take upon me, after two such authorities, to say, that neither of these is right. The accounts are so positive, that many curious people have rid thither to see this place, call'd Swallow, and to see this Beechworth Castle, at the foot of which the river is swallow'd up, not doubting but they should see some wonderful gulph, in which a whole river should be at once as it were bury'd alive; for Mr. Camden says, "Swallow is the place": The bishop says, "near Beechworth-Castle the river is swallowed up"; nay, and to make the wonder appear more conformable to the relation, the map of the county of Surrey, plac'd in Mr. Camden, makes a large blank between the river as swallowed up, a little off of Darking, and its rising again as at Leatherhead, breaking the river off abruptly, as if pouring its waters all at once into a great gulph, like one of the common-shores of the streets of London, and bringing it out again at once, just as the water of the brook running into Fleet-Ditch, comes out from under Holbourn-Bridge.

Now after all these plausible stories, the matter of fact is this, and no more; and even of this, the thing is wonderful enough too: But I say, it is thus, and no more, (viz.)

The river Mole passes by Beechworth Castle in a full stream; and for near a mile farther on the west of the castle, it takes into its stream Darking-Brook, as they call it, and has upon it a large corn-mill, call'd Darking-Mill; below this it runs close at the foot of Box-Hill, near that part of the hill, which is call'd the Stomacher; then, as if obstructed by the hill, it turns a little south, and runs cross the road which leads from Darking to Leatherhead, where it is apparently rapid and strong; and then fetches a circuit round a park, formerly belonging to Sir Richard Studdolph, and which is part of it, within sight of Leatherhead, and so keeps a continued chanel to the very town of Leatherhead; so that there is no such thing as a natural bridge, or a river lost, no, not at all; and in the winter, in time of floods the stream will be very large, and rapid all the way above ground, which I affirm of my own knowledge, having seen it so, on many occasions.

But the true state of the case is this, the current of the river being much obstructed by the interposition of those hills, call'd Box-Hill, which tho' descending in a kind of vale, as if parted to admit the river to pass, and making that descent so low as to have the appearance of a level, near a village call'd Mickleham; I say, these hills yet interrupting the free course of the river, it forces the waters as it were to find their way thro' as well as they can; and in order to this, beginning, I say, where the river comes close to the foot of the precipice of Box-Hill, call'd the Stomacher, the waters sink insensibly away, and in some places are to be seen (and I have seen them) little chanels which go out on the sides of the river, where the water in a stream not so big as would fill a pipe of a quarter of an inch diameter, trills away out of the river, and sinks insensibly into the ground.

In this manner it goes away, lessening the stream for above a mile, near two, and these they call the Swallows; and the whole ground on the bank of the river, where it is flat and low, is full of these subterraneous passages; so that if on any sudden rain the river swells over the banks, it is observ'd not to go back into the chanel again when the flood abates, but to sink away into the earth in the meadows, where it spreads; a remarkable proof of which I shall give presently.

But now take this with you as you go, that these Swallows, for they are many, and not one call'd the Swallow, as is said in Mr. Camden; these Swallows (I say) tho' they diminish the stream much, do not so drink it up as to make it disappear: But that, where it crosses the road near Mickleham, it runs, as I have said, very sharp and broad, nor did I ever know it dry in the dryest summer in that place, tho' I liv'd in the neighbourhood several years: On the contrary I have known it so deep, that waggons and carriages have not dar'd to go thro'; but never knew it, I say, dry in the greatest time of drought.

Below this place the hills rise again on the other side very high, and particularly on the ridge, which the country people call the Ashcom-Hills, and they seem to force the river again west; so it surrounds most of the park I mentioned above, and has several bridges upon it, and by this time indeed, so much of it is sunk away, that in a very dry summer the chanel, tho' full of water in pits and holes cannot be perceiv'd to run; but this must be, I say, in a very dry season, and still there is the chanel visible where it runs at other times fiercely enough.

This part which I say has the least water, continuing about half a mile, we then perceive the chanel insensibly to have more water than before: That is to say, that as it sunk in gradually and insensibly, so it takes vent again in the like manner in thousands of little springs, and unseen places, very few in any quantity, till in another half mile, it is a full river again, and passes in full streams under Leatherhead-Bridge, as above, and for the truth of this, I appeal to the knowledge of the inhabitants of Darking, Mickleham, Leatherhead, and all the country round.

A farther proof of this, and which is the account which I promised above, relating to the gradual sinking away of the water, take as follows: It was in the year 1676, in the month of October, or thereabouts, that there happen'd a very sudden hasty land flood, which swell'd the river to a very great height; and particularly so high, that at Beechworth-Castle, and other gentlemen's seats, near the river, where they had fish-ponds that were fed by the river, it over-flowed their ponds, and carry'd off all their fish, or at least they thought so: Sir Adam Brown liv'd then at Beechworth-Castle, a gentleman in those days, well known in the country, for he was many years Knight of the Shire, of the family of Browns, a branch of the house of Montacutes at Midhurst, mentioned before, but a collateral line; another of the Browns liv'd at Bucknal, another at

Darking, which I mention chiefly, because some ignorant writers, particularly the late Atlas, has confounded the title of Montacute with the sirname of Montague, which is quite another family, and generation, not at all ally'd, and nothing near so antient, but this by the by.

Sir Adam Brown's son, and the young gentlemen of these, and other neighbouring families, disturb'd at the loss of their fish, and mov'd by the report, came all down to Darking; where they raised a little troop of the young fellows and boys of the town, and all went together, to that part of the river which runs by the foot of the Stomacher, as I said they call it, on Box-Hill.

There was a low flat piece of meadow ground, lying close to the river on one side; just opposite to which, the hill lying also close to the river, made up the bank on the other: This piece of ground might contain about four or five acres, and lying hollow in the middle, like the shape of a dripping-pan, was by the overflowing of the river full of water, and so full, that the bank, which lay close to the river, tho' higher than the rest, was not to be seen.

The gentlemen set themselves and all their little army at work, to raise this bank, which I say, lay between the river and the hollow of the field, so as to separate the water in the hollow part of the field from that in the river, and having so many hands, they effected that part the first day; and made a solid dam or bank, so that they cou'd walk upon it dry footed; then they made a return to it, at the upper, or east end of the field; so that in short, no more water could run into the field from any part of the river.

When this was done, they built hutts or booths, and made fires, and sent for victuals and drink to treat their young company, and there they encamp'd, as if they waited some great event; and so indeed they did, for in about two nights and a day, exclusive of the time they took in making their dams, the water sunk all away in the field; and the consequence of that was, that the fish being surrounded, were catch'd, as it were, in a trap, for they cou'd not be swallow'd up with the water; and the purchase fully recompenc'd their labour, for the like quantity of fish, great and small, I believe was never taken at once in this kingdom, out of so small a river.

This story would have nothing in it wonderful, or to make it worth recording, were it not so evident a demonstration of the manner of this river losing it self under ground, or being swallowed up, as they call it; for this field where the water sunk away is just at the place, which Mr. Cambden calls the Swallows, near the village of Mickleham; and under the precipice of the hill, and yet the water was two nights and a day, as I say, sinking leisurely off; and in this manner, and in no other, does the whole river, or so much of it as passes under ground, sink away.

The town of Darking is eminent for several little things worth observation; as first, for the great Roman highway, call'd Stonny-street, which Mr. Cambden says, passes through the very church-yard of this town: Secondly, for a little common or heath, call'd the Cottman Dean, or the dean or heath of poor cottagers, for so the word signifies, belonging to the town; and where their alms-house stands; which some learned physicians have singled out for the best air in England: Thirdly, for Mr. Howard's house and garden, call'd Deaden, the garden is so naturally mounded with hills, that it makes a compleat amphitheatre, being an oblong square, the area about eighty yards by forty, and the hills unpassably steep, serve instead of walls, and are handsomely planted with trees, whose tops rising above one another gradually, as the hill rises at their roots, make a most beautiful green wall, of perhaps fifty or sixty foot high; at the north end, which is the entrance, is the house, which closes it wholly; and at the south end, the antient possessor, Mr. Howard, by what we call perforation, caused a vault or cave to be made quite through the hill, which came out again into a fine vineyard, which he planted the same year, on the south side, or slope of the hill, and which they say has produced since most excellent good wines, and a very great quantity of them.

Mr. Howard was an honourable and antient gentleman, younger brother to the old Duke of Norfolk, then living: (viz.) In the year 1676, for in that year, or the year before, was that vineyard planted, and tho' Mr. Howard was then upwards of sixty years of age, he enjoy'd that pleasant seat near thirty years after.

At this town liv'd another antient gentleman and his son, of a very good family; (viz.) Augustin Bellson, Esq; or as some write it Belschon, the father was measur'd seven foot and half an inch high, allowing all that he might have sunk, for his age, being seventy one years old; and the son measur'd two inches taller than his father.

These families were Roman, as were several others thereabouts at that time; but were soon after that, upon the breaking out of the Popish Plot, dispers'd; some one way, and some another, as the fate of those times oblig'd them to do; tho' I do not remember that any part of the scenes of treason were lay'd about Darking, or that any of the Romish gentlemen thereabout were charg'd with being concern'd with them.

The market of Darking cannot be omitted, as it relates to my design of giving an account of the several parts of England; from whence this great city of London, and all the dainty doings, which are to be seen there, as to eating, is supply'd with provisions.

This market is of all the markets in England famous for poultry; and particularly for the fattest geese, and the largest capons, the name of a Darking Capon being well known among the poulterers in Leaden-Hall Market; in a word, they are brought to this market from as far as Horsham in Sussex; and 'tis the business of all the country, on that side for many miles, to breed and fatten them up, insomuch, that 'tis like a manufacture to the country people; and some of these capons are so large, as that they are little inferior to turkeys; and I have seen them sold for 4s. to 4s. 6d. each, and weighing from 4l. to 5 or 6l. a peice.

Once a year here is also a fair, (viz.) on Holy Thursday, chiefly for lambs, and the greatest fair in England of that kind: I have pass'd over the so much celebrated house of Mr. Evelyn at Wotton, near Darking, not that it is not worth notice, but because so many other writers have said so much of it.

On the top of Box-Hill, and in view of this town, grows a very great beech-tree, which by way of distinction is call'd the Great Beech, and a very great tree it is; but I mention it on the following account, under the shade of this tree, was a little vault or cave, and here every Sunday, during the summer season, there used to be a rendezvous of coaches and horsemen, with abundance of gentlemen and ladies from Epsome to take the air, and walk in the box-woods; and in a word, divert, or debauch, or perhaps both, as they thought fit, and the game encreased so much, that it began almost on a sudden, to make a great noise in the country.

A vintner who kept the King's-Arms-Inn, at Darking, taking notice of the constant and unusual flux of company thither, took the hint from the prospect of his advantage, which offer'd, and obtaining leave of Sir Adam Brown, whose mannor and land it was, furnish'd this little cellar or vault with tables, chairs, &c. and with wine and eatables to entertain the ladies and gentlemen on Sunday nights, as above; and this was so agreeable to them as that it encreased the company exceedingly; in a word, by these means, the concourse of gentry, and in consequence of the country people, became so great, that the place was like a little fair; so that at length the country began to take notice of it, and it was very offensive, especially to the best governed people; this lasted some years, I think two or three, and tho' complaint was made of it to Sir Adam Brown, and the neighbouring justices; alledging the revelling, and the indecent mirth that was among them, and on the Sabbath Day too, yet it did not obtain a suitable redress: whereupon a certain set of young men, of the town of Darking, and perhaps prompted by some others, resenting the thing also, made an unwelcome visit to the place once on a Saturday night, just before the usual time of their wicked mirth, and behold when the coaches and ladies, &c. from Epsome appear'd the next afternoon, they found the cellar or vault, and all that was in it, blown up with gun-powder; and so secret was it kept, that upon the utmost enquiry it cou'd never be heard, or found out who were the persons that did it: That action put an end to their revels for a great while; nor was the place ever repair'd that I heard of, at least it was not put to the same wicked use that it was employ'd in before.

From this hill, and particularly from this part of it, is a fair view in clear weather quite over the Wild of Sussex, to the South-Downs; and by the help of glasses, those who know where things are scituated, may plainly see the town of Horsham, Ashdown-Forest, the Duke of Somerset's house at Petworth, and the South-Downs, as they range between Brighthelmston and Arundel; besides an unbounded prospect into Kent.

The vale beneath this hill is for many miles east and west, call'd the Holmward, by some the Holm-Wood, others Holmsdale; but more vulgarly the Homeward: In the woody part of which are often found outlying red deer, and in the days of King James II. or while he was Duke of York, they have hunted the largest stags here that have been seen in England; the duke took great care to have them preserv'd for his own sport, and they were so preserv'd for many years; but have since that been most of them destroy'd.

This Homeward, or Holmwood, is a vale, which is now chiefly grown with furz, famous for the country people gathering such quantities of strawberries, as they carry them to market by horse-loads: I saw neither town or village, for many miles on it, much less any gentlemen's seats, only cottages and single houses; but vast quantities of geese and poultry, which as is said above, employs all the country in breeding them up: There has been large timber here, (they say) but most of it is cut down and gone, except that where there are any woods standing, the timber is still exceeding good and large.

It is suggested that this place was in antient times so unpassable a wild, or overgrown waste, the woods so thick, and the extent so large, reaching far into Sussex, that it was the retreat for many ages of the native Britons, who the Romans cou'd never drive out; and after that it was the like to the Saxons, when the Danes harrass'd the nation with their troops, and ravag'd the country wherever they came; and on this account they retain here in memory the following lines.

> This is Holmes Dale,
> Never conquer'd, never shall.

But this is a peice of history, which I leave as I find it; the country tho' wild still, and perhaps having the same countenance now in many places, as it had above a thousand years ago; yet in other places is cultivated, and has roads passable enough in the summer quite thro' it, on every side, and the woods are clear'd off in a great measure as above.

Keeping at the bottom of these hills, and yet not enter'd into this vale, the county is dry, and rather sandy or gravel, and is full of gentlemen's houses, and of good towns; but if we go but a little to the right hand south, into the said wild part, 'tis a deep, strong, and in the wet season, an unpassable clay.

Here travelling east at the foot of the hills, we came to Rygate, a large market-town with a castle, and a mansion-house, inhabited for some years by Sir John Parsons, once Lord Mayor of London, and whose son is in a fair way to be so also; being one of the aldermen and sheriffs of the said city at the writing these sheets.

Here are two miserable borough towns too, which nevertheless send each of them two members to Parliament, to wit, Gatton under the side of the hill, almost at Rygate; and Bleechingly, more eastward on the same cross-road, which we were upon before: In the first of these Sir John Thomson, (afterwards Lord Haversham) having purchas'd the mannor, was always elected; as Mr. Paul Docminique, an Italian merchant, has been since: The last was for many years, the estate of Sir Robert Clayton, a known citizen, and benefactor to the city of London, whose posterity still enjoy it: And at either town the purchasers seem to buy the election with the property.

At Nutfield, between Rygate and Bleechingly, is another branch of the family of Evelyn, who have flourish'd there many years, tho' in a kind of retreat, and are often chosen representatives for the town of Bleechingly, which is just at their door.

From hence, crossing still the roads leading from London into Sussex, we come to a village call'd Godstone, which lyes on the road from London to Lewis; and keeping on (east) we come to Westerham, the first market town in Kent on that side: This is a neat handsome well built market-town, and is full of gentry, and consequently of good company. The late Earl of Jersey built, or rather finished, for it was begun by a private gentleman, a very noble house here, which still remains in the family, and is every year made finer and finer.

All this part of the country is very agreeably pleasant, wholesome and fruitful, I mean quite from Guildford to this place; and is accordingly overspread with good towns, gentlemen's houses, populous villages, abundance of fruit, with hop-grounds and cherry orchards, and the lands well cultivated; but all on the right-hand, that is to say, south, is exceedingly grown with timber, has abundance of waste and wild grounds, and forests, and woods, with many large iron-works, at which they cast great quantities of iron caldrons, chimney-backs, furnaces, retorts, boiling pots, and all such necessary things of iron; besides iron cannon, bomb-shells, stink-pots, hand-grenadoes, and cannon ball, &c. in an infinite quantity, and which turn to very great account; tho' at the same time the works are prodigiously expensive, and the quantity of wood they consume is exceeding great, which keeps up that complaint I mention'd before; that timber would grow scarce, and consequently dear, from the great quantity consum'd in the iron-works in Sussex.

From hence going forward east, we come to Riverhead, a town on the road from London to Tunbridge; and then having little to speak of in Kent, except some petty market-towns, such as Wrotham, commonly call'd Rootham, Town-Malling, Cranbrook, and the like; of which something had been observ'd, as I travell'd forward, in the beginning of this circuit, I turn'd north, and came to Bromley, a market-town, made famous by an hospital, lately built there by Dr. Warner, Lord Bishop of Rochester, for the relief of the widows of clergy-men, which was not only well endow'd at first, but has had many gifts and charities bestow'd on it since, and is a very noble foundation for the best of charities in the world; besides it has been an example, and an encouragement to the like in other places, and has already been imitated, as Mr. Camden's most reverend continuator assures us, by the Bishops of Winchester and Salisbury in their dioceses.

Near this town we turn'd away by Beckenham, and thro' Norwood to Croydon; in the way we saw Dullige or Sydenham Wells, where great crouds of people throng every summer from London to drink the waters, as at Epsome and Tunbridge; only with this difference, that as at Epsome and Tunbridge, they go more for the diversion of the season, for the mirth and the company; for gaming, or intrieguing, and the like, here they go for meer physick, and this causes another difference; Namely, that as the nobility and gentry go to Tunbridge, the merchants and rich citizens to Epsome; so the common people go chiefly to Dullwich and Stretham; and the rather also, because it lyes so near London, that they can walk to it in the morning, and return at night; which abundance do; that is to say, especially of a Sunday, or on holidays, which makes the better sort also decline the place; the croud on those days being both unruly and unmannerly.

Croydon is a great corn-market, but chiefly for oats and oatmeal, all for London still; the town is large and full of citizens from London, which makes it so populous; it is the antient palace of the Archbishops of Canterbury, and several of them lye buried here; particularly that great man, Archbishop Whitgift, who not only repair'd the palace, but built the famous hospital and school, which remains there to this day, to the singular honour of the giver.

In the gardens of this episcopal palace, the Lady Dowager Onslow, mother of the present lord of that name, of whom mention has been made, was very unhappily drown'd about two year since, in one of the fish-ponds, whether she did it herself, or whether by accident, or how, 'tis not the business of such a work as this to enquire; her daughter being the wife of Sir John Williams, merchant of London, had hired the house, and she was in his family.

From hence we pass'd by Beddington, where is still the seat or mansion house of Sir Nicholas Carew, it was a fine building in Mr. Camden's time; but is now almost rebuilt from the ground, by the present owner, Sir Nicholas Carew, who now possesses that estate, and who is one of the representatives for the county of Surrey; the house is magnificently great, and the gardens are exquisitely fine; yet architects say, that the two wings are too deep for the body of the house, that they should either have been wider asunder, or not so long; the court before them is extreamly fine, and the canal in the park, before the court, is so well that nothing can be better, having a river running through it; the gardens are exceedingly enlarged, they take up all the flat part of the park, with vista's, or prospects thro' the park, for two or three miles; the orange-trees continue, and are indeed wonderful; they are the only standard orange-trees in England, and have moving houses to cover them in the winter; they are loaded with fruit in the summer, and the gardners told us, they have stood in the ground where they now grow above 80 years.

I am sorry to record it to the reproach of any person in their grave, that the ancestor of this family, tho' otherwise a very honest gentleman, if fame lyes not, was so addicted to gaming, and so unfortunately over-match'd in his play, that he lost this noble seat and parks, and all the fine addenda which were then about it, at one night's play, some say, at one cast of dice, to Mr. Harvey of Comb, near Kingston; What misery had befallen the family, if the right of the winner had been prosecuted with rigour, as by what I have heard it would have been, is hard to write: But God had better things in store for the gentleman's posterity than he took thought for himself; and the estate being entail'd upon the heir, the loser dy'd before it came into possession of the winner, and so it has been preserv'd, and the present gentleman has not only recover'd the disaster, but as above, has exceedingly improv'd it all.

From hence it is but a little mile to Cashalton, a country village scituate among innumerable springs of water, which all together, form a river in the very street of the town, and joining the other springs which come from Croydon and Bedington, make one stream, which are call'd the river Wandell: This village seated among such delightful springs, is yet all standing upon firm chalk; and having the Downs close adjoining, makes the most agreeable spot on all this side of London, as is abundantly testify'd by its being, as it were, crouded with fine houses of the citizens of London; some of which are built with such a profusion of expence, that they look rather like seats of the nobility, than the country houses of citizens and merchants; particularly those of Sir William Scawen, lately deceased; who besides an immense estate in money has left, as I was told, one article of nine thousand pounds a year to his heir; and was himself since the Fire of London, only Mr. Scawen, a Hamborough merchant, dealing by commission, and not in any view of such an encrease of wealth, or any thing like it.

The other house is that of Sir John Fellows, late sub-governor of the South-Sea Company, who having the misfortune to fall in the general calamity of the late directors, lost all his unhappy wealth, which he had gain'd in the company, and a good and honestly gotten estate of his own into the bargain: I cannot dwell on the description of all the fine houses in this and the neighbouring vilages; I shall speak of them again in bulk with their neighbours, of Mitcham, Stretham, Tooting, Clapham, and others; but I must take a trip here cross the Downs to Epsome.

Banstead Downs need no description other than this, that their being so near London, and surrounded as they are with pleasant villages, and being in themselves perfectly agreeable, the ground smooth, soft, level and dry; (even in but a few hours after rain) they conspire to make the most delightful spot of ground, of that kind in all this part of Britain.

When on the publick race days they are cover'd with coaches and ladies, and an innumerable company of horsemen, as well gentlemen as citizens, attending the sport; and then adding to the beauty of the sight, the racers flying over the course, as if they either touch'd not, or felt not the ground they run upon; I think no sight, except that of a victorious army, under the command of a Protestant King of Great Britain could exceed it.

About four miles, over those delicious Downs, brings us to Epsome, and if you will suppose me to come there in the month of July, or thereabouts, you may think me to come in the middle of the season, when the town is full of company, and all disposed to mirth and pleasantry; for abating one unhappy stock jobbing year, when England took leave to act the frantick, for a little while; and when every body's heads were turn'd with projects and stocks, I say, except this year, we see nothing of business in the whole conversation of Epsome; even the men of business, who are really so when in London; whether it be at the Exchange, the Alley, or the Treasury-Offices, and the Court; yet here they look as if they had left all their London thoughts behind them, and had separated themselves to mirth and good company; as if they came hither to unbend the bow of the mind, and to give themselves a loose to their innocent pleasures;

I say, innocent, for such they may enjoy here, and such any man may make his being here, if he pleases.

As, I say, this place seems adapted wholly to pleasure, so the town is suited to it; 'tis all rural, the houses are built at large, not many together, with gardens and ground about them; that the people who come out of their confin'd dwellings in London, may have air and liberty, suited to the design of country lodgings.

You have no sooner taken lodgings, and enter'd the apartments, but if you are any thing known, you walk out, to see who and who's together; for 'tis the general language of the place, Come let's go see the town, folks don't come to Epsome to stay within doors.

The next morning you are welcom'd with the musick under your chamber window; but for a shilling or two you get rid of them, and prepare for going to the Wells.

Here you have the compliment of the place, are enter'd into the list of the pleasant company, so you become a citizen of Epsome for that summer; and this costs you another shilling, or if you please, half a crown: Then you drink the waters, or walk about as if you did; dance with the ladies, tho' it be in your gown and slippers; have musick and company of what kind you like, for every man may sort himself as he pleases; The grave with the grave, and the gay with the gay, the bright, and the wicked; all may be match'd if they seek for it, and perhaps some of the last may be over-match'd, if they are not upon their guard.

After the morning diversions are over, and every one are walk'd home to their lodgings, the town is perfectly quiet again; nothing is to be seen, the Green, the Great Room, the raffling-shops all are (as if it was a trading town on a holiday) shut up; there's little stirring, except footmen, and maid servants, going to and fro of errands, and higglers and butchers, carrying provisions to people's lodgings.

This takes up the town till dinner is over, and the company have repos'd for two or three hours in the heat of the day; then the first thing you observe is, that the ladies come to the shady seats, at their doors, and to the benches in the groves, and cover'd walks; (of which, every house that can have them, is generally supply'd with several). Here they refresh with cooling liquors, agreeable conversation, and innocent mirth.

Those that have coaches, or horses (as soon as the sun declines) take the air on the Downs, and those that have not, content themselves with staying a little later, and when the air grows cool, and the sun low, they walk out under the shade of the hedges and trees, as they find it for their diversion: In the mean time, towards evening the Bowling-green begins to fill, the musick strikes up in the Great Room, and company draws together a-pace: And here they never fail of abundance of mirth, every night being a kind of ball; the gentlemen bowl, the ladies dance, others raffle, and some rattle; conversation is the general pleasure of the place, till it grows late, and then the company draws off; and, generally speaking, they are pretty well as to keeping good hours; so that by eleven a clock the dancing generally ends, and the day closes with good wishes, and appointments to meet the next morning at the Wells, or somewhere else.

The retir'd part of the world, of which also there are very many here, have the waters brought home to their apartments in the morning, where they drink and walk about a little, for assisting the physical operation, till near noon, then dress dinner, and repose for the heat as others do; after which they visit, drink tea, walk abroad, come to their lodgings to supper, then walk again till it grows dark, and then to bed: The greatest part of the men, I mean of this grave sort, may be supposed to be men of business, who are at London upon business all the day, and thronging to their lodgings at night, make the families, generally speaking, rather provide suppers than dinners; for 'tis very frequent for the trading part of the company to place their families here, and take their horses every morning to London, to the Exchange, to the Alley, or to the warehouse, and be at Epsome again at night; and I know one citizen that practis'd it for several years together, and scarce ever lay a night in London during the whole season.

This, I say, makes the good wives satisfy themselves with providing for the family, rather at night than at noon, that their husbands may eat with them; after which they walk abroad as above, and these they call the sober citizens, and those are not much at the Wells, or at the Green; except sometimes, when they give themselves a holiday, or when they get sooner home than usual.

Nor are these which I call the more retir'd part the company, the least part of those that fill up the town of Epsome, nor is their way of living so retir'd, but that there is a great deal of society, mirth, and good manners, and good company among these too.

The fine park of the late Earl of Berkeley, near Epsome, was formerly a great addition to the pleasure of the place, by the fine walks and cool retreats there; but the earl finding it absolutely necessary, for a known reason, to shut it up, and not permit any walking there, that relief to the company was abated for some years; but the pleasures of nature are so many round the town, the shady trees so every where planted, and now generally well grown, that it makes Epsome like a great park fill'd with little groves, lodges and retreats for coolness of air, and shade from the sun; and I believe, I may say, it is not to be match'd in the world, on that account; at least, not in so little a space of ground.

It is to be observ'd too, that for shady walks, and innumerable numbers of trees planted before the houses, Epsome differs much from it self, that is to say, as it was twenty or thirty years ago; for then those trees that were planted, were generally young, and not grown; and now not only all the trees then young, are grown large and fair, but thousands are planted since; so that the town, at a distance, looks like a great wood full of houses, scatter'd every where, all over it.

In the winter this is no place for pleasure indeed; as it is full of mirth and gayety in the summer, so the prospect in the winter presents you with little, but good houses shut up, and windows fasten'd; the furniture taken down, the families remov'd, the walks out of repair, the leaves off of the trees, and the people out of the town; and which is still worse, the ordinary roads both to it, and near it, except only on the side of the Downs, are deep, stiff, full of sloughs, and, in a word, unpassable; for all the country, the side of the Downs, as I have said, only excepted, is a deep stiff clay; so that there's no riding in the winter without the utmost fatiegue, and some hazard, and this is the reason that Epsome is not (like Hampstead or Richmond) full of company in winter as well as summer.

From Epsome that I might thoroughly visit the county of Surrey, I rode over those clays, and through very bad roads to Kingstone, and from thence keeping the bank of the river on my right hand, I had a fine view of Hampton-Court, at a distance, but had reserv'd it for another journey; and was bound now in search of a piece of antiquity to satisfy my own curiosity, this was to Oatland, that I might see the famous place where Julius Cæsar pass'd the river Thames in the sight of the British army, and notwithstanding they had stuck the river full of sharp stakes for three miles together.

The people said several of those stakes were still to be seen in the bottom of the river, having stood there for now above 1760 years; but they cou'd show me none of them, tho' they call the place Coway Stakes to this day; I cou'd make little judgment of the thing, only from this, that it really seems probable, that this was the first place where Cæsar at that time cou'd find the river fordable, or any way passable to him, who had no boats, no pontons, and no way to make bridges over, in the teeth of so powerful, and so furious an enemy; but the Roman valour and discipline surmounted all difficulties, and he pass'd the army, routing the Britons; whose king and general, Cassibellanus, never offer'd a pitch'd battle to the Romans afterward.

Satisfy'd with what little I cou'd see here, which indeed was nothing at all, but the meer place, said to be so; and which it behov'd me to believe, only because it was not unlikely to be true; I say, satisfy'd with this, I came back directly to King-stone, a good market-town, but remarkable for little, only that they say, the antient British and Saxon kings were usually crown'd here in former times, which I will neither assert or deny.

But keeping the river now on my left, as I did before on my right-hand, drawing near to London, we came to Hame and Peterson, little villages; the first, famous for a most pleasant pallace of the late Duke of Lauderdale, close by the river; a house King Charles II. used to be frequently at, and be exceedingly pleased with; the avenues of this fine house to the land side, come up to the end of the village of Peterson, where the wall of New Park comes also close to the town, on the other side; in an angle of which stood a most delicious house, built by the late Earl of Rochester, Lord High Treasurer in King James II's. reign, as also in part of Queen Ann's reign, which place he discharg'd so well, that we never heard of any misapplications, so much as suggested, much less inquir'd after.

I am oblig'd to say only, that this house *stood* here; for even while this is writing the place seems to be but smoaking with the ruins of a most unhappy disaster, the whole house being a few months ago burnt down to the ground with a fire, so sudden, and so furious, that the family who were all at home, had scarce time to save their lives.

Nor was the house, tho' so exquisitely finished, so beautiful within and without, the greatest loss sustained; the rich furniture, the curious collection of paintings; and above all, the most curious collection of books, being the library of the first Earl of Clarendon, Lord Chancellor of England, and author of that most excellent History of the Rebellion, of which the world knows so much; I say, this library, as I am assur'd, was here wholly consum'd; a loss irreparable, and not to be sufficiently regretted by all lovers of learning, having among other valuable things, several manuscripts relating to those times, and to things transacted by himself, and by the king his master, both at home and abroad; and of other antient things, collected by that noble and learned author in foreign countries; which both for their rariety, antiquity, and authority, were of an inestimable value.

From hence we come to Richmond, the delightful retreat of their royal highnesses, the Prince and Princess of Wales, and where they have spent the fine season every summer for some years: The prince's Court being so near must needs have fill'd Richmond, which was before a most agreeable retreat for the first and second rate gentry, with a great deal of the best company in England: This town and the country adjacent, encrease daily in buildings, many noble houses for the accommodation of such, being lately rais'd and more in prospect: But 'tis fear'd should the prince come, for any cause that may happen, to quit that side of the country, those numerous buildings must abate in the value which is now set upon them: The company however, at Richmond, is very great in the winter, when the prince's Court is not there; because of the neighbourhood of so many gentlemen, who live constantly there, and thereabouts; and of its nearness to London also; and in this it has the advantage both of Epsome and Tunbridge.

Here are wells likewise, and a mineral-water, which tho' not so much us'd as that at Epsome and Tunbridge, are yet sufficient to keep up the forms of the place, and bring the company together in the morning, as the musick does in the evening; and as there is more of quality in and about the place than is ordinarily to be seen at Epsome, the company is more shining, and sometimes even illustriously bright.

Mr. Temple created Baron Temple, of the kingdom of Ireland, even since this circuit was perform'd; and who is the son and successor to the honour, estate, and great part of the character of the great Sir William Temple, has a fine seat and gardens (hard by) at Shene; The gardens are indeed exquisitely fine, being finished, and even contriv'd by the great genius of Sir William, his father; and as they were his last delight in life, so they were every way suited to be so, to a man of his sense and capacity, who knew what kind of life was best fitted to make a man's last days happy

It is not easy to describe the beauty with which the banks of the Thames shine on either side of the river, from hence to London, much more than our ancestors, even of but one age ago, knew any thing of: If for pleasant villages, great houses, palaces, gardens, &c. it was true in Queen Elizabeth's time, according to the poet, that

> The Thames with royal Tyber may compare.

I say, if this were true at that time, what may be said of it now? when for one fine house that was to be seen then, there are a hundred; nay, for ought I know, five hundred to be seen now, even as you sit still in a boat, and pass up and down the river.

First beginning from Ham-House, as above, the prince's palace salutes the eye, being formerly no more than a lodge in the park, and by that means belonging to the ranger, who was then, the (since unhappy) Duke of Ormond, and who, with other branches of a noble estate, lost this among the rest by his precipitate retreat from the Parliamentary justice: I have seen many of the seats of the nobility in France, and some larger, but none finer than this, except such as had been lay'd out at the royal expence.

From Richmond to London, the river sides are full of villages, and those villages so full of beautiful buildings, charming gardens, and rich habitations of gentlemen of quality, that nothing in the world can imitate it; no, not the country for twenty miles round Paris, tho' that indeed is a kind of prodigy.

To enumerate the gentlemen's houses in their view, would be too long for this work to describe them, would fill a large folio; it shall suffice to observe something concerning the original of the strange passion, for fine gardens, which has so commendably possess'd the English gentlemen of late years, for 'tis evident it is but of late years.

It is since the Revolution that our English gentlemen, began so universally, to adorn their gardens with those plants, we call ever greens, which leads me to a particular observation that may not be improper in this place; King William and Queen Mary introduced each of them two customs, which by the people's imitating them became the two idols of the town, and indeed of the whole kingdom; the queen brought in (1.) the love of fine East-India callicoes, such as were then call'd Masslapatan chints, atlasses, and fine painted callicoes, which afterwards descended into the humours of the common people so much, as to make them greivous to our trade, and ruining to our manufactures and the poor; so that the Parliament were oblig'd to make two Acts at several times to restrain, and at last prohibit the use of them: (2.) The queen brought in the custom or humour, as I may call it, of furnishing houses with china-ware, which increased to a strange degree afterwards, piling their china upon the tops of cabinets, scrutores, and every chymney-piece, to the tops of the ceilings, and even setting up shelves for their china-ware, where they wanted such places, till it became a grievance in the expence of it, and even injurious to their families and estates.

The good queen far from designing any injury to the country where she was so entirely belov'd, little thought she was in either of these laying a foundation for such fatal excesses, and would no doubt have been the first to have reform'd them had she lived to see it.

The king on his part introduc'd (1.) the love of gardening; and (2.) of painting: In the first his majesty was particularly delighted with the decoration of ever greens, as the greatest addition to the beauty of a garden, preserving the figure of the place, even in the roughest part of an inclement and tempestuous winter.

Sir Stephen Fox's gardens at Istleworth, and Sir William Temple's at Eastshene, mentioned above, were the only two gardens where they had entirely persued this method at that time, and of Sir Stephen's garden, this was to be said, that almost all his fine ever-greens were raised in the places where they stood; Sir Stephen taking as much delight to see them rise gradually, and form them into what they were to be, as to buy them of the nursery gardeners, finish'd to his hand; besides that by this method his greens, the finest in England, cost him nothing but the labour of his servants, and about ten years patience; which if they were to have been purchased, would not have cost so little as ten thousand pounds, especially at that time: It was here that King William was so pleased that according to his majesty's usual expression, when he lik'd a place very well, he stood, and looking round him from the head of one of the canals, Well says his majesty, I cou'd dwell here five days; every thing was so exquisitely contriv'd, finish'd, and well kept, that the king, who was allow'd to be the best judge of such things then living in the world, did not so much as once say, this or that thing cou'd have been better.

With the particular judgment of the king, all the gentlemen

in England began to fall in; and in a few years fine gardens,
and fine houses began to grow up in every corner; the king
began with the gardens at Hampton-Court and Kensington,
and the gentlemen follow'd every where, with such a gust that
the alteration is indeed wonderful thro' the whole kingdom;
but no where more than in the two counties of Middlesex and
Surrey, as they border on the river Thames; the beauty and
expence of which are only to be wonder'd at, not describ'd; they
may indeed be guess'd at, by what is seen in one or two such
as these nam'd: But I think to enter into a particular of them
would be an intollerable task, and tedious to the reader.

That these houses and gardens are admirably beautiful in
their kind, and in their separate, and distinct beauties, such as
their scituation, decoration, architect, furniture, and the like,
must be granted; and many descriptions have been accurately
given of them, as of Ham-House, Qew-Green, the Prince's House,
Sir William Temple's, Sir Charles Hedges, Sion-House, Osterly,
Lord Ranelagh's at Chelsea-Hospital; the many noble seats
in Istleworth, Twittenham, Hamersmith, Fullham, Puttney,
Chelsea, Battersea, and the like.

But I find none has spoken of what I call the distant glory of
all these buildings: There is a beauty in these things at a
distance, taking them *en passant*, and in perspective, which few
people value, and fewer understand; and yet here they are more
truly great, than in all their private beauties whatsoever; Here
they reflect beauty, and magnificence upon the whole country,
and give a kind of a character to the island of Great Britain in
general. The banks of the Sein are not thus adorn'd from Paris
to Roan, or from Paris to the Loign above the city: The Danube
can show nothing like it above and below Vienna, or the Po
above and below Turin; the whole country here shines with
a lustre not to be describ'd; Take them in a remote view, the
fine seats shine among the trees as jewels shine in a rich coronet;
in a near sight they are meer pictures and paintings; at a
distance they are all nature, near hand all art; but both in the
extreamest beauty.

In a word, nothing can be more beautiful; here is a plain and
pleasant country, a rich fertile soil, cultivated and enclosed to
the utmost perfection of husbandry, then bespangled with
villages; those villages fill'd with these houses, and the houses
surrounded with gardens, walks, vistas, avenues, representing
all the beauties of building, and all the pleasures of planting:
It is impossible to view these countries from any rising ground

and not be ravish'd with the delightful prospect: For example, suppose you take your view from the little rising hills about Clapham, if you look to the east, there you see the pleasant villages of Peckham and Camberwell, with some of the finest dwellings about London; as (1) the Lord Powis's at Peckham: (2) a house built by a merchant, one Collins, but now standing empty at Camberwell, but justly call'd a picture of a house, and several others: Then turning south, we see Loughborough-House near Kennington, Mr. Howland's, now the Dutchess of Bedford's, at Stretham; Sir Richard Temple's house near Croydon; a whole town of fine houses at Cashalton; Sir Nicholas Carew's, and Sir John Lake's at Bedington; Sir Theodore Janssen another South-Sea forfeiture at Wimbleton; Sir James Bateman's at Tooting; besides an innumerable number in Clapham it self: On the south west also you have Mr. Harvey's at Coomb, formerly the palace of a king; with all the villages mentioned above, and the country adjoining fill'd with the palaces of the British nobility and gentry already spoken of; looking north, behold, to crown all, a fair prospect of the whole city of London it self; the most glorious sight without exception, that the whole world at present can show, or perhaps ever cou'd show since the sacking of Rome in the European, and the burning the Temple of Jerusalem in the Asian part of the world.

Add to all this, that these fine houses and innumerable more, which cannot be spoken of here, are not, at least very few of them, the mansion houses of families, the antient residences of ancestors, the capital messuages of the estates; nor have the rich possessors any lands to a considerable value about them; but these are all houses of retreat, like the Bastides of Marseilles, gentlemen's meer summer-houses, or citizen's country-houses; whither they retire from the hurries of business, and from getting money, to draw their breath in a clear air, and to divert themselves and families in the hot weather; and they that are shut up, and as it were strip'd of their inhabitants in the winter, who return to smoke and dirt, sin and seacoal, (as it was coursly express'd) in the busy city; so that in short all this variety, this beauty, this glorious show of wealth and plenty, is really a view of the luxuriant age which we live in, and of the overflowing riches of the citizens, who in their abundance make these gay excursions, and live thus deliciously all the summer, retiring within themselves in the winter, the better to lay up for the next summer's expence.

If this then is produc'd from the gay part of the town only, what must be the immense wealth of the city it self, where such a produce is brought forth? where such prodigious estates are raised in one man's age; instances of which we have seen in those of Sir Josiah Child, Sir John Lethulier, Sir James Bateman, Sir Robert Clayton, Sir William Scawen, and hundreds more; whose beginnings were small, or but small compar'd, and who have exceeded even the greatest part of the nobility of England in wealth, at their death, and all of their own getting.

It is impossible in one journey to describe effectually this part of the county of Surrey, lying from Kingston to London and Greenwich, where I set out: That is, including the villages of Richmond, Petersham, Eastshene, Mortlock, Putney, Wandsworth, Barn-Elms, Battersey, Wimbleton, Tooting, Clapham, Camberwell, Peckham and Deptford; the description would swell with the stories of private families, and of the reasons of these opulent foundations, more than with their history.

It would also take up a large chapter in this book, to but mention the overthrow, and catastrophe of innumerable wealthy city families, who after they have thought their houses establish'd, and have built their magnificent country seats, as well as others, have sunk under the misfortunes of business, and the disasters of trade, after the world has thought them pass'd all possibility of danger; such as Sir Joseph Hodges, Sir Justus Beck, the widow Cock at Camberwell, and many others; besides all the late South-Sea directors, all which I chuse to have forgotten, as no doubt they desire to be, in recording the wealth and opulence of this part of England, which I doubt not to convince you infinitely out does the whole world.

I am come now to Southwark, a suburb to, rather than a part of London; but of which this may be said with justice.

A royal city were not London by.

To give you a brief description of Southwark, it might be call'd a long street, of about nine miles in length, as it is now built on eastward; reaching from Vaux-Hall to London-Bridge, and from the bridge to Deptford, all up to Deptford-Bridge, which parts it from Greenwich, all the way winding and turning as the river winds and turns; except only in that part, which reaches from Cuckold's-Point to Deptford, which indeed winds more than the river does.

In the center, which is opposite to the bridge, it is thicken'd with buildings, and may be reckon'd near a mile broad; (viz.) from the bridge to the end of Kent-street and Blackman-street, and about the Mint; but else the whole building is but narrow, nor indeed can it be otherwise; considering the length of it.

The principal beauty of the borrough of Southwark, consists in the prodigious number of its inhabitants: Take it as it was antiently bounded, it contain'd nine parishes; but as it is now extended, and, as I say, joins with Deptford, it contains eleven large parishes: According to the weekly-bills, for the year 1722, the nine parishes only bury'd 4166, which is about one sixth part of the whole body, call'd London; the bill of mortallity for that year, amounting in all to 25750.

The first thing we meet with considerable, is at the Spring-Garden, just at the corner, where the road turns away to go from Vaux-Hall Turnpike, towards Newington, there are the remains of the old lines cast up in the times of the Rebellion, to fortify this side of the town; and at that corner was a very large bastion, or rather a fort, and such indeed they call it; which commanded all the pass on that side, and farther on, where the openings near St. George's-Fields are, which they now call the Ducking-Pond, there was another; the water they call the Ducking-Pond, is evidently to this day the moat of the fort, and the lines are so high, and so undemolish'd still, that a very little matter would repair and perfect them again.

From hence they turn'd south east, and went to the windmill, at the end of Blackman-street, where they cross'd the road, and going to the end of Kent-street, we see another great bastion; and then turning S.E. till they come to the end of Barnaby-street, or rather beyond, among the tanners, and there you see another fort, so plain, and so undemolish'd, the grass growing now over the works, that it is as plain as it was, even when it was thrown down.

Here is also another remain of antiquity, the vestiges of which are easy to be traced; (viz.) The place where by strength of men's hands, they turn'd the channel of this great river of Thames, and made a new course for the waters, while the great bridge, which is now standing, was built: Here it is evident they turn'd the waters out: (viz.) About a place call'd Nine Elms, just beyond Vaux-Hall, where now a little brook, from the Wash-way at Kennington, and which they once attempted to make navigable, enters the Thames, from thence it cross'd the great road, a little beyond the end of the houses in Newington; between which and Kennington Common, on the left of the road, as you go south, there is a very large pond, or lake of water, part of the channel not fill'd up to this day; from thence it enter'd the marshes between Rotherif and Deptford, where for many years after there remained a drain for the water, upon which was a large mill-pond and dam, and where since was built the second great wet-dock, said to belong to the Duke of Bedford's estate, and call'd at first Snellgrove's-Dock, because built by one Mr. Snellgrove, a shipwright, whose building-yards adjoin'd it. A farther description of Southwark, I refer till I come to speak of London, as one general appellation for the two cities of London and Westminster; and all the burrough of Southwark, and all the buildings and villages included within the bills of mortallity, make but one London, in the general appellation, of which in its order. I am, &c.

THE END OF THE SECOND LETTER

LETTER III

CONTAINING A DESCRIPTION OF THE SOUTH COASTS OF HAMPSHIRE,
WILTS, DORSETSHIRE, SOMERSETSHIRE, DEVONSHIRE, AND
CORNWALL

SIR,—I find so much left to speak of, and so many things to say
in every part of England, that my journey cannot be barren of
intelligence, which way soever I turn; no, tho' I were to oblige
myself to say nothing of any thing that had been spoken of
before.

I intended once to have gone due west this journey; but then
I should have been obliged to croud my observations so close,
(to bring Hampton-Court, Windsor, Blenheim, Oxford, the
Bath and Bristol, all into one letter; all those remarkable places
lying in a line, as it were, in one point of the compass) as to
have made my letter too long, or my observations too light and
superficial, as others have done before me.

This letter will divide the weighty task, and consequently
make it fit lighter on the memory, be pleasanter to the reader,
and make my progress the more regular: I shall therefore take
in Hampton-Court and Windsor in this journey; the first at
my setting out, and the last at my return, and the rest as their
situation demands.

As I came down from Kingston, in my last circuit, by the
south bank of the Thames, on the Surrey side of the river; so
I go up to Hampton Court, now, on the north bank, and on the
Middlesex side, which I mention, because as the sides of the
country bordering on the river, lie parallel, so the beauty of
the country, the pleasant situations, the glory of innumerable
fine buildings, noblemens and gentlemens houses, and citizens
retreats, are so equal a match to what I had describ'd on the
other side, that one knows not which to give the preference to:
But as I must speak of them again, when I come to write of the
county of Middlesex, which I have now purposely omitted;
so I pass them over here, except the palace of Hampton only,
which I mention'd in Middlesex, for the reasons above.

Hampton Court lyes on the north bank of the river Thames,

about two small miles from Kingston, and on the road from Stanes to Kingston Bridge; so that the road straightening the parks a little, they were obliged to part the parks, and leave the Paddock, and the Great Park, part on the other side the road; a testimony of that just regard that the Kings of England always had, and still have, to the common good, and to the service of the country, that they would not interrupt the course of the road, or cause the poor people to go out of the way of their business, to or from the markets and fairs, for any pleasure of their own whatsoever.

The palace of Hampton-Court was first founded, and built from the ground, by that great statesman, and favourite of King Henry VIII. Cardinal Wolsey; and if it be a just observation any where, as is made from the situation of the old abbies and monasteries, the clergy were excellent judges of the beauty and pleasantness of the country, and chose always to plant in the best; I say, if it was a just observation in any case, it was in this; for if there be a situation on the whole river between Stanes-Bridge and Windsor-Bridge, pleasanter than another, it is this of Hampton; close to the river, yet not offended by the rising of its waters in floods, or storms, near to the reflux of the tides, but not quite so near as to be affected with any foulness of the water, which the flowing of the tides generally is the occasion of. The gardens extend almost to the bank of the river, yet are never overflow'd; nor are there any marshes on either side the river to make the waters stagnate, or the air unwholesome on that account. The river is high enough to be navigable, and low enough to be a little pleasantly rapid; so that the stream looks always chearful, not slow and sleeping, like a pond. This keeps the waters always clear and clean, the bottom in view, the fish playing, and in sight; and, in a word, it has every thing that can make an inland; or, as I may call it, a country river, pleasant and agreeable.

I shall sing you no songs here of the river in the first person of a water nymph, a goddess, (and I know not what) according to the humour of the ancient poets. I shall talk nothing of the marriage of old Isis, the male river, with the beautiful Thame, the female river, a whimsy as simple as the subject was empty, but I shall speak of the river as occasion presents, as it really is made glorious by the splendor of its shores, gilded with noble palaces, strong fortifications, large hospitals, and publick buildings; with the greatest bridge, and the greatest city in the world, made famous by the opulence of its merchants, the encrease and extensiveness of its commerce; by its invincible navies, and by the innumerable fleets of ships sailing upon it, to and from all parts of the world.

As I meet with the river upwards in my travels thro' the inland country, I shall speak of it, as it is the chanel for conveying an infinite quantity of provisions from remote counties to London, and enriching all the counties again that lye near it, by the return of wealth and trade from the city; and in describing these things I expect both to inform and divert my readers, and speak, in a more masculine manner, more to the dignity of the subject, and also more to their satisfaction, than I could do any other way.

There is little more to be said of the Thames, relating to Hampton-Court, than that it adds, by its neighbourhood, to the pleasure of the situation; for as to passing by water too and from London; tho' in summer 'tis exceeding pleasant, yet the passage is a little too long to make it easy to the ladies, especially to be crowded up in the small boats, which usually go upon the Thames for pleasure.

The prince and princess, indeed, I remember came once down by water, upon the occasion of her royal highness's being great with child, and near her time; so near, that she was deliver'd within two or three days after: But this passage being in the royal barges, with strength of oars, and the day exceeding fine, the passage, I say, was made very pleasant, and still the more so, for being short. Again, this passage is all the way with the stream, whereas, in the common passage, upwards, great part of the way is against the stream, which is slow and heavy.

But be the going and coming how it will by water, 'tis an exceeding pleasant passage by land, whether we go by the Surrey side or the Middlesex side of the water, of which I shall say more in its place.

The situation of Hampton-Court being thus mention'd, and its founder, 'tis to be mention'd next, that it fell to the Crown in the forfeiture of his eminence the cardinal, when the king seiz'd his effects and estate, by which this and Whitehall, another house of his own building also, came to King Henry VIII. two palaces fit for the Kings of England, erected by one cardinal, are standing monuments of the excessive pride, as well as the immense wealth of that prelate, who knew no bounds of his insolence and ambition, till he was overthrown at once by the displeasure of his master.

Whoever knew Hampton-Court before it was begun to be rebuilt, or alter'd, by the late King William, must acknowledge it was a very compleat palace before, and fit for a king; and tho' it might not, according to the modern method of building, or of gardening, pass for a thing exquisitely fine; yet it had this remaining to itself, and perhaps peculiar; namely, that it shewed a situation exceedingly capable of improvement, and of being made one of the most delightful palaces in Europe.

This Her Majesty Queen Mary was so sensible of, that while the king had order'd the pulling down the old apartments, and building it up in that most beautiful form, which we see them now appear in, her majesty, impatient of enjoying so agreeable a retreat, fix'd upon a building formerly made use of chiefly for landing from the river, and therefore call'd the Water Gallery; and here, as if she had been conscious that she had but a few years to enjoy it, she order'd all the little neat curious things to be done, which suited her own conveniences, and made it the pleasantest little thing within doors that could possibly be made, tho' its situation being such, as it could not be allowed to stand after the great building was finish'd; we now see no remains of it.

The queen had here her gallery of beauties, being the pictures, at full length, of the principal ladies attending upon her majesty, or who were frequently in her retinue; and this was the more beautiful sight, because the originals were all in being, and often to be compar'd with their pictures. Her majesty had here a fine apartment, with a sett of lodgings, for her private retreat only, but most exquisitely furnish'd; particularly a fine chints bed, then a great curiosity; another of her own work, while in Holland, very magnificent, and several others; and here was also her majesty's fine collection of Delft ware, which indeed was very large and fine; and here was also a vast stock of fine China ware, the like whereof was not then to be seen in England; the long gallery, as above, was fill'd with this china, and every other place, where it could be plac'd, with advantage.

The queen had here also a small bathing-room, made very fine, suited either to hot or cold bathing, as the season should invite; also a dairy, with all its conveniences, in which her majesty took great delight: All these things were finish'd with expedition, that here their majesties might repose while they saw the main building go forward. While this was doing, the gardens were laid out, the plan of them devised by the king himself; and especially the amendments and alterations were

*G 820

made by the king, or the queen's particular special command, or by both; for their majesties agreed so well in their fancy, and had both so good judgment in the just proportions of things, which are the principal beauties of a garden, that it may be said they both order'd every thing that was done.

Here the fine parcel of limes, which form the semi-circle on the south front of the house, by the iron gates, looking into the park, were by the dextrous hand of the head gardener, remov'd, after some of them had been almost thirty years planted in other places, tho' not far of. I know the King of France, in the decoration of the gardens of Versailles, had oaks remov'd, which, by their dimensions, must have been above an hundred years old, and yet were taken up with so much art, and by the strength of such engines, by which such a monsterous quantity of earth was raised with them, that the trees could not feel their remove; that is to say, their growth was not at all hinder'd. This I confess, makes the wonder much the less in those trees at Hampton-Court gardens; but the performance was not the less difficult or nice, however, in these, and they thrive perfectly well.

While the gardens were thus laid out, the king also directed the laying the pipes for the fountain and *jette d'eau's*; and particularly the dimensions of them, and what quantity of water they should cast up, and encreas'd the number of them after the first design.

The ground on the side of the other front, has receiv'd some alterations since the taking down the water gallery; but not that part immediately next the lodgings: The orange trees, and fine Dutch bays, are plac'd within the arches of the building under the first floor: so that the lower part of the house was all one as a green house for some time: Here stands advanced, on two pedestals of stone, two marble vases, or flower pots, of most exquisite workmanship; the one done by an Englishman, and the other by a German: 'Tis hard to say which is the best performance, tho' the doing of it was a kind of tryal of skill between them; but it gives us room, without partiality, to say they were both masters of their art.

The parterre on that side descends from the terrass walk by steps, and on the left a terrass goes down to the water-side, from which the garden on the eastward front is overlook'd, and gives a most pleasant prospect.

The fine scrolls and bordure of these gardens were at first edg'd with box; but on the queen's disliking the smell, those edgings were taken up, but have since been planted again, at least in many places, nothing making so fair and regular an edging as box, or is so soon brought to its perfection.

On the north side of the house, where the gardens seem'd to want skreening from the weather, or the view of the chapel, and some part of the old building requir'd to be cover'd from the eye; the vacant ground, which was large, is very happily cast into a wilderness, with a labyrinth, and espaliers so high, that they effectually take off all that part of the old building, which would have been offensive to the sight. This labyrinth and wilderness is not only well design'd, and compleatly finish'd, but is perfectly well kept, and the espaliers fill'd exactly, at bottom to the very ground, and are led up to proportion'd heights on the top; so that nothing of that kind can be more beautiful.

The house itself is every way answerable on the outside to the beautiful prospect, and the two fronts are the largest, and, beyond comparison, the finest of the kind in England: The great stairs go up from the second court of the palace on the right hand, and lead you to the south prospect.

I hinted in my last that King William brought into England the love of fine paintings, as well as that of fine gardens; and you have an example of it in the cartoons, as they are call'd, being five pieces of such paintings, as, if you will believe men of nice judgment and great travelling, are not to be match'd in Europe: The stories are known, but especially two of them, viz. that of St. Paul preaching on Mars-Hill to the self-wise Athenians, and that of St. Peter passing sentence of death on Ananias; I say, these two strike the mind with the utmost surprize; the passions are so drawn to the life, astonishment, terror and death in the face of Ananias; zeal and a sacred fire in the eyes of the blessed apostle; fright and surprize upon the countenances of the beholders in the piece of Ananias; all these describe themselves so naturally, that you cannot but seem to discover something of the like passions, even in seeing them.

In the other, there is the boldness and courage with which St. Paul undertook to talk to a sett of men, who he knew despis'd all the world, as thinking themselves able to teach them any thing: In the audience, there is anticipating pride and conceit in some, a smile or fleer of contempt in others, but a kind of sensible conviction, tho' crush'd in its beginning, on the faces of the rest; and all together appear confounded, but have little to say, and know nothing at all of it, they gravely put him off to hear him another time; all these are seen here in the very dress of the face; that is, the very countenances which they hold while they listen to the new doctrine, which the apostle preached to a people at that time ignorant of it.

The other of the cartoons are exceeding fine; but I mention these as the particular two which are most lively, which strike the fancy the soonest at first view: 'Tis reported, but with what truth I know not, that the late French king offer'd an hundred thousand louis d'ors for these pictures; but this, I say, is but a report: The king brought a great many other fine pieces to England, and with them the love of fine paintings so universally spread itself among the nobility and persons of figure all over the kingdom, that it is incredible what collections have been made by English gentlemen since that time; and how all Europe has been rumag'd, as we may say, for pictures to bring over hither, where, for twenty years, they yielded the purchasers, such as collected them for sale, immense profit: But the rates are abated since that, and we begin to be glutted with the copies and frauds of the Dutch and Flemish painters, who have imposed grossly upon us. But to return to the palace of Hampton-Court: Queen Mary liv'd not to see it compleatly finish'd; and her death, with the other difficulties of that reign, put a stop to the works for some time, till the king reviving his good liking of the place, set them to work again, and it was finish'd, as we see it: But I have been assur'd, that had the peace continu'd, and the king liv'd to enjoy the continuance of it, his majesty had resolv'd to have pull'd down all the remains of the old building; such as the chapel, and the large court within the first gate, and to have built up the whole palace after the manner of those two fronts already done. In these would have been an entire sett of rooms of state for the receiving, and, if need had been, lodging, and entertaining any foreign prince, with his retinue; also offices for all the Secretaries of State, Lords of the Treasury, and of trade; to have repair'd to for the dispatch of such business, as it might be necessary to have done there upon the king's longer residence there than ordinary; as also apartments for all the great officers of the houshold; so that had the house had two great squares added, as was design'd, there would have been no room to spare, or that would not have been very well fill'd: But the king's death put an end to all these things.

Since the death of King William, Hampton-Court seem'd abandon'd of its patron: They have gotten a kind of proverbial saying relating to Hampton-Court, viz. That it has been generally chosen by every other prince, since it became a house of note. King Charles was the first that delighted in it since Queen Elizabeth's time; as for the reigns before, it was but newly forfeited to the Crown, and was not made a royal house till King Charles I. who was not only a prince that delighted in country retirements, but knew how to make choice of them by the beauty of their situation, the goodness of the air, &c. he took great delight here, and, had he liv'd to enjoy it in peace, had purpos'd to make it another thing than it was: But we all know what took him off from that felicity, and all others; and this house was at last made one of his prisons by his rebellious subjects.

His son, King Charles II. may well be said to have an aversion to the place, for the reason just mention'd, namely, the treatment his royal father met with there; and particularly that the rebel and murtherer of his father, Cromwell, afterwards possess'd this palace, and revel'd here in the blood of the royal party, as he had done in that of his sovereign; King Charles II. therefore chose Windsor, and bestow'd a vast sum in beautifying the castle there, and which brought it to the perfection we see it in at this day; some few alterations excepted, done in the time of King William.

King William, for King James is not to be nam'd as to his choice of retir'd palaces, his delight running quite another way; I say, King William fix'd upon Hampton Court; and it was in his reign that Hampton Court put on new cloaths, and being dress'd gay and glorious, made the figure we now see it in.

The late queen, taken up for part of her reign in her kind regards to the prince her spouse, was oblig'd to reside where her care of his health confin'd her, and in this case kept for the most part at Kensington, where he died; but her majesty always discover'd her delight to be at Windsor, where she chose the little house, as 'twas call'd, opposite to the castle, and took the air in her chaise in the parks and forest, as she saw occasion.

Now Hampton Court, by the like alternative, is come into request again; and we find his present majesty, who is a good judge too of the pleasantness and situation of a place of that kind, has taken Hampton-Court into his favour, and has made it much his choice for the summer's retreat of the Court, and where they may best enjoy the diversions of the season: When Hampton Court will find such another favourable juncture as in King William's time, when the remainder of her ashes shall be swept away, and her compleat fabric, as design'd by King

William, shall be finish'd, I cannot tell; but if ever that shall be, I know no palace in Europe, Versailles excepted, which can come up to her, either for beauty and magnificence, or for extent of building, and the ornaments attending it.

From Hampton Court I directed my course for a journey into the south west part of England; and, to take up my beginning where I concluded my last, I cross'd to Chertsey on the Thames, a town I mention'd before; from whence crossing the Black Desert, as I call'd it, of Bagshot-Heath, I directed my course for Hampshire, or Hantshire, and particularly for Basingstoke; that is to say, that a little before I pass'd into the great western road upon the heath, somewhat west of Bagshot, at a village call'd Blackwater, and enter'd Hampshire, near Hartleroe.

Before we reach Basingstoke, we get rid of that unpleasant country, which I so often call a desart, and enter into a pleasant fertile country, enclosed and cultivated like the rest of England; and passing a village or two, we enter Basingstoke, in the midst of woods and pastures, rich and fertile, and the country accordingly spread with the houses of the nobility and gentry, as in other places: On the right hand, a little before we come to the town, we pass at a small distance the famous fortress, so it was then, of Basing, being a house belonging then to the Marquis of Winchester, the great ancestor of the present family of the Dukes of Bolton.

This house, garrison'd by a resolute band of old soldiers, was a great curb to the rebels of the Parliament Party, almost thro' that whole war; till it was, after a vigorous defence, yielded to the conquerors, by the inevitable fate of things at that time. The old house is indeed demolish'd; but the successor of the family, the first Duke of Bolton, has erected a very noble fabrick in the same place, or near it, which, however, is not equal to the magnificence which fame gives to the ancient house, whose strength of building only, besides the out-works, withstood the battery of cannon in several attacks, and repuls'd the Roundheads, three or four times, when they attempted to besiege it: 'Tis incredible what booty the garrison of this place pick'd up, lying, as they did, just on the great western road, where they intercepted the carriers, plunder'd the waggons, and suffer'd nothing to pass; to the great interruption of the trade of the city of London.

Basingstoke is a large populous market town, has a good market for corn, and lately, within a very few years, is fallen into a manufacture, viz. of making druggets and shalloons, and such slight goods, which, however, employs a good number of the poor people, and enables them to get their bread, which knew not how to get it before.

From hence the great western road goes on to Whitchurch and Andover, two market towns, and sending members to Parliament; at the last of which, the Downs, or open country, begins, which we in general, tho' falsly, call Salisbury-Plain: But my resolution being to take in my view what I had pass'd by before; I was oblig'd to go off to the left hand, to Alresford and Winchester.

Alresford was a flourishing market town, and remarkable for this; That tho' it had no great trade, and particularly very little, if any manufactures, yet there was no collection in the town for the poor, nor any poor low enough to take alms of the parish, which is what I do not think can be said of any town in England besides.

But this happy circumstance, which so distinguish'd Alresford from all her neighbours, was brought to an end in the year ——, when, by a sudden and surprizing fire, the whole town, with both the church and the market-house, was reduc'd to a heap of rubbish; and, except a few poor hutts at the remotest ends of the town, not a house left standing: The town is since that very handsomely rebuilt, and the neighbouring gentlemen contributed largely to the relief of the people, especially, by sending in timber towards their building; also their Market-house is handsomely built; but the church not yet, tho' we hear there is a fund raising likewise for that.

Here is a very large pond, or lake of water, kept up to a head, by a strong *batterd'eau*, or dam, which the people tell us was made by the Romans; and that it is to this day part of the great Roman highway, which leads from Winchester to Alton, and, as 'tis supposed, went on to London, tho' we no where see any remains of it, except between Winchester and Alton, and chiefly between this town and Alton.

Near this town, a little north-west, the Duke of Bolton has another seat, which, tho' not large, is a very handsome beautiful palace, and the gardens not only very exact, but very finely situate, the prospect and visto's noble and great, and the whole very well kept.

From hence, at the end of seven miles over the Downs, we come to the very ancient city of Winchester; not only the great church, which is so famous all over Europe, and has been so much talk'd of, but even the whole city has, at a distance, the face of venerable, and looks ancient a far off; and yet here are many modern buildings too, and some very handsome; as the college schools; with the bishop's palace, built by Bishop Morley, since the late wars; the old palace of the bishop having been ruin'd by that known church incendiary, Sir William Waller, and his crew of plunderers; who, if my information is not wrong, as I believe it is not, destroy'd more monuments of the dead, and defac'd more churches, than all the Round-heads in England beside.

This church, and the schools, also are accurately describ'd by several writers, especially by the *Monasticon*, where their antiquity and original is fully set forth: The outside of the church is as plain and course, as if the founders had abhor'd ornaments, or that William of Wickham had been a Quaker, or at least a Quietist: There is neither statue, or a nich for a statue, to be seen on all the outside; no carv'd work, no spires, towers, pinacles, balustrades, or any thing; but meer walls, buttresses, windows, and coins, necessary to the support and order of the building: It has no steeple, but a short tower cover'd flat, as if the top of it had fallen down, and it had been cover'd in haste to keep the rain out, till they had time to build it up again.

But the inside of the church has many very good things in it, and worth observation; it was for some ages the burying place of the English Saxon kings; whose reliques, at the repair of the church, were collected by Bishop Fox, and, being put together into large wooden chests, lin'd with lead, were again interr'd at the foot of the great wall in the choir, three on one side, and three on the other; with an account whose bones are in each chest, whether the division of the reliques might be depended upon, has been doubted, but is not thought material, so that we do but believe they are all there.

The choir of the church appears very magnificent; the roof is very high, and the Gothick work in the arch'd part is very fine, tho' very old; the painting in the windows is admirably good, and easy to be distinguish'd by those that understand those things: The steps ascending to the choir make a very fine show, having the statues of King James, and his son King Charles, in copper, finely cast; the first on the right hand, and the other on the left, as you go up to the choir.

The choir is said to be the longest in England; and as the number of prebendaries, canons, &c. are many, it requir'd such a length. The ornaments of the choir are the effects of the bounty of several bishops; the fine altar (the noblest in England by much) was done by Bishop Morley; the roof, and the coat of arms of the Saxon and Norman kings, were done by Bishop Fox; and the fine throne, for the bishop in the choir, was given by Bishop Mew, in his life-time; and it was well it was; for if he had order'd it by will, there is reason to believe it had never been done. That reverend prelate, notwithstanding he enjoy'd so rich a bishoprick, scarce leaving money enough behind him, to pay for his coffin.

There are a great many persons of rank bury'd in this church, besides the Saxon kings, mention'd above; and besides several of the most eminent bishops of the see: Just under the altar lyes a son of William the Conqueror, without any monument; and behind the altar, under a very fine and venerable monument, lyes the famous Lord Treasurer, Weston, late Earl of Portland, Lord High Treasurer of England under King Charles I. His effigy is in copper armour, at full length, with his head rais'd on three cushions of the same, and is a very magnificent work: There is also a very fine monument of Cardinal Beaufort, in his cardinal's robes and hat.

The monument of Sir John Cloberry is extraordinary, but more, because it puts strangers upon enquiring into his story, than for any thing wonderful in the figure, it being cut in a modern dress; the habit gentlemen wore in those times, which, being now so much out of fashion, appears mean enough: But this gentleman's story is particular, being the person solely entrusted with the secret of the Restoration of King Charles II. as the messenger that pass'd between General Monk on one hand, and Mr. Montague, and others entrusted by King Charles II. on the other hand; which he manag'd so faithfully, as to effect that memorable event, to which England owes the felicity of all her happy days since that time; by which faithful service, Sir John Cloberry, then a private musqueteer only, rais'd himself to the honour of a knight, with the reward of a good estate from the bounty of the king.

Every body that goes into this church, and reads what is to be read there, will be told, that the body of the church was built by the famous William of Wickham; whose monument, intimating his fame, lyes in the middle of that part, which was built at his expence.

He was a courtier before a bishop; and tho' he had no great share of learning, he was a great promoter of it, and a lover of learned men: His natural genius was much beyond his acquir'd parts, and his skill in politicks beyond his ecclesiastick knowledge: He is said to have put his master, King Edward III. to whom he was Secretary of State, upon the two great projects which made his reign so glorious, viz. First, upon setting up his claim to the crown of France, and pushing that claim by force of arms, which brought on the war with France, in which that prince was three times victorious in battle. (2.) Upon setting up, or instituting the Order of the Garter; in which he (being before that made Bishop of Winchester) obtain'd the honour for the Bishops of Winchester, of being always prelates of the Order, as an appendix to the bishoprick; and he himself was the first prelate of the Order, and the ensigns of that honour are joyn'd with his episcopal ornaments, in the robing of his effigy on the monument above.

To the honour of this bishop, there are other foundations of his, as much to his fame as that of this church, of which I shall speak in their order; but particularly the college in this city, which is a noble foundation indeed: The building consists of two large courts, in which are the lodgings for the masters and scholars, and in the center a very noble chapel; beyond that, in the second court, are the schools, with a large cloyster beyond them, and some enclosures laid open for the diversion of the scholars. There also is a great hall, where the scholars dine: The funds for the support of this college are very considerable; the masters live in a very good figure, and their maintenance is sufficient to support it: They have all seperate dwellings in the house, and all possible conveniences appointed them.

The scholars have exhibitions at a certain time of continuance here, if they please to study, in the new college at Oxford, built by the same noble benefactor, of which I shall speak in its order.

The clergy here live at large, and very handsomely, in the close belonging to the cathedral; where, besides the bishop's palace, mention'd above, are very good houses, and very handsomely built, for the prebendaries, canons, and other dignitaries of this church: The deanary is a very pleasant dwelling, the gardens very large, and the river running thro' them; but the floods in winter sometimes incommode the gardens very much.

This school has fully answer'd the end of the founder, who, tho' he was no great scholar, resolv'd to erect a house for the making the ages to come more learned than those that went before; and it had, I say, fully answer'd the end, for many learned and great men have been rais'd here, some of whom we shall have occasion to mention as we go on.

Among the many private inscriptions in this church, we found one made by Dr. Over, once an eminent physician in this city, on a mother and child, who, being his patients, died together, and were bury'd in the same grave, and which intimate, that one died of a fever, and the other of a dropsy.

> Surrepuit natum febris matrem Abstulit Hydrops,
> Igne Prior fatis, altera Cessit Aqua.

As the city it self stands in a vale on the bank, and at the conjunction of two small rivers, so the country rising every way, but just as the course of the water keeps the valley open, you must necessarily, as you go out of the gates, go up hill every way: But when once ascended, you come to the most charming plains, and most pleasant country of that kind in England; which continues, with very small intersections of rivers and valleys, for above fifty miles, as shall appear in the sequel of this journey.

At the west gate of this city was anciently a castle, known to be so by the ruins, more than by any extraordinary notice taken of it in history: What they say of it, that the Saxon kings kept their Court here, is doubtful, and must be meant of the West Saxons only; and as to the tale of King Arthur's round table, which, they pretend, was kept here for him, and his two dozen of knights; which table hangs up still, as a piece of antiquity, to the tune of 1200 years, and has, as they pretend, the names of the said knights in Saxon characters, and yet such as no man can read: All this story I see so little ground to give the least credit to, that I look upon it, and 't shall please you, to be no better than a FIBB.

Where this castle stood, or whatever else it was, for some say there was no castle there, the late King Charles II. mark'd out, a very noble design; which had he liv'd, would certainly have made that part of the country, the New-Market of the ages to come; for the country hereabout far excels that of New-Market Heath, for all kinds of sport and diversion, fit for a prince, no body can dispute; and as the design included a noble palace, sufficient like Windsor, for a summer residence of the whole Court, it would certainly have diverted the king from his cursory journeys to New-Market.

The plan of this house has receiv'd several alterations; and as it is never like to be finish'd, 'tis scarce worth recording the variety: The building is begun, and the front next the city carry'd up to the roof, and cover'd; but the remainder is not begun: There was a street of houses design'd from the gate of the palace down to the town, but it was never begun to be built; the park mark'd out was exceeding large, near ten miles in circumference, and ended west upon the open downs, in view of the town of Stockbridge.

This house was afterwards settled with a royal revenue also, as an appenage, establish'd by Parliament upon Prince George of Denmark for his life, in case he had out-liv'd the queen: But his royal highness dying before her majesty, all hope of seeing this design perfected, or the house finish'd, is now vanish'd.

I cannot omit that there are several publick edifices in this city, and in the neighbourhood; as the hospitals, and the building adjoining near the east gate; and towards the north, a piece of an old monastry undemolish'd, and which is still preserv'd to the religion, being the residence of some private Roman Catholick gentlemen, where they have an oratory, and, as they say, live still according to the rules of St. Benedict. This building is call'd Hide-House; and, as they live very usefully and, to the highest degree, obliging among their neighbours, they meet with no obstruction or disturbance from any body.

Winchester is a place of no trade, other than is naturally occasion'd by the inhabitants of the city and neighbouring villages, one with another: Here is no manufacture, no navigation; there was indeed an attempt to make the river navigable from Southampton; and it was once made practicable, but it never answer'd the expence, so as to give encouragement to the undertakers.

Here is a great deal of good company; and abundance of gentry being in the neighbourhood, it adds to the sociableness of the place: The clergy also here are, generally speaking, very rich, and very numerous.

As there is such good company, so they are gotten into that new-fashion'd way of conversing by assemblies: I shall do no more than mention them here; they are pleasant and agreeable to the young people, and some times fatal to them, of which, in its place; Winchester has its share of the mirth: May it escape the ill consequences.

The hospital on the south of this city, at a miles distance on the road to Southampton, is worth notice: 'Tis said to be founded by King William Rufus, but was not endow'd or appointed till later times by Cardinal Beaufort. Every traveller that knocks at the door of this house, in his way, and asks for it, claims the relief of a piece of white bread and a cup of beer; and this donation is still continued; a quantity of good beer is set apart every day to be given away; and what is left, is distributed to other poor, but none of it kept to the next day.

How the revenues of this hospital, which should maintain the master and thirty private gentlemen, who they call Fellows, but ought to call Brothers, is now reduc'd to maintain only fourteen, while the master lives in a figure equal to the best gentleman in the country, would be well worth the enquiry of a proper visitor, if such can be nam'd: 'Tis a thing worthy of complaint, when publick charaties, design'd for the relief of the poor, are embezzel'd and depredated by the rich, and turn'd to the support of luxury and pride.

From Winchester, is about 25 miles, and over the most charming plains that can any where be seen, (far in my opinion) excelling the plains of Mecca, we come to Salisbury; the vast flocks of sheep, which one every where sees upon these downs, and the great number of those flocks, is a sight truly worth observation; 'tis ordinary for these flocks to contain from 3 to 5000 in a flock; and several private farmers hereabouts have two or three such flocks.

But 'tis more remarkable still; how a great part of these downs comes by a new method of husbandry, to be not only made arable, which they never were in former days, but to bear excellent wheat, and great crops too, tho' otherwise poor barren land, and never known to our ancestors to be capable of any such thing; nay, they would perhaps have laugh'd at any one that would have gone about to plough up the wild downs and hills, where the sheep were wont to go: But experience has made the present age wiser, and more skilful in husbandry; for by only folding the sheep upon the plow'd lands, those lands, which otherwise are barren, and where the plow goes within three or four inches of the solid rock of chalk, are made fruitful, and bear very good wheat, as well as rye and barley: I shall say more of this when I come to speak of the same practice farther in the country.

This plain country continues in length from Winchester to Salisbury 25 miles, from thence to Dorchester 22 miles, thence to Weymouth 6 miles, so that they lye near 50 miles in length, and breadth; they reach also in some places 35 to 40 miles: They who would make any practicable guess at the number of sheep usually fed on these downs, may take it from a calculation

made, as I was told, at Dorchester, that there were 600000 sheep
fed within 6 miles of that town, measuring every way round,
and the town in the center.

As we pass'd this plain country, we saw a great many old
camps, as well Roman as British, and several remains of the
ancient inhabitants of this kingdom, and of their wars, battles,
entrenchments, encampments, buildings, and other fortifications, which are indeed very agreeable to a traveller, that has
read any thing of the history of the country. Old Sarum is as
remarkable as any of these, where there is a double entrench-
ment, with a deep graffe, or ditch, to either of them; the area
about 100 yards in diameter, taking in the whole crown of the
hill, and thereby rendering the ascent very difficult: Near this,
there is one farm house, which is all the remains I could see
of any town in or near the place, for the encampment has no
resemblance of a town; and yet this is call'd the borough of
Old Sarum, and sends two members to Parliament, who, those
members can justly say, they represent, would be hard for them
to answer.

Some will have it, that the old city of Sorbiodunum, or
Salisbury, stood here, and was afterwards, for I know not
what reasons, remov'd to the low marshy grounds, among
the rivers, where it now stands: But as I see no authority for
it, other than mere tradition, I believe my share of it, and
take it *ad referendum.*

Salisbury itself is indeed a large and pleasant city; tho' I do
not think it at all the pleasanter for that which they boast so
much of; namely, the water running thro' the middle of every
street, or that it adds any thing to the beauty of the place, but
just the contrary; it keeps the streets always dirty, full of wet
and filth, and weeds, even in the middle of summer.

The city is plac'd upon the confluence of two large rivers,
the Avon and the Willy, either of them considerable rivers, but
very large, when joyn'd together, and yet larger when they
receive a third river, viz. the Naddir, which joyns them near
Clarendon Park, about three miles below the city; then, with
a deep channel, and a current less rapid, they run down to
Christ Church, which is their port, and where they empty
themselves into the sea; from that town upwards, towards
Salisbury, they are made navigable too within two miles, and
might be so quite into the city, were it not for the strength of
the stream.

As the city of Winchester is a city without trade, that is to

say, without any particular manufactures; so this city of
Salisbury, and all the county of Wilts, of which it is the capital,
are full of a great variety of manufactures; and those some of
the most considerable in England; namely, the cloathing trade,
and the trade of flannels, drugets, and several other sorts of
manufactures, of which in their order.

The city of Salisbury has two remarkable manufactures
carried on in it, and which employ the poor of great part of the
country round; namely, fine flannels, and long cloths for the
Turkey trade, call'd Salisbury Whites: The people of Salisbury
are gay and rich, and have a flourishing trade; and there is a
great deal of good manners and good company among them;
I mean, among the citizens, besides what is found among the
gentlemen; for there are many good families in Salisbury,
besides the citizens.

This society has a great addition from the Closs, that is to
say, the circle of ground wall'd in adjacent to the cathedral; in
which the families of the prebendaries and commons, and others
of the clergy belonging to the cathedral have their houses, as
is usual in all cities where there are cathedral churches. These
are so considerable here, and the place so large, that it is (as it
is call'd in general) like another city.

The cathedral is famous for the height of its spire, which is
without exception the highest, and the handsomest in England,
being from the ground 410 foot, and yet the walls so exceeding
thin, that at the upper part of the spire upon a view made by
the late Christopher Wren, the wall was found to be less than
five inches thick; upon which a consultation was had, whether
the spire, or at least the upper part of it should be taken down,
it being suppos'd to have receiv'd some damage by the great
storm in the year 1703; but it was resolv'd in the negative, and
Sir Christopher order'd it to be so strengthen'd with bands of
iron plates, as has effectually secur'd it; and I have heard some
of the best architects say, it is stronger now than when it was
first built.

They tell us here long stories of the great art us'd in laying
the first foundations of this church; the ground being marshy
and wet, occasion'd by the channels of the rivers; that it was
laid upon piles according to some, and upon woolpacks according
to others; but this is not suppos'd by those who know, that the
whole country is one rock of chalk, even from the tops of the
highest hills, to the bottom of the deepest rivers.

They tell us, this church was 40 years a building, and cost

an immense sum of money, but it must be acknowledged that
the inside of the work is not answerable in the decoration of
things, to the workmanship without; the painting in the choir
is mean, and more like the ordinary method of common drawing
room, or tavern painting, than that of a church; the carving
is good, but very little of it, and it is rather a fine church than
finely set off.

The ordinary boast of this building, that there were as many
gates as months, as many windows as days, as many marble
pillars as hours in the year, is now no recommendation at all.
However the mention of it must be preserv'd.

> As many days as in one year there be,
> So many windows in one church we see;
> As many marble pillars there appear,
> As there are hours throughout the fleeting year;
> As many gates as moons one year do view:
> Strange tale to tell, yet not more strange than true.

There are however some very fine monuments in this church;
particularly one belonging to the noble family of Seymours,
since Dukes of Somerset, (and ancestors of the present flourishing
family,) which on a most melancholly occasion has been now
lately open'd again to receive the body of the late Dutchess of
Somerset, the happy consort for almost 40 years of his grace
the present duke; and only daughter and heiress of the antient
and noble family of Piercy, Earls of Northumberland, whose
great estate she brought into the family of Somerset, who now
enjoy it.

With her was bury'd at the same time her graces daughter
the Marchioness of Caermarthen, being married to the Marquess
of Caermarthen, son and heir apparent to the Lord of Leeds,
who dy'd for grief at the loss of the dutchess her mother, and
was buried with her; also her second son the Duke Piercy
Somerset, who dyed a few months before, and had been buryed
in the abby-church of Westminster, but was order'd to be
remov'd and laid here with the ancestors of his house; and I hear
his grace designs to have a yet more magnificent monument
erected in this cathedral for them, just by the other, which is
there already.

How the Dukes of Somerset came to quit this church for
their burying-place, and be laid in Westminster-Abbey, that
I know not; but 'tis certain that the present duke has chosen to
have his family laid here with their ancestors, and to that end
has caused the corps of his son the Lord Piercy, as above, and

one of his daughters who had been buryed in the Abbey, to be remov'd and brought down to this vault, which lyes in that they call the Virgin Mary's Chappel behind the altar. There is, as above, a noble monument for a late Duke and Dutchess of Somerset in the place already; with their pourtraits at full length, their heads lying upon cushions, the whole perfectly well wrought in fine polish'd Italian marble, and their sons kneeling by them; those I suppose to be the father of the great Duke of Somerset, uncle to King Edward IV, but after this the family lay in Westminster-Abbey, where there is also a fine monument for that very duke who was beheaded by Edward VI, and who was the great patron of the Reformation.

Among other monuments of noble men in this cathedral they show you one that is very extraordinary, and to which there hangs a tale: There was in the reign of Philip and Mary a very unhappy murther committed by the then Lord Sturton, or Stourton, a family since extinct, but well known till within a few years in that country.

This Lord Stourton being guilty of the said murther, which also was aggravated with very bad circumstances, could not obtain the usual grace of the Crown, (viz.) to be beheaded, but Queen Mary positively ordered that like a common malefactor he should die at the gallows: After he was hang'd, his friends desiring to have him bury'd at Salisbury, the bishop would not consent that he should be buryed in the cathedral, unless as a farther mark of infamy, his friends would submit to this condition (viz.) That the silken halter in which he was hang'd should be hanged up over his grave in the church, as a monument of his crime; which was accordingly done, and there it is to be seen to this day.

The putting this halter up here, was not so wonderful to me as it was, that the posterity of that lord, who remain'd in good rank sometime after, should never prevail to have that mark of infamy taken off from the memory of their ancestor.

There are several other monuments in this cathedral, as particularly of two noblemen of antient families in Scotland, one of the name of Hay, and one of the name of Gordon; but they give us nothing of their history, so that we must be content to say there they lye, and that's all.

The cloyster, and the chapter-house adjoyning to the church, are the finest here of any I have seen in England; the latter is octogon, or eight square, and is 150 foot in its circumference; the roof bearing all upon one small marble pillar in the center, which you may shake with your hands; and it is hardly to be imagin'd it can be any great support to the roof, which makes it the more curious, it is not indeed to be match'd I believe in Europe.

From hence directing my course to the sea-side in pursuit of my first design, viz. of viewing the whole coast of England, I left the great road, and went down the east side of the river towards New-Forest, and Lymington; and here I saw the antient house and seat of Clarendon, the mansion of the antient family of Hide, ancestors of the great Earl of Clarendon, and from whence his lordship was honour'd with that title, or the house erected into an honour in favour of his family.

But this being a large county, and full of memorable branches of antiquity, and modern curiosity, I cannot quit my observations so soon, but being happily fix'd by the favour of a particular friend at so beautiful a spot of ground as this of Clarendon Park, I made several little excursions from hence to view the northern parts of this county; a county so fruitful of wonders, that tho' I do not make antiquity my chief search, yet I must not pass it over entirely, where so much of it, and so well worth observation is to be found, which would look as if I either understood not the value of the study, or expected my readers should be satisfy'd with a total omission of it.

I have mention'd that this county is generally a vast continu'd body of high chalky hills, whose tops spread themselves into fruitful and pleasant downs and plains, upon which great flocks of sheep are fed, &c. But the reader is desir'd to observe these hills and plains are most beautifully intersected, and cut thro' by the course of divers pleasant and profitable rivers; in the course, and near the banks, of which there always is a chain of fruitful meadows, and rich pastures, and those interspers'd with innumerable pleasant towns, villages, and houses, and among them many of considerable magnitude; so that while you view the downs, and think the country wild and uninhabited; yet when you come to descend into these vales you are surpris'd with the most pleasant and fertile country in England.

There are no less than four of these rivers which meet all together, at, or near the city of Salisbury, especially the waters of three of them run thro' the streets of the city; the Nadder and the Willy, and the Avon, and the course of these three lead us thro' the whole mountainous part of the county, the two first joyn their waters at Wilton; the shire-town, tho' a place of no great notice now; and these are the waters which run

thro' the canal, and the gardens of Wilton House, the seat of
that ornament of nobility and learning, the Earl of Pembroke.

One cannot be said to have seen any thing that a man of
curiosity would think worth seeing in this county, and not have
been at Wilton House; but not the beautiful building, not the
antient trophy of a great family, not the noble scituation, not
all the pleasures of the gardens, parks, fountains, hare-warren,
or of whatever is rare either in art or nature are equal to, that
yet more glorious sight, of a noble princely palace, constantly
filled with its noble and proper inhabitants; viz. the lord and
proprietor, who is indeed a true patriarchal monarch, reigns
here with an authority agreeable to all his subjects (family);
and his reign is made agreeable, by his first practising the most
exquisite government of himself, and then guiding all under
him by the rules of honour and vertue; being also himself
perfectly master of all the needful arts of family government;
I mean needful to make that government, both easy, and pleasant to those who are under it, and who therefore willingly,
and by choice conform to it.

Here an exhaulted genius is the instructor, a glorious example
the guide, and a gentle well directed hand the governour and
law-giver to the whole; and the family like a well govern'd
city appears happy, flourishing and regular, groaning under
no grievance, pleas'd with what they enjoy, and enjoying every
thing which they ought to be pleas'd with.

Nor is the blessing of this noble resident extended to the
family only, but even to all the country round, who in their
degree feel the effects of the general beneficence; and where the
neighbourhood, however poor, receive all the good they can
expect, and are sure to have no injury, or oppression.

The canal before the house lyes parallel with the road, and
receives into it the whole river Willey, or at least is able to do
so; it may indeed be said, that the river is made into a canal;
when we come into the court-yards before the house there are
several peices of antiquity to entertain the curious; as particularly, a noble column of porphyry, with a marble statue
of Venus on the top of it. In Italy, and especially at Rome and
Naples, we see a great variety of fine columns, and some of
them of excellent workmanship, and antiquity, and at some of
the Courts of the Princes of Italy the like is seen; as especially at
the Court of Florence; but in England I do not remember to have
seen any thing like this, which as they told me is two and thirty
foot high and of excellent workmanship, and that it came last

from Candia, but formerly from Alexandria; what may belong to the history of it any further, I suppose is not known, at least they could tell me no more of it, who shew'd it me.

On the left of the court was formerly a large grotto, and curious water-works, and in a house, or shed, or part of the building which open'd with two folding doors, like a coach-house, a large equestrian statue of one of the ancestors of the family in compleat armour, as also another of a Roman emperor in brass, but the last time I had the curiosity to see this house, I mist that part; so that I suppos'd they were remov'd.

As the present Earl of Pembroke, the lord of this fine palace, is a nobleman of great personal merit, many other ways; so he is a man of learning, and reading, beyond most men of his lordship's high rank in this nation, if not in the world; and as his reading has made him a master of antiquity, and judge of such peices of antiquity, as he has had opportunity to meet with in his own travels, and otherwise in the world; so it has given him a love of the study, and made him a collector of valuable things, as well in painting as in sculpture, and other excellencies of art, as also of nature; in so much that Wilton-House is now a meer musæum, or a chamber of rarities, and we meet with several things there, which are to be found no where else in the world.

As his lordship is a great collector of fine paintings; so I know no nobleman's house in England, so prepar'd, as if built on purpose to receive them; the largest, and the finest peices that can be imagin'd extant in the world, might have found a place here capable to receive them; I say, they might have found, as if they could not now, which is in part true; for at present the whole house is so compleatly fill'd, that I see no room for any new peice to crowd in, without displacing some other fine peice that hung there before; as for the value of the peice, that might so offer to succeed the displac'd, that the great judge of the whole collection, the earl himself, must determine, and as his judgment is perfectly good, the best picture would be sure to possess the place. In a word: Here is without doubt the best, if not the greatest collection of rarities, and paintings, that are to be seen together, in any one nobleman's, or gentleman's house in England. The peice of our Saviour washing his disciples feet, which they shew you in one of the first rooms you go into, must be spoken of by every body that has any knowledge of painting, and is an admirable peice indeed.

You ascend the great stair case, at the upper end of the

hall, which is very large; at the foot of the stair-case you have a Bacchus large as the life, done in fine Peloponesian marble; carrying a young Bacchus on his arm, the young one eating grapes, and letting you see by his countenance, that he is pleas'd with the tast of them; nothing can be done finer, or more lively represent the thing intended; namely the gust of the appetite, which if it be not a passion, 'tis an affection, which is as much seen in the countenance, perhaps more than any other: One ought to stop every two steps of this stair-case, as we go up, to contemplate the vast variety of pictures, that cover the walls, and of some of the best masters in Europe, and yet this is but an introduction to what is beyond them.

When you are enter'd the appartments, such variety seizes you every way, that you scarce know to which hand to turn your self: First, on one side you see several rooms fill'd with paintings, as before, all so curious, and the variety such, that 'tis with reluctance, that you can turn from them; while looking another way, you are call'd off by a vast collection of busto's, and peices of the greatest antiquity of the kind, both Greek, and Romans; among these, there is one of the Roman emperor, Marcus Aurelius in *basso relievo*; I never saw any thing like what appears here, except in the chamber of rarieties at Munick in Bavaria.

Passing these, you come into several large rooms, as if contriv'd for the reception of the beautiful guests that take them up; one of these is near 70 foot long and the ceiling 26 foot high, with another adjoyning of the same height, and breadth, but not so long: Those together might be call'd the Great Gallery of Wilton, and might vie for paintings with the gallery of Luxemburg in the Fauxbourg of Paris.

These two rooms are fill'd with the family peices of the house of Herbert, most of them by Lilly, or Vandyke, and one in particularly, out does all that ever I met with, either at home, or abroad, 'tis done, as was the mode of painting at that time, after the manner of a family peice of King Charles I. with his queen, and children, which before the burning of White-Hall, I remember to hang at the east end of the Long Gallery in the palace.

This peice fills the farther end of the great room which I just now mention'd, it contains the Earl of Montgomery, ancestor of the house of Herbert, not then Earls of Pembroke, and his lady, sitting, and as big as the life; there are about them, their own five sons, and one daughter, and their daughter-in-law, who was daughter of the Duke of Buckingham, marry'd to the elder Lord Herbert, their eldest son; it is enough to say of this peice, 'tis worth the labour of any lover of art to go 500 miles to see it; and I am inform'd several gentlemen of quality have come from France almost on purpose; It would be endless to describe the whole set of the family pictures, which take up this room, unless we would enter into the roof-tree of the family, and set down a genealogical line of the whole house.

After we have seen this fine range of beauties, for such indeed they are; far from being at an end of your surprize, you have three or four rooms still upon the same floor, fill'd with wonders, as before: Nothing can be finer than the pictures themselves, nothing more surprising than the number of them; at length you descend the back-stairs, which are in themselves large, tho' not like the other: However, not a hands breadth is left to crowd a picture in of the smallest size, and even the upper rooms, which might be call'd garrets, are not naked, but have some very good peices in them.

Upon the whole, the genius of the noble collector may be seen in this glorious collection, than which, take them together, there is not a finer in any private hand in Europe, and in no hand at all in Britain, private or publick.

The gardens are on the south of the house, and extend themselves beyond the river, a branch of which runs thro' one part of them, and still south of the gardens in the great park, which extending beyond the vale, mounts the hill opening at the last to the great down, which is properly call'd by way of distinction, Salisbury-Plain, and leads from the city of Salisbury, to Shaftesbury; here also his lordship has a hare-warren (as 'tis call'd) tho' improperly; it has indeed been a sanctuary for the hares for many years; but the gentlemen complain that it marrs their game, for that as soon as they put up a hare for their sport, if it be any where within two or three miles, away she runs for the warren, and there is an end of their pursuits; on the other hand, it makes all the countrymen turn poachers, and destroy the hares, by what means they can; but this is a smaller matter, and of no great import one way or other.

From this pleasant and agreeable days work, I return'd to Clarendon, and the next day took another short tour to the hills, to see that celebrated peice of antiquity, the wonderful Stone-Henge, being six miles from Salisbury north, and upon the side of the river Avon, near the town of Amesbury: 'Tis needless, that I should enter here into any part of the dispute about which our learned antiquaries have so puzzl'd themselves, that several books, and one of them, in folio, has been publish'd about it; some alledging it to be a heathen, or pagan temple, and altar, or place of sacrifice, as Mr. Jones; others, a monument, or trophy of victory; others a monument for the dead, as Mr. Aubury, and the like: Again, some will have it be British, some Danish, some Saxon, some Roman, and some before them all, Phenician.

I shall suppose it, as the majority of all writers do, to be a monument for the dead, and the rather, because men's bones have been frequently dug up in the ground near them. The common opinion that no man could ever count them, that a baker carry'd a basket of bread, and laid a loaf upon every stone, and yet could never make out the same number twice; This, I take, as a meer country fiction, and a ridiculous one too; the reason why they cannot easily be told, is, that many of them lye half, or part buryed in the ground, and a peice here, and a peice there, only appearing above the grass, it cannot be known easily, which belong to one stone, and which to another, or which are separate stones, and which are joyned under ground to one another; otherwise, as to those which appear, they are easie to be told, and I have seen them told four times after one another, beginning every time at a different place, and every time they amounted to 72 in all; but then this was counting every peice of a stone of bulk, which appear'd at above the surface of the earth, and was not evidently part of, and adjoyning to another, to be a distinct and separate body, or stone by it self.

The form of this monument is not only describ'd but delineated in most authors, and indeed 'tis hard to know the first, but by the last; the figure was at first circular, and there were at least four rows or circles, within one another; the main stones were placed upright, and they were joyn'd on the top by cross stones, laid from one to another, and fastn'd with vast mortices and tenants: Length of time has so decay'd them, that not only most of the cross stones which lay on the top are fallen down, but many of the upright also, notwithstanding the weight of them is so prodigious great: How they came thither, or from whence, no stones of that kind being now to be found in any part of England near it, is still the mistery, for they are of such immense bulk that no engines, or carriages which we have in use in this age could stir them.

Doubtless they had some method in former days in foreign

countries, as well as here, to move heavier weights than we find practicable now; How else did Solomons workmen build the battlement, or additional wall to support the precipeice of Mount Moriah, on which the temple was built? which was all built of great stones of Parian marble, each stone being forty cubits long, and fourteen cubits broad, and eight cubits high, or thick, which reckoning each cubit at two foot and half of our measure, as the learned agree to do, was 100 foot long, 35 foot broad, and 20 foot thick.

These stones at Stonehenge, as Mr. Cambden describes them, and in which others agree, were very large, tho' not so large, the upright stones 24 foot high, 7 foot broad, 16 foot round; and weight 12 ton each; and the cross stones on the top, which he calls coronets, were 6 or 7 ton, but this does not seem equal, for if the cross stones weigh'd six, or seven ton, the others, as they appear now, were at least 5 or 6 times as big, and must weigh in proportion; and therefore, I must think their judgment much nearer the case who judge the upright stones at 16 ton, or thereabouts, supposing them to stand a great way into the earth, as 'tis not doubted but they do; and the coronets, or cross stones, at about two ton, which is very large too, and as much as their bulk can be thought to allow.

Upon the whole, we must take them as our ancestors have done; Namely, for an erection, or building so antient, that no history has handed down to us the original, as we find it then uncertain, we must leave it so: 'Tis indeed a reverend peice of antiquity, and 'tis a great loss that the true history of it is not known; But since it is not, I think the making so many conjectures at the reality, when they know they can but guess at it, and above all the insisting so long, and warmly on their private opinions, is but amusing themselves and us with a doubt, which perhaps lyes the deeper for their search into it.

The downs and plains in this part of England being so open, and the surface so little subject to alteration, there are more remains of antiquity to be seen upon them, than in other places; for example, I think they tell us there are three and fifty antient encampments, or fortifications to be seen in this one county, some whereof are exceeding plain to be seen, some of one form, some of another; some of one nation, some of another, British, Danish, Saxon, Roman, as at Ebb-down, Burywood, Oldburgh-Hill, Cummerford, Roundway-Down, St. Ann's-Hill, Bratton-Castle, Clay-Hill, Stournton-Park, Whitecole-Hill, Battlebury, Scrathbury, Yanesbury, Frippsbury, Suthbury-Hill, Amesbury,

Great Bodwyn, Easterley, Merdon, Aubery, Martenscil-Hill, Barbury-Castle, and many more.

Also the Barrows, as we all agree to call them, are very many in number in this county, and very obvious, having suffer'd very little decay. These are large hillocks of earth cast up, as the antients agree, by the soldiers over the bodies of their dead comrades slain in battle; several hundreds of these are to be seen, especially in the north part of this county, about Marlbro' and the downs, from thence to St. Ann's-Hill, and even every way, the downs are full of them.

I have done with matters of antiquity for this county, unless you will admit me to mention the famous parliament in the reign of Hen. II. held at Clarendon, where I am now writing, and another intended to be held there in Rich. 2d's time, but prevented by the barons, being then up in arms against the king.

Near this place at Farlo was the birth-place of the late Sir Stephen Fox, and where the town sharing in his good fortune, shews several marks of his bounty, as particularly, the building a new church from the foundation, and getting an Act of Parliament past, for making it parochial, it being but a chappel of ease before to an adjoyning parish: Also Sir Stephen built and endow'd an alms-house here for six poor women, with a master and a free-school; the master is to be a clergyman, and to officiate in the church, that is to say, is to have the living, which including the school is very sufficient.

I am now to pursue my first design, and shall take the west part of Wiltshire in my return, where are several things still to be taken notice of, and some very well worth our stay. In the mean time I went on to Langbro' a fine seat of my Lord Colerain, which is very well kept, tho' the family it seems is not much in this country, having another estate, and dwelling at Tottenham-High-Cross near London.

From hence in my way to the sea-side I came to New-Forest, of which I have said something already with relation to the great extent of ground, which lyes wast, and in which there is so great a quantity of large timber, as I have spoken of already.

This wast and wild part of the country was, as some record, lay'd open, and wast for a forest, and for game, by that violent tyrant William the Conqueror, and for which purpose he un- peopled the country, pull'd down the houses, and which was worse, the churches of several parishes or towns, and of abundance of villages, turning the poor people out of their habitations, and possessions, and laying all open for his deer: The same histories likewise record that two of his own blood and posterity, and particularly his immediate successor William Rufus lost their lives in this forest: One (viz.) the said William Rufus being shot with an arrow directed at a deer, which the king, and his company were hunting, and the arrow glancing on a tree, chang'd his course and struck the king full on the breast, and kill'd him; This they relate as a just judgment of God on the cruel devastation made here by the Conqueror; Be it so or not, as heaven pleases; but that the king was so kill'd, is certain, and they show the tree, on which the arrow glanc'd, to this day; in King Charles II. time, it was ordered to be surrounded with a pale, but as great part of the paleing is down with age; whether the tree be really so old, or not, is to me a great question; the action being near 700 year ago.

I cannot omit to mention here a proposal made a few years ago to the late Lord Treasurer, Godolphin, for re-peopling this forest, which for some reasons I can be more particular in, than any man now left alive, because I had the honour to draw up the scheme, and argue it before that noble lord, and some others who were principally concern'd at that time in bringing over, or rather providing for when they were come over, the poor inhabitants of the Palatinate; a thing in it self commendable, but as it was manag'd, made scandalous to England, and miserable to those poor people.

Some persons being ordered by that noble lord, above mention'd, to consider of measures, how the said poor people should be provided for, and whether they could be provided for, or no, without injury to the publick: The answer was grounded upon this maxim, that the number of inhabitants is the wealth and strength of a kingdom, provided those inhabitants were such, as by honest industry applied themselves to live by their labour, to whatsoever trades, or employments they were brought up: In the next place it was inquir'd, what employments those poor people were brought up to? It was answer'd, there were husbandmen, and artificers of all sorts, upon which the proposal was as follows.

NEW FOREST in Hampshire was singl'd out to
be the place.

Here it was propos'd to draw a great square-line, containing four thousand acres of land, marking out two large highways, or roads thro' the center, crossing both ways, so that there should be a thousand acres in each division, exclusive of the land contain'd in the said cross roads.

Then it was propos'd to single out twenty men, and their families, who should be recommended as honest industrious men, expert in, or at least capable of being instructed in husbandry, curing and cultivating of land, breeding and feeding cattle, and the like; To each of these should be parcell'd out in equal distributions, two hundred acres of this land, so that the whole four thousand acres should be fully distributed to the said twenty families, for which they should have no rent to pay, and be liable to no taxes, but such as provided for their own sick or poor, repairing their own roads, and the like: This exemption from rent and taxes, to continue for twenty years, and then to pay each 50l. a year to the queen; that is to say, to the Crown.

The form of the several farms would be laid out thus.

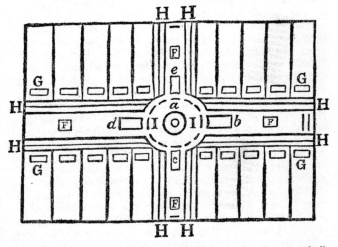

a the church, *b* the shambles, *c* the market house, *d* a town hall, *e* a conduit with stocks, &c. *F* the conduits, or wells, *G* houses, *H* the lands enclosed behind, *I* streets of houses for tradesmen.

To each of these families, who I wou'd now call farmers, it was propos'd to advance 200l. in ready money, as a stock to set them to work, to furnish them with cattle, horses, cows, hogs, &c. and to hire and pay labourers, to enclose, clear, and cure the land; which it would be suppos'd the first year would not be so much to their advantage as afterwards; allowing them timber out of the forest to build themselves houses, and barns, sheds, and offices, as they should have occasion; also for carts, waggons, ploughs, harrows, and the like necessary things, care to be taken, that the men and their families went to work forthwith according to the design.

Thus twenty families would be immediately supplyed, and provided for, for there would be no doubt, but these families with so much land given them gratis, and so much money to work with, would live very well; but what would this do for the support of the rest? who were suppos'd to be to every twenty farmers, forty or fifty families of other people; some of one trade, some of another, with women and children? to this it was answer'd, that these twenty farmers would by the consequence of their own settlements, provide for, and employ such a proportion of others of their own people, that by thus providing for twenty families in a place, the whole number of Palatinates would have been provided for, had they been 20000 more in number than they were, and that without being any burthen upon, or injury to the people of England; on the contrary, they would have been an advantage, and an addition of wealth and strength to the nation, and to the country in particular where they should be thus seated: For example;

As soon as the land was mark'd out, the farmers put in possession of it, and the money given them, they should be oblig'd to go to work, in order to their settlement; suppose it then to be in the spring of the year, when such work was most proper; First all hands would be requir'd, to fence, and part off the land, and clear it of the timber, or bushes, or what ever else was upon it, which requir'd to be remov'd: The first thing therefore which the farmers would do, would be to single out from the rest of their number, every one three servants, that is to say, two men, and a maid; less cou'd not answer the preparations they would be oblig'd to make, and yet work hard themselves also; by the help of these, they would with good management soon get so much of their land cur'd, fenc'd off, plow'd, and sow'd, as should yeild them a sufficiency of corn and kitchin stuff, the very first year, both for horse-meat, hog-meat, food for the family, and some to carry to market too, by which to bring in money to go farther on, as above.

At the first enterance, they were to have the tents allow'd

them to live in, which they then had from the Tower; but as soon as leisure, and conveniences admitted, every farmer was oblig'd to begin to build him a farm house, which he would do gradually, some and some, as he could spare time from his other works, and money from his little stock.

In order to furnish himself with carts, waggons, plows, harrows, wheel-barrows, hurdles, and all such necessary utentisils of husbandry; there would be an absolute necessity of wheelwrights, or cartwrights, one at least to each division.

Thus by the way, there would be employ'd three servants to each farmer, that makes sixty persons.

Four families of wheelwrights, one to each division: which suppose five in a family, makes 20 persons; suppose four head carpenters, with each three men, and as at first all would be building together, they would to every house building have at least one labourer, four families of carpenters, five to each family, and three servants, is thirty two persons, one labourer to each house building, is twenty persons more.

Thus here would be necessarily brought together, in the very first of the work 132 persons, besides the head farmers, who at five also to each family are hundred more, in all two hundred thirty two.

For the necessary supply of these with provisions, cloaths, houshold-stuff, &c. for all should be done among themselves; first, they must have at least four butchers with their families; twenty persons, four shoemakers with their families, and each shoemaker two journeymen for every trade; would encrease the number of customers to every trade: This is twenty eight persons more.

They would then require a hatmaker, a glover, at least two ropemakers, four taylors, three weavers of woollen, and three weavers of linnen, two basketmakers, two common brewers, ten or twelve shop-keepers to furnish chandlery and grocery wares; and as many for drapery and mercery, over and above what they could work, this makes two and forty families more, each at five in a family, which is two hundred and ten persons; all the labouring part of these must have at least two servants, the brewers more, which I cast up at forty more.

Add to these two ministers, one clerk, one sexton, or gravedigger with their families, two physicians, three apothecaries, two surgeons, less there could not be, only that for the beginning it might be said the physicians should be surgeons, and I take them so; this is forty five persons, besides servants; so that in short, to omit many tradesmen more who would be wanted among them, there would necessarily, and voluntarily follow, to these twenty families of farmers at least six hundred more of their own people.

It is no difficult thing to show that the ready money of 4000*l.* which the government was to advance to those twenty farmers, would employ and pay, and consequently subsist all these numerous dependants, in the works which must severally be done for them, for the first year; after which the farmers would begin to receive their own money back again; for all these tradesmen must come to their own market to buy corn, flesh, milk, butter, cheese, bacon, &c. which after the first year the farmers having no rent to pay, would have to spare sufficiently, and so take back their own money with advantage; I need not go on to mention, how by consequence provisions encreasing, and money circulating, this town should encrease in a very little time.

It was propos'd also that for the encouragement of all the handicraftsmen, and labouring poor, who either as servants, or as labourers for day-work, assisted the farmers or other tradesmen, they should have every man three acres of ground given them, with leave to build cottages upon the same, the allotments to be upon the waste, at the end of the cross-roads where they entered the town.

In the center of the square was laid out a circle of twelve acres of ground, to be cast into streets for inhabitants to build on, as their ability would permit; all that would build to have ground gratis for twenty years, timber out of the forest, and convenient yards, gardens and orchards allotted to every house.

In the great streets near where they cross each other, was to be built a handsome market-house, with a town-hall for parish or corporation business, doing justice and the like; also shambles, and in a handsome part of the ground mention'd to be laid out for streets, as near the center as might be, was to be ground laid out for the building a church, which every man should either contribute to the building of, in money, or give every tenth day of his time to assist in labouring at the building.

I have omitted many tradesmen, who would be wanted here, and would find a good livelihood among their country folks; only to get accidental work, as daymen, or labourers; of which such a town would constantly employ many, as also poor women for assistance in families, such as midwives, nurses, &c.

Adjacent to the town was to be a certain quantity of common land, for the benefit of the cottages; that the poor might have a few sheep, or cows as their circumstances requir'd; and this to be appointed at the several ends of the town.

There was a calculation made of what encrease here would be, both of wealth and people in twenty years in this town; what a vast consumption of provisions they would cause, more than the four thousand acres of land given them would produce; by which consumption and encrease, so much advantage would accrue to the publick stock, and so many subjects be added to the many thousands of Great Britain; who in the next age would be all true born Englishmen, and forget both the language, and nation from whence they came; and it was in order to this that two ministers were appointed, one of which should officiate in English, and the other in High Dutch; and withal to have them oblig'd by a law to teach all their children both to speak, read and write the English language.

Upon their encrease they would also want barbers, and glasiers, painters also, and plumbers; a wind-mill or two, and the millers and their families, a fulling-mill, and a cloth worker; as also a master clothier, or two, for making a manufacture among them for their own wear, and for employing the women and children; a dyer or two, for dying their manufactures; and, which above all, is not to be omitted, four families at least of smiths, with every one two servants; considering that besides all the family work, which continually employs a smith, all the shoeing of horses, all the iron-work of plows, carts, waggons, harrows, &c. must be wrought by them.

There was no allowance made for inns, and ale-houses, seeing it would be frequent that those who kept publick houses of any sort, would likewise have some other employment to carry on.

This was the scheme for settling the Palatinates, by which means twenty families of farmers, handsomely set up, and supported, would lay a foundation, as I have said, for six or seven hundred of the rest of their people; and as the land in New Forest is undoubtedly good, and capable of improvement by such cultivation, so other wastes in England are to be found as fruitful as that; and twenty such villages might have been erected, the poor strangers maintain'd, and the nation evidently be better'd by it; as to the money to be advanc'd, which in the case of twenty such settlements, at 4000*l.* each, would be 80000*l.* two things were answer'd to it.

1. That the annual rent to be receiv'd for all those lands after twenty years, would abundantly pay the publick for the first disbursses on the scheme above, that rent being then to amount to 40000*l*. per ann.

2. More money than would have done this, was expended, or rather thrown away upon them here, to keep them in suspense, and afterwards starve them; sending them a begging all over the nation, and shipping them off to perish in other countries: Where the mistake lay, is none of my business to enquire.

I reserv'd this account for this place, because I pass'd in this journey over the very spot where the design was laid out; namely, near Lindhurst, in the road from Rumsey to Limington, whither I now directed my course.

Limington is a little, but populous sea port, standing opposite to the Isle of Wight, in the narrow part of the streight, which ships some times pass thro', in fair weather, call'd, the Needles; and right against an ancient town of that island call'd Yarmouth, and which, in distinction from the great town of Yarmouth in Norfolk, is call'd South Yarmouth: This town of Limington is chiefly noted for making fine salt, which is indeed excellent good; and from whence all these south parts of England are supply'd, as well by water as by land carriage; and sometimes, tho' not often, they send salt to London, when contrary winds having kept the northern fleets back, the price at London has been very high; but this is very seldom and uncertain. Limington sends two members to Parliament, and this and her salt trade is all I can say to her; for tho' she is very well situated, as to the convenience of shipping, I do not find they have any foreign commerce, except it be what we call smugling, and roguing; which, I may say, is the reigning commerce of all this part of the English coast, from the mouth of the Thames to the Land's End of Cornwall.

From hence there are but few towns on the sea coast west, tho' there are several considerable rivers empty themselves into the sea, nor are there any harbours, or sea ports of any note, except Pool: As for Christ Church, tho' it stands at the mouth of the Avon, which, as I have said, comes down from Salisbury, and brings with it all the waters of the south and east parts of Wiltshire; and receives also the Stour and Piddle, two Dorsetshire rivers, which bring with them all the waters of the north part of Dorsetshire; yet it is a very inconsiderable poor place, scarce worth seeing, and less worth mentioning in this account;

only, that it sends two members to Parliament, which many poor towns in this part of England do, as well as that.

From hence I stept up into the country north-west, to see the ancient town of Wimburn, or Wimburnminster; There I found nothing remarkable, but the church, which is indeed a very great one, ancient, and yet very well built, with a very firm strong square tower, considerably high; but was, without doubt, much finer, when on the top of it, stood a most exquisite spire, finer and taller, if fame lyes not, than that at Salisbury, and, by its situation, in a plainer, flatter country, visible, no question, much farther: But this most beautiful ornament was blown down by a sudden tempest of wind, as they tell us, in the year 1622.

The church remains a venerable piece of antiquity, and has in it the remains of a place, once, much more in request than it is now; for here are the monuments of several noble families; and in particular of one king, viz. King Etheldred, who was slain in battle by the Danes: He was a prince fam'd for piety and religion, and, according to the zeal of these times, was esteem'd as a martyr; because venturing his life against the Danes, who were heathens, he died fighting for his religion and his country. The inscription upon his grave is preserv'd, and has been carefully repair'd, so as to be easily read, and is as follows:

In hoc loco quiescit Corpus S. Etheldredi, Regis West Saxonum, Martyris, qui Anno Dom. DCCCLXXII. xxiii. Aprilis per Manus Danorum Paganorum Occubuit.

In English thus:

Here rests the body of Holy Etheldred, King of the West Saxons, and martyr, who fell by the hands of the pagan Danes, in the year of our Lord 872, the 23d of April.

Here are also the monuments of the great Marchioness of Exeter, mother of Edward Courtney, Earl of Devonshire, and last of the family of Courtneys who enjoy'd that honour; as also of John de Beaufort Duke of Somerset, and his wife, grand-mother of King Henry VII. by her daughter Margaret, Countess of Richmond.

This last lady I mention, because she was foundress of a very fine free-school, which has since been enlarg'd, and had a new benefactress in Queen Elizabeth, who has enlarg'd the stipend and annex'd it to the foundation: The famous Cardinal Pool was dean of this church before his exaltation.

Having said this of the church, I have said all that is worth naming of the town; except that the inhabitants, who are

many, and poor, are chiefly maintain'd by the manufacture of
knitting stockings, which employs great part indeed of the
county of Dorset, of which this is the first town eastward.

South of this town, over a sandy wild and barren country,
we came to Pool, a considerable sea-port, and indeed the most
considerable in all this part of England; for here I found some
ships, some merchants, and some trade; especially, here were
a good number of ships fitted out every year to the Newfoundland fishing, in which the Pool men were said to have been
particularly successful for many years past.

The town sits in the bottom of a great bay, or inlet of the
sea, which entring at one narrow mouth opens to a very great
breadth within the entrance, and comes up to the very shoar of
this town; it runs also west up almost to the town of Wareham,
a little below which, it receives the rivers Froom and Piddle, the
two principal rivers of the county.

This place is famous for the best, and biggest oysters in all
this part of England, which the people of Pool pretend to be
famous for pickling, and they are barrell'd up here, and sent
not only to London, but to the West Indies, and to Spain, and
Italy, and other parts. 'Tis observ'd more pearl are found in the
Pool oysters, and larger than in any other oysters about England.

As the entrance into this large bay is narrow, so it is made
narrower by an island, call'd Branksey, which lying in the very
mouth of the passage, divides it into two, and where there is an
old castle, call'd Branksey Castle, built to defend the entrance,
and this strength was very great advantage to the trade of this
port, in the time of the late war with France.

Wareham is a neat town, and full of people, having a share
of trade with Pool it self, it shows the ruins of a large town,
and 'tis apparent has had eight churches, of which they have
three remaining.

South of Wareham, and between the bay I have mention'd
and the sea, lyes a large tract of land, which being surrounded
by the sea, except on one side is call'd an island, tho' it is really
what should be call'd a peninsula; this tract of land is better
inhabited than the sea coast of this west end of Dorsetshire
generally is, and the manufacture of stockings is carry'd on
there also; it is called the Isle of Purbeck, and has in the middle
of it a large market-town, call'd Corf, and from the famous
castle there, the whole town is now call'd Corf-Castle, it is a
corporation, sending members to Parliaments.

This part of the country is eminent for vast quarreys of

stone, which is cut out flat, and us'd in London in great quantities
for paving court-yards, alleys, avenues to houses, kitchins, foot-
ways on the sides of the high-streets, and the like; and is very
profitable to the place, as also in the number of shipping employ'd
in bringing it to London. There are also several rocks of very
good marble, only that the veins in the stone are not black and
white, as the Italian, but grey, red, and other colours.

From hence to Weymouth, which is —— miles we rode in
view of the sea; the country is open, and in some respects
pleasant, but not like the northern parts of the county, which
are all fine carpet ground, soft as velvet, and the herbage,
sweet as garden herbs, which makes their sheep be the best in
England, if not in the world, and their wool fine to an extream.

I cannot omit here a small adventure, which was very surprizing to me on this journey; passing this plain country, we
came to an open peice of ground where a neighbouring gentleman had at a great expence laid out a proper peice of land for
a Decoy, or Duck-coy, as some call it; the works were but newly
done, the planting young, the ponds very large, and well made;
but the proper places for shelter of the fowl not cover'd, the trees
not being grown, and men were still at work improving, and
enlarging, and planting on the adjoyning heath, or common:
Near the decoy keeper's house, were some places where young
decoy-ducks were hatch'd, or otherwise kept to fit them for their
work; To preserve them from vermin, polecats, kites, and such
like, they had set traps, as is usual in such cases, and a gibbet
by it, where abundance of such creatures as were taken were
hang'd up for show.

While the decoy man was busy showing the new-works,
he was alarm'd with a great cry about this house for Help,
Help, and away he run, like the wind, guessing, as we suppos'd,
that something was catch'd in the trap.

It was a good big boy about 13 or 14 year old, that cry'd out,
for coming to the place, he found a great fowl catch'd by the
leg in the trap, which yet was so strong, and so outrageous,
that the boy going too near him, he flew at him, and frighted
him, bit him, and beat him with his wings, for he was too strong
for the boy; as the master ran from the decoy, so another man-
servant ran from the house, and finding a strange creature fast
in the trap, not knowing what it was, laid at him with a great
stick; the creature fought him a good while, but at length he
struck him an unlucky blow, which quieted him; after this we
all came up to see what was the matter, and found a monstruous

eagle caught by the leg in the trap, and kill'd by the fellow's cudgel, as above.

When the master came to know what it was, and that his man had kill'd it, he was ready to kill the fellow for his pains, for it was a noble creature indeed, and would have been worth a great deal to the man to have it shown about the country, or to have sold to any gentleman curious in such things; but the eagle was dead, and there we left it: 'Tis probable this eagle had flown over the sea from France, either there, or at the Isle of Weight, where the Channel is not so wide; for we do not find that any eagles are known to breed in those parts of Britain.

From hence we turn'd up to Dorchester, the county town, tho' not the largest town in the county; Dorchester is indeed a pleasant agreeable town to live in, and where I thought the people seem'd less divided into factions and parties, than in other places; for though here are divisions and the people are not all of one mind, either as to religion, or politicks, yet they did not seem to separate with so much animosity as in other places: Here I saw the Church of England clergymen, and the Dissenting minister, or preacher drinking tea together, and conversing with civility and good neighbourhood, like catholick Christians, and men of a catholick, and extensive charity: The town is populous, tho' not large, the streets broad, but the buildings old, and low; however, there is good company and a good deal of it; and a man that coveted a retreat in this world might as agreeably spend his time, and as well in Dorchester, as in any town I know in England.

The downs round this town are exceeding pleasant, and come up on every side, even to the very streets end; and here it was that they told me, that there were 600 thousand sheep fed on the downs, within six miles of the town; that is, six miles every way, which is twelve miles in diameter, and thirty six miles in circumference. This I say, I was told, I do not affirm it to be true; but when I viewed the country round, I confess I could not but incline to believe it.

It is observable of these sheep, that they are exceeding fruitful, and the ews generally bringing two lambs, and they are for that reason bought by all the farmers thro' the east part of England, who come to Burford Fair in this country to buy them, and carry them into Kent and Surry eastward, and into Buckinghamshire, and Bedfordshire, and Oxfordshire north, even our Bansted Downs in Surrey, so fam'd for good mutton, is supply'd from this place: The grass, or herbage of these downs is full of the sweetest, and the most aromatick plants, such as nourish the sheep to a strange degree, and the sheeps dung again nourishes that herbage to a strange degree; so that the valleys are render'd extreamly fruitful, by the washing of the water in hasty showers from off these hills.

An eminent instance of this is seen at Amesbury in Wiltshire, the next county to this, for it is the same thing in proportion over this whole county: I was told that at this town there was a meadow on the bank of the river Avon, which runs thence to Salisbury, which was let for 12l. a year per acre for the grass only: This I enquir'd particularly after, at the place, and was assur'd by the inhabitants as one man, that the fact was true, and was shew'd the meadows; the grass which grew on them was such as grew to the length of ten or twelve foot, rising up to a good height, and then taking root again, and was of so rich a nature as to answer very well such an extravagant rent.

The reason they gave for this, was the extraordinary richness of the soil, made so, as above, by the falling, or washing of the rains from the hills adjacent, by which tho' no other land thereabouts had such a kind of grass, yet all other meadows, and low grounds of the valley were extreamly rich in proportion.

There are abundance of good families, and of very antient lines in the neighbourhood of this town of Dorchester, as the Napiers, the Courtneys, Strangeways, Seymours, Banks, Tregonells, Sedenhams, and many others, some of which have very great estates in the county, and in particular Colonel Strangeways, Napier, and Courtney. The first of these is master of the famous swannery, or nursery of swans, the like of which I believe is not in Europe; I wonder any man should pretend to travel over this country, and pass by it too, and then write his account, and take no notice of it.

From Dorchester it is six miles to the sea side south, and the ocean in view almost all the way: The first town you come to is Weymouth, or Weymouth and Melcomb, two towns lying at the mouth of a little rivulet, which they call the Wey, but scarce claims the name of a river; however, the entrance makes a very good, tho' small harbour, and they are joyn'd by a wooden bridge; so that nothing but the harbour parts them; yet they are seperate corporations, and choose each of them two Members of Parliament, just as London and Southwark.

Weymouth is a sweet, clean, agreeable town, considering its low situation, and close to the sea; 'tis well built, and has a great many good substantial merchants in it; who drive a considerable trade, and have a good number of ships belonging to the town: They carry on now, in time of peace, a trade with France; but besides this, they trade also to Portugal, Spain, Newfoundland, and Virginia; and they have a large correspondence also up in the country for the consumption of their returns; especially the wine trade, and the Newfoundland trade are considerable here.

Without the harbour is an old castle, call'd Sandfoot Castle, and over-against them, where there is a good road for ships to put in on occasions of bad weather, is Portland Castle, and the road is call'd Portland Road: While I was here once, there came a merchant ship into that road, call'd Portland Road, under a very hard storm of wind; she was homeward bound from Oporto for London, laden with wines, and as she came in, she made signals of distress to the town, firing guns for help, and the like, as is usual in such cases; it was in the dark of the night that the ship came in, and, by the help of her own pilot, found her way into the road, where she came to an anchor, but, as I say, fir'd guns for help.

The venturous Weymouth-men went off, even before it was light, with two boats to see who she was, and what condition she was in, and found she was come to an anchor, and had struck her top-masts; but that she had been in bad weather, had lost an anchor and cable before, and had but one cable to trust to, which did hold her, but was weak; and as the storm continued to blow, they expected every hour to go on shore, and split to pieces.

Upon this, the Weymouth boats came back with such diligence, that, in less than three hours, they were on board them again with an anchor and cable, which they immediately bent in its place, and let go to assist the other, and thereby secur'd the ship: 'Tis true, that they took a good price of the master for the help they gave him; for they made him draw a bill on his owners at London for 12l. for the use of the anchor, cable, and boat, besides some gratuities to the men: But they sav'd the ship and cargo by it, and in three or four days the weather was calm, and he proceeded on his voyage, returning the anchor and cable again; so that, upon the whole, it was not so extravagant as at first I thought it to be.

The Isle of Portland, on which the castle I mention'd stands, lies right against this port of Weymouth: Hence it is, that our best and whitest free stone comes, with which the cathedral of

St. Paul's, the Monument, and all the publick edifices in the city of London, are chiefly built; and 'tis wonderful, and well worth the observation of a traveller to see the quarries in the rocks, from whence they are cut out, what stones, and of what prodigious a size are cut out there.

The island is indeed little more than one continued rock of free stone, and the height of the land is such, that from this island they see, in clear weather, above half over the Channel to France, tho' the Channel here is very broad; the sea off of this island, and especially to the west of it, is counted the most dangerous part of the British Channel: Due south, there is almost a continued disturbance in the waters, by reason of what they call two tides meeting, which I take to be no more than the setts of the currents from the French coast, and from the English shore meeting: This they call Portland Race; and several ships, not aware of these currents, have been embay'd to the west of Portland, and been driven on shore on the beach, (of which I shall speak presently) and there lost.

To prevent this danger, and guide the mariner in these distresses, they have, within these few months, set up two light-houses on the two points of that island; and they had not been many months set up, with the directions given to the publick for their bearings, but we found three outward-bound East-India ships which were in distress in the night, in a hard extream gale of wind, were so directed by those lights, that they avoided going on shore by it, which, if the lights had not been there, would inevitably happen'd to their destruction.

This island, tho' seemingly miserable, and thinly inhabited, yet the inhabitants being almost all stone-cutters, we found there was no very poor people among them; and when they collected money for the rebuilding St. Paul's, they got more in this island than in the great town of Dorchester, as we were told.

Tho' Portland stands a league off from the main land of Britain, yet it is almost joyn'd by a prodigious riffe of beach, that is to say, of small stones cast up by the sea, which runs from the island so near the shore of England, that they ferry over with a boat and a rope, the water not being above half a stones throw over; and the said riffe of beach ending, as it were, at that inlet of water, turns away west, and runs parallel with the shore quite to Abbotsbury, which is a town about seven miles beyond Weymouth.

I name this for two reasons; first, to explain again what I said before, of ships being embay'd and lost here: This is when ships coming from the westward omit to keep a good offing, or are taken short by contrary winds, and cannot weather the high land of Portland, but are driven between Portland and the main land; if they can come to an anchor, and ride it out, well and good, and if not, they run on shore on that vast beach, and are lost without remedy.

On the inside of this beach, and between it, and the land, there is, as I have said, an inlet of water, which they ferry over, as above, to pass and repass to and from Portland: This inlet opens at about two miles west, and grows very broad, and makes a kind of lake within the land of a mile and a half broad, and near three miles in length, the breadth unequal. At the farthest end west of this water is a large duck-coy, and the verge of the water well grown with wood, and proper groves of trees for cover for the foul; in the open lake, or broad part, is a continual assembly of swans: Here they live, feed and breed, and the number of them is such, that, I believe, I did not see so few as 7 or 8000. Here they are protected, and here they breed in abundance; we saw several of them upon the wing, very high in the air, whence we supposed, that they flew over the riffe of beach, which parts the lake from the sea to feed on the shores as they thought fit, and so came home again at their leisure.

From this duck-coy west, the lake narrows, and at last almost closes, till the beach joyns the shore; and so Portland may be said not to be an island, but part of the continent; and now we came to Abbotsbury, a town anciently famous for a great monastery, and now eminent for nothing but its ruins.

From hence we went on to Bridport, a pretty large corporation town on the sea shore, tho' without a harbour: Here we saw boats all the way on the shore fishing for mackerell, which they take in the easiest manner imaginable; for they fix one end of the net to a pole, set deep into the sand, then the net being in a boat, they row right out into the water some length, then turn, and row parallel with the shore, vering out the net all the while, till they have let go all the net, except the line at the end, and then the boat rows on shore, when the men haling the net to the shore at both ends, bring to shore with it such fish, as they surrounded in the little way they rowed; this, at that time, proved to be an incredible number, insomuch, that the men could hardly draw them on shore: As soon as the boats had brought their fish on shore, we observed a guard, or watch, placed on the shore in several places, who we found had their eye not on the fishermen, but on the country people, who came down to the shore to buy their fish; and very sharp we found they were; and some that came with small carts were obliged to go back empty, without any fish. When we came to enquire into the particulars of this, we found, that these were officers placed on the shore by the justices and magistrates of the towns about, who were order'd to prevent the country farmers buying the mackerell to dung their land with them, which was thought to be dangerous, as to infection: In short, such was the plenty of fish that year, that mackerell, the finest and largest I ever saw, were sold at the sea side a hundred for a penny.

From Bridport, a town in which we see nothing remarkable, we came to Lime, the town particularly made famous by the landing of the Duke of Monmouth, and his unfortunate troop, in the time of King James II. of which I need say nothing, the history of it being so recent in the memory of so many living.

This is a town of good figure, and has in it several eminent merchants, who carry on a considerable trade to France, Spain, Newfoundland, and the Streights; and tho' they have neither creek or bay, road, or river, they have a good harbour; but 'tis such a one as is not in all Britain besides, if there is such a one in any part of the world.

It is a massy pile of building, consisting of high and thick walls of stone, rais'd, at first, with all the methods that skill and art could devise, but maintain'd now with very little difficulty: The walls are rais'd in the main sea, at a good distance from the shore; it consists of one main and solid wall of stone, large enough for carts and carriages to pass on the top, and to admit houses and ware houses to be built on it; so that it is broad as a street; opposite to this, but farther into the sea, is another wall of the same workmanship, which crosses the end of the first wall, and comes about with a tail, parallel to the first wall.

Between the point of the first or main wall, is the entrance into the port, and the second, or opposite wall, breaking the violence of the sea from the entrance, the ships go into the basin, as into a peer, or harbour, and ride there as secure as in a mill pond, or as in a wet dock.

The town's people have the benefit of this wonderful harbour, and it is carefully kept in repair, as indeed it behoves them to do; but they could give me nothing of the history of it; nor do they, as I could perceive, know anything of the original of it, or who built it; it was lately almost beaten down by a storm, but is repair'd again.

This work is call'd the COBB: The custom-house officers have a lodge and warehouse upon it, and there were several ships of very good force, and rich in value, in the basin of it when I was there: It might be strengthen'd with a fort, and the walls themselves are firm enough to carry what guns they please to plant upon it; but they did not seem to think it needful; and as the shore is convenient for batteries, they have some guns planted in proper places, both for the defence of the COBB, and the town also.

This town is under the government of a mayor and aldermen, and may pass for a place of wealth, considering the bigness of it: Here we found the merchants began to trade in the pitchard fishing, tho' not to so considerable a degree as they do farther west; the pitchards seldom coming up so high eastward as Portland, and not very often so high as Lime.

It was in sight of these hills that Queen Elizabeth's fleet, under the command of the Lord Howard of Effingham, then admiral, began first to engage in a close, and resolv'd fight with the invincible Spanish Armada, in 1588: Maintaining the fight, the Spaniards making eastward, till they came the length of Portland Race, where they gave it over; the Spaniards having receiv'd considerable damage, and keeping then closer together. Off of the same place was a desperate engagement in the year 1672, between the English and Dutch, in which the Dutch were worsted, and driven over to the coast of France, and then glad to make home to refit and repair.

While we stay'd here some time viewing this town and coast, we had opportunity to observe the pleasant way of conversation, as it is manag'd among the gentlemen of this county, and their families, which are without reflection some of the most polite and well bred people in the isle of Britain: As their hospitality is very great, and their bounty to the poor remarkable, so their generous friendly way of living with, visiting, and associating one with another is as hard to be describ'd, as it is really to be admir'd; they seem to have a mutual confidence in, and friendship with one another, as if they were all relations; nor did I observe the sharping tricking temper, which is too much crept in among the gameing and horse-racing gentry in some parts of England, to be so much known among them, any otherwise than to be abhorr'd; and yet they sometimes play too, and make matches, and horse-races, as they see occasion.

The ladies here do not want the help of assemblies to assist in match-making; or half-pay officers to run away with their daughters, which the meetings, call'd assemblies in some other parts of England, are recommended for: Here's no Bury Fair, where the women are scandalously said to carry themselves to market, and where every night they meet at the play, or at the assembly for intreague, and yet I observ'd that the women do not seem to stick on hand so much in this country, as in those countries, where those assemblies are so lately set up; the reason of which I cannot help saying, if my opinion may bear any weight, is, that the Dorsetshire ladies are equal in beauty, and may be superiour in reputation; In a word, their reputation seems here to be better kept; guarded by better conduct, and manag'd with more prudence, and yet the Dorsetshire ladies, I assure you, are not nuns, they do not go vail'd about streets, or hide themselves when visited; but a general freedom of conversation, agreeable, mannerly, kind, and good runs thro' the whole body of the gentry of both sexes, mix'd with the best of behaviour, and yet govern'd by prudence and modesty; such as I no where see better in all my observation, thro' the whole isle of Britain. In this little interval also I visited some of the biggest towns in the north-west part of this county, as Blandford, a town on the river Stour in the road between Salisbury and Dorchester, a handsome well built town, but chiefly famous for making the finest bonelace in England, and where they shew'd me some so exquisitely fine, as I think I never saw better in Flanders, France or Italy, and which they said, they rated at above 30*l.* sterling a yard; but I suppose there was not much of this to be had, but 'tis most certain, that they make exceeding rich lace in that county, such as no part of England can equal.

From thence I went west to Stourbridge, vulgarly call'd Strabridge; the town, and the country round is employ'd in the manufacture of stockings, and which was once famous for making the finest, best, and highest priz'd knit stockings in England; but that trade now is much decay'd by the encrease of the knitting-stocking engine, or frame, which has destroyed the hand knitting-trade for fine stockings thro' the whole kingdom, of which I shall speak more in its place.

From hence I came to Shireburn, a large and populous town, with one collegiate, or conventual church, and may properly claim to have more inhabitants in it than any town in Dorsetshire, tho' it is neither the county town, or does it send members to Parliament; the church is still a reverend pile, and shews the face of great antiquity. Here begins the Wiltshire medley cloathing, tho' this town be in Dorsetshire; of which I shall speak at large in its place, and therefore I omit any discourse of it here.

Shaftsbury is also on the edge of this county, adjoining to Wiltshire and Dorsetshire, being 14 miles from Salisbury, over that fine down or carpet ground, which they call particularly, or properly Salisbury Plain. It has neither house or town in view all the way, and the road which often lyes very broad, and branches off insensibly, might easily cause a traveller to loose his way, but there is a certain never failing assistance upon all these downs for telling a stranger his way, and that is the number of shepherds feeding, or keeping their vast flocks of sheep, which are every where in the way, and who, with a very little pains, a traveller may always speak with. Nothing can be like it, the Arcadians plains of which we read so much pastoral trumpery in the poets, could be nothing to them.

This Shaftsbury is now a sorry town, upon the top of a high hill, and which closes the plain, or downs, and whence nature presents you a new scene or prospect, (viz.) of Somerset and Wiltshire, where 'tis all enclosed, and grown with woods, forests, and planted hedge-rows: The country rich, fertile and populous, the towns and houses standing thick, and being large and full of inhabitants, and those inhabitants fully employ'd in the richest and most valuable manufacture in the world, (viz.) the English cloathing, as well, the medley, or mixt clothing, as whites; as well for the home trade, as the foreign trade; of which I shall take leave to be very particular in my return thro' the west and north part of Wiltshire, in the latter part of this work.

In my return to my western progress, I pass'd some little part of Somersetshire, as thro' Evil, or Yeovil, upon the river Ivil, in going to which we go down a long steep hill, which they call Babylon-Hill; but from what original I could find none of the country people to inform me.

This Yeovil is a market town of good resort, and some clothing is carry'd on, in, and near it, but not much, its main manufacture at this time is making of gloves.

It cannot pass my observation here, that when we are come this length from London, the dialect of the English tongue, or the country way of expressing themselves is not easily understood, it is so strangely altered; it is true, that it is so in many parts of England besides, but in none in so gross a degree as in this part; This way of boorish country speech, as in Ireland, it is call'd the brogue upon the tongue; so here 'tis call'd *jouring* and 'tis certain, that tho' the tongue be all meer natural English, yet those that are but a little acquainted with them, cannot understand one half of what they say: It is not possible to explain this fully by writing, because the difference is not so much in the orthography of words, as in the tone, and diction; their abridging the speech, *cham* for *I am*, *chil* for *I will*, *don*, for *put on*, and *doff*, for *put off*, and the like. And I cannot omit a short story here on this subject; coming to a relations house, who was a school-master at Martock in Somersetshire, I went into his school to beg the boys a play day, as is usual in such cases; I should have said to beg the master a play day, but that by the way; coming into the school, I observ'd one of the lowest scholars was reading his lesson to the usher, which lesson it seems was a chapter in the Bible, so I sat down by the master, till the boy had read out his chapter: I observ'd the boy read a little oddly in the tone of the country, which made me the more attentive, because on enquiry, I found that the words were the same, and the orthography the same as in all our Bibles. I observ'd also the boy read it out with his eyes still on the book, and his head like a meer boy, moving from side to side, as the lines reach'd cross the columns of the book; his lesson was in the Cant. 5. 3. of which the words are these,

"I have put off my coat, how shall I put it on, I have wash'd my feet, how shall I defile them?"

The boy read thus, with his eyes, as I say, full on the text.

"Chav a doffed my cooat, how shall I don't, chav a wash'd my veet, how shall I moil'em?"

How the dexterous dunce could form his mouth to express so readily the words, (which stood right printed in the book) in his country jargon, I could not but admire; I shall add to this another peice as diverting, which also happen'd in my knowledge at this very town of Yeovil, tho' some years ago.

There liv'd a good substantial family in the town, not far from the Angel Inn, a well known house, which was then, and I suppose is still the chief inn of the town. This family had a dog, which among his other good qualities, for which they kept him (for he was a rare house dog) had this bad one, that he was a most notorious thief; but withal, so cunning a dog, and managed himself so warily, that he preserved a mighty good reputation among the neighbourhood; as the family was well beloved in the town, so was the dog; he was known to be a very useful servant to them, especially in the night, when he was fierce as a lion, but in the day the gentlest, lovingest creature that could be, and as they said, all the neighbours had a good word for this dog.

It happen'd that the good wife, or mistress at the Angel Inn, had frequently missed several peices of meat out of the pail, as they say, or powdering-tub, as we call it; and that some very large peices; 'tis also to be observ'd the dog did not stay to eat (what he took) upon the spot, in which case some peices, or bones, or fragments might be left, and so it might be discover'd to be a dog; but he made cleaner work, and when he fasten'd upon a peice of meat he was sure to carry it quite away, to such retreats as he knew he could be safe in, and so feast upon it at leisure.

It happen'd at last, as with most thieves it does, that the inn-keeper was too cunning for him, and the poor dog was nabb'd, taken in the fact, and could make no defence.

Having found the thief, and got him in custody, the master of the house, a good humour'd fellow, and loth to disoblige the dog's master, by executing the criminal, as the dog-law directs; mitigates his sentence, and handled him as follows; first taking out his knife, he cut off both his ears, and then bringing him to the threshold, he chop'd off his tail; and having thus effectually dishonour'd the poor cur among his neighbours, he tyed a string about his neck, and a peice of paper to the string directed to his master, and with these witty west country verses on it.

To my honour'd master —— Esq;

> Hail master a cham a' com hoam
> So cut as an ape, and tail have I noan,
> For stealing of beef, and pork, out of the pail,
> For thease they'v cut my ears, for th' wother my tail;
> Nea measter, and us tell thee more nor that
> And's come there again, my brains will be flat.

I could give many more accounts of the different dialects of the people of this country, in some of which they are really not to be understood, but the particulars have little or no diversion in them, they carry it such a length, that we see their jouring speech even upon their monuments, and grave-stones; As for example, even in some of the church-yards of the city of Bristol, I saw this excellent poetry after some other lines—

> And when that thou doest hear of thick,
> Think of the glass that runneth quick.

But I proceed into Devonshire, from Evil we came to Crookorn, thence to Chard, and from thence into the same road I was in before at Honiton.

This is a large and beautiful market-town, very populous, and well built, and is so very remarkably pav'd with small pebbles, that on either sides the way a little channel is left shouldered up on the sides of it; so that it holds a small stream of fine clear running water with a little square dipping place left at every door, so that every family in the town has a clear clean running river, (as it may be call'd) just at their own door, and this so much finer, so much pleasanter, and agreeable to look on, then that at Salisbury, which they boast so much of, that in my opinion, there is no comparison.

Here we see the first of the great serge manufacture of Devonshire, a trade too great to be describ'd in miniature, as it must be, if I undertake it here; and which takes up this whole county, which is the largest and most populous in England, Yorkshire excepted, (which ought to be esteem'd three counties, and is indeed divided as such into the East, West and North Riding;) but Devonshire one entire county, is so full of great towns, and those towns so full of people, and those people so universally employ'd in trade, and manufactures, that not only it cannot be equall'd in England, but perhaps not in Europe.

In my travel thro' Dorsetshire, I ought to have observ'd that the biggest towns in that county sent no members to Parliament, and that the smallest did; that is to say, that Sherborn, Blandford, Winbornminster, Sturmister, and several other towns choose no members, whereas Weymouth, Melcom, and Bridport, were all burgess towns; but now we come to Devonshire, we find almost all the great towns, and some smaller choosing members also; It is true, there are some large populous towns that do not choose, but then there are so many that do, that the county seems to have no injustice, for they send up six and twenty members.

However, as I say above, there are several great towns which do not choose Parliament men, of which Bidiford is one, Crediton or Kirton another, Ilfracomb a third, but those excepted the principal towns in the county do all choose Members of Parliament.

Honiton is one of those, and may pass not only for a pleasant good town, as before, but stands in the best and pleasantest part of the whole county; and I cannot but recommend it to any gentlemen that travel this road, that if they please to observe the prospect for half a mile, till their coming down the hill, and to the entrance into Honiton, the view of the country is the most beautiful landskip in the world, a meer picture; and I do not remember the like in any one place in England; 'tis observable that the market of this town was kept originally on the Sunday, till it was chang'd by the direction of King John.

From Honiton the country is exceeding pleasant still, and on the road they have a beautiful prospect almost all the way to Exeter, which is twelve miles; on the left hand of this road lyes that part of the county, which they call the South Hams, and which is famous for the best cyder in that part of England; also the town of St. Mary Oterey, commonly call'd St. Mary Autree: They tell us the name is deriv'd from the river Ottery, and that, from the multitude of otters found always in that river, which however to me seems fabulous; nor does there appear to be any such great number of otters in that water, or in the county about, more than is usual in other counties, or in other parts of the county about them; they tell us they send 20000 hogsheds of cyder hence every year to London, and which is still worse, that it is most of it bought there by the merchants to mix with their wines, which if true, is not much to the reputations of the London vintners; but that by the by.

From hence we came to Exeter, a city famous for two things, which we seldom find unite in the same town, (viz.) that 'tis full of gentry, and good company, and yet full of trade and manufactures also; the serge market held here every week is very well worth a strangers seeing, and next to the Brigg-Market at Leeds in Yorkshire, is the greatest in England. The people assur'd me that at this market is generally sold from 60 to 70 to 80, and sometimes a hundred thousand pounds value in serges in a week. I think 'tis kept on Mondays.

They have the river Esk here, a very considerable river, and principal in the whole county; and within three miles, or thereabouts, it receives ships of any ordinary burthen, the port there being call'd Topsham; but now by the application, and at the expence of the citizens, the channel of the river is so widened, deepen'd, and cleans'd from the shoal, which would otherwise interrupt the navigation, that the ships come now quite up to the city, and there with ease both deliver and take in their lading.

This city drives a very great correspondence with Holland, as also directly to Portugal, Spain and Italy; shipping off vast quantities of the woollen-manufactures, especially, to Holland, the Dutch giving very large commissions here for the buying of serges perpetuan's, and such goods; which are made not only in and about Exeter, but at Crediton, Honiton, Culliton, St. Mary Autry, Newton-Bushell, Ashburton and especially at Tiverton, Cullumbton, Bampton, and all the north east part of the county, which part of the county is, as it may be said, fully employ'd, the people made rich, and the poor that are properly so call'd, well subsisted, and employ'd by it.

Excester is a large rich, beautiful, populous, and was once a very strong city; but as to the last, as the castle, the walls, and all the old works are demolish'd, so were they standing, the way of managing seiges, and attacks of towns is such now, and so alter'd from what it was in those days, that Excester in the utmost strength it could ever boast, would not now hold out five days open trenches; nay, would hardly put an army to the trouble of opening trenches against it at all. This city was famous in the late civil unnatural war, for its loyalty to the king, and for being a sanctuary to the queen, where her majesty resid'd for sometime, and here she was deliver'd of a daughter, being the Princess Henrietta Maria, of whom our histories give a particular account, so I need say no more of it here.

The cathedral church of this city is an antient beauty, or as it may be said, it is beautiful for its antiquity; But it has been so fully, and often described that it would look like a meer coppying from others to mention it: There is a good library kept in it, in which are some manuscripts, and particularly an old missal, or mass-book, the leaves of velum, and famous for its most exquisite writing.

This county, and this part of it in particular, has been famous for the birth of several eminent men, as well for learning, as for arts, and for war, as particularly: (1.) Sir William Petre, who the learn'd Dr. Wake, now Archbishop of Canterbury, and author of the Additions to Mr. Cambden, says, was Secretary of State, and Privy Counsellor to King Hen. VIII. Ed. VI. Queen Mary, and Queen Elizabeth, and seven times sent ambassador into foreign countries.

2. Sir Thomas Bodley, famous, and of grateful memory to all learned men, and lovers of letters, for his collecting, and establishing, the best library in Britain; which is now at Oxford, and is call'd after his name the Bodleian Library to this day.

3. Also Sir Francis Drake, born at Plymouth.

4. Sir Walter Raleigh, of both those I need say nothing: Fame publishes their merit upon every mention of their names.

5. That great patron of learning --- Hooker, author of the *Ecclesiastical Polity*, and of several other valuable peices.

6. Of Dr. Arthur Duck, a fam'd civilian, and well known by his works among the learned advocates of Doctors Commons.

7. Dr. John Moreman of Southold, famous for being the first clergyman in England, who ventured to teach his parishoners the Lord's Prayer, Creed, and Ten Commandments in the English tongue; and reading them so publickly in the parish church of Mayenhennet, in this county, of which he was vicar.

8. Dr. John De Brampton, a man of great learning, who flourish'd in the reign of Hen. VI. was famous, for being the first that read Aristotle publickly in the University of Cambridge, and for several learned books of his writing, which are now lost.

9. Peter Blundel, a clothier, who built the free-school at Tiverton, and endowed it very handsomely, of which in its place.

10. Sir John Glanvill, a noted lawyer, and one of the judges of the Common Pleas.

11. Sergeant Glanvill his son, as great a lawyer as his father.

12. Sir John Maynard, an eminent lawyer of later years; one of the Commissioners of the Great Seal under King William III. all these three were born at Tavistock.

13. Sir Peter King, the present Lord Chief Justice of the Common Pleas, and many others.

I shall take the north part of this county in my return from Cornwall; so I must now lean to the south, that is to say, to the south coast, for in going on indeed, we go south west.

About 22 miles from Excester we go to Totness, on the river Dart. This is a very good town; of some trade, but has more gentlemen in it than tradesmen of note; they have a very fine stone-bridge here over the river, which being within seven or eight miles of the sea, is very large, and the tide flows 10 or 12 foot at the bridge. Here we had the diversion of seeing them catch fish, with the assistance of a dog. The case is this, on the south side of the river, and on a slip, or narrow cut or channel made on purpose for a mill, there stands a corn-mill; the mill tayl, or floor for the water below the wheels is wharft up on either side with stone, above high-water mark, and for above 20 or 30 foot in length below it, on that part of the river towards the sea; at the end of this wharfing is a grating of wood, the cross-bars of which stand bearing inward, sharp at the end, and pointing inward towards one another, as the wyers of a mouse-trap.

When the tide flows up, the fish can with ease go in between the points of these cross-bars, but the mill being shut down they can go no farther upwards; and when the water ebbs again, they are left behind, not being able to pass the points of the grating, as above, outwards; which like a mouse-trap keeps them in, so that they are left at the bottom with about a foot, or a foot and half water. We were carryed hither at low water, where we saw about 50 or 60 small salmon, about 17 to 20 inches long, which the country people call salmon peal, and to catch these, the person who went with us, who was our landlord at a great inn next the bridge, put in a net on a hoop at the end of a pole, the pole going cross the hoop, which we call in this country a shove net: The net being fix'd at one end of the place they put in a dog, who was taught his trade before hand, at the other end of the place, and he drives all the fish into the net, so that only holding the net still in its place, the man took up two or three and thirty salmon peal at the first time.

Of these we took six for our dinner, for which they ask'd a shilling, (viz.) two pence a peice, and for such fish not at all bigger, and not so fresh, I have seen 6s. 6d. each given at a London fish-market, whither they are some time brought from Chichester by land carriage.

This excessive plenty of so good fish, and other provisions being likewise very cheap in proportion, makes the town of Totness a very good place to live in; especially for such as have large families, and but small estates, and many such are said to come into those parts on purpose for saving money, and to live in proportion to their income.

From hence we went still south about seven miles, (all in view of this river) to Dartmouth, a town of note, seated at the mouth of the river Dart, and where it enters into the sea at a very narrow, but safe entrance; The opening into Dartmouth Harbour is not broad, but the channel deep enough for the biggest ship in the royal navy; the sides of the entrance are high mounded with rocks; without which just at the first narrowing of the passage, stands a good strong fort without a platform of guns, which commands the port.

The narrow entrance is not much above half a mile, when it opens and makes a basin, or harbour able to receive 500 sail of ships of any size, and where they may ride with the greatest safety, even as in a mill-pond, or wet-dock: I had the curiosity here with the assistance of a merchant of the town to go out to the mouth of the haven in a boat to see the entrance, and castle, or fort that commands it; and coming back with the tide of flood, I observ'd some small fish to skip, and play upon the surface of the water, upon which I ask'd my friend what fish they were; immediately one of the rowers or seamen starts up in the boat, and throwing his arms abroad, as if he had been betwitch'd, cryes out as loud as he could baul, "a scool, a scool." The word was taken to the shore as hastily as it would have been on land if he had cry'd fire; and by that time we reach'd the keys, the town was all in a kind of an uproar.

The matter was, that a great shoal, or as they call it a *scool* of pilchards came swimming with the tide of flood directly, out of the sea into the harbour. My friend whose boat we were in, told me this was a surprize which he would have been very glad of, if he could but have had a days or two's warning, for he might have taken 200 tun of them, and the like was the case of other merchants in town; for in short, no body was ready for them, except a small fishing boat, or two; one of which went out into the middle of the harbour, and at two or three hawls, took about forty thousand of them. We sent our servant to the key to buy some, who for a half-penny, brought us seventeen, and if he would have taken them, might have had as many more for the same money; with these we went to dinner; the cook at the inn broil'd them for us, which is their way of dressing them, with pepper and salt, which cost us about a farthing; so that two of us, and a servant din'd, and at a tavern too, for three farthings, dressing and all, and this is the reason of telling the tale; What drink, wine, or beer we had, I do not remember, but whatever it was, that we paid for by it self; but for our food we really din'd for *three farthings*, and very well too: Our friend treated us the next day with a dish of large lobsters, and I being curious to know the value of such things, and having freedom enough with him to enquire; I found that for 6*d*. or 8*d*. they bought as good lobsters there, as would have cost in London 3*s*. to 3*s*. 6*d*. each.

In observing the coming in of those pilchards, as above, we found that out at sea, in the offing, beyond the mouth of the harbour there was a whole army of porpuses, which as they told us pursued the pilchards, and 'tis probable drove them into the harbour, as above. The scool it seems drove up the river a great way, even as high as Totness Bridge, as we heard afterwards; so that the country people who had boats, and nets, catch'd as many as they knew what to do with, and perhaps liv'd upon pilchards for several days; but as to the merchant's and trade, their coming was so suddain, that it was no advantage to them.

Round the west side of this basin, or harbour in a kind of

a semicircle, lyes the town of Dartmouth, a very large and populous town, tho' but meanly built, and standing on the side of a steep hill; yet the key is large, and the street before it spacious. Here are some very flourishing merchants, who trade very prosperously, and to the most considerable trading ports of Spain, Portugal, Italy, and the Plantations; but especially, they are great traders to Newfoundland, and from thence to Spain, and Italy with fish, and they drive a good trade also, in their own fishery of pilchards, which is hereabouts carried on with the greatest number of vessels of any port, in the west, except Falmouth.

A little to the southward of this town, and to the east of the port, is Torbay, of which I know nothing proper to my observation, more than that it is a very good road for ships, tho' sometimes, especially with a southerly, or S.E. wind, ships have been oblig'd to quit the bay, and put out to sea, or run into Dartmouth for shelter.

I suppose I need not mention, that they had from the hilly part of this town, and especially from the hills opposite to it, the noble prospect, and at that time particularly delightful, of the Prince of Orange's fleet, when he came to that coast, and as they entered into Torbay, to land; the prince and his army being in a fleet of about 600 sail of transport ships, besides 50 sail of men of war of the line, all which with a fair wind, and fine weather came to an anchor there at once.

This town as most of the towns of Devonshire are, is full of Dissenters, and a very large meeting-house they have here; how they act here with respect to the great dispute about the doctrine of the Trinity, which has caus'd such a breach among those people at Excester, and other parts of the county, I cannot give any account of. This town sends two members to Parliament.

From hence we went to Plympton, a poor and thinly inhabited town, tho' blest with the like privilege of sending members to the Parliament; of which I have little more to say, but that from thence the road lyes to Plymouth, distance about six miles.

Plymouth is indeed a town of consideration, and of great importance to the publick. The situation of it between two very large inlets of the sea, and in the bottom of a large bay, which is very remarkable for the advantage of navigation. The Sound, or bay is compass'd on every side with hills, and the shoar generally steep and rocky, tho' the anchorage is good, and it is pretty safe riding: In the entrance to this bay, lyes a large and most dangerous rock, which at high-water is cover'd, but at low-tide lyes bare, where many a good ship has been lost, even in the view of safety, and many a ships crew drown'd in the night, before help could be had for them.

Upon this rock, which was call'd the Edystone, from its situation, the famous Mr. Winstanley undertook to build a light-house for the direction of sailors, and with great art, and expedition finish'd it; which work considering its height, the magnitude of its building, and the little hold there was, by which it was possible to fasten it to the rock, stood to admiration, and bore out many a bitter storm.

Mr. Winstanly often visited, and frequently strengthen'd the building, by new works, and was so confident of its firmness, and stability, that he usually said, he only desir'd to be in it when a storm should happen, for many people had told him, it would certainly fall, if it came to blow a little harder than ordinary.

But he happen'd at last to be in it once too often; Namely, when that dreadful tempest blew, Nov. the 27, 1703. This tempest began on the Wednesday before, and blew with such violence, and shook the light-house so much, that as they told me there, Mr. Winstanly would fain have been on shoar, and made signals for help, but no boats durst go off to him; and to finish the tragedy, on the Friday, Nov. 26, when the tempest was so redoubled, that it became a terror to the whole nation; the first sight there seaward, that the people of Plymouth, were presented with in the morning after the storm, was the bare Eddystone, the light-house being gone; in which Mr. Winstanly, and all that were with him perish'd, and were never seen, or heard of since: But that which was a worse loss still, was, that a few days after a merchant's ship call'd the *Winchelsea* homeward bound from Virginia, not knowing the Eddystone light-house was down; for want of the light that should have been seen run foul of the rock it self, and was lost with all her lading, and most of her men, but there is now another light-house built on the same rock.

What other disasters happen'd at the same time, in the Sound, and in the roads about Plymouth, is not my business: They are also publish'd in other books, to which I refer.

One thing, which I was a witness too, on a former journey to this place, I cannot omit: It was the next year after that great storm, and but a little sooner in the year, being in August, I was at Plymouth, and walking on the Hoo, which is a plain on the edge of the sea, looking to the road, I observ'd the evening so serene, so calm, so bright, and the sea so smooth, that a finer sight, I think, I never saw; there was very little wind, but what was, seem'd to be westerly; and, about an hour after, it blew a little breeze at south west, with which wind there came into the Sound, that night, and the next morning, a fleet of fourteen sail of ships, from Barbadoes; richly loaden, for London: Having been long at sea, most of the captains and passengers came on shore to refresh themselves, as is usual, after such tedious voyages, and the ships rode all in the Sound on that side next to Catwater: As is customary, upon safe arriving to their native country, there was a general joy and rejoycing, both on board and on shore.

The next day the wind began to freshen, especially in the afternoon, and the sea to be disturb'd, and very hard it blew at night, but all was well for that time; but the night after it blew a dreadful storm, not much inferior, for the time it lasted, to the storm mention'd above, which blew down the light-house on the Eddy Stone; about midnight the noise indeed was very dreadful, what with the roaring of the sea, and of the wind, intermix'd with the firing of guns for help from the ships, the cries of the seamen and people on shore, and, which was worse, the cries of those, which were driven on shore by the tempest, and dash'd in pieces. In a word, all the fleet, except three, or thereabouts, were dash'd to pieces against the rocks, and sunk in the sea, most of the men being drowned: Those three, who were sav'd, receiv'd so much damage, that their lading was almost all spoil'd: One ship in the dark of the night, the men not knowing where they were, run into Catwater, and run on shore there, by which she was however sav'd from shipwreck, and the lives of her crew were saved also.

This was a melancholly morning indeed; nothing was to be seen but wrecks of the ships, and a foaming furious sea, in that very place where they rode all in joy and triumph, but the evening before: The captains, passengers and officers who were, as I have said, gone on shoar, between the joy of saving their lives, and the affliction of having lost their ships, their cargoes, and their friends, were objects indeed worth our compassion and observation; and there was a great variety of the passions to be observ'd in them: Now lamenting their losses, then giving thanks for their deliverance, many of the passengers had lost their all, and were, as they express'd themselves, utterly undone; they were, I say, now lamenting their losses, with violent excesses of grief; then giving thanks for their lives, and that they should be brought on shore, as it were, on purpose to be sav'd from death; then again in tears for such as were drowned; the various cases were indeed very affecting, and, in many things, very instructing.

As, I say, Plymouth lyes in the bottom of this Sound, in the center between the two waters, so there lies against it, in the same position, an island, which they call St. Nicholas, on which there is a castle, which commands the entrance into Ham-Oze, and indeed that also into Catwater in some degree: In this island the famous General Lambert, one of Cromwell's great agents, or officers in the Rebellion was imprison'd for life, and liv'd many years there.

On the shore, over-against this island, is the citadel of Plymouth, a small, but regular fortification, inaccessible by sea, but not exceeding strong by land, except that they say the works are of a stone, hard as marble, and would not soon yield to the batteries of an enemy: But that is a language our modern engineers now laugh at.

The town stands above this, upon the same rock, and lyes sloping on the side of it, towards the east; the inlet of the sea, which is call'd Catwater, and which is a harbour, capable of receiving any number of ships, and of any size, washing the eastern shore of the town, where they have a kind of natural mole, or haven, with a key, and all other conveniencies for bringing in vessels for loading and unloading; nor is the trade carried on here inconsiderable in it self, or the number of merchants small.

The other inlet of the sea, as I term it, is on the other side of the town, and is call'd Ham-Oze, being the mouth of the river Tamar, a considerable river, which parts the two counties of Devon and Cornwall: Here the war with France making it necessary that the ships of war should have a retreat nearer hand than at Portsmouth, the late King William order'd a wet dock, with yards, dry docks, launches, and conveniencies of all kinds for building, and repairing of ships to be built; and with these follow'd necessarily the building of store-houses and warehouses, for the rigging, sails, naval and military stores, &c. of such ships as may be appointed to be laid up there, as now several are, with very handsome houses for the commissioners, clerks, and officers of all kinds usual in the kings yards, to dwell in: It is in short, now become as compleat an arsenal, or yard, for building and fitting men of war as any of the government are masters of, and perhaps much more convenient than some of them, tho' not so large.

The building of these things, with the addition of rope walks, and mast-yards, &c. as it brought abundance of trades-people, and workmen to the place, so they began by little and little to build houses on the lands adjacent, till at length there appeared a very handsome street, spacious and large, and as well inhabited, and so many houses are since added, that it is become a considerable town, and must of consequence in time draw abundance of people from Plymouth it self.

However, the town of Plymouth is, and will always be a very considerable town, while that excellent harbour makes it such a general port for the receiving all the fleets of merchants ships from the southward, as from Spain, Italy, the West-Indies, &c. who generally make it the first port to put in at for refreshment, or safety, from either weather or enemies.

The town is populous and wealthy, having, as above, several considerable merchants, and abundance of wealthy shop-keepers, whose trade depends upon supplying the sea-faring people, that upon so many occasions put into that port; as for gentlemen, I mean those that are such by family, and birth, and way of living, it cannot be expected to find many such in a town, meerly depending on trade, shipping and sea-faring business, yet I found here some men of value, persons of liberal education, general knowledge, and excellent behaviour, whose society obliges me to say, that a gentleman might find very agreeable company in Plymouth.

From Plymouth we pass the Tamar, over a ferry to Saltash, a little poor shatter'd town, the first we sat foot on in the county of Cornwall. The Tamar here is very wide, and the ferry boats bad, so that I thought my self well escap'd, when I got safe on shore in Cornwall.

Saltash seems to be the ruins of a larger place, and we saw many houses as it were falling down, and I doubt not but the mice and rats have abandoned many more, as they say they will, when they are likely to fall; yet this town is govern'd by a mayor and aldermen, has many privileges, sends members to Parliament, takes toll of all vessels that pass the river, and have the sole oyster fishing in the whole river, which is considerable. Mr. Carew, author of the *Survey of Cornwall*, tells us a strange story of a dog in this town, of whom it was observ'd, that if they gave him any large bone, or piece of meat, he immediately went out of doors with it, and after having disappeared for

I 820

some time, would return again, upon which after some time they watch'd him, when to their great surprise they found that the poor charitable creature carryed what he so got to an old decrip'd mastiff, which lay in a nest that he had made among the brakes a little way out of the town, and was blind; so that he could not help himself, and there this creature fed him; he adds, also, that on Sundays, or hollydays, when he found they made good chear in the house, where he liv'd, he would go out, and bring this old blind dog to the door, and feed him there till he had enough, and then go with him back to his habitation in the country again, and see him safe in; if this story is true, it is very remarkable indeed, and I thought it worth telling, because the author was a person, who they say might be credited.

This town has a kind of jurisdiction upon the river Tamar down to the mouth of the port, so that they claim anchorage of all small ships that enter the river, their coroner sits upon all dead bodies that are found drown'd in the river, and the like, but they make not much profit of them. There is a good market here, and that is the best thing to be said of the town, it is also very much encreased since the number of the inhabitants are encreased at the new town, as I mentioned, as near the dock at the mouth of Ham Oaze, for those people choose rather to go to Saltash to market by water, then to walk to Plymouth by land for their provisions; because, first, as they go in the town boat, the same boat brings home what they buy; so that it is much less trouble, (second,) because provisions are bought much cheaper at Saltash, than at Plymouth: This I say, is like to be a very great advantage to the town of Saltash, and may in time put a new face of wealth upon the place.

They talk of some merchants beginning to trade here, and they have some ships that use the Newfoundland fishery; but I could not hear of any thing considerable they do in it, there is no other considerable town up the Tamar, till we come to Lanceston, the county town, which I shall take in my return, so I turn'd west, keeping the south shore of the county, to the Lands End.

From Saltash I went to Liskard, about 7 miles. This is a considerable town, well built, has people of fashion in it, and a very great market; it also sends two members to Parliament, and is one of the five towns, call'd Stannary Towns, that is to say, where the blocks of TINN are brought to the coinage, of which by it self; this coinage of tinn is an article very much to the advantage of the towns where it is settled, tho' the money paid goes another way.

This town of Liskard was once eminent, had a good castle, and a large house, where the antient Dukes of Cornwall kept their Court in those days; also it enjoy'd several privileges, especially by the favour of the Black Prince, who, as Prince of Wales, and Duke of Cornwall resided here; and in return, they say this town, and the country round it, rais'd a great body of stout young fellows, who entered into his service, and followed his fortunes in his wars in France, as also in Spain; But these buildings are so decay'd, that there are now scarce any of the ruins of the castle, or of the prince's Court remaining.

The only publick edifices they have now to show, are the guild, or town-hall, on which there is a turret with a fine clock; a very good free-school, well provided; a very fine conduit in the market-place; an antient large church, and which is something rare, for the county of Cornwall, a large new built meeting-house for the Dissenters, which I name, because they assur'd me there was but three more, and those very inconsiderable in all the county of Cornwall; whereas in Devonshire, which is the next county, there are reckon'd about seventy, some of which are exceeding large and fine.

This town is also remarkable for a very great trade in all manufactures of leather, such as boots, shoes, gloves, purses, breeches, &c. and some spinning of late years is set up here, encourag'd by the woollen manufacturers of Devonshire.

Between these two towns of Saltash and Liskard, is St. Germans, now a village, decay'd, and without any market, but the largest parish in the whole county; in the bounds of which is contained, as they report, 17 villages, and the town of Saltash among them, for Saltash has no parish church, it seems of it self but as a chappel of ease to St. Germans: In the neighbourhood of these towns are many pleasant seats of the Cornish gentry, who are indeed very numerous, tho' their estates may not be so large, as is usual in England; yet neither are they despicable in that part, and in particular this may be said of them, that as they generally live cheap, and are more at home than in other counties, so they live more like gentlemen, and keep more within bounds of their estates than the English generally do, take them altogether.

Add to this, that they are the most sociable, generous, and to one another, the kindest neighbours that are to be found; and as they generally live, as we may say, together, for they are almost always at one anothers houses, so they generally inter-marry among themselves, the gentlemen seldom going out of the county for a wife, or the ladies for a husband, from whence they say, that proverb upon them was rais'd (viz.) That all the Cornish gentlemen are cousins.

On the hills north of Liskard, and in the way between Liskard and Lanceston, there are many tinn mines, and as they told us some of the richest veins of that metal are found there, that are in the whole county; the metal when cast at the blowing houses into blocks, being as above, carry'd to Liskard to be coin'd.

From Liskard, in our course west, we are necessarily carry'd to the sea coast, because of the river Fowey, or Fowath, which empties it self into the sea, at a very large mouth, and hereby this river rising in the middle of the breadth of the county, and running south, and the river Camel rising not far from it, and running north, with a like large channel, the land from Bodmyn to the western part of the county is almost made an island, and in a manner cut off from the eastern part, the peninsula, or neck of land between, being not above twelve miles over.

On this south side we come to Foy, or Fowey, an antient town, and formerly very large; nay, not large only, but powerful and potent, for the Foyens, as they were then call'd, were able to fit out large fleets, not only for merchant's ships, but even of men of war; and with these not only fought with, but several times vanquished, and routed the squadron of the Cinque Port men, who in those days were thought very powerful.

Mr. Cambden observes, that the town of Foy quarters some part of the arms of every one of those Cinque Ports with their own; intimating, that they had at several times trampled over them all; certain it is, they did often beat them, and took their ships, and brought them as good prizes into their haven of Foy, and carry'd it so high, that they fitted out their fleets against the French, and took several of their men of war when they were at war with England, and enrich'd their town by the spoil of their enemies.

Edward IV. favour'd them much, and because the French threaten'd them, to come up their river with a powerful navy to burn their town, he caus'd two forts to be built at the publick charge, for security of the town and river, which forts at least some show of them remain there still, but the same King Edward was some time after so disgusted at the townsmen for officiously falling upon the French after a truce was made, and proclaim'd, that he effectually disarm'd them, took away their whole fleet, ships, tackle, apparel and furniture; and since that time we do not read of any of their naval exploits, nor that they ever recover'd, or attempted to recover their strength at sea: However, Foy, at this time, is a very fair town, it lyes extended on the east side of the river for above a mile, the buildings fair; and there are a great many flourishing merchants in it, who have a great share in the fishing trade, especially for pilchards, of which they take a great quantity here abouts. In this town, is also a coinage for the TINN, of which a great quantity is dug up in the country, north and west of the town.

The river Fowey, which is very broad and deep here, was formerly navigable by ships of good burthen as high as Lest-withiel an antient, and once a flourishing, but now a decay'd town, and as to trade and navigation quite destitute, which is occasioned by the river being fill'd up with sands, which some say, the tides drive up in stormy weather from the sea; others say 'tis by sands wash'd from the lead mines in the hills; the last of which, (by the way) I take to be a mistake, the sand from the hills being not of quantity sufficient to fill up the channel of a navigable river, and if it had, might easily have been stopped by the towns people from falling into the river; but that the sea has choak'd up the river with sand, is not only probable but true, and there are other rivers which suffer in the like manner in this same country.

This town of Lestwithiel, retains however several advantages, which support its figure, as first, that it is one of the Coinage Towns, as I call them, or Stannary Towns, as others call them. (2.) The common gaol for the whole Stannary is here, as are also the county courts for the whole county of Cornwall.

There is a mock cavalcade kept up at this town, which is very remarkable, the particulars, as they are related by Mr. Carew in his *Survey of Cornwall*, take as follows.

Upon little Easter Sunday, the free-holders of this town and mannour by themselves, or their deputies, did there assemble: Amongst whom, one (as it fell to his lot by turn) bravely apparall'd, gallantly mounted, with a crown on his head, a scepter in his hand, and a sword borne before him, and dutifully attended by all the rest also on horseback, rode thro' the principal street to the church: The curate in his best beseen solemnly received him at the church-yard stile, and conducted him to hear divine service: After which, he repaired with the same pomp, to a house provided for that purpose, made a feast to his attendants, kept the tables-end himself, and was served with kneeling assay, and all other rights due to the estate of a prince: With which dinner, the ceremony ended, and every man returned home again. The pedigree of this usage is deriv'd from so many descents of ages that the cause and author out-reach the remembrance: Howbeit, these circumstances afford a conjecture, that it should betoken royalties appertaining to the honour of Cornwal.

Behind Foye, and nearer to the coast at the mouth of a small river, which some call Lowe, tho' without any authority, there stand two towns opposite to one another, bearing the name of the river Loe, that is to say, distinguish'd by the addition of East Loe, and West Loe. These are both good trading towns, and especially fishing towns and which is very particular, are like Weymouth and Melcomb, in Dorsetshire, seperated only by the creek, or river; and yet each of them send members to Parliaments: These towns are joyn'd together by a very beautiful and stately stone bridge having fifteen arches.

East Loo, was the antienter corporation of the two, and for some ages ago the greater and more considerable town; but now they tell us West Loo is the richest, and has the most ships belonging to it: Were they put together, they would make a very handsome seaport town. They have a great fishing trade here, as well for supply of the country, as for merchandize, and the towns are not dispisable; but as to sending four members to the British Parliament, which is as many as the city of London chooses, that I confess seems a little scandalous, but to who, is none of my business to enquire.

Passing from hence, and ferrying over Foy river, or the river Foweth, call it as ye please, we come into a large country without many towns in it of note, but very well furnished with gentlemen's seats, and a little higher up with tinn works.

The sea making several deep bays here, they who travel by land are oblig'd to go higher into the country to pass above the water, especially at Trewardreth Bay, which lyes very broad, above ten miles within the country, which passing at Trewardreth, a town of no great note, tho' the bay takes its name from it, the next inlet of the sea, is the famous firth, or inlet, call'd Falmouth Haven. It is certainly next to Milford Haven in South Wales, the fairest and best road for shipping that is in the whole isle of Britain, when there be considered the depth of water for above twenty miles within land; the safety of riding, shelter'd from all kind of winds or storms, the good anchorage, and the many creeks, all navigable, where ships may run in and be safe, so that the like is no where to be found.

There are six or seven very considerable places upon this

haven, and the rivers from it, (viz.) Grampound, Tregony, Truro, Penryn, Falmouth, St. Mawes, and Pendennis. The three first of these send members to Parliament, the town of Falmouth, as big as all the three, and richer than ten of them sends none, which imports no more than this, that Falmouth it self is not of so great antiquity, as to its rising, as those other towns are; and yet the whole haven takes its name from Falmouth too, unless as some think the town took its name from the haven, which however they give no authority to suggest.

St. Mawes and Pendennis are two fortifications placed at the points, or enterance of this haven, opposite to one another, tho' not with a communication, or view; they are very strong; the first principally by sea, having a good plat form of guns, pointing thwart the channel, and planted on a level with the water; but Pendennis Castle is strong by land as well as by water, is regularly fortified, has good out works, and generally a strong garrison; St. Mawes, otherwise call'd St. Mary's has a town annex'd to the castle, and is a borough, sending members to the Parliament. Pendennis is a meer fortress, tho' there are some habitations in it too, and some at a small distance near the sea side, but not of any great consideration.

The town of Falmouth is by much the richest, and best trading town in this county, tho' not so antient as its neighbour town of Truro; and indeed, is in some things oblig'd to acknowledge the seigniorty; Namely, that in the corporation of Truro, the person who they choose to be their mayor of Truro, is also mayor of Falmouth of course. How the jurisdiction is manag'd, is an account too long for this place; the Truro men also receive several duties collected in Falmouth, particularly wharfage for the merchandizes landed, or shipp'd off; but let these advantages be what they will, the town of Falmouth has gotten the trade, at least the best part of it from the other, which is chiefly owing to the situation, for that Falmouth lying upon the sea, but within the entrance, ships of the greatest burthen come up to the very keys, and the whole royal navy might ride safely in the road, whereas the town of Truro lying far within, and at the mouth of two fresh rivers, is not navigable for vessels of above 150 tons, or thereabouts.

Some have suggested that the original of Falmouth, was the having so large a key, and so good a depth of water at it. The merchants of Truro formerly us'd it for the place of lading and unlading their ships, as the merchants of Exceter did at Topsham, and this is the more probable in that, as above, the wharfage of those landing places is still the property of the corporation of Truro.

But let this be as it will, the trade is now in a manner wholly gone to Falmouth, the trade at Truro, being now chiefly if not only for shipping off of block TINN and copper oar, the latter being lately found in large quantities in some of the mountains between Truro, and St. Michaels, and which is much improv'd since the several mills are erected at Bristol, and other parts, for the manufactures of battery ware or, as 'tis call'd, brass, which is made out of English copper, most of it dug in these parts; the oar it self also being found very rich and good.

Falmouth is well built, has abundance of shipping belonging to it, is full of rich merchants, and has a flourishing and encreasing trade. I say encreasing, because by the late setting up the English packets between this port and Lisbon, there is a new commerce between Portugal and this town, carried on to a very great value.

It is true, part of this trade was founded in a clandestine commerce, carried on by the said packets at Lisbon, where being the king's ships, and claiming the privilege of not being searched, or visited by the custom-house officers, they found means to carry off great quantities of British manufactures, which they sold on board to the Portuguese merchants, and they convey'd them on shoar, as 'tis supposed without paying custom.

But the government there, getting intelligence of it, and complaint being made in England also, where it was found to be very prejudicial to the fair merchant, that trade has been effectually stopp'd, but the Falmouth merchants having by this means gotten a taste of the Portuguese trade, have maintain'd it ever since in ships of their own: These packets bring over such vast quantities of gold in specie, either in moidores, which is the Portugal coin, or in bars of gold, that I am very credibly inform'd the carryer from Falmouth, brought by land from thence to London, at one time, in the month of January, 1722, or near it, eighty thousand moidores in gold, which came from Lisbon in the pacquet boats, for account of the merchants at London, and that it was attended with a guard of 12 horsemen well arm'd, for which the said carryer had half per cent for his hazard.

This is a specimen of the Portugal trade, and how considerable it is in it self, as well as how advantageous to England, but as that is not to the present case, I proceed; the custom-house for all the towns in this port, and the head collector is establish'd at this town, where the duties, including the other ports is very considerable: Here is also a very great fishing for pilchards, and the merchants for Falmouth have the chief stroke in that gainful trade.

Truro is however a very considerable town too; it stands up the water north and by east from Falmouth in the utmost extended branch of the haven, in the middle, between the conflux of two rivers, which tho' not of any long course, have a very good appearance for a port, and make a large wharf between them in the front of the town; and the water here makes a good port for small ships, tho' it be at the influx, but not for ships of burthen. This is the particular town where the lord warden of the Stannaries always holds his famous Parliament of Miners, and for stamping of TINN. The town is well built, but shews that it has been much fuller, both of houses and inhabitants, than it is now; nor will it probably ever rise, while the town of Falmouth stands where it does, and while the trade is settled in it, as it is. There are at least three churches in it, but no Dissenter's meeting house, that I could hear of.

Tregony, is upon the same water north east from Falmouth, distance about sixteen miles from it, but is a town of very little trade, nor indeed have any of the towns so far within the shoar, notwithstanding the benefit of the water any considerable trade but what is carried on under the merchants of Falmouth, or Truro; the chief thing that is to be said of this town, is, that it sends members to Parliament, as does also

Grandpound, a market-town, and burro' about 4 miles farther up the water. This place indeed has a claim to antiquity, and is an appendix to the Dutchy of Cornwall, of which it holds at a fee farm rent, and pays to the Prince of Wales, as duke, 10l. 11s. 1d. per annum; it has no parish church, but only a chappel of ease to an adjacent parish.

Penryn, is up the same branch of the haven, as Falmouth, but stands four miles higher towards the west, yet ships come to it of as great a size, as can come to Truro it self; it is a very pleasant agreeable town, and for that reason has many merchants in it, who would perhaps otherwise live at Falmouth. The chief commerce of these towns, as to their sea affairs, is the pilchards, and Newfoundland fishing, which is very profitable to them all; it had formerly a conventual church, with a chantry, and a religious house, a cel to Kirton, but they are all demolish'd, and scarce the ruins of them distinguishable enough to know one part from another.

Quiting Falmouth Haven from Penryn west, we came to

Helsten, about 7 miles, and stands upon the little river Cober, which however admits the sea so into its bosom as to make a tolerable good harbour for ships a little below the town. It is the fifth town, allow'd for the coining TINN, and several of the ships call'd "tinn" ships are loaden here.

This town is large and populous, and has four spacious streets, a handsome church, and a good trade: This town also sends members to Parliament. Beyond this is a market town tho' of no resort for trade, call'd Market Jew, it lyes indeed on the sea-side, but has no harbour or safe road for shipping.

At Helford is a small, but good harbour between Falmouth and this port, where many times the TINN ships go in to load for London; also here are a good number of fishing vessels for the pilchard trade, and abundance of skilful fishermen: It was from this town that in the great storm, which happened, Nov. 27, 1703, a ship loaden with tinn, was blown out to sea, and driven to the Isle of Wight, in seven hours, having on board only one man, and two boys; the story is as follows, (viz.)

The beginning of the storm, there lay a ship laden with tinn, in Helford Haven, about two leagues and a half west of Falmouth. The tinn was taken on board at a place call'd Guague Wharf, five or six miles up the river, and the vessel was come down to Helford, in order to pursue her voyage to London.

About 8 a-clock in the evening the commander, whose name was Anthony Jenkins, went on board with his mate to see that every thing was safe, and to give orders, but went both on shoar again, leaving only a man, and two boys on board, not apprehending any danger, they being in safe harbour; however, he ordered them, that if it should blow hard, they should carry out the small bower anchor, and so to moor the ship by two anchors, and then giving what other orders he thought to be needful, he went ashore, as above.

About 9 o'clock, the wind beginning to blow harder, they carryed out the anchor according to the master's order; but the wind encreasing about 10, the ship began to drive, so they carry'd out their best bower, which having a good new cable, brought the ship up. The storm still encreasing they let go the kedge anchor; so that they then rode by four anchors a head, which were all they had.

But between 11 and 12 o'clock, the wind came about west and by south, and blew in so violent and terrible a manner, that tho' they rid under the lee of a high shore, yet the ship was driven from all her anchors, and about midnight drove quite out of the harbour (the opening of the harbour lying due east and west) into the open sea, the men having neither anchor or cable, or boat to help themselves.

In this dreadful condition, they driving, I say, out of the harbour: Their first and chief care was to go clear of the rocks, which lye on either side the harbour's mouth, and which they perform'd pretty well; then, seeing no remedy, they consulted what to do next. They cou'd carry no sail at first, no not a knot, nor do any thing but run

away afore it: The only thing they had to think on, was to keep
her out at sea as far as they could, for fear of a point of land, call'd
The Dead Man's Head, which lyes to the eastward of Falmouth
Haven, and then if they could escape the land, thought to run in
for Plymouth, next morning, so if possible, to save their lives.

In this frighted condition they drove away at a prodigious rate,
having sometimes the bonnet of their foresail a little out, but the
yard lower'd almost to the deck; sometimes the ship almost under
water, and sometimes above, keeping still in the offing, for fear of
the land, till they might see daylight; but when the day brake they
found they were to think no more of Plymouth, for they were far
enough beyond it, and the first land they made was Peverel Point,
being the southernmost land of the Isle of Purbeck, in Dorsetshire,
and a little to the westward of the Isle of Wight; so that now they
were in a terrible consternation, and driving still at a prodigious
rate, by seven a clock they found themselves broad side of the
Isle of Wight.

Here they consulted again what to do to save their lives; one of
the boys was for running her into the Downs, but the man objected,
that having no anchor or cable, nor boat to go on shore with, and
the storm blowing off shore, in the Downs, they should be inevitably
blown off, and lost upon the unfortunate Goodwin, which it seems
the man had been on once before, and narrowly escaped.

Now came the last consultation for their lives; the other of the
boys said, he had been in a certain creek in the Isle of Wight, where
between the rocks he knew there was room to run the ship in, and
at least to save their lives, and that he saw the place just that
moment; so he desir'd the man to let him have the helm, and he
would do his best, and venture it. The man gave him the helm, and
he stood directly in among the rocks, the people standing on the
shore, thinking they were mad, and that they would in a few
minutes be dashed in a thousand pieces.

But when they came nearer, and the people found they steer'd
as if they knew the place, they made signals to them to direct them,
as well as they could, and the young bold fellow run her into a small
cove, where she stuck fast, as it were, between the rocks on both
sides, there being but just room enough for the breadth of the ship;
the ship indeed giving two or three knocks stav'd, and sunk, but
the man and the two youths jump't a shore, and were safe, and the
lading being tinn was afterwards secur'd. *N.B.* The merchants very
well rewarded the three sailors, especially the lad that ran her into
that place.

Pensance is the farthest town of any note west, being 254
miles from London, and within about ten miles of the promontory, call'd the Lands End; so that this promontory is from
London 264 miles, or thereabouts: This town of Pensance is
a place of good business, well built and populous, has a good
trade, and a great many ships belonging to it, notwithstanding
it is so remote. Here are also a great many good families of
gentlemen, tho' in this utmost angle of the nation; and, which

is yet more strange, the veins of lead, tinn, and copper oar, are said to be seen, even to the utmost extent of land at low water mark, and in the very sea; so rich, so valuable a treasure is contain'd in these parts of Great Britain, tho' they are suppos'd to be so poor, because so very remote from London, which is the center of our wealth.

Between this town and St. Burien, a town midway between it and the Land's End, stands a circle of great stones, not unlike those at Stonehenge in Wiltshire, with one bigger than the rest in the middle; they stand about 12 foot asunder, but have no inscription, neither does tradition offer to leave any part of their history upon record; as whether it was a trophy, or a monument of burial, or an altar for worship, or what else; so that all that can be learn'd of them, is, That here they are: The parish where they stand is call'd Boscawone, from whence the ancient and honourable family of Boscawen derive their names.

Near Pensance, but open to the sea, is that gulph they call Mounts Bay, nam'd so from a high hill standing in the water, which they call St. Michael's Mount; the seamen call it only, the Cornish Mount; It has been fortify'd, tho' the situation of it makes it so difficult of access, that like the Bass in Scotland, there needs no fortification; like the Bass too, it was once made a prison for prisoners of State, but now it is wholly neglected; there is a very good road here for shipping, which makes the town of Pensance be a place of good resort.

A little up in the county towards the north west is Godolchan, which tho' a hill, rather than a town, gives name to the noble and ancient family of Godolphin; and nearer on the northern coast is Royalton, which since the late Sydney Godolphin, Esq; a younger brother of the family, was created Earl of Godolphin, gave title of lord to his eldest son, who was call'd Lord Royalton during the life of his father. This place also is infinitely rich in tinn mines.

I am now at my journey's end; As to the islands of Scilly, which lye beyond the Land's End, I shall say something of them presently: I must now return *sur mes pas*, as the French call it; tho' not literally so, for I shall not come back the same way I went; but as I have coasted the south shore to the Land's End, I shall come back by the north coast, and my observations in my return will furnish very well materials for a fourth letter.

I am, &c.

THE END OF THE THIRD LETTER

APPENDIX TO LETTER III

I HAVE ended this account at the utmost extent of the island of Great Britain west, without visiting those excrescences of the island, as I think I may call them, (viz.) the rocks of Scilly, of which, what is most famous, is their infamy, or reproach; Namely, how many good ships are, almost *continually* dash'd in pieces there, and how many brave lives lost, in spight of the mariners best skill, or the light-houses, and other sea-marks best notice.

These islands lye so in the middle between the two vast openings of the north and south narrow seas, or as the sailors call them, the Bristol Channel, and The Channel, (so call'd by way of eminence) that it cannot, or perhaps never will be avoided, but that several ships in the dark of the night, and in stress of weather may by being out in their reckonings, or other unavoidable accidents mistake, and if they do, they are sure, as the sailors call it, to run bump a shore upon Scilly, where they find no quarter among the breakers, but are beat to pieces, without any possibility of escape.

One can hardly mention the Bishop and his Clerks, as they are call'd, or the rocks of Scilly, without letting fall a tear to the memory of Sir Cloudesly Shovel, and all the gallant spirits that were with him at one blow, and without a moments warning dash'd into a state of immortality; the admiral with three men of war, and all their men (running upon these rocks, right afore the wind, and in a dark night) being lost there, and not a man sav'd. But all our annals and histories are full of this, so I need say no more.

They tell us of eleven sail of merchant ships homeward-bound, and richly laden from the southward, who had the like fate, in the same place, a great many years ago; and that some of them coming from Spain, and having a great quantity of bullion, or pieces of eight on board, the money frequently drives on shore still, and that in good quantities, especially after stormy weather.

This may be the reason why, as we observed during our short

stay here, several mornings after, it had blown something hard in the night, the sands were cover'd with country people running too and fro' to see if the sea had cast up any thing of value. This the seamen call "going a shoring"; and it seems they do often find good purchase: Sometimes also dead bodies are cast up here, the consequence of shipwrecks among those fatal rocks and islands; as also broken pieces of ships, casks, chests, and almost every thing that will float, or roll on shore by the surges of the sea.

Nor is it seldom that the voracious country people scuffle and fight about the right to what they find, and that in a desperate manner, so that this part of Cornwall may truly be said to be inhabited by a fierce and ravenous people; for they are so greedy, and eager for the prey, that they are charg'd with strange, bloody, and cruel dealings, even sometimes with one another; but especially with poor distress'd seamen when they come on shore by force of a tempest, and seek help for their lives, and where they find the rocks themselves not more merciless than the people who range about them for their prey.

Here also, as a farther testimony of the immense riches which have been lost at several times upon this coast, we found several engineers, and projectors; some with one sort of diving engine, and some with another; some claiming such a wreck, and some such and such others; where they alledg'd, they were assur'd there were great quantities of money; and strange unprecedented ways were us'd by them to come at it; Some, I say, with one kind of engine, and some another; and tho' we thought several of them very strange impracticable methods, yet, I was assur'd by the country people, that they had done wonders with them under water, and that some of them had taken up things of great weight, and in a great depth of water; others had split open the wrecks they had found, in a manner one would have thought not possible to be done, so far under water, and had taken out things from the very holds of the ships; but we could not learn, that they had come at any pieces of eight, which was the thing they seem'd most to aim at, and depend upon; at least they had not found any great quantity, as they said they expected.

However, we left them as busy as we found them, and far from being discouraged; and if half the golden mountains, or silver mountains either, which they promise themselves, should appear, they will be very well paid for their labour.

From the tops of the hills, on this extremity of the land, you may see out into that they call the Chops of the Channel, which, as it is the greatest inlet of commerce, and the most frequented by merchant-ships of any place in the world; so one seldom looks out to seaward, but something new presents; that is to say, of ships passing, or repassing, either on the great or lesser channel.

Upon a former accidental journey into this part of the country, during the war with France, it was with a mixture of pleasure and horror that we saw from the hills at the Lizard, which is the southermost point of this land, an obstinate fight between three French-men of war, and two English, with a privateer, and three merchant-ships in their company; the English had the misfortune, not only to be fewer ships of war in number, but of less force; so that while the two biggest French ships engaged the English, the third in the mean time took the two merchant-ships, and went off with them; as to the piccaroon, or privateer, she was able to do little in the matter, not daring to come so near the men of war, as to take a broadside, which her thin sides would not have been able to bear, but would have sent her to the bottom at once; so that the English men of war had no assistance from her, nor could she prevent the taking the two merchant-ships; yet we observ'd that the English captains manag'd their fight so well, and their seamen behav'd so briskly, that in about three hours both the French-men stood off, and being sufficiently bang'd, let us see that they had no more stomach to fight; after which the English, having damage enough too no doubt, stood away to the eastward, as we suppos'd, to refit.

This point of the Lizard, which runs out to the southward, and the other promontory mention'd above, make the two angles, or horns, as they are call'd, from whence 'tis suppos'd this county receiv'd its first name of Cornwall, or as Mr. Cambden says, *Cornubia* in the Latin, and in the British *Kernaw*, as running out in two vastly extended horns; and indeed it seems, as if nature had form'd this situation for the direction of mariners, as foreknowing of what importance it should be, and how in future ages these seas should be thus throng'd with merchant ships, the protection of whose wealth, and the safety of the people navigating them, was so much her early care, that she stretched out the land so very many ways, and extended the points and promontories so far, and in so many different places into the sea, that the land might be more easily discover'd at a due distance, which way soever the ships should come.

Nor is the Lizard Point less useful (tho' not so far west) than the other, which is more properly call'd the Land's End; but if we may credit our mariners, it is more frequently, first discover'd from the sea; for as our mariners knowing by the soundings when they are in the mouth of the Channel, do then most naturally stand to the southward, to avoid mistaking the Channel, and to shun the Severn Sea, or Bristol Channel, but still more to avoid running upon Scilly, and the rocks about it, as is observ'd before: I say, as they carefully keep to the southward, till they think they are fair with the Channel, and then stand to the northward again, or north east, to make the land; this is the reason why the Lizard is generally speaking, the first land they make, and not the Land's End.

Then having made the Lizard, they either (first) run in for Falmouth, which is the next port, if they are taken short with easterly winds, or are in want of provisions and refreshment, or have any thing out of order, so that they care not to keep the sea; or (2dly) stand away for the Ram Head, and Plymouth-Sound, or (3dly) keep an offing to run up the Channel.

So that the Lizard is the general guide, and of more use in these cases than the other point, and is therefore the land which the ships choose to make first, for then also they are sure that they are past Scilly, and all the dangers of that part of the island.

Nature has fortify'd this part of the island of Britain in a strange manner, and so as is worth a traveller's observation, as if she knew the force and violence of the mighty ocean, which beats upon it, and which indeed, if the land was not made firm in proportion, could not withstand, but would have been wash'd away long ago.

First, there are the islands of Scilly, and the rocks about them, these are plac'd like outworks to resist the first assaults of this enemy, and so break the force of it; as the piles, or starlings (as they are call'd) are plac'd before the solid stonework of London-Bridge, to fence off the force, either of the water, or ice, or any thing else that might be dangerous to the work.

Then there are a vast number of sunk rocks, (so the seamen call them,) besides such as are visible, and above water; which gradually lessen the quantity of water, that would otherwise lye with an infinite weight and force upon the land; 'tis observ'd, that these rocks lye under water for a great way off into the sea on every side the said two horns or points of land; so breaking the force of the water, and as above lessening the weight of it.

But besides this, the whole terra firma, or body of the land, which makes this part of the isle of Britain, seems to be one solid rock, as if it was formed by Nature to resist the otherwise irresistible power of the ocean; and indeed if one was to observe with what fury the sea comes on sometimes against the shore here, especially at the Lizard Point, where there are but few, if any outworks, (as I call them) to resist it; How high the waves come rowling forward, storming on the neck of one another; particularly when the wind blows off sea, one would wonder, that even the strongest rocks themselves should be able to resist, and repel them. But, as I said, the country seems to be as it were one great body of stone, and prepar'd so on purpose.

And yet, as if all this was not enough, Nature has provided another strong fence, and that is, that these vast rocks are, as it were, cemented together by the solid and weighty oar of TINN and copper, especially the last, which is plentifully found upon the very outmost edge of the land, and with which the stones may be said to be soder'd together, lest the force of the sea should separate and disjoynt them, and so break in upon these fortifications of the island, to destroy its chief security.

This is certain, that there is a more than ordinary quantity of tinn, copper, and lead also, placed by the Great Director of nature in these very remote angles and, as I have said above, the oar is found upon the very surface of the rocks a good way into the sea, and that it does not only lye, as it were, upon, or between the stones among the earth, which in that case might be washed from it by the sea, but that it is even blended or mix'd in with the stones themselves, that the stones must be split into pieces to come at it; by this mixture the rocks are made infinitely weighty and solid, and thereby still the more qualified to repel the force of the sea.

Upon this remote part of the island we saw great numbers of that famous kind of crows, which is known by the name of the Cornish cough, or chough, so the country people call them: They are the same kind, which are found in Switzerland among the Alps, and which Pliny pretended, were peculiar to those mountains, and calls the Pyrrhocorax; the body is black, the legs, feet, and bill of a deep yellow, almost to a red; I could not find that it was affected for any good quality it had, nor is the flesh good to eat, for it feeds much on fish and carrion; it is counted little better than a kite, for it is of ravenous quality, and is very mischievous; it will steal and carry away any thing it finds about the house, that is not too heavy, tho' not fit for its food; as knives, forks, spoons and linnen cloths, or whatever it can fly away with, sometimes they say it has stolen bits of firebrands, or lighted candles, and lodged them in the stacks of corn, and the thatch of barns and houses, and set them on fire; but this I only had by oral tradition.

I might take up many sheets in describing the valuable curiosities of this little Cherosonese, or neck land, call'd the Land's End, in which there lyes an immense treasure, and many things worth notice, I mean besides those to be found upon the surface: But I am too near the end of this letter. If I have opportunity, I shall take notice of some part of what I omit here, in my return by the northern shore of the county.

THE END OF THE THIRD LETTER

ADDENDA TO THE FIRST VOLUME

SINCE the closing this volume there are several great and magnificent buildings begun to be erected, within the circuit of these letters, which however, not being finish'd, cannot now be fully described, (viz.)

1. Sir Gregory Page's house on Black-Heath, which they tell us, will be a more magnificent work than any private gentleman's seat in this part of Great-Britain.

2. The Lord Onslow's seat, re-edifying near Guildford.

3. Sir John Williams's seat all new, at Stoke, near Nayland-Bridge, in Suffolk.

4. A new square, almost a new town, at the east-side of Greenwich, on the Heath, in the way to Charleton.

5. And, lastly, the famous addition, or square begun at King's College Chapel in Cambridge, of which the foundation is but even now lay'd.

THE AUTHOR'S PREFACE TO THE
SECOND VOLUME

THE reception which the first part of this work has met with, has not been so mean as to discourage the performance of the second volume, nor to slacken the diligence in our endeavours to perform it well: It is not an easy thing to travel over a whole kingdom, and in so critical a manner too, as will enable the traveller to give an account of things fit for the use of those that shall come after him.

To describe a country by other mens accounts of it, would soon expose the writer to a discovery of the fraud; and to describe it by survey, requires a preparation too great for any thing but a publick purse, and persons appointed by authority; This was the case in Mr. Cambden's travelling, by which means he had access to every curiosity, publick and private. But to describe a country by way of journey, in a private capacity, as has been the case here, though it requires a particular application, to what may be learn'd from due enquiry and from conversation, yet it admits not the observer to dwell upon every nicety, to measure the distances, and determine exactly the scite, the dimensions, or the extent of places, or read the histories of them. But it is giving an account by way of essay, or, as the moderns call it, by memoirs of the present state of things, in a familiar manner.

This we have perform'd in the best manner we could, and have taken care to have it come fully up to our proposals. We are not to boast of the performance, but are content to have it compar'd with any that have gone before it; if it may be done with impartiality and a fair design of determining according to truth: Our manner is plain, and suited to the nature of familiar letters; our relations have no blusters, no rhodomontadoes of our own abilities; but we keep close to the first design of giving, as near as possible, such an account of things, as may entertain the reader, and give him a view of our country, such as may tempt him to travel over it himself, in which case it will be not a little assisting to him, or qualify him to discourse of it, as one that had a tolerable knowledge of it, tho' he stay'd at home.

As we observ'd in the first volume, and frequently in this, there will always be something new, for those that come after; and if an account of Great Britain was to be written every year, there would be something found out, which was overlook'd before, or something to describe, which had its birth since the former accounts: New foundations are always laying, new buildings always raising, highways repairing, churches and publick buildings erecting, fires and other calamities happening, fortunes of families taking different turns, new trades are every day erected, new projects enterpriz'd, new designs laid; so that as long as England is a trading, improving nation, no perfect description either of the place, the people, or the conditions and state of things can be given.

For example; since the finishing of the last volume, the South Sea Company have engaged in the Greenland Fishery, and have fitted out a fleet of twelve great ships, which they have built new from the stocks, and have made that great wet-dock between Deptford and Redriff, the center of all that commerce and the buildings, the works, and the management, of that they call their cookery; that is, the boyling their blubber into oyl. 'Tis well if they do not make stink enough, and gain too little, especially to the neighbouring places of Deptford and Redriff.

Another article has happened, even between the writing the Appendix to this work, and this Preface; namely, That an Act of Parliament is passing, and will soon, we suppose, be pass'd for making the river Nyne navigable from Peterborough to Northampton, a work which will be of infinite advantage to the country, because the river pierces so far into the heart of the island, where there is no navigation for between twenty or thirty miles any way: 'Tis true, this may be long in doing, it being above fifty miles in length by the river; and they had once before an Act granted for the same thing; yet, 'tis said, they intend now to go about it in good earnest, and that they will be content with performing it piece-meal, that is to say, some and some, that they may see how practicable it may be, and how well it will turn to account.

It is not design'd to make apologies here for the performance; there were so few mistakes in the former volume, that were of any importance, and those few so easily rectify'd, that tho' this circuit is much greater, and perhaps the variety the greatest of all the three, yet 'tis hop'd there will be so few exceptions, as they may be easily accounted for hereafter.

The saying that Sudbury was not a corporation, when really it was so; that Chelmsford was the first and chief plantation of hops in Essex, when it seems Castle Henningham claims precedence: The debate whether Dunwich has now any trade left, or, whether it be quite devour'd of the sea; or whether Woodbridge or Ipswich are the chief ports for exporting Suffolk butter; are all so easily to be rectify'd by any reader, tho' they are among the chief mistakes of the last volume, that we cannot but hope the candor of the reader will make allowances for it, if such should unavoidably have slipt observation, in this part also, tho' we hope not.

We have now finish'd the whole south of Trent, which being the most populous part of the country, and infinitely fuller of great towns, of people, and of trade, has also the greatest variety of incidents in its passing over.

But the northern part being also to include Scotland, and being the greatest in extent, will have its beauties, we can assure you; and tho' the country may in some respects, be called barren, the history of it will not be so.

Scotland will have justice done it, without the flattery and ridiculous encomiums which have already so much exposed two Scotish writers upon that subject.[1]

The great and once wasted countries of Northumberland, Cumberland, and Durham, shall be truly and not slightly describ'd, with their real improvements, without loading our work with fragments of antiquity, and dressing up the wilds of the borders as a paradise, which are indeed but a wilderness.

In the mean time we recommend our performance to the candor of the reader, and whatever may be objected, we doubt not to have obtained the just reputation of having written with impartiality and with truth.

[1] Scotland may follow in a later Everyman volume.

LETTER IV

CONTAINING A DESCRIPTION OF THE NORTH SHORE OF THE
COUNTIES OF CORNWALL, AND DEVON, AND SOME PARTS OF
SOMERSETSHIRE, WILTSHIRE, DORSETSHIRE, GLOUCESTER-
SHIRE, BUCKINGHAMSHIRE AND BERKSHIRE

SIR,—My last letter ended the account of my travels, where
Nature ended her account, when she meeted out the island,
and where she fix'd the utmost western bounds of Britain; and,
being resolved to see the very extremity of it, I set my foot
into the sea, as it were, beyond the farthest inch of dry land
west, as I had done before near the town of Dover, at the foot
of the rocks of the South-Foreland in Kent, which, I think, is
the farthest point east in a line; And as I had done, also, at
Leostoff in Suffolk, which is another promontory on the eastern
coast, and is reckon'd the farthest land eastward of the island
in general: Likewise, I had used the same ceremony at Selsy
near Chichester, which I take to be the farthest land south,
except at Portland only, which, as it is not really an island,
may be called, the farthest land south; so, in its place, I shall
give you an account of the same curiosity at John a Grot's
House in Caithness, the farthest piece of ground in Great
Britain, north.

I had once, indeed, resolved to have coasted the whole circuit
of Britain by sea, as 'tis said, Agricola the Roman general, did;
and in this voyage I would have gone about every promontory,
and into the bottom of every bay, and had provided myself
a good yacht, and an able commander for that purpose; but
I found it would be too hazardous an undertaking for any man
to justify himself in the doing it upon the meer foundation of
curiosity, and having no other business at all; so I gave it over.

There was another difficulty also, upon which my navigator,
or commander, as I called him, who was an old experienced
seaman, dissuaded me from the undertaking; and that was, the
necessity of getting pilots to every part of the coast, and to
every port, river, and creek, and the danger of not getting
them: The necessity was plain; For that, as I proposed to keep
all the way near, or under the shore, to enter into all the bays,

and mouths of rivers, and creeks, as above; 1. It would be impracticable to find any single man that knew so perfectly the whole coast, as to venture in without pilots. 2. Pilots would not always be found, especially on the north and west coasts of Scotland; so I laid it aside, I say, as a hopeless, and too dangerous adventure, and satisfied myself, to make the circuit very near as perfect by land, which I have done with much less hazard, though with much more pains and expence; the fruit of which, you have, in part, communicated in these letters.

I now turned about to the east, and as, when I went west, I kept to the southern coast of this long county of Cornwall, and of Devonshire also, so in going east, I shall keep the north-shore on board. The first place, of any note, we came to, is St. Ives, a pretty good town, and grown rich by the fishing-trade; it is situated on the west side of a deep bay, called St. Ives Bay, from the name of the town. This bay is opposite, on the land side, to Mount's Bay, which I spoke of in my last, in my account of Pensance.

It is a very pleasant view we have at Madern Hills, and the plain by them, in the way from the Land's-End to St. Ives, where, at one sight, there is a prospect of the ocean at the Land's-End west; of the British Channel at Mount's Bay south; and the Bristol Channel, or Severn Sea, north; At St. Ives, the land between the two bays being not above four or five miles over, is so situated, that upon the hill, neither of the two seas are above three miles off, and very plain to be seen; and also, in a clear day, the islands of Scilly, though above thirty miles off.

From this town and port of St. Ives, we have no town of any note on the coast; no, not a market town, except Redruth, which is of no consideration, 'till we come to Padstow-Haven, which is near thirty miles: The country is, indeed, both fruitful and pleasant, and several houses of gentlemen are seen as we pass; the sands, also, are very pleasant to the eye, and to travel upon; Among the gentlemens houses, is, Lanhidrock, the seat of the Earls of Radnor, who are Barons of Truro, and were so, long before they obtained the title of Radnor; also a good house belonging to the ancient family of Trefusis.

In viewing these things, we observ'd the hills fruitful of tin, copper, and lead, all the way on our right hand, the product of which, is carried all to the other shore; so that we shall have little to say of it here. The chief business on this shore, is in the herring fishing; the herrings, about October, come driving up the Severn Sea, and from the coast of Ireland, in prodigious

shoals, and beat all upon this coast as high as Biddeford, and
Barnstable, in Devonshire, and are caught in great quantities
by the fishermen, chiefly on account of the merchants of Falmouth, Foy, and Plymouth, and other ports on the south.

Padstow is a large town, and stands on a very good harbour
for such shipping as use that coast, that is to say, for the Irish
trade: The harbour is the mouth of the river Camel, or Camal,
which rising at Camelford, runs down by Bodmyn to Wodbridge,
or Wardbridge, a large stone bridge of eight arches, or thereabouts, built by the general good will of the country gentlemen;
but at the motion of a religious man, named Lovibond, moved
in mere charity; the passage over the river there, before, being
very dangerous, and having been the loss of some lives, as well
as goods. The passage from this town of Padstow to Ireland, is
called, by writers, to be no more than twenty-four hours, but
not justly: It is true, that Padstow being the first, and best, if
not the only haven on this shore, the trade from Ireland settled
here of course, and a great many ships in this harbour, are
imploy'd in the commerce; but to say, they make the voyage in
four-and-twenty hours, is to say, It has been so, or, on extraordinary gales of fair wind, it may be done; but not one in
twenty-four ships makes its voyage in twenty-four hours; and,
I believe, it may be said, they are oftener five or six days in
the passage.

A little way within the land S.W. from Padstow, lies
St. Columb, eminent for nothing but its being the antient
estate of the famous Arundel of Trerice, of late years made
noble by King Charles II., being still famous in the present
Lord Arundel of Trerice; also between them, is a very antient
seat of a family of the name of Prideaux who, in Queen
Elizabeth's time, built a very noble seat there, which remains
to this day, tho' time makes the architect of it look a little
out of fashion.

Higher within the land, lies the town of Bodmyn, once one
of the coining towns for tin, but lost it to Lestwithyel: However, this town enjoys several privileges, some of which are
also tokens of its antiquity.

The coinage towns were, in Queen Elizabeth's time, four;
namely,

| Leskard, | Truro, |
| Lestwithyel, | Helston. |

Since that, in King James's time, was added,
Pensance.

Tintagel Castle lies upon this coast a little farther, a mark of great antiquity, and every writer has mentioned it; but as antiquity is not my work, I leave the ruins of Tintagel to those that search into antiquity; little or nothing, that I could hear, is to be seen at it; and as for the story of King Arthur being both born and killed there, 'tis a piece of tradition, only on oral history, and not any authority to be produced for it.

We have nothing more of note in this county, that I could see, or hear of, but a set of monumental stones, found standing not far from Bodmyn, called The Hurlers, of which the country, nor all the writers of the country, can give us no good account; so I must leave them as I found them.

The game called the Hurlers, is a thing the Cornish men value themselves much upon; I confess, I see nothing in it, but that it is a rude violent play among the boors, or country people; brutish and furious, and a sort of an evidence, that they were, once, a kind of barbarians: It seems, to me, something to resemble the old way of play, as it was then called, with whirle-bats, with which Hercules slew the gyant, when he undertook to clean the Augean stable.

The wrestling in Cornwall, is, indeed, a much more manly and generous exercise, and that closure, which they call the Cornish Hug, has made them eminent in the wrestling rings all over England, as the Norfolk, and Suffolk men, are for their dexterity at the hand and foot, and throwing up the heels of their adversary, without taking hold of him.

I came out of Cornwall by passing the river Tamar at Launceston, the last, or rather, the first, town in the county, the town shewing little else, but marks of its antiquity; for great part of it is so old, as it may, in a manner, pass for an old, ragged, decay'd place, in general. It stands at a distance, almost two miles from the river, over which, there is a very good bridge; the town is eminent, however, for being, as we call it, the county town, where the assizes are always kept.

In the time when Richard, Earl of Cornwall, had the absolute government of this county, and was, we might say, king of the country, it was a frontier town, walled about, and well fortified, and had, also, a strong castle to defend it; but these are seen, now, only in their old cloaths, and lie all in ruins and heaps of rubbish.

It is a principal gain to the people of this town, that they let lodgings to the gentlemen, who attend here in the time of the assizes, and other publick meetings; as particularly, that of electing knights of the shire, and at the county sessions, which are held here; for which purposes, the town's people have their rooms better furnished than in other places of this country, though their houses are but low; nor do they fail to make a good price to their lodgers, for the conveniences they afford them.

The town sends two members to Parliament, and so does Newport, a little village adjoining, and which, indeed, is but a part of Launceston itself; so that the town may be said, almost, to choose four Members of Parliament. There is a fine image, or figure of Mary Magdalen, upon the tower of the church, which the Catholicks fail not to pay their reverences to, as they pass by. There is no tin, or copper, or lead, found hereabouts, as I could find, nor any manufacture in the place; there are a pretty many attorneys here, who manage business for the rest of their fraternity at the assizes: As to trade, it has not much to boast of, and yet there are people enough in it to excuse those who call it a populous place: There is a long nook of the county, runs north from this place, which is called the Hundred of Stratton, and in which there is one market town, and no more, the name of which, is Stratton; but has nothing in, or about it, worth our making any remarks. Passing the river Tamar, as above, about two miles from Launceston, we enter the great county of Devon, and as we enter Devonshire, in the most wild and barren part of the county, and where, formerly, tin mines were found, though now they are either quite exhausted, or not to be found without more charge than the purchase, if found, would be worth; so we must expect it a little to resemble its neighbour country for a while.

The river Tamar, here, is so full of fresh salmon, and those so exceeding fat, and good, that they are esteemed, in both counties, above the fish, of the same kind, found in other places; and the quantity is so great, as supplies the country in abundance, which is occasioned by the mouth of the river being so very large, and the water so deep for two leagues before it opens into Plymouth Sound, so that the fish have a secure retreat in the salt water for their harbour and shelter, and from thence they shoot up into the fresh water, in such vast numbers to cast their spawn, that the country people cannot take too many.

It is observed of Cornwall, as of one or two counties more in England, that all the rivers that are in the county, rise within the bounds of the same county; and this must needs be because this river Tamar, which parts the two counties, rises in the upper edge, within a little more than two miles of the North, or Severn Sea, and runs into the South, or British Channel, cross the whole limits, so that no river out of Devonshire, can enter Cornwall, that little piece in the north excepted; unless we should suppose it to run cross the Tamar, which is not to be thought of.

As we are just entered Devonshire, as I said above, it seems, at first sight, a wild, barren, poor country; but we ride but a few miles, 'till we find an alteration in several things: 1. More people; 2. Larger towns; 3. The people all busy, and in full employ upon their manufactures.

At the uppermost, and extreme part of the county, N.W. there runs a huge promontory, a mountain like proboscis, into the sea, beyond all the land on either side, whether of Devonshire, or of Cornwall. This they would fain have called Hercules's Promontory, and Mr. Cambden, in his writing, and his map-maker also, calls it Herculis Promontorium; but the honest sailers, and after them, the plain country people, call it, in down-right modern English, Hartland Point, or, Hearty Point, from the town of Hartland, which stands just within the shore, and is on the very utmost edge of the county of Devon: It is a market town, though so remote, and of good resort too, the people coming to it out of Cornwall, as well as out of Devonshire; and particularly the fisher-boats of Barnstaple, Bidiford, and other towns on the coast, lying often under the lee, as they call it, of these rocks, for shelter from the S.W. or S.E. winds; the seamen go on shore here, and supply themselves with provisions; nor is the town unconcerned in that gainful fishing trade, which is carried on for the herrings on this coast, many seamen and fishing vessels belonging to the town.

From this point or promontory, the land, falling away for some miles, makes a gulph or bay, which, reaching to the head land, or point of Barnstable River or Haven, is called from thence, Barnstable Bay; into this bay, or at the W. end of this bay, the rivers Taw and Tower empty themselves at one mouth, that is to say, in one channel; and it is very particular, that as two rivers join in one channel, so here are two great trading towns in one port, a thing which as it is not usual, so I cannot say 'tis any advantage to either of them; for it naturally follows, that they rival one another, and lessen both; whereas, had they been join'd together in one town, or were it possible to join them, they would make the most considerable town, or city rather, in all this part of England.

These are the towns of Barnstable and Biddiford, or, as some write it, Bediford; the first of these is the most antient, the last the most flourishing; the harbour or river is in its entrance the same to both, and when they part, the Tower turning to the right, or south west, and the Taw to the S.E. yet they seem to be both so safe, so easy in the channel, so equally good with respect to shipping, so equi-distant from the sea, and so equally advantageous, that neither town complains of the bounty of the sea to them, or their situation by land; and yet, of late years, the town of Biddiford has flourished, and the town of Barnstable rather declin'd.

Biddiford is a pleasant, clean, well-built town; the more antient street which lies next the river, is very pleasant, where is the bridge, a very noble key, and the custom-house; this part also is very well built and populous, and fronts the river for above three quarters of a mile: But besides this, there is a new spacious street, which runs N. and S. or rather N.W. and S.E. a great length, broad as the High Street of Excester, well-built, and, which is more than all, well inhabited, with considerable and wealthy merchants, who trade to most parts of the trading world.

Here, as is to be seen in almost all the market towns of Devonshire, is a very large, well-built, and well-finish'd meeting-house, and, by the multitude of people which I saw come out of it, and the appearance of them, I thought all the town had gone thither, and began to enquire for the church: But when I came to the church, I found that also, large, spacious, and well filled too, and that with people of the best fashion. The person who officiates at the meeting-house in this town, I happened to have some conversation with, and found him to be not only a learned man, and master of good reading; but a most acceptable gentlemanly person, and one, who, contrary to our receiv'd opinion of those people, had not only good learning, and good sense, but abundance of good manners, and good humour; nothing soure, cynical, or morose in him, and, in a word, a very valuable man: And as such a character always recommends a man to men of sense and good breeding, so I found this gentleman was very well received in the place, even by those who he differ'd from in matters of religion, and those differences did not, as is usual, make any breach in their conversing with him: His name, as I remember, was Bartlet. But this is a digression: I wish I could say the like of all the rest of his brethren.

The trade of this town being very much in fish, as it is also of all the towns on this coast, I observed here, that several ships were employ'd to go to Leverpool, and up the river Mersey to Warrington, to fetch the rock salt, which is found in that county, (and of which I shall say more in my remarks on those parts) which rock salt they bring to Biddiford and Barnstable, and here they dissolve it into brine in the sea water, joyning the strength of two bodies into one, and then boil it up again into a new salt, as the Dutch do by the French and Portuguese salt: This is justly call'd salt upon salt, and with this they cure their herrings; and as this is a trade which can be but of a few years standing, because the rock itself has not been discover'd in England much above twenty years; so the difference in curing the fish has been such, and it has so recommended their herrings in foreign markets, that the demand for them has considerably increased, and consequently the trade.

There is indeed, a very fine stone bridge over the river here, but the passage over it is so narrow, and they are so chary of it, that few carriages go over it; but as the water ebbs quite out of the river every low water, the carts and waggons go over the sand with great ease and safety; the arches of the bridge are beautiful and stately; but as for saying one of them is so big, that a ship of 60 tons may sail under it, &c. as a late author asserts, I leave that where I find it, for the people of Bidiford to laugh at: If it had been said the hull of such a ship might pass under the bridge, it might have been let go; But, as he says, It may SAIL under it, which must suppose some or one of its masts standing too; this puts it past all possibility of belief, at least to those who judge of such things by rules of mechanism, or by what is to be seen in other parts of the world, no such thing being practicable either at London Bridge, Rochester Bridge, or even at York, where the largest arch in England is supposed to be.

Bidiford was antiently the inheritance of the family of Granville, or Greenfield, as formerly call'd, and the Earl of Bath, who is the heir and chief of the family, is now Baron of Bidiford, Viscount Lansdown, and Earl of Bath.

As Biddiford has a fine bridge over the Tower or Towridge, so Barnstable has a very noble bridge over the Taw, and though not longer, is counted larger and stronger than the other. These two rival towns are really very considerable; both of them have a large share in the trade to Ireland, and in the herring fishery, and in a trade to the British colonies in America; if Biddiford

cures more fish, Barnstable imports more wine, and other
merchandizes; they are both establish'd ports for landing wooll
from Ireland; of which by itself.

If Biddiford has a greater number of merchants, Barnstable
has a greater commerce within land, by its great market for
Irish wooll and yarn, &c. with the serge-makers of Tiverton
and Excester, who come up hither to buy. So that, in a word,
Barnstable, though it has lost ground to Biddiford, yet, take it
in all its trade compleatly, is full as considerable as Biddiford;
only, that perhaps, it was formerly far superior to it, and the
other has risen up to be a match to it.

Barnstable is a large, spacious, well built town, more populous
than Biddiford, but not better built, and stands lower; insomuch,
that at high water in spring tides, it is, as it were, surrounded
with water; the bridge here, was built by the generous gift
of one Stamford, a citizen and merchant of London, who, it
seems, was not a native of this place, but by trading here to
his gain, had kindness enough for the town, to offer such a
benefaction to them as they enjoy the benefit of to this day.

The bridge at Biddiford as above, was likewise a gift; but
was, as they say, done by collections among the clergy, by
grant of indulgences and the like church management: But
be it how it will, both the towns are infinitely obliged to the
benefactors.

Behind Biddiford, that is as we come from Launceston, are
several good towns, though I observ'd that the country was
wild and barren; as Tavistock, belonging to the house of Bedford,
and giving the title of marquis, to the eldest son of that illustrious ducal family; the town of Torrington, on the same river
Towridge that Biddiford stands on; the title of Earl of Torrington, was first given to the late General Monk, Duke of
Albemarle, in honour, and for a reward of his loyalty, in
restoring King Charles II. and the line being extinct in his
son, it was given by King William III. to Admiral Herbert,
who came over with him, and was immediately made admiral
of the British fleet, to defend the possession of the crown in
the person of that prince; and since that to Sir George Bing,
one of our present admirals, and one who asserted the authority
and power of the British navy against the Spaniards, at the
late sea fight near Cape Passaro in Sicily: So that the town of
Torrington, seems to be appropriated to the honour of the
defenders of the British sovereignty at sea.

Another town in this part of the country is Okehampton,

vulgarly Okington, a good market town, which gave title of
baron to the Lord Mohun, and sends two members to the
Parliament; it is a manufacturing town, as all the towns this
way now are, and pretty rich; and having said this, I have said
all, unless it be, that in the records of antiquity, it appears to
have been much more considerable than it is now, having 92
knights fees belonging to it. But as I studiously avoid medling
with antiquity in these accounts, studying to give you the
present state of the countries and towns through which I travel,
rather than what they have been; so I say no more of those
things than needs must.

A little above Barnstable, N.E. upon the coast, stands a good
market and port town, call'd Ilfar-Comb, a town of good trade,
populous and rich, all which is owing to its having a very good
harbour and road for ships, and where ships from Ireland often
put in, when, in bad weather, they cannot, without the extremest
hazard, run into the mouth of the Taw, which they call Barnstable Water; and this is one reason, which causes the merchants
at Barnstable, to do much of their business at this port of
Ilfar-comb.

Antiquity tells us long stories, of the Danes landing on this
coast; of Hubba, the Danish king, being slain here, that is at
Kennith Castle, between this place and the mouth of the Taw
and Towridge, and that the place was call'd Hubbestow ever
after, from the burying of this prince there; All this may be
true, for ought we know, but I could neither find or hear of
this castle of Kennith, or burial place, Hubbestow, or any
thing of the ruins or remains of them in the country; so I shall
trouble you no farther about them.

The sea coast in this county, runs a little farther east by
north, but I found there was nothing of moment to be seen
there, except fishing towns, and small creeks, on which are
two small market towns, such as Combemerton, and Porlock,
'till we came to Minehead.

Leaving the coast, we came, in our going southward, to the
great river Ex, or Isca, which rises in the hills on this north
side of the county, and that so far, as, like the Tamar, it begins
within four or five miles of the Severn Sea; the country it
rises in, is called Exmore, Cambden calls it a filthy, barren,
ground, and, indeed, so it is; but as soon as the Ex comes off
from the moors, and hilly country, and descends into the lower
grounds, we found the alteration; for then we saw Devonshire
in its other countenance, viz. cultivated, populous, and fruitful;

and continuing so 'till we came to Tiverton, a town which I mentioned before, but did not fully describe.

Next to Excester, this is the greatest manufacturing town in the county, and, of all the inland towns, is next to it in wealth, and in numbers of people; it stands on the river Ex, and has over it, a very fine bridge, with another over the little river Loman, which, immediately after, falls into the Ex just below the town: Antiquity says, before those bridges were built, there were two fords here, one through each river, and that the town was from thence called Twyford-ton, that is, the town upon the two fords, and so by abbreviating the sounds Twy-for-ton, then Tiverton; but that I leave to the learned searchers into antient things.

But the beauty of Tiverton is the Free-School, at the east entrance into the town, a noble building, but a much nobler foundation; it was erected by one Peter Blundel, a clothier, and a lover of learning, who used the saying of William of Wickham to the king when he founded the royal school at Winchester, viz. That if he was not himself a scholar, he would be the occasion of making more scholars, than any scholar in England; to which end he founded this school: He has endowed it with so liberal a maintenance, that, as I was informed, the school-master has, at least, sixty pounds per annum, besides a very good house to live in, and the advantage of scholars not on the foundation, and the usher in proportion; and to this he added two fellowships, and two scholarships, which he gave the maintenance for to Sydney-College in Cambridge, and one fellowship, and two scholarships, to Baliol-College in Oxford, all which are appointed for the scholars bred up in this school, and the present reverend master, was a scholar upon the foundation in the same school.

As this is a manufacturing country, as above, we found the people, here, all fully employ'd, and very few, if any, out of work, except such as need not be unemploy'd, but were so from mere sloth and idleness, of which, some will be found every where.

From this town, there is little belonging to Devonshire, but what has been spoken of, except what lies in the road to Taunton, which we took next, where we meet with the river Columb, a river rising also in the utmost limits of the shire towards Somersetshire, and giving name to so many towns on its banks, as leaves no room to doubt of its own name being right, such as Columb David's, Ufcolumbe, Columstock, and Columbton;

the last is a market town, and they are all full of manufacturers, depending much on the master manufacturers of Tiverton.

With this town, we leave the county of Devon, and entering Somersetshire, have really a taste of a different country from Devonshire; for entering Wellington, the first town we came at in Somersetshire, though partly employ'd in manufacturing too, we were immediately surrounded with beggars, to such a degree, that we had some difficulty to keep them from under our horse heels.

It was our misfortune at first, that we threw some farthings, and halfpence, such as we had, among them; for thinking by this to be rid of them, on the contrary, it brought out such a croud of them, as if the whole town was come out into the street, and they ran in this manner after us through the whole street, and a great way after we were quite out of the town; so that we were glad to ride as fast as we could through the town to get clear of them; I was, indeed, astonish'd at such a sight, in a country where the people were so generally full of work, as they were here; for in Cornwall, where there are hardly any manufacturers, and where there are, indeed, abundance of poor, yet we never found any thing like this.

Before I quite leave Devonshire, I must mention one thing, which I observed at my first setting out; namely, That I would take notice how every county in England furnish'd something of its produce towards the supply of the city of London: Now I must allow, that Cornwall is, in some respects, an exception to this rule, because, though it is fruitful enough for the supply of its own inhabitants, yet, in the first place, the waste grounds are so many, the inhabitants so numerous, and the county so narrow, that, except the herrings, a few of which may be brought to London for sale, they have not much overplus to furnish other parts with; but then they make us amends by sending up an immense wealth in their tin, lead, and copper, from the bowels of their barren mountains, and the export of the pilchards, and herrings, from both their shores to Spain and Italy, from whence much of the returns are again brought to London for their vent and consumption.

In like manner, the county of Devon has been rich in mines of tin and lead, though they seem at present, wrought out; and they had their stannary towns and coinage, as well as in Cornwall; nay, so numerous were the miners or tinners, as they are called in this county, that they were, on occasion of a national muster, or defence, regimented by themselves, arm'd, and officer'd by themselves, and were, in short, a separate militia from the train'd bands, or militia of the county; but now we see the tin works in Devonshire is quite laid aside, not one tin mine being at work in the whole county: There are, indeed, some copper-works undertaken on the north side, as we were told; but I do not find, that they are yet brought to any perfection, and about Ilfarcomb, Comb Mertin, also at Delverton, in the north part of the county, they have been at work to see if they can recover some silver mines, which, in the time of King Edward III. were so large, that they employed three hundred miners, besides other workmen, and brought that prince great sums of money for the carrying on his wars against France: What progress they are now like to make in it, I cannot yet learn.

But there is one article in the produce of Devonshire, which makes good what I have written before, That every county contributes something towards the supply of London; and this is, the cyder which I have mentioned already, and which takes up the south part of the county, between Topsham and Axminster, where they have so vast a quantity of fruit, and so much cyder made, that sometimes they have sent ten, or twenty thousand hogsheads of it in a year to London, and at a very reasonable rate too.

The county of Somerset joins to the N.E. part of Devonshire. I touch'd only upon one point of the county in my last, as I went west. The whole county is worth a more particular account, than can be given within the space of a letter.

I entered the county, as I observed above, by Wellington, where we had the entertainment of the beggars; from whence we came to Taunton, vulgarly called Taunton Dean upon the River Ton; this is a large, wealthy, and exceedingly populous, town: One of the chief manufacturers of the town told us, That there was at that time so good a trade in the town, that they had then eleven hundred looms going for the weaving of sagathies, du roys, and such kind of stuffs, which are made there; and that which added to the thing very much, was, that not one of those looms wanted work: He farther added, That there was not a child in the town, or in the villages round it, of above five years old, but, if it was not neglected by its parents, and untaught, could earn its own bread. This was what I never met with in any place in England, except at Colchester in Essex.

This town chooses two Members of Parliament, and their

way of choosing is, by those who they call "pot-walloners," that is to say, every inhabitant, whether house-keeper or lodger, that dresses their own victuals; to make out which, several inmates, or lodgers, will, sometime before the election, bring out their pots, and make fires in the street, and boil their victuals in the sight of their neighbours, that their votes may not be called in question.

There are two large parish churches in this town, and two or three meeting-houses, whereof one, is said to be the largest in the county. The inhabitants have been noted for the number of Dissenters; for among them it was always counted a seminary of such: They suffered deeply in the Duke of Monmouth's Rebellion, but paid King James home for the cruelty exercised by Jeffries among them; for when the Prince of Orange arrived, the whole town ran in to him, with so universal a joy, that, 'twas thought, if he had wanted it, he might have raised a little army there, and in the adjacent part of the country.

There was, and, I suppose, is still, a private college, or academy, for the Dissenters in this town; the tutor, who then managed it, was named Warren, who told me, that there were threescore and twelve ministers then preaching, whereof six had conformed to the Church, the rest were among the Dissenters, who had been his scholars, whereupon, one of his own sort had, it seems, stiled him the Father of the Faithful: The academy, since his death, is continued, but not kept up to the degree it was, in the days of the said Mr. Warren.

From this town of Taunton, which is by far the greatest in all this part of the country, and has more people in it, than the city of York, we went north to take a view of the coast. Exmore, of which mention was made above, where the River Ex rises, lies in the way, part of it in this country, and extending to the sea side: It gives, indeed, but a melancholy view, being a vast tract of barren, and desolate lands; yet on the coast, there are some very good sea-ports. As,

1. Porlock, on the very utmost extent of the country; it has a small harbour, but of no importance, nor has it any thing of trade, so I need but name it. 2. Minhead, the best port, and safest harbour, in all these counties, at least, on this side: No ship is so big, but it may come in, and no weather so bad, but the ships are safe when they are in; and they told me, that in the great storm anno 1703, when in all the harbours and rivers in the county, the ships were blown on shore, wreck'd, and lost, they suffered little or no damage in this harbour.

The trade of this town lies chiefly with Ireland, and this was, for many years, the chief port in this part of England, where wool from Ireland was allowed to be imported; but that liberty is since inlarged to several other ports by Act of Parliament.

This corporation sends two members to the Parliament, which are chosen also, as at Taunton, by the pot-walloners; the town is well built, is full of rich merchants, and has some trade also to Virginia, and the West Indies: They correspond much with the merchants of Barnstable, and Bristol, in their foreign trade.

There are some very good families, and of very antient standing, in this part of the county, among which, the families of Seymour, of Portman, of Orchard, Wyndham, Popham of Wellington, Mallet, an antient family of Norman extraction, Mohun, Beauchamp, and some others, are most eminent; the Mohuns in particular were antiently lords of Dunstar Castle, at a small distance from the sea, and very strong. Here formerly was the antient mansion, or inheritance, of the Lords Mohun, who, as above, long enjoy'd it: Who it will now descend to, that antient family being extinct in the person of the late unhappy Lord Mohun, who was kill'd in a duel with Duke Hamilton, I could not learn.

From hence the coast bears back west to Watchet, a small port also, but of no importance, that is to say, 'tis of no importance now; for if we may calculate things present, by things past, the town of Minhead is risen out of the decay of the towns of Porlock and Watchet, which were once important places; and the reason is clear, since the increase of shipping and trade, and the improvement of the navigating skill, bigger ships being brought into use, than were formerly built; accordingly, larger ports, and deeper water, were requisite to harbour such vessels, than would serve for that purpose before; and the harbour at Minhead being fairer, and much deeper, than those at Watchet and Porlock, and therefore able to secure those greater ships, which the others were not, the merchants removed to it; and thus, in time, the town grew up, to what we now find it to be.

From hence the winding shore brings us to Bridgewater. This is an antient and very considerable town and port, it stands at the mouth of the river Parrat, or Perot, which comes from the south, after having received the river Tone from the west, which is made navigable up to Taunton, by a very fine new channel, cut at the expence of the people of Taunton, and which, by the navigation of it, is infinitely advantagious to that town, and well worth all their expence, first by bringing up coals, which are brought from Swanzy in Wales by sea to Bridgewater, and thence by barges up this river to Taunton; also for bringing all heavy goods and merchandizes from Bristol, such as iron, lead, oyl, wine, hemp, flax, pitch, tar, grocery, and dye stuffs, and the like; their tobacco they generally received from Barnstable by land, which is about sixteen miles west

This town of Bridgewater, is a populous, trading town, is well built, and as well inhabited, and has many families of good fashion dwelling in it, besides merchants. The famous Admiral Blake, was a native of this town. Here it was, that the Duke of Monmouth, finding himself defeated in his expectation of the city of Bristol, and repuls'd at the city of Bath, and press'd by the approach of the king's troops, who endeavour'd to surround him, made his retreat; where, finding the king's troops followed him, and seem'd resolved to attack him, he went up to the top of the steeple, with some of his officers, and viewing the situation of the king's army, by the help of perspectives, resolved to make an attempt upon them the same night, by way of prevention, and accordingly march'd out of the town in the dead of the night to attack them, and had he not, either by the treachery, or mistake of his guides, been brought to an unpassable ditch, where he could not get over, in the interval of which, the king's troops took the alarm, by the firing a pistol among the duke's men, whether, also, by accident, or treachery, was not known; I say, had not those accidents, and his own fate, conspired to his defeat, he had certainly cut the Lord Feversham's army (for he commanded them) all to pieces; but by these circumstances, he was brought to a battle on unequal terms, and defeated: The rest I need not mention.

This town was regularly fortified in the late civil wars, and sustained two sieges, if not more; the situation of it renders it easy to be fortified, the river and haven taking one chief part of the circumference; over the river, they have a very good bridge of stone, and the tide rises here, at high water, near six fathoms, whereof, sometimes it comes in with such furious haste, as to come two fathoms deep at a time, and when it does so, by surprize, it often does great damage to ships, driving them foul of one another, and oftentimes oversetting them. This sudden rage of the tide, is called, the "boar," and is frequent in all the rivers of this channel, especially in the Severn itself; 'tis also known in the north, particularly in the Trent, and the Ouse, at their entrance into Humber, and in several other places.

In this town of Bridgewater, besides a very large church, there is a fine new-built meeting-house, that is to say, built since the Toleration, in which 'tis remarkable, that they have an advanc'd seat for the mayor and aldermen, when any of the magistrates should be of their Communion, as sometimes has happened. Here, also, is a college, or private academy, for the Dissenters to breed up their preaching youth; the tutor was one Mr. Moor, a man who, it is own'd, was a master of good literature; what talent he had at erudition, I can give no account of, for it is not every master of learning, that makes a good instructor of others, as I shall observe on some other occasions.

From Bridgewater, there is a road to Bristol, which they call the Lower Way; the Upper Way, and which is the more frequented road, being over Mendip Hills. This Lower Way also is not always passable, being subject to floods, and dangerous inundations, I mean, dangerous to travel through, especially for strangers: All this part of the country, viz. between Bridgewater, and the sea, and on northward upon the coast, lies low, and is wholly imployed in breeding and feeding of cattle, as are also the moors, or marsh grounds, which extend themselves up the rivers Perrot, and Ivill, into the heart of the country; of which in its place.

This low part of the country, between Bridgewater and Bristol, suffered exceedingly in that terrible inundation of the sea, which was occasioned by the violence of the wind in the great storm, anno 1703, and the country people have set up marks upon their houses and trees, with this note upon them, "Thus high the waters came in the great storm": "Thus far the great tide flowed up in the last violent tempest"; and the like.

And in one place they shewed us, where a ship was, by the force of the water, and the rage of the tempest, driven up upon the shore, several hundred yards from the ordinary high water mark, and was left in that surprizing condition upon dry land.

As this country is all a grazing, rich, feeding soil, so a great number of large oxen are fed here, which are sent up to London; so that now we come into the reach of my former observation, viz. That every county furnishes something for the supply of London, and no county in England furnishes more effectual provisions, nor, in proportion, a greater value than this. These supplies are in three articles.

1. Fat oxen (as above) as large, and good, as any in England.
2. Large Cheddar cheese, the greatest, and best of the kind in England.
3. Colts bred in great numbers in the moors, and sold into the northern counties, where the horse copers, as they are called, in Staffordshire, and Leicestershire, buy them again, and sell them to London for cart horses, and coach horses, the breed being very large.

As the low part of this county is thus imployed in grazing and feeding cattle, so all the rest of this large extended country is imployed in the woollen manufactures, and in the best, and most profitable part of it, viz.

In Taunton - -	The serges, druggets, &c. and several other kinds of stuffs.
In Wells, Shepton, Glastenbury, &c.	Knitting of stockings, principally for the Spanish trade.
In Bristol, and many towns on the Somerset-shire side - - -	Druggets, cantaloons, and other stuffs.
In Froom, Philips-Norton, and all the country bordering upon Wiltshire - - -	Fine Spanish medley cloths, especially on that part of the county from Wincanton, and Meer, to Warminster, Bruton, Castle-cary, Temple Comb, down to Gillingham, and Shaftsbury, in Dorsetshire.

I mention this at large, because this trade of fine Spanish medley cloth, being the mix'd colours and cloths, with which all the gentlemen and persons of any fashion in England, are cloth'd, and vast quantities of which are exported to all parts of Europe, is so very considerable, so vast an advantage to England, maintains and supports so many poor families, and makes so many rich ones, that no man can be just in the description of things, and in a survey of this part of England, and not enter into a particular description of it; the above you may take as an introduction to it, only I shall add but a little more, concerning this county of Somerset, and shall, upon my entering into the north-west and west parts of Wiltshire, where the center of this prodigy of a trade is, sum it all up together, and shew you the extent of land which it spreads itself upon, and give you room, at least, to make some guess at the numbers of poor people, who are sustain'd and inrich'd by it.

But I must first go back again a little while into Somersetshire: The northern part of the county, I did not visit in this journey, which, as I hinted before, is only a return from my long travel to the Land's End. In omitting this part, I, of course, leave the two cities of Bristol and Bath, and that high part of the county called Mendip Hill, to my next western journey, which will include all the counties due west from London; for these now spoken of, though ordinarily called the west country, are rather S.W. than west.

But as I made a little trip from Bridgewater north, into the body of the county, I must take notice of what I observed in that part of it: The first place I came to was Glastenbury, where, indeed, the venerable marks of antiquity, however I have declin'd the observation of them, struck me with some unusual awe, and I resolved to hear all that could be told me upon that subject; and first they told me (for there are two pieces of antiquity, which were to be inquired of in this place) that King Arthur was buried here, and that his coffin had been found here.

Secondly, that Joseph of Arimathea was here, and that when he fix'd his staff in the ground, which was on Christmas Day, it immediately took root, budded, put forth white-thorn leaves, and the next day, was in full blossom, white as a sheet, and that the plant is preserved, and blows every Christmas Day, as at first, to this very day.

I took all this *ad referendum*, but took guides afterward, to see what demonstrations there could be given of all these things; they went over the ruins of the place with me, telling me, which part every particular piece of building had been; and as for the white-thorn, they carried me to a gentleman's garden in the town, where it was preserved, and I brought a piece of it away in my hat, but took it upon their honour, that it really does blow in such manner, as above, on Christmas Day. However, it must be confess'd, that it is universally attested.

Where I had the sight of the white-thorn tree, I obtained a sight of Mr. Cambden, and his continuator, and was, at first, a little concern'd, that a person of Mr. Cambden's judgment, gave such an account of the legendary part of the history of this place, with a taste of his crediting the whole story; and from him I began to believe also, that Joseph of Arimathea, was really here, and that the Christian religion was preached in this island within thirty seven years after the death of our Saviour.

This, however, prompted me to farther inquiry, and the following account occurred, which is to be found, as they say, in the manuscript History of the Church of Glastenbury, now deposited in the Cottonian Library, and taken from it by Mr. Dugdale, in his *Monasticon*. Fol. 1, 2.

GLASTONBURY MONASTERY IN SOMERSETSHIRE,
OF THE ORDER OF ST. BENEDICT

In the year 31 after the Passion of our Lord, twelve of St. Philip the Apostle's disciples (the chief of whom was Joseph of Arimathea) came into this country, and preached the Christian faith to Arviragus, who refused to embrace it, and yet granted them this place, with twelve hides of land; where they made walls of wattles, and erected the first church in this kingdom, which Christ personally dedicated to the honour of His Mother, and the place for burial of His servants, as is said in the manuscript History of the Monastery of Glastenbury in the Cotton Library. These twelve, and their successors, continuing long the same number, and leading an eremetical life, converted a great multitude of pagans to the faith of Christ. They being all, at length, dead and buried here, the most holy men Phaganus and Diruvianus, coming into these parts, and baptizing King Lucius and his people, had the aforesaid hides confirm'd to them and their successors, the same number of twelve being kept up 'till the coming of St. Patrick, who, instructing them in the monastical life, became their abbot: After whom, the holy fathers Benignus, Kolumkil, and Gildas, led a most holy life there. Next came St. David Archbishop of Menevia, now called St. David's, who added a new chapel to the church, dedicating it to the blessed Virgin, and erected a rich altar; and near the said chapel, Joseph of Arimathea, and other holy men, are said to have been buried. Tho' the church was afterwards several times rebuilt, this place still remained under the former consecration, and was held in such veneration, that kings, bishops, and all the greatest persons, thought themselves happy in adding something to its possessions, or being buried with any small parcel of its earth. St. Dunstan, and other holy abbots, always preserving the number of twelve monks, added to them several clergymen that sung well.

This church, by reason of its antiquity, was by the English called Ealdchurch, that is, Old Church; and the people of the country about it, thought no oath more sacred, than to swear by the Old Church; as being the first, and oldest church in England, and held in such veneration, that it was called a second Rome, for sanctity;

because, as Rome was honoured with a multitude of martyrs, so this place was renowned for many confessors.

This island, in which this church stands, was, by the Britons, first called Ynswyrtryn, that is, the Glass Island, by reason of the river, as it were of the colour of glass, incompassing the marsh. It was called an island, because inclosed about by a deep marsh. It was called Avallonia, either from the British word *aval*, signifying an apple, as being full of fruit-trees, or from Avallon, who was once lord of that territory. The Saxons gave it the name of Glastingebury, that is, the Town of Glass. There are several islands about this, all belonging to it, all which together were reduced to make up the twelve hides above-mentioned, the bounds whereof may be seen in Dugdale, p. 2. and 3. All the places within those bounds enjoy all sorts of immunities, from the first times of Christianity, granted and confirmed to the church of Glastonbury by the British, English, and Norman kings.

This church was the sacred repository of the ashes of a multitude of saints, insomuch that no corner of it, or of the church-yard, is destitute of the same. There lie the twelve disciples (above-mentioned) of St. Philip the Apostle, with their chief, Joseph of Arimathea, and his son Josephus; also St. Patrick, the apostle of Ireland; St. Benignus, disciple to St. Patrick; St. Pinius, disciple to Benignus; St. Gildas, the British historian; St. David, Bishop of Menevia; St. Dunstan; St. Indrastus, martyr, and his seven companions; St. Urban, martyr; St. Apollinaris, bishop and martyr, disciple to St. Peter the Apostle; St. Vincentius, archdeacon and martyr; three of the Holy Innocents; St. Besilius, martyr; part of St. Oswald, king and martyr; St. Valerius, and St. Salvius, bishops and martyrs; St. Canon, Anastatius, Renignius, Casanius, Abdon, and Sennen, martyrs; St. Paulinus, Bishop of the Northumbrians; St. Aidan, Bishop of Lindisfarn; Coelfrid and Boisilus, abbots; Venerable Bede; St. Benedict, bishop; Hesterpine, Sigfride, and Herbert, abbots; St. Idamus, bishop; St. Teison, abbot, and his twelve companions; St. Iltwich; St. Lilianus, abbot; part of Guthlac, the anchorite; St. Poppa, Archbishop of Treves; St. Geminianus, confessor; the holy virgins Hilda, Hebbe, Begu, Crisante, Udilia, Mary, Martha, Lucy, Walburge, Gertrude, Cecily, Wenta, Mamilla, Edberga, Elfleda, Batildis, Ursula, Daria, Ealswitha; the last of these affirmed to be intire many years after she had been interred. Many more names of holy men and women were lost by the burning of the antient church, and time has worn out the memory of a still greater number.

Many holy relicks were also preserved in this church: Of those relating to the Old Testament, part of Rachel's tomb; of the altar on which Moses pour'd out oyl; of his book; of the tomb of Isaiah; some manna: relicks of the prophet Daniel; of the three children delivered from the fiery furnace; six gilt stones of the pavement of the Temple, and some of the gate. Relating to our Lord Jesus Christ: Some of the linen He was wrapp'd in; two pieces of the manger; some of the gold offer'd by the Wise Men; five stones out of Jordan, where our Saviour was baptized; one of the vessels in which Christ turned water into wine; of the stones the Devil proposed

to Christ to convert into bread; of the five loaves with which our
Lord fed five thousand persons; of the place where He was trans-
figured; of the stone He stood on in the Temple; of His hair; of the
hem of His garment; and many more, too tedious for this place:
Also relicks of the Blessed Virgin; of St. John Baptist; of the
Apostles; of many martyrs, confessors, and holy virgins.

On this account, Glastonbury was every where held in the greatest
veneration; and, as has been said, the greatest persons coveted to
be buried there; most of whose names have been lost, and of some,
mention has been made above.

A few feet from the Old Church stood two pyramids; that next
to the church twenty-six feet high, on which were many antiquities
worn out by age. On the uppermost story of it, was a pontifical
image; on the second, the image of a king, with these letter, *Heri,
Sexi,* and *Blisier;* on the third, were these words, *Wemerest, Bantomp,
Wineweng;* on the fourth, *Hate, Wulfred,* and *Eanfled;* on the fifth,
and lowest, an image, and this inscription, *Logior, Weslicas, Bregden,
Swelves, Hwingendes, Bera.* The other pyramid was eighteen feet
high, and had four stages, on which was to be read, *Hedde* Bishop
Bregored, and *Breorward.* What these words signify is not known;
but it is guess'd, they were the names of the persons deposited
within the pyramid. So great was the respect paid by our ancestors
to this place, that they durst not utter any idle words, nor so much
as spit in the church, or church-yard, unless compell'd by the utmost
necessity, and even then with the utmost reluctancy and remorse:
Neither durst any man bring a hawk, horse, or dog into the church,
because it had been often observed, that such as had been acci-
dentally brought in, immediately died. Even from foreign countries
the earth of this church-yard was sent for, to bury with the greatest
persons; and it is reported, that even a Mahometan sultan, having
taken an English gentleman in the Holy Land, gave him his liberty,
upon promise, that he would bring him a gantlet full of that earth,
which was accordingly perform'd, and the gentleman returning to
Glastonbury, declared the same upon oath.

As to the burial of King Arthur, Mr. Cambden makes no
doubt of it, and gives us from Giraldus Cambrensis, an account
how King Henry II. caused search to be made for his tomb,
and before they had dug seven foot, they came to a great stone,
having a cross of lead on the inside of it, and the subsequent
letters, or inscription upon it, and in the following rude character; which the said Giraldus Cambrensis, Mr. Cambden says,
was an eye-witness of, as well as of a coffin of hollow'd oak,
which they found by digging nine foot deeper than the inscription, wherein were deposited the bones of that great prince.

On the top of a high hill, near a mile from the town, stands an
old tower, which the people vulgarly call the TORR; what it was,
we are not certain; but it is made famous by one thing in particular; that here King Henry VIII. caused Richard Whitingus,

the last Abbot of Glastonbury, to be hanged for refusing to surrender the monastery.

I must confess, that I cannot so much blame the Catholicks in those early days, for reverencing this place as they did, or, at least, 'till they came to found idolatry upon their respect, if they really believed all these things; but my business is to relate, rather than make remarks.

The inscription on King Arthur's coffin, is as follows:

Four miles from Glastonbury, lies the little city of Wells, where is one of the neatest, and, in some respects, the most beautiful, cathedrals in England, particularly the west front of it, is one complete draught of imagery, very fine, and yet very antient.

This is a neat, clean city, and the clergy, in particular, live very handsomly; the Closs, or part of the city, where the Bishop's Palace is, is very properly called so; for it is walled in, and lock'd up like a little fortification, and has a ditch round it.

The dignified clergy live in the inside of it, and the prebendaries, and canons, which are very numerous, have very agreeable dwellings, and live very pleasantly. Here are no less than seven-and-twenty prebends, and nineteen canons, belonging to this church, besides a dean, a chancellor, a precentor, and three arch deacons; a number which very few cathedrals in England have, besides this.

Dugdale, in his *Monasticon*, tells us, that the church of Wells has given to the kingdom, one Cardinal, six High Chancellors, five High Treasurers, one Lord Privy Seal, one Lord President of Wales, one Secretary of State, all of them bishops of this diocess; the county is the diocess, and contains three hundred eighty-eight parishes, and the arch deaconries are of Wells, Bath, and Taunton.

The city lies just at the foot of the mountains called Mendip Hills, and is itself built on a stony foundation. Its manufacture is chiefly of stockings, as is mentioned already; 'tis well built, and populous, and has several good families in it; so that there is no want of good company there.

Near this city, and just under the hills, is the famous, and so much talk'd of Wokey Hole, which, to me, that had been in Pool's Hole, in the Peak of Derby, has nothing of wonder or curiosity in it; the chief thing I observ'd in this, is, what is generally found in all such subterraneous caverns; namely, That the water dropping from the roof of the vault, petrifies, and hangs in long pieces like isicles, as if it would, in time, turn into a column to support the arch. As to the stories of a witch dwelling here, as of a gyant dwelling in the other (I mean in Pool's Hole) I take them to be equally fabulous, and worth no notice.

In the low country, on the other side Mendip Hills, lies Chedder, a village pleasantly situated under the very ridge of the mountains; before the village is a large green, or common, a piece of ground, in which the whole herd of the cows, belonging to the town, do feed; the ground is exceeding rich, and as the whole village are cowkeepers, they take care to keep up the goodness of the soil, by agreeing to lay on large quantities of dung for manuring, and inriching the land.

The milk of all the town cows, is brought together every day into a common room, where the persons appointed, or trusted for the management, measure every man's quantity, and set it down in a book; when the quantities are adjusted, the milk is all put together, and every meal's milk makes one cheese, and no more; so that the cheese is bigger, or less, as the cows yield more, or less, milk. By this method, the goodness of the cheese is preserved, and, without all dispute, it is the best cheese that England affords, if not, that the whole world affords.

As the cheeses are, by this means, very large, for they often weigh a hundred weight, sometimes much more, so the poorer inhabitants, who have but few cows, are obliged to stay the longer for the return of their milk; for no man has any such return, 'till his share comes to a whole cheese, and then he has it; and if the quantity of his milk deliver'd in, comes to above a cheese, the overplus rests in account to his credit, 'till another cheese comes to his share; and thus every man has equal justice, and though he should have but one cow, he shall, in time, have one whole cheese. This cheese is often sold for six pence to eight pence per pound, when the Cheshire cheese is sold but for two pence to two pence halfpenny.

Here is a deep, frightful chasm in the mountain, in the hollow of which, the road goes, by which they travel towards Bristol; and out of the same hollow, springs a little river, which flows with such a full stream, that, it is said, it drives twelve mills within a quarter of a mile of the spring; but this is not to be understood, without supposing it to fetch some winding reaches in the way; there would not, otherwise, be room for twelve mills to stand, and have any head of water above the mill, within so small a space of ground. The water of this spring, grows quickly into a river, and runs down into the marshes, and joins another little river called Axe, about Axbridge, and thence into the Bristol Channel, or Severn Sea.

I must now turn east, and south-east, for I resolved not to go up the hills of Mendip at all, this journey, leaving that part to another tour, when I shall give an account of these mountains, as also of the cities of Bath and Bristol, to which they are very near, all in one letter.

I come now to that part of the country, which joins itself to Wiltshire, which I reserved, in particular, to this place, in order to give some account of the broad-cloth manufacture, which

I several times mentioned in my first journey, and which is carried on here, and that to such a degree, as deserves a place in all the descriptions, or histories, which shall be given of this country.

As the east, and south parts of Wiltshire are, as I have already observed, all hilly, spreading themselves far and wide, in plains, and grassy downs, for breeding, and feeding, vast flocks of sheep, and a prodigious number of them: And as the west and north parts of Somersetshire are, on the contrary, low, and marshy, or moorish, for feeding, and breeding, of black cattle, and horses, or for lead-mines, &c. So all the south west part of Wiltshire, and the east part of Somersetshire, are low and flat, being a rich, inclosed country, full of rivers and towns, and infinitely populous, insomuch, that some of the market towns are equal to cities in bigness, and superior to them in numbers of people.

This low, flat country, contains part of the three counties of Somerset, Wilts, and Gloucester, and that the extent of it may be the easier understood by those who know any thing of the situation of the country, it reaches from Cirencester in the north, to Sherburn on the edge of Dorsetshire south, and from the Devizes east, to Bristol west, which may take in about fifty miles in length where longest, and twenty in breadth where narrowest.

In this extent of country, we have the following market towns, which are principally employ'd in the clothing trade, that is to say, in that part of it, which I am now speaking of; namely, fine medley, or mix'd cloths, such as are usually worn in England by the better sort of people; and, also, exported in great quantities to Holland, Hamburgh, Sweden, Denmark, Spain, Italy, &c. The principal clothing towns in this part of the country, are these,

Somersetshire	Frome, Pensford, Philip's Norton, Bruton, Shepton Mallet, Castle Carey, and Wincanton.
Wiltshire	Malmsbury, Castlecomb, Chippenham, Caln, Devizes, Bradford, Trubridge, Westbury, Warminster, Meer.
Dorsetshire	Gillingham, Shaftsbury, Bemister, and Bere, Sturminster, Shireborn.
Gloucester	Cirencester, Tetbury, Marshfield, Minchinghampton, and Fairford.

These towns, as they stand thin, and at considerable distance from one another; for, except the two towns of Bradford and Trubridge, the other stand at an unusual distance; I say, these towns are interspers'd with a very great number of villages, I had almost said, innumerable villages, hamlets, and scattered houses, in which, generally speaking, the spinning work of all this manufacture is performed by the poor people; the master clothiers, who generally live in the greater towns, sending out the wooll weekly to their houses, by their servants and horses, and, at the same time, bringing back the yarn that they have spun and finished, which then is fitted for the loom.

The increasing and flourishing circumstances of this trade, are happily visible by the great concourse of people to, and increase of buildings and inhabitants in these principal clothing towns where this trade is carried on, and the wealth of the clothiers. The town of Froom, or, as it is written in our maps, Frome Sellwood, is a specimen of this, which is so prodigiously increased within these last twenty or thirty years, that they have built a new church, and so many new streets of houses, and those houses are so full of inhabitants, that Frome is now reckoned to have more people in it, than the city of Bath, and some say, than even Salisbury itself, and if their trade continues to increase for a few years more, as it has done for those past, it is very likely to be one of the greatest and wealthiest inland towns in England.

I call it an inland town, because it is particularly distinguish'd as such, being, not only no sea-port, but not near any sea-port, having no manner of communication by water, no navigable river at it, or near it. Its trade is wholly clothing, and the cloths they make, are, generally speaking, all conveyed to London: Blackwell-Hall is their market, and thither they send up the gross of their clothing product; and, if we may believe common fame, there are above ten thousand people in Frome now, more than lived in it twenty years ago, and yet it was a considerable town then too.

Here are, also, several large meeting-houses, as well as churches, as there are, generally, in all the manufacturing, trading towns in England, especially in the western counties.

The Devizes is, next to this, a large and important town, and full of wealthy clothiers; but this town has, lately, run pretty much into the drugget-making trade; a business, which has made some invasion upon the broad-cloth trade, and great quantities of druggets are worn in England, as also, exported beyond the seas, even in the place of our broad-cloths, and where they usually were worn and exported; but this is much the same as to the trade still; for as it is all a woollen manufacture, and that the druggets may properly be called cloth, though narrow, and of a different make, so the makers are all called clothiers.

The River Avon, a noble and large fresh river, branching itself into many parts, and receiving almost all the rivers on that side the hills, waters this whole fruitful vale; and the water of this river seems particularly qualified for the use of the clothiers; that is to say, for dying the best colours, and for fulling and dressing the cloth, so that the clothiers generally plant themselves upon this river, but especially the dyers, as at Trubridge, and Bradford, which are the two most eminent cloathing towns in that part of the vale for the making fine Spanish cloths, and of the nicest mixtures.

From these towns south, to Westbury, and to Warminster, the same trade continues, and the finest medley Spanish cloths, not in England only, but in the whole world, are made in this part. They told me at Bradford, That it was no extraordinary thing to have clothiers in that country worth, from ten thousand, to forty thousand pounds a man, and many of the great families, who now pass for gentry in those counties, have been originally raised from, and built up by this truly noble manufacture.

If I may speak here from the authority of the antient inhabitants of the place, and who have been curious observers upon this subject, the country which I have now described, as principally imploy'd in, and maintained by this prodigy of a trade, contains two million, three hundred and thirty thousand acres of land, and has in it seven hundred eighty-eight parishes, and three hundred and seventy-four thousand people. It is true, that this is all guess-work; but I must confess myself very willing to believe, that the reckoning is far short of the account; for the county is exceeding large and populous.

It may be worth enquiry, by the curious, how the manufacturers, in so vast a consumption of the wooll, as such a trade must take up, can be supplied with wooll for their trade; and, indeed, it would be something strange, if the answer were not at hand.

1. We may reasonably conclude, that this manufacture was at first seated in this county, or, as we may say, planted itself here at first, because of the infinite numbers of sheep, which

were fed at that time upon the downs and plains of Dorset, Wilts, and Hampshire, all adjoining, as a trading town is seated, or rises gradually upon some large river, because of the benefit of navigation; and as gentlemen place the mansion houses of their estates, and seats of their families, as near the pleasant rivers, woods, and fine prospects as possible, for the delight of their living; so the first planters of the clothing manufacture, doubtless, chose this delightful vale for its seat, because of the neighbourhood of those plains, which might be supposed to be a fund of wooll for the carrying it on. Thus the manufacture of white cloth was planted in Stroud Water in Gloucestershire, for the sake of the excellent water there for the dying scarlets, and all colours that are dyed in grain, which are better dyed there, than in any other place of England, some towns near London excepted. Hence, therefore, we first observe, they are supplied yearly with the fleeces of two or three millions of sheep.

2. But as the number of sheep fed on these downs is lessened, rather than increased, because of the many thousand acres of the carpet ground being, of late years, turned into arable land, and sowed with wheat; which, by the way, has made Warminster a market town, on the edge of Somersetshire, as it now is, without exception, the greatest market for wheat in England, with this exception only, viz. Where none of it is bought to send to London.

I say, The number of sheep, and consequently the quantity of wooll, decreasing, and at the same time the manufacture, as has been said, prodigiously increasing, the manufacturers applied themselves to other parts for a supply, and hence began the influx of north-country wooll to come in from the counties of Northampton, Leicester, and Lincoln, the center of which trade, is about Tetbury and Cirencester, where are the markets for the north-country wooll, and where, as they say, several hundred packs of wooll are sold every week, for the supply of this prodigious consumption.

3. From London, they have great quantities of wooll, which is generally called Kentish wooll, in the fleece, which is brought up from thence by the farmers, since the late severe Acts against their selling it within a certain number of miles of the sea, also fell-wooll for the combers, bought of the wooll-staplers in Barnabystreet, and sent back by the carriers, which bring up the cloths to market.

4. They have also, sometimes, large quantities of Irish wooll,

by the way of Bristol, or of Mynhead, in Somersetshire; but this is uncertain, and only on extraordinary occasions. I omit the Spanish wooll, as being an article by itself.

Thus, in short, as those that see the numbers of sheep fed on the downs and plains, as above, and that see the quantity of wooll brought to the markets of Tetbury, and other towns, and the quantity sent from London, all into this one vale, would wonder how it was possible to be consumed, manufactured, and wrought up; so on the other hand, those that saw the numbers of people imploy'd, and the vast quantity of goods made in this part of England, would wonder where the whole nation should be able to supply them with wooll.

And yet, notwithstanding the whole country is thus imploy'd in the broad-cloth manufacture, as above, I must not omit to mention, that here is a very great application to another trade or two, which I am obliged, by my first scheme, not to forget to mention, viz. The supplying the city of London with provisions; though it is true, that the general imployment of the people in all this county, is in the woollen manufacture; yet, as the spinning is generally the work of the women and children, and that the land is here exceeding rich and fertile, so it cannot be supposed, but that here are farmers in great numbers, whose business it is to cultivate the land, and supply the rest of the inhabitants with provisions; and this they do so well, that notwithstanding the county is so exceeding populous, yet provisions of all sorts are very cheap, the quantity very great, and a great overplus sent every day to London for the supply of their demand, which, as I said before, is great enough to exhaust a whole nation.

All the lower part of this county, and also of Gloucestershire, adjoining, is full of large feeding farms, which we call dairies, and the cheese they make, as it is excellent good of its kind, so being a different kind from the Cheshire, being soft and thin, is eaten newer than that from Cheshire. Of this, a vast quantity is every week sent up to London, where, though it is called Gloucestershire cheese, yet a great part of it is made in Wiltshire, and the greatest part of that which comes to London, the Gloucestershire cheese being more generally carried to Bristol, and Bath, where a very great quantity is consumed, as well by the inhabitants of two populous cities, as also for the shipping off to our West-India colonies, and other places.

This Wiltshire cheese is carried to the river of Thames, which runs through part of the county, by land carriage, and so by barges to London.

Again, in the spring of the year, they make a vast quantity of that we call green cheese, which is a thin, and very soft cheese, resembling cream cheeses, only thicker, and very rich. These are brought to market new, and eaten so, and the quantity is so great, and this sort of cheese is so universally liked and accepted in London, that all the low, rich lands of this county, are little enough to supply the market; but then this holds only for the two first summer months of the year, May and June, or little more.

Besides this, the farmers in Wiltshire, and the part of Gloucestershire adjoining, send a very great quantity of bacon up to London, which is esteemed as the best bacon in England, Hampshire only excepted: This bacon is raised in such quantities here, by reason of the great dairies, as above, the hogs being fed with the vast quantity of whey, and skim'd milk, which so many farmers have to spare, and which must, otherwise, be thrown away.

But this is not all, for as the north part of Wiltshire, as well the downs, as the vales, border upon the river Thames, and, in some places, comes up even to the banks of it; so most of that part of the county being arable land, they sow a very great quantity of barley, which is carried to the markets at Abingdon, at Farrington, and such places, where it is made into malt, and carried to London. This imploys all the hill country from above Malmsbury to Marlbro, and on the side of the Vale of White Horse, as 'tis called, which is in Barkshire, and the hills adjoyning, a tract of ground, able to furnish, considering its fertility, a prodigious quantity of barley, and does so.

Thus Wiltshire itself helps to supply London with cheese, bacon, and malt, three very considerable articles, besides that vast manufacture of fine Spanish cloths, which I have said so much of, and I may, without being partial, say, that it is thereby rendered one of the most important counties in England, that is to say, important to the publick wealth of the kingdom. The bare product is in itself prodigious great; the downs are an inexhausted store-house of wooll, and of corn, and the valley, or low part of it, is the like for cheese and bacon.

One thing here is worth while to mention, for the observation of those counties in England, where they are not yet arrived to that perfection of husbandry, as in this county, and I have purposely reserved it to this place: The case is this, The downs or

plains, which are generally called Salisbury Plain; but, particularly, extend themselves over the counties of Southampton,
Wilts, and Dorset, were formerly all left open to be fed by the
large flocks of sheep so often mentioned; but now, so much of
these downs are plowed up, as has increased the quantity of
corn produced in this county, in a prodigious manner, and
lessened their quantity of wooll, as above; all which has been
done by folding their sheep upon the plow'd lands, removing the
fold every night to a fresh place, 'till the whole piece of ground
has been folded on; this, and this alone, has made these lands,
which in themselves are poor, and where, in some places, the
earth is not above six inches above the solid chalk rock, able
to bear as good wheat, as any of the richer lands in the vales,
though not quite so much: I say this alone; for many of these
lands lie so remote from the farmers houses, and up such high
hills, for the farmers live always in the valleys, and by the
rivers, that it could not be worth their while to carry dung
from those farm-houses, to those remote lands; besides, the
draught up hill would be so heavy, and the ways so bad, that
it would kill all their cattle.

If this way of folding sheep upon the fallows, and plowed
lands, were practised, in some parts of England, and especially
in Scotland, they would find it turn to such account, and so
effectually improve the waste lands, which now are useless and
uncultivated, that the sheep would be more valuable, and lands
turn to a better account than was ever yet known among them.
In Wiltshire it appears to be so very significant, that if a farmer
has a thousand of sheep, and no fallows to fold them on, his
neighbours will give him ten shillings a night for every thousand.

I am come now to Marlborough: On the downs, about two
or three miles from the town, are abundance of loose stones,
lying scattered about the plain; some whereof are very large, and
appear to be of the same kind with those at Stonehenge, and
some larger. They are called by the country people, not for
want of ignorance, The Gray Weathers. I do not find any
account given of them in history, or by the greatest of our
antiquaries, so I must leave them as I find them.

At Marlborough, and in several villages near, as well as on
the downs, there are several of those round rising mounts,
which the country people call barrows, and which all our
writers agree, were monuments of the dead, and particularly
of soldiers slain in fight. This in Marlborough, stands in the
Duke of Somerset's garden, and is, by that means, kept up to

its due height. There is a winding way cut out of the mount, that goes several times round it, 'till insensibly it brings you to the top, where there is a seat, and a small pleasant green, from whence you look over great part of the town.

This is an antient town, and, at present, has a pretty good shop-keeping trade, but not much of the manufacturing part. The river Kennet, lately made navigable by Act of Parliament, rises just by this town, and running from hence to Hungerford, and Newbery, becomes a large stream, and passing by Reading, runs into the Thames near the town. This river is famous for craw-fish, which they help travellers to at Newbery; but they seldom want for price.

Between this town of Marlborough, and Abington, westward, is the Vale of White Horse: The inhabitants tell a great many fabulous stories of the original of its being so called; but there is nothing of foundation in them all, that I could see; the whole of the story is this; Looking south from the vale, we see a trench cut on the side of a high green hill, this trench is cut in the shape of a horse, and not ill-shap'd I assure you. The trench is about two yards wide on the top, about a yard deep, and filled almost up with chalk, so that at a distance, for it is seen many miles off, you see the exact shape of a White Horse; but so large, as to take up near an acre of ground, some say, almost two acres. From this figure the hill is called, in our maps, White Horse Hill, and the low, or flat country under it, the Vale of White Horse.

It is a very fertile and fruitful vale, and extends itself from Farrington almost to Abington, tho' not exactly in a line: Some think 'twas done by the Saxons, whose device was a white horse, and is so still.

Having spoken of what is most remarkable, or at least, what most occurred to my observation from the Land's End to Newbery in Barkshire, I must here take the liberty to look round upon some passages in later times, which have made this part of the country more famous than before. 1. On the hills on this side the Devizes, is Roundway Down, where the Lord Wilmot, and the king's forces, beat, and intirely routed, the famous Sir William Waller, in the late Rebellion, or Civil War; from whence the place is called, by some, Runaway Down to this day. A little nearer towards Marlborough, is St. Ann's Hill, where, notwithstanding several high hills between, and the distance of twenty-two miles, or more, is a fair view of Salisbury-steeple, or spire, which is, without all dispute, the highest in

England. The defeat of Sir William Waller, take in the few words of one of the most impartial historians of those times.—
The action was, in short, thus,

Waller had always the misfortune to be beaten when he pursued his enemy to force a fight. This was his case now: He heard that the Lord Wilmot, with a body of the king's forces, were marched into the west to joyn Colonel Greenville, Sir Arthur Slanning, and the loyal troops in Dorsetshire: Upon this, he makes long marches to overtake, and intercept them, pretending to fight them, joyn'd, or not joyn'd; but my Lord Wilmot advancing with 1500 horse of the king's best troops, joyn'd the western forces at the Devizes, and facing about upon Waller, met him upon Roundway Down, not far from St. Ann's Hill, mentioned above.

As I said, he who was seeking out his enemy, must himself be easy to be found, and therefore they soon came together; for though Waller seeing too late, that he was in an error, would have been glad to have got off without fighting, yet seeing the king's troops advance in full march to attack him, boldly drew up in order of battle, and marched forward to meet them: Upon which ensued an obstinate, and very bloody, fight; for Waller was brave, and his men had been enur'd to victory, especially his infantry, and though they were gallantly attacked by Colonel Slanning, and Greenville, the latter of whom was slain, yet they stood their ground, and could not be broken, but rather gain'd upon the Royalists: But the Lord Wilmot charging with an irresistable fury at the head of the cavalry, the rebel horse were broken, and put into confusion, a body of Wilmot's horse pushing them quite out of the field: Lord Wilmot then falling with the like fury upon the rear of the foot, while the king's foot lay hard upon them in the front: They were, at last, broken also; and, in a word, quite overthrown: And there being no way to escape the horse, upon an open wild down, as that is, they were most of them cut in pieces, or taken prisoners. All their cannon and baggage were also taken, with their arms and ammunition; and Waller himself, with great difficulty, escaped. This was in the month of August, 1643.

From this action, as I said, this place was ever after called Runaway-Down, instead of Roundway-Down.

At Newbery there was another, or rather a double scene of blood; for here were two obstinate, and hard fought, battles, at two several times, between the king's army, and the Parliament's, the king being present at them both, and both fought almost upon the same spot of ground. In these two battles, said an old experienced soldier, that served in the king's army, there was more generalship shewn on both sides, than in any other battle through the whole course of the war; his meaning was, That the generals, on both sides, shewed the most exquisite skill in the managing, posting, bringing up, and drawing off their troops; and as the men fought with great bravery on both sides, so the generals, and officers, shewed both their bravery, and their judgment. In the first of these battles, the success was doubtful, and both sides pretended to the advantage: In the last, the king's army had apparently the worst of it, and yet the king, in a very few days, with a great body of horse, fetch'd off his cannon, which he had, in the close of the battle, thrust into Dunington Castle, and carried them away to Oxford, the head quarter of his army, or his place of arms, as it would be called now; and this he did in the sight of the victorious army, facing them at the same time, with a body of six thousand horse, and they, on the other hand, did not think fit to draw out to attack him. That retreat, in point of honour, was equal to a victory, and gave new courage, as well as reputation, to the king's troops. Indeed the Parliament's army was out-general'd in that part; for as they had beaten the king's army out of the field, and obliged them to shelter their train of artillery and carriages in the castle, which was in itself a place of no great strength; they ought immediately, even the same night, to have invested the place, and posted their army so, as to cover the siege; in which case, the cannon, and all that was in the castle, had been their own; for though the king had indeed, a gallant body of horse, and superior to the Parliament cavalry by almost three thousand, yet his best regiments of foot had been roughly handled in the battle, and some of them quite cut in pieces; so that his majesty would not have been in condition to have attacked them in their posts, in order to have raised the siege.

But this is not my business: This town of Newbery is an antient cloathing town, though, now, little of that part remains to it; but it retains still a manufacturing genius, and the people are generally imployed in making shalloons, a kind of stuff, which, though it be used only for the lineing and insides of mens cloaths, for women use but little of it, nor the men for any thing but as above, yet it becomes so generally worn, both at home and abroad, that it is increased to a manufacture by itself, and is more considerable, than any single manufacture of stuffs in the nation. This imploys the town of Newbery, as also, Andover, another town on the side of Wiltshire, about twelve miles from it, and abundance of other towns, in other counties of England, of which I shall speak in their place.

And, having mentioned Andover, though out of the road that I was in, I must digress to tell you, that the town of

Andover lies on the very edge of the downs which I have so often mentioned, and is in the road from Newbery to Salisbury, as it is from London to Taunton, and all the manufacturing part of Somersetshire; 'tis a handsom town, well built, populous, and much inrich'd by the manufacture, as above, and may be called a thriving town: It sends two members to Parliament, and is an antient corporation.

But the chief reason of my making this digression, is to mention, that within a mile, or thereabouts, of this town, at the place where the open down country begins, is Wey-Hill, where the greatest fair for sheep is kept, that this nation can shew. I confess, though I once saw the fair, yet I could make no estimate of the number brought thither for sale; but asking the opinion of a grasier, who had used to buy sheep there, he boldly answered, There were many hundred thousands. This being too general, I press'd him farther; at length he said, He believed there were five hundred thousand sheep sold there in one fair. Now, tho' this might, I believe, be too many, yet 'tis sufficient to note, that there are a prodigious quantity of sheep sold here; nor can it be otherwise, if it be considered, that the sheep sold here, are not for immediate killing, but are generally ewes for store sheep for the farmers, and they send for them from all the following counties, Berks, Oxford, Bucks, Bedford, Hertford, Middlesex, Kent, Surrey, and Sussex: The custom of these farmers, is, to send one farmer in behalf of (perhaps) twenty, and so the sheep come up together, and they part them when they come home. These ewes have alsc this property, that they generally bring two lambs at a time. What weathers are bought here, are carried off by the farmers, who have feeding grounds, in order to fat them for killing; but they are but few compared to the ewes.

But to go back to Newbery: Not to insist upon the famous Jack of Newbery, who was so great a clothier, that when King James met his waggons loaden with cloths going to London, and inquiring whose they were, was answered by them all, They were Jack of Newbery's, the king returned, if the story be true, That this Jack of Newbery was richer than he: But not to insist upon this man's story, which is almost grown fabulous, yet another story is fact, and to be proved, viz. That this is one of the two legatee towns (as they were called) in the will of the late famous Mr. Kenrick, who being the son of a clothier of Newbery, and afterwards a merchant in London, left four thousand pounds to Newbery, and seven thousand five hundred pounds to Reading, to incourage the cloathing trade, and set the poor at work, besides other gifts of extraordinary value to the poor, as such. This gentleman I shall have occasion to mention again, and therefore I say no more now, only, that his effigie, or picture, was to be seen, before the Fire, in S. Christopher's Church in Thread Needle Street, London, where he is buried, and where the benefaction he left for prayers every morning at six a clock, winter and summer, in that church, is still injoyed, and the prayers performed there accordingly: As likewise, it is at Reading, and at Newbery.

This extraordinary will is to be seen at large in Stow's *Survey of London*, to which I refer, and which it is well worth the reader's while to look over, the like not being heard of in England, before. It seems he died a batchelor, or, at least, without children, and his legacies, all in ready money, cannot amount to less than forty thousand to fifty thousand pounds, besides what might be included in the general clause of leaving all the rest of his estate to him who he made his universal heir; which estate, as I have heard, amounted to a very great value. That forty or fifty thousand pounds also, being considered at the time it was left, might well be rated at four times the value, as the rate of things goes now, it being in the year 1624. What improvement the town of Newbery, or the town of Reading, has made of the great sums he left to their management, that I did not inquire into.

Near this town of Newbery, the late Earl of Craven built a very stately pile of buildings for his own dwelling, called Spine; but as it was never quite finished, so I do not understand, that his lordship ever came to live in it, and, within these few years, it was, by a sudden fire, which no-body can, or no-body will, tell how it began, burnt down to the ground. It was reported, the old lord built this magnificent palace, for such it really was, at a time when he (flatter'd himself, at least, with expectation, and) had hopes of marrying Madam Royal, as she was then called, the Queen of Bohemia, sister to King Charles I. who was then a widow, and lived under the shadow of the English Court; but being frustrated afterwards in that view, his lordship went no farther in his building.

Here it was that the vanguard, or first line of the Prince of Orange's army, was posted, when the Irish dragoons, who were posted in Reading, finding they should be attacked in a few days, had put the town's people into such a fright, by threatening to burn and plunder the town, and cut all the peoples throats, hat they sent express messengers to the Dutch general officer Grave Van Nassau for help; who sent them a detachment of but two hundred and eighty dragoons, though the troops in he town were near seven hundred men. What success they met with, I shall mention presently.

The next town of note, I say, is Reading, a very large and wealthy town, handsomly built, the inhabitants rich, and driving a very great trade. The town lies on the River Kennet, but so near the Thames, that the largest barges which they use, may come up to the town bridge, and there they have wharfs to load, and unload them. Their chief trade is by this water-navigation to and from London, though they have necessarily a great trade into the country, for the consumption of the goods which they bring by their barges from London, and particularly coals, salt, grocery wares, tobacco, oyls, and all heavy goods.

They send from hence to London by these barges, very great quantities of malt, and meal, and these are the two principal articles of their loadings, of which, so large are those barges, that some of them, as I was told, bring a thousand, or twelve hundred quarters of malt at a time, which, according to the ordinary computation of tonnage in the freight of other vessels, is from a hundred, to an hundred and twenty ton, dead weight.

They also send very great quantities of timber from Reading; for Berkshire being a very-well wooded county, and the River Thames a convenient conveyance for the timber, they send most of it, and especially the largest and fairest of the timber, to London, which is generally bought by the shipwrights in the river, for the building merchant ships; as also, the like trade of timber is at Henley, another town on the Thames, and at Maidenhead, of which by itself.

Here was a large manufacture of sail-cloth set up in this town, by the late Sir Owen Buckingham, Lord Mayor of London, and many of the poor people were, profitably (to them) imployed in it; but Sir Owen himself dying, and his son being unhappily killed in a duel, a little while after, that manufacture died also.

There is, however, still a remnant of the woollen manufacture here; I say a remnant, because this was once a very considerable cloathing town, much greater than it is now; and this town, as well as Newbery, and principally before Newbery, has injoyed the munificent legacies of that generous merchant I mentioned before, I mean Mr. Kenrick, who left them 750*l.* to set the poor at work, and encourage the cloathing trade. How they manage for the poor, that they can give the best account of.

Mr. Cambden's continuator, Dr. Gibson, says, there was once a hundred and forty master-clothiers in this one town; but that now, they are almost all gone. During the civil wars in England, this town was strongly fortified, and the remains of the bastions, and other works are still to be seen; but the Royalists abandoning it afterwards, it was possess'd by the Parliament, soon after the battle at Newbery.

There are three churches, and two large meeting houses in this town, besides that of the Quakers; and the town, Cambden calls it a little city, is said to contain about eight thousand people, including a little hamlet at the bridge over the Thames.

Here was once a most famous monastery, founded by King Henry I. younger son of William the Conqueror, who lies buried in it with his queen, and his daughter Maud; of whom it was said, She was a king's daughter, a king's wife, and a king's mother, but herself no queen; this is made out, in that she was daughter to Henry I. wife to the Emperor of Germany, and mother to King Henry II. so she was an empress, but not a queen. This abbey is now so demolished, that scarce any remains of it are found, or the place of it known.

As I have noted above, it was here that the Dutch with two hundred and eighty horse and dragoons, attacked the forces of the late King James, in aid of the distress'd town's-men, who they threatened to murther and plunder that very day. It was on a Sunday morning, that the Irish dragoons had resolved on the design'd mischief, if they really intended it: In order to it, they posted a guard at the principal church in the piazza there, and might, indeed, easily have lock'd all the people in, and have cut their throats; also they placed a company of foot in the church-yard of another church, over-against the Bear Inn; so that if they really did not intend to massacre the people, as their officers said they did not, yet that way of posting their men, joyn'd to the loud oaths and protestations, that they would do it, made it look as like such a design, as any thing unexecuted, or unattempted, could do.

In this posture things stood when the Dutch entered the town: The Irish had placed a centinel on the top of the steeple of the great church, with orders, if he saw any troops advance, to fire his piece, and ring the bell; the fellow, being surprised with the sight, for he discover'd the Dutch but a little before they reached the town, fired his musquet, but forgot to ring the bell, and came down. However, his firing gave the alarm sufficiently, and the troops in the town, who were all under arms before, whether for the design'd execution, or not, I will not determine; but, I say, being under arms before, they had little more to do, but to post their troops, which they did with skill enough, being commanded by Sir John Lanier, an experienced officer, and colonel of a regiment of horse in King James's army; and had the men done their duty, they might easily have repuls'd the few troops that attacked them; but the Dutch entering the town in two places, one by the ordinary road from Newbery, and the other by the Broad Street near where the horse-fair is kept, forc'd both the posts, and entered the market place, where the main body of the Irish troops were drawn up.

The first party of the Dutch found a company of foot drawn up in the church-yard over-against the Bear Inn, and a troop of dragoons in the Bear Inn yard; the dragoons hearing the Dutch were at hand, their officer bravely drew them out of the inn yard, and faced the Dutch in the open road, the church-yard wall being lined with musquetiers to flank the street; the Dutch, who came on full gallop, fell in upon the dragoons, sword in hand, and with such irresistable fury, that the Irish were immediately put into confusion, and after three or four minutes bearing the charge, they were driven clear out of the street. At the very same instant, another party of the Dutch dragoons, dismounting, entered the church-yard, and the whole body posted there, fled also, with little or no resistance, not sufficient, indeed, to be called resistance. After this, the dragoons, mounting again, forced their squadrons, and entered the market place.

Here, the troops being numerous, made two or three regular discharges; but finding themselves charged in the rear by the other Dutchmen, who had by this time entered the said Broad Street, they not knowing the strength, or weakness of their enemy, presently broke, and fled by all the ways possible. Sir John Lanier, having a calash and six horses, got away with the first, though he was twice headed by a Dutch trooper, who endeavoured to shoot one of the horses, but miss'd his shot, so the colonel got away.

The Dutch having cleared the town, pursued some of them as far as Twyford, and such was the terror that they were in, that a person, from whom I had this part of the relation, told me, he saw one Dutch trooper chase twelve of the Irish dragoons to the river near Twyford, and ride into the water a good way after them; nor durst Sir John Lanier's regiment of horse, and Sir John Fenwick's, and a third, whose colonel I do not remember, advance to relieve their friends, though they, having had the alarm, stood drawn up on the hill on Twyford side of the river, where they might see by what a contemptible number their numerous party was pursued; for there were not above five and forty, or fifty at most, of the Dutch, that pursued about three hundred of the Irish dragoons to Twyford.

Thus the town of Reading was delivered from the danger they were threatned with, and which they as really expected, as they expected the sun would rise. It is true, the Irish officers denied afterwards, that there was any such design, or that they intended to offer the people any violence; but it is true, that several of their soldiers confess'd it, and gave private intimations of it, to the people in the houses where they quartered, especially some that had been kindly treated in their quarters, and had a little more gratitude and humanity than the rest.

I cannot omit to observe one thing here, to which I was an eye-witness, and which will resolve a difficulty that to this day has puzzled the understandings of a great many people, if not of the whole nation; namely, That here began the universal alarm that spread over the whole kingdom (almost at the same time) of the Irish being coming to cut every bodies throats: The brief account of which, because it has something curious in it, I believe will be agreeable to you. The state of it is thus:

As the terror which the threatnings of these Irishmen had brought upon the whole town of Reading, obliged the magistrates, and chief of the inhabitants, to apply to the Prince of Orange's army for immediate help, so you cannot doubt, but that many of the inhabitants fled for their lives by all the ways that they could; and this was chiefly in the night; for in the day, the soldiers, who had their eyes every where, stopped them, and would not permit them to stir, which still increased their terror.

Those that got away, you may be sure, were in the utmost fright and amazement, and they had nothing less in their mouths, but that the Irish would (and by that time had) burnt the town, and cut the throats of all the people, men, women, and children. I was then at Windsor, and in the very interval of all this fright, King James being gone, and the army retreated from Salisbury, the Lord Feversham calls the troops together, and causing them to lay down their arms, disbands them, and gives them leave, every man, to go whither they would.

The Irish dragoons, which had fled from Reading, rallied at Twyford, and having not lost many of their number (for there were not above twelve men killed) they marched on for Maidenhead, swearing, and cursing, after most soldierly a manner, that they would burn all the towns where-ever they came, and cut the throats of all the people. However, whether it was, that they thought themselves too near the Dutch at Maidenhead, or what else was the matter, they did not offer to take quarters at Maidenhead, the town also being full of King James's troops, so they marched on for Colebrook, blustering in the same manner, of what they would do when they came there. The town of Colebrook had notice of their coming, and how they had publickly threatened to burn the town, and murther all the people; but, happily for them, they had quartered there a regiment of Scots foot, of those regiments which King James had caused to march from Scotland to his aid on this occasion; and they had with them, as was the usage of all the foot in those times, two pieces of cannon, that is to say, field-pieces, and they stood just in the market-place, pointing westward to the street where these gentlemen were to come.

The people of Colebrook applied immediately to the Scots colonel, whose name I am very sorry I cannot remember, because it is to his honour that I should mention it, and begged his protection. The colonel calling together a council of his officers, immediately resolved, they would make good their quarters, unless they received orders from their superior officers to quit them, and that they would defend the town from plunder; and upon this, immediately the drums beat to arms, and the regiment came together in a few moments: It was in the depth of winter, and, by consequence, was night, and being a wet day, the evening was exceeding dark, when some advanced centinels gave notice, that they heard the drums beat the dragoons march, at some distance upon the road.

Upon this the colonel ordered a lieutenant, with thirty musqueteers, to make an advanced guard at the extreme part of the town, and he was supported by another party of forty men, most pikes, at a small distance, who were to advance upon a signal; and if these last should ingage, the drums of the whole regiment were to beat a march, and half the battalion, to advance with the two pieces of cannon.

It was near ten a clock at night before the dragoons reached the town, when the two advanced dragoons, which, by the discipline at that time, always rode at a distance from the regiment, were challenged by the centinels placed by the lieutenant, as above; upon which they gave notice to the regiment, who immediately halted, and an officer, with some dragoons (they could not tell how many, because it was dark) came up, and demanded, Who they were that challenged? the centinel called his corporal, and he the serjeant, with three files of musqueteers, and they told the officer what regiment they belong'd to, and that they had orders to stop any troops from entering the town, 'till their colonel should be acquainted with it, and give farther orders.

The dragoons, as the ground would admit, drew up in front, and their officers began to huff and threaten, that they were the king's troops, and within the line of the army; that they must have quarters in the town, and ought not to be refused by their own side.

By this time the lieutenant came up also: He gave the officer of dragoons very good words, and told him, He knew too well what belonged to the duty of a subaltern officer, to blame him for doing his duty; but that the regiment was under arms, and the colonel at the head of them in the market-house, and he would immediately send to him for orders, and doubted not, but that the colonel would give them quarters in the town. The dragoons, not satisfied with this civil usage, threatened, swore, rag'd, and damning the colonel, and the regiment, though not present, said they would have quarters without asking leave of any man, and the officer turning about to a serjeant, bid him go back, and cause the regiment to advance.

The lieutenant told him calmly, He was sorry to see him act so; but if that was his resolution, he was ready for him, and immediately called out to his serjeant to give the signal to the next party to advance, and told the officer of dragoons, that if he stirred one foot forward, or any of his men, he would fire upon them immediately. The forty men advanced, and in two minutes after, they could hear the drums of the regiment beat the Scots march.

Upon this, the dragoons halted again, and the major of the dragoons advancing to the parlee, the lieutenant colonel of the foot, was also come up to the lieutenant's party, with the forty men, and with the colonel's answer to the demand of quarters; namely, That if the dragoons had any orders in writing from the general for quartering in the town, or for marching that way, he was very ready to give them admittance; but if not, they were his quarters, and he would defend them to the last man, and no-body should come in there, especially at that time of night.

The dragoons, however, insulted and menac'd the major also, and that at such a rate, that he gave orders immediately to acquaint the colonel of it, who instantly advanced, in full march, with the whole regiment, having about one hundred links lighted to let them see the way, the night being exceeding dark.

When the dragoons saw this, and having no stomach to engage, they desisted; but raged and stormed at such a rate, as I cannot express, and taking the road to Stanes, swore, they would go thither, and burn the town, and kill man, woman and child.

Those blusters were so loud, and the fellows, by nation, such as from whom it might be expected, as put the people of Colebrook, the fright they had been in for themselves being a little over, into a second concern for their neighbours at Stanes, and some of them shewed the concern to be so real, that they sent express upon express to Stanes, to acquaint the people there of their danger, knowing there was, at that time, only two companies of foot, of Colonel ——'s regiment, in the town. When these messengers came there, they found the people already alarmed by others, who had come from the same town of Colebrook, in the first fright, with the news, that the Irish were coming to burn the said town of Colebrook, and that, by that time, they did not question but they had done it, and they were surprized to hear now, that it was not done; but upon the arriving of these messengers, bringing word, that they had burnt Colebrook, but for the assistance of the Scots regiment; and that they were coming to Stanes, and swore, they would kill man, woman and child; it is impossible to express the consternation of the people: Away they run out of the town, dark, and rainy, and midnight as it was, some to Kingston, some over the heath to Hownslow, and Brentford, some to Egham, and some to Windsor, with the dreadful news; and by that time they reached those places, their fears had turned their story from saying, they would burn and kill, to they had burned and killed, and were coming after you to do the like.

The same alarm was carried by others from Colebrook to Uxbridge; for thither the dragoons were for marching at first; and thus, some one way, and some another, it spread like the undulations of the water in a pond, when a flat stone is cast upon the surface: From Brentford and Kingston, and from

Uxbridge, it came severally, and by different roads, to London, and so, as I may say, all over England; nor is it wonderful, that it seemed to be all over the nation in one day, which was the next after this beginning; Fear gave wings to the news, no post could carry it as it flew from town to town, and still every messenger had two articles with him. 1. Not that such and such towns were to be burnt and plundered by them; but that they were already burnt; and 2. That the Irish were at their heels to do the like.

This, I think, is a clear account of this alarm, and what can be more natural? Colebrook was not the case, for where-ever the Colebrook men came, they were asked, If their town was down? I rode the next morning to Maidenhead: At Slough they told me, Maidenhead was burnt, and Uxbridge, and Reading, and I know not how many more, were destroy'd; and when I came to Reading, they told me, Maidenhead and Okingham were burnt, and the like. From thence I went to Henley, where the Prince of Orange, with the second line of his army, entered that very afternoon, and there they had had the same account, with the news of King James's flight; and thus it spread every way insensibly. The manner is too recent in memory, to need my giving any description of it.

My next stage from Reading, was to Great Marlow in Buckinghamshire, which, though not in the direct road, yet lying on the banks of the river of Thames, is, in my course, proper enough to be spoken of, and is particularly worth notice for several things.

1. It is a town of very great embarkation on the Thames, not so much for goods wrought here, (for the trade of the town is chiefly in bone-lace) but for goods from the neighbouring towns, and particularly, a very great quantity of malt, and meal, is brought hither from High-Wickham, a large market town, about —— miles off, which is one of the greatest corn markets on this side of England, and lies on the road from London to Oxford.

2. Between High Wickham and Marlow, is a little river called the Loddon, on which are a great many mills, and particularly corn mills, and paper mills; the first of these, grind and dress the wheat, and then the meal is sent to Marlow, and loaded on board the barges for London: And the second makes great quantities of printing paper, and that, very good of its kind, and cheap, such as generally is made use of in printing our news

papers, journals, &c. and smaller pamphlets; but not much fine, or large, for bound books, or writing.

3. On the river of Thames, just by the side of this town, though on the other bank, are three very remarkable mills, which are called the Temple-Mills, and are called also, the Brass-Mills, and are for making Bisham Abbey Battery Work, as they call it, viz. brass kettles, and pans, &c. of all sorts. They have first a foundary, where, by the help of *lapis caliminaris*, they convert copper into brass, and then, having cast the brass in large broad plates, they beat them out by force of great hammers, wrought by the water mills, into what shape they think fit for sale. Those mills went on by the strength of a good stock of money in a company or partnership, and with very good success, 'till at last, they turned it into what they call a Bubble, brought it to Exchange-Alley, set it a stock-jobbing in the days of our South Sea madness, and brought it up to be sold at one hundred pounds per share, whose intrinsick worth was perhaps ten pounds, 'till, with the fall of all those things together, it fell to nothing again. Their treasurer, a tradesman in London, failed, having misapply'd about thirty thousand pounds of their money, and then, as it is usual where want of success goes before, quarelling among themselves followed after, and so the whole affair sunk into a piece of mere confusion and loss, which otherwise was certainly a very beneficial undertaking.

4. Next to these are two mills, both extraordinary in themselves, one for making of thimbles, a work excellently well finished, and which performs to admiration, and another for pressing of oyl from rape-seed, and flax-seed, both which, as I was told, turn to very good accouut to the proprietors.

Here is also brought down a vast quantity of beech wood, which grows in the woods of Buckinghamshire more plentifully than in any other part of England. This is the most useful wood, for some uses, that grows, and without which, the city of London would be put to more difficulty, than for any thing of its kind in the nation.

1. For fellies for the great carrs, as they are called, which ply in London streets for carrying of merchandizes, and for cole-carts, dust-carts, and such like sorts of voiture, which are not, by the city laws, allowed to draw with shod wheels, or wheels tyr'd with iron.

2. For billet wood for the king's palaces, and for the plate and flint glass houses, and other such nice purposes.

3. Beech quarters for divers uses, particularly chairmakers,

and turnery wares. The quantity of this, brought from hence, is almost incredible, and yet so is the country overgrown with beech in those parts, that it is bought very reasonable, nor is there like to be any scarcity of it for time to come.

At Bisham, over against this town, was formerly an abbey, and the remains of it are still to be seen there: The estate belongs to the antient family of the name of Hobby. Some of the heads of this family, were very eminent in former days, particularly Sir William Hobby, and Sir Edward Hobby, the latter having been imployed by Queen Elizabeth in the most important foreign negotiations. Their monuments, with those of their ladies, and sons, are now to be seen, and well worth seeing they are, in the little church of Bisham. The seat of the family, is now in Dorsetshire, where Sir Thomas Hobby is still living; but they are generally all brought hither, when they die, to be buried with their ancestors.

A little higher, on the same side of the river, is Hurley, an antient seat of the Lord Lovelace, and that family being extinct, it came, by the daughter and heiress, to Sir Henry Johnson of Blackwall, near Ratcliff, who originally was only a shipwright, or master-builder, at the great yard and dock there, of which I shall speak in their place. This lady left only one daughter, married to the Earl of Strafford, and who now enjoys the Hurly estate, in the right of the above marriages of the daughters.

There are two other towns on the Thames, which I have already mentioned, viz. Henly and Maidenhead, which have little or nothing remarkable in them; but that they have great business also, by the trade for malt and meal and timber for London, which they ship, or load, on their great barges for London, as the other towns do.

And now I am, by just degrees, come to Windsor, where I must leave talking of trade, river, navigation, meal, and malt, and describe the most beautiful, and most pleasantly situated castle, and royal palace, in the whole isle of Britain.

Windsor Castle, founded, as some say, by William the Conqueror, if there was any thing in that part, was at least rebuilt, by Edward III. But the truth of the story is this, William the Conqueror did pitch upon it as a pleasant situation, in a delightful sporting country, and agreeable to him, who delighted much in hunting; and, as he says of it, a place fitted for the entertainment of kings, and therefore treated with the Abbot of Westminster for an exchange, and so took possession of it. He also had several little lodges, or hunting houses, in the forest adjoyning, and frequently lodg'd, for the conveniency of his game, in a house which the monks before injoy'd, near, or in the town of Windsor, for the town is much more antient than the castle, and was an eminent pass upon the Thames in the reign of the Saxon kings: But to pass over the antiquity or history of the town, this is certain, That King Edward III. took an extreme liking to the place, because of its beautiful situation, and pleasing prospect, which, indeed, is not to be out-done in any part of the kingdom: Here, at length, the king resolved to fix his summer residence, and himself laid out the plan of a most magnificent palace, the same, as to the outward form and building, as we now see it; for whatever has been done for beautifying, altering, or amending the inside and apartments, there has nothing been added to the building itself, except that noble terras, which runs under the north front, and leads to the green on the park, at the east side, or end of it, along which east end, the fine lodgings, and royal apartments, were at first built, all the north part being then taken up in rooms of state, and halls for publick balls, &c.

The house itself was, indeed, a palace, and without any appearance of a fortification; but when the building was brought on to the slope of the hill on the town side, the king added ditches, ramparts, the round tower, and several addenda of strength; and so it was immediately called a castle.

The pretence which some made to an old story, that William of Wickham built this castle, is a story so evidently fabulous, and so plainly detected, that the very relations which pretend to it, discover the contrary; owning, that the king was so incensed against him, but for a suggestion, that he had a project of assuming the honour of being the founder, that it had like to have cost William all his interest in the king's favour, which, at that time, was very great; and the Duke of Lancaster, who was his irreconcilable enemy, took the advantage of prompting the king to make that suggestion; but he cleared himself by denying, that he ever made any pretence to being the founder, only put this construction upon the words, That the money, and the reputation he had gained by building that castle for the king, had been the making of him. The words were these,

THIS MADE WICKHAM.

These words, they say, he had caused to be cut on a stone in the inner wall of the little tower, which, from him, is to this day called Winchester Tower.

But to pass over this fiction, this is certain, King Edward was the founder of the whole work, and the plan of it was much of his own contrivance; but he committed the overseeing, and direction of the works, to William of Wickham, or, if you please, William of Wickham was the Sir Christopher Wren of that Court; for William was then a layman, not having had a liberal education, but had a good genius, a mighty lover of building, and had applied his head much that way; nor, indeed, does the building itself fail to do the head, or master-builder, a great deal of honour; for in all the decorations and ornaments, which have been made since by the princes who have liked Windsor best, they have found no occasion to alter any of the front, or to pull down, or build up, add, or diminish, except it be some small matter at the entrance to the great stair-case, the kitchen, and offices below stairs, and the like; but the great north, and east fronts, the square of the inner court, the great gates at the entering from the town, with the Round Tower, and the walls annexed, are all standing in the very form in which King Edward III. left them.

The only addition in the inside, is a fine equestrian statue of King Charles II. which stands over the great well, sunk, as may be supposed, in the first building, for the supply of the castle with water, and in which was an engine for raising the water, notwithstanding the great depth, by very little labour; the contrivance and performance done by the great Sir Samuel Morland, one of the best-natur'd mechanicks of his time, and as good a mathematician.

On the outside was added, the terrace walk, built by Queen Elizabeth, and where she usually walked for an hour every day before her dinner, if not hindered by windy weather, which she had a peculiar aversion to; for as to rainy weather, it would not always hinder her; but she rather loved to walk in a mild, calm rain, with an umbrella over her head.

This walk was really a magnificent work; for as it is raised on the side of a precipice, or steep declivity of the hill, so that hill was necessarily cut down a very great depth to bring the foundation to a flat equal to the breadth, which was to be formed above. From the foundation it was raised by solid stone work, of a vast thickness, with cross walls of stone, for banding the front, and preventing any thrust from the weight of earth within. Then this work was all to be filled up again within, after all was first taken out, was thrown down the front of the hill, to push out the precipices still farther, that it might be the same slope from the terrace, as it was before from the foot of the castle.

This noble walk is covered with fine gravel, and has cavities, with dreins, to carry off all the water; so that let it rain as it will, not a drop of it is seen to rest on the walk, but it is dry, hard, and fit to walk on immediately. The breadth of this walk is very spacious on the north side, on the east side it is narrower; but neither at Versailles, or at any of the royal palaces in France, or at Rome, or Naples, have I ever seen any thing like it. The grand seignior's terrace in the outer court of the Seraglio, next the sea, is the nearest to it, that I have read of, and yet not equal to it, if I may believe the account of those who have seen it; for that, I acknowledge, I have not seen. At the north-east corner of this terrace, where it turns south, to run on by the east side of the castle, there are steps, by which you go off upon the plain of the park, which is kept smooth as a carpet, and on the edge of which, the prospect of the terrace is doubled by a vista, south over the park, and quite up to the great park, and towards the forest. Here also is a small seat, fit for one, or but two at the most, with a high back, and cover for the head, which turns so easily, the whole being fix'd on a pin of iron, or brass, of strength sufficient, that the persons who sit in it, may turn it from the wind, and which way soever the wind blows, or how hard soever, yet they may sit in a perfect tranquillity, and enjoy a compleat calm. This is said also, to be Queen Elizabeth's own invention, who, though she delighted in being abroad in the air, yet hated to be ruffled with the wind. It is also an admirable contrivance for the person sitting in it, to shelter himself from the sun.

This lofty terrace makes the castle quite another thing, and gives an egress to the people within to the park, and to a most beautiful walk, which King Edward III. nor his successors for some hundreds of years, knew nothing of, all their prospect being from the windows of the castle.

On that side of the building which looks out upon the terrace, are all the royal apartments, King Edward III's were on the east side. The east side is now allotted to great officers of state, who are obliged to attend whenever the Court removes to Windsor, such as the Lord Treasurers, Secretaries of State, Lord High Chancellor, Lord Archbishop of Canterbury, and the like; and below they have proper offices for business, if they please to order any to be done there.

You mount into the royal apartments, by several back stairs; but the publick way is up a small ascent to a flat, or half pace (for I love to make my account speak English) where there are two entries of state, by two large stair-cases, one on the left hand to the royal apartments, and the other, on the right, to St. George's-Hall, and the royal chapel.

Before the enterance to these, on either side, you pass through the guard chambers, where you see the walls furnished with arms, and the king's Beef-eaters, as they call the yeomen of the guard, keep their station, or, as it may be called, their main guard. These rooms lead either way, towards the fine lodgings, or towards St. George's Hall, which you please.

In the royal lodgings, there have been so many alterations of furniture, that there can be no entering upon the particular description. In one of those lodgings, the late Queen Mary set up a rich atlas, and chints bed, which, in those times, was invaluable, the chints being of Masslapatan, on the coast of Coromandel, the finest that was ever seen before that time in England; but the rate of those things have suffered much alteration since that time. Also here was, some time before that, the picture of the late Dutchess of Portsmouth at full length, a noble piece, and of which 'twas said, King Charles II. should say, 'Twas the finest painting, of the finest woman in Christendom; but our English ladies of Queen Mary's court, were of another opinion, and the Gallery of Beauties, as it was called, which her majesty placed in the water gallery at Hampton Court, shews several as good faces, and as good painting.

In the chimney-piece of one of these apartments, is a piece of needle-work exquisitely fine, performed, as they say, by the Queen of Scots, during the time of her confinement in Fotheringay Castle. There are several family pieces in the chimney-pieces, and other parts of those lodgings, that are valuable, because of the persons they represent: But the finery of painting is to come.

These rooms look all out north towards the terrace, and over part of the finest, and richest, vale in the world; for the same vale attending the course of the River Thames, with very little interruption, reaches to, and includes the city of London east, and the city of Oxford west: The river, with a winding, and beautiful stream, gliding gently through the middle of it, and inriching by its navigation, both the land and the people on every side.

It must be confess'd, that, as William the Conqueror expresses it in his letter to the monks at Windsor, it was a place fit for the entertainment of kings, so it is; for it seems, by nature, to be formed for a palace; and for delight; all kinds of pleasure and convenience, that any country, at least in England, can afford, are to be found here.

It may be proper here to say something to the beauties and ornaments of St. George's Hall, though nothing can be said equal to what the eye would be witness to; 'tis surprizing, at the first entrance, to see at the upper end, the picture of King William on horseback, under him, an ascent with marble steps, a balustrade, and a half pace, which, formerly, was actually there, with room for a throne, or chair of state, for the sovereign to sit on, when on publick days he thought fit to appear in ceremony.

No man that had seen the former steps or ascent, and had gone up to the balustrade and throne, as I had done, could avoid supposing, they were there still; and as on a casual view, having been absent some years out of the nation, I was going forward towards the end of the hall, intending to go up the steps, as I had done formerly, I was confounded, when I came nearer, to see that the ascent was taken down, the marble steps gone, the chair of state, or throne, quite away, and that all I saw, was only painted upon the wall below the king and his horse; indeed it was so lively, so bright, so exquisitely performed, that I was perfectly deceived, though I had some pretension to judgment in pictures too; nor was my eye alone deceived, others were under the same deception, who were then with me.

When I came to the farther end, and look'd from the throne, as I called it, down the hall. I was again surprized, though most agreeably, I confess, viz. The painting on the side of the hall, which was the representation of Prince Edward's triumph, in imitation of Cæsar's glorious entry into Rome, and which was drawn marching from the lower end of the room, to the upper, that is to say, from the door, which is in the corner on the north side of the hall, was now wholly inverted, and the same triumph was performed again; but the march turned just the other way.

That this could be done no other way, but by wiping the whole work out, and painting it all over again, was easy to conclude, seeing it was not done upon cloth, but upon the mere plaister of the wall, as appeared by the salts of the lime in the wall, having work'd out, and spoiled a great piece of the paint; besides, the nature of the thing forbids; for if it had been a canvas, turning it would have been impracticable, for then all the imagery would have stood heels up, unless it had been carried on to the directly opposite part of the hall, and that could not be, because there were the windows, looking all into the inner court of the castle.

The first painting was done by Mr. Varrio, who, after finishing this work, was entertained for 12 years at Burley House, near Stamford, by that great lover of art, and particularly of fine painting, the Earl of Excester: After which King William entertained him again, and, as they told me, he performed this second painting of the hall, with greater mastership of hand, than he had done the first. The painting of the cielings generally remain, being finished by the same hand in a most exquisite manner at first.

At the west end of the hall, is the chapel royal, the neatest and finest of the kind in England; the carv'd work is beyond any that can be seen in England, the altar-piece is that of the institution, or, as we may call it, our Lord's first supper. I remember, that going with some friends to shew them this magnificent palace, it chanced to be at the time when the Dissenters were a little uneasy at being obliged to kneel at the Sacrament; one of my friends, who, as I said, I carried to see Windsor Castle, was a Dissenter, and when he came into the chapel, he fix'd his eyes upon the altar-piece with such a fix'd, steady posture, and held it so long, that I could not but take notice of it, and asked him, Whether it was not a fine piece? Yes, says he, it is; but, whispering to me, he added, How can your people prosecute us for refusing to kneel at the Sacrament? Don't you see there, that though our Saviour himself officiates, they are all sitting about the table?

I confess it surprized me, and, at first, I knew not what answer to make to him; but I told him, That was not a place for him and I to dispute it, we would talk of it afterwards, and so we did, but brought it to no conclusion, so 'tis needless to mention it any more here.

After we had spent some hours in viewing all that was curious on this side, we came down to the dungeon, or Round Tower, which goes up a long, but easy, ascent of steps, and is very high. Here we were obliged to deliver up our swords, but no where else.

There is nothing curious here: The governor, or constable's

lodgings, are very well, and neatly furnished, but nothing extraordinary, especially they will not look so, after seeing the fine lodgings, as above. From this tower, you see St. Paul's Cathedral at London, very plainly: Coming down from hence, we came into the other court, where is the great Chapel of the Garter, and the house or college for the poor knights, as they are called.

The late Duke of Northumberland, who was constable of this castle, met with a very strange, and uncommon accident in coming hither from Stanes in his coach; for being benighted, as we call it in England, the night also very dark, and passing by a place where there are some houses, tho' not a town, and where the road goes close to the river, whether his coachman did not see the water, or mistook it for the water in the road, I know not, but he plunged in the horses, coach and all, into the river, and at a place where the water was exceeding deep, and the bank steep; so that if help had not come immediately from a gentleman's house, which was close to the road, the servants crying out loud enough to alarm them, his grace, and a gentleman who was in the coach with him, had unavoidably perished; and, as it was, he was a considerable time under water, so that he was in the extremity of danger.

I might go back here to the history of the Order of the Garter, the institution of which by King Edward III. not only had its original here, but seems to be seated here, as a native of the place; and that this is the place where the ceremonies of it, the instalments, feasts, &c. are always to be performed: But this is done so fully in other authors, and by so many, that it would be falling into that error, which I condemn in others, and making my accounts be, what I resolved, from the beginning, they should not be; namely, A copy of other men's performances. I shall only give you out of Mr. Ashmole, a list of the first knights who had the honour of this Order, and who have been succeeded by so many kings, dukes, and sovereign princes abroad, as well as noble-men, and peers of this kingdom at home. The names of the first knights are as follow.

King Edward III.
His Son Edward the Black Prince,
Henry, Duke of Lancaster,
Thomas, Earl of Warwick,
Peers Capitow de la Bouch,
Ralph, Earl of Stafford,
William Montacute, Earl of Salisbury,
Roger Mortimer, Earl of March,
John de Lysle,
Bartholomew Burghersh,

John de Beauchamp,	Hugh Wrotesley,
John de Mohun,	Nele Loring,
Hugh Courtenay,	John Chandos,
Thomas Holland,	James de Audeley,
John de Grey,	Otho Holland,
Richard Fitz Simon,	Henry Eam,
Miles Stapleton,	Sanchet Daubricourt,
Thomas Wale,	Walter Paveley, *alias* Pevrell.

It is true, these were not all noble-men, that is to say, not all peers, neither does the institution confine the order to such; but 'tis certain, they were all men of great characters and stations, either in the army, or in the civil administration, and such as the sovereign did not think it below him to make his companions; for so they are called.

The lower court, as I mentioned, of the castle, though not so beautiful, for the stately lodgings, rooms of state, &c. is particularly glorious for this fine chapel of the Order, a most beautiful and magnificent work, and which shews the greatness, not only of the Court in those days, but the spirit and genius of the magnanimous founder. The chapel is not only fine within, but the workmanship without is extraordinary; nothing so antient is to be seen so very beautiful. The chapel of St. Stephen's in Westminster-Abby, called Henry VIIth's Chapel, and King's College Chapel at Cambridge, built by Henry VI. are fine buildings; but they are modern, compared to this, which was begun, as by the inscribed dates upon the works appears, in the year 1337.

The coats of arms, and the various imagery &c. even inside and outside, not only of the king, but of several of the first Knights Companions, are most admirably finished, and the work has stood out the injury of time to admiration; the beauty of the building remains without any addition, and, indeed, requiring none.

'Tis observable, that King Edward owns this chapel was begun by his ancestors, and some think it was by King Edward I. and that he himself was baptized in it, and that there was a castle built by William the Conqueror also: As to the chapel, which was then called a church, or a convent, King Edward III. did not pull down the old building intirely, but he added all the choir to the first model, and several other proper parts for the purposes intended; as houses and handsome apartments for the canons, dignitaries, and other persons belonging to the church, which are generally situated on the north side of the square, out of sight, or rather skreen'd from the common view by the church itself, which dwellings are, notwithstanding, very good, and well accommodated for the persons who are possessors of them; then the king finished it in the manner we now see it: As for the old castle, the building of William the Conqueror, the king pulled it intirely down, even to the very foundation, forming a new building according to the present plan, and which stood, as above, to the time of King Charles II. without any alteration.

The establishment for this chapel was very considerable, by the donation of divers subjects, before it was set apart to be the chapel of the Order; the Duke of Suffolk in particular, as appears in Dugdale's *Monasticon*, gave near three thousand acres of land, nineteen manors, one hundred seventy messuages and tofts, and several advowsons of churches to it, which, with other gifts afterwards, made the revenue above one thousand pounds a year in those days, which was a prodigious sum, as money went at that time.

In the choir are the stalls for the knights of the Order, with a throne for the sovereign; also stalls in the middle of it for the poor knights pensioners, who live in their house or hospital on the south side of the square or court which the church stands in.

Here are to be seen, the banners of the knights who now enjoy the honour of the Garter: When they die, those banners are taken down, and the coat of arms of the deceased knight set up in the place allotted for those arms over the same stall, so that those coats of arms are a living history, or rather a record of all the knights that ever have been since the first institution of the Order, and how they succeeded one another; by which it appears, that kings, emperors and sovereign princes, have not thought it below them to accept of the honour of being Knights Companions of this Order; while, at the same time, it must be noted to the honour of the English Crown, that our kings have never thought fit to accept of any of their Orders abroad, of what kind soever, whether Popish or Protestant; that of the Cordon Blue, or the Cordon Blanc, the Cordon Noir, or the Cordon Rouge, the Golden Fleece of Spain, the Holy Ghost of France, or the Black Eagle of Prussia, or any other; whereas of the Garter, there is an account by the register of the Order, that there are reckoned up of this most noble company,

Eight Emperors of Germany.
Three Kings of Sweden.
Five Kings of Denmark.
Two Kings of Prussia.
Three Kings of Spain,
Five Princes of Orange.
Five Kings of France.
Four Dukes, Peers of France.
Two Noblemen of the House of Duras in France, viz. Galliard de Duras, & Lewis de Duras, Earl of Feversham.
One King of Scotland, besides James VI. who became Sovereign of the Order.
Five Kings of Portugal.
One King of Poland.
Two Kings of Naples.
One King of Aragon.
Three Infants of Portugal.

One Prince of the House of the King of Bohemia, Prince Rupert.
One Prince of Denmark, Prince George.
One Bishop of Osnaburg.
Five Princes of Lunenburg.
One Elector of Brandeburg.
Seven Electors Palatines.
Two Electors of Saxony.
Two Dukes of Lorrain.
Three Dukes of Wirtemberg.
Two Dukes of Holstein.
Two Grandees of Spain.
Two Dukes de Urbino in Italy.
One Duke of Savoy.
Three Princes of England not Kings, viz. Edward the Black Prince, the Duke of Gloucester, and Prince Frederick.

Several kings, and persons of high rank have been buried also in this chapel; as Edward IV. and Charles I. Also here is the family repository, or burying ground of the Dukes of Beauford, who are a natural branch of the royal family, by the antient House of Lancaster; and in the chapel where the vault is there is a very noble monument of the last duke save one.

All the ceremonies observed here in the installment of the knights, are so perfectly and fully set down in Mr. Ashmole's *History of the Order of the Garter*, that nothing can be said, but what must be a copy from him, which, as above, I studiously decline, and therefore refer you to him.

Besides the foreign princes, Companions of this famous Order as above; there is a little gallaxie of English nobility, the flower of so many Courts, and so many ages, to whose families the ensigns of the Order have been an honour, and who are not the least of the honour this Order has to boast of.

In the first institution, there was but one duke, namely, the great Duke of Lancaster; but as that order of nobility is since much increased in England, since the days of King Edward III. so in the present list of knights, we find no less than fifteen dukes, including the Prince of Wales, who is also Duke of Cornwall. The list of the present knights are as follow, viz.

King George,
George Prince of Wales,
Duke of York, the king's
 brother,
Prince Frederick,
Duke of Cleveland and South-
 ampton,
Duke of Somerset,
Duke of Richmond,
Duke of St. Albans,
Duke of Devonshire,
Duke of Argyle,
Duke of Newcastle,
Duke of Kent,

Duke of Kingstone,
Duke of Montague,
Duke of Grafton,
Duke of Dorset,
Duke of Rutland,
Earl of Lincoln,
Earl of Pembroke,
Earl of Berkley,
Earl Paulet,
Earl of Peterborough,
Earl of Strafford,
Earl of Scarborough,
Lord Visc. Townshend.

As the upper court and building are fronted with the fine
terrace as above, so the lower court, where this fine chapel
stands, is walled round with a very high wall, so that no buildings, if there was room for any, could overlook it, which wall
goes round the west end of the court to the gate, which looking
south, leads into the town, as the gate of the upper court looks
likewise S.E. into the park, which they call the Little Park.

The parks about Windsor are very agreeable, and suitable to
the rest; the little park, which is so, only compared to the great
park, is above three miles round, the great one fourteen, and
the forest above thirty: This park is particular to the Court, the
other are open for riding, hunting, and taking the air for any
gentlemen that please.

The lodges in those parks, are no more lodges, tho' they
retain the name, but palaces, and might pass for such in other
countries; but as they are all eclipsed by the palace itself, so it
need only be added, That those lodges are principally beautified
by the grandeur of the persons to whom the post of rangers
have been assigned, who, having been inriched by other advance-
ments, honours and profitable employments, thought nothing
too much to lay out to beautify their apartments, in a place,
which it was so much to their honour, as well as conveniency,
to reside; such is the lodge, which belongs to Admiral Churchill,
the Dutchess of Marlborough and others.

I cannot leave Windsor, without taking notice, that we
crossed the Thames upon a wooden bridge, for all the bridges
on the river, between London and Oxford, are of timber, for
the conveniency of the barges: Here we saw Eaton College, the

finest school for what we call grammar learning, for it extends only to the humanity class, that is in Britain, or, perhaps, in Europe.

The building, except the great school room, is antient, the chapel truly Gothick; but all has been repaired, at a very great expence, out of the college stock, within these few years.

The gardens are very fine, and extended from the college, down, almost, to the bank of the Thames; they are extremely well planted, and perfectly well kept.

This college was founded by King Henry VI. a prince munificent in his gifts, for the encouragement of learning, to profusion; Witness, besides this noble foundation, that of King's College in Cambridge, to which the scholars of Eaton are annually removed

This college has a settled revenue of about five thousand pounds per annum, and maintains as follows.

A provost.

A vice provost, who is also a fellow.

Seven fellows, inclusive of the vice provost.

Seventy scholars on the foundation, besides a full choir for the chapel, with officers, and servants usual.

The school is divided into the upper and lower, and each into three classes.

Each school has one master, and each master four assistants, or ushers.

None are received into the upper school, 'till they can make Latin verse, and have a tolerable knowledge of the Greek.

In the lower school, the children are received very young, and are initiated into all school-learning.

Besides the seventy scholars upon the foundation, there are always abundance of children, generally speaking, of the best families, and of persons of distinction, who are boarded in the houses of the masters, and within the college.

The number of scholars instructed here, is from 400 to 550; but has not been under 400 for many years past.

The elections of scholars for the university out of this school, is worth taking notice of: It being a time of jubilee to the school.

The election is once every year, and is made on the first Tuesday in August. In order to the election, there are deputed from King's College in Cambridge, three persons, viz. The Provost of King's College for the time being, with one senior, and one junior poser, fellows of the same college. To these are joyn'd, on the part of Eaton College, the provost, the vice provost, and the head master.

These calling the scholars of the upper class, called the sixth class, before them, and examining them in the several parts of their learning, choose out twelve such as they think best qualified, and these are entered in a roll, or list, for the university. The youths thus chosen, are not immediately removed from the school, but must wait till vacancies fall in the said King's College, to make room to receive them; and as such vacancies happen, they are then called up, as they stand in seniority in the said list, or roll of election.

When a scholar from Eaton, comes to King's College, he is received upon the foundation, and pursues his studies there for three years, after which, he claims a Fellowship, unless forfeited in the terms of the statutes; that is to say, by marriage, accepting of ecclesiastick preferments, &c. The present governors at Eaton, are,

The Provost, The Reverend and Honourable Dr. Godolphin, Dean of St. Paul's.

Vice Provost, and Senior Fellow, The Right Reverend Dr. Wiston, Bishop of Excester.

Second Fellow, The Right Reverend Dr. Waddington, Bishop of Chichester.

Third Fellow, The Reverend Dr. Richardson, Master of Peter House in Cambridge.

Fourth Fellow, The Reverend Dr. Evans.

Fifth Fellow, The Reverend Dr. Carter.

Sixth Fellow, The Reverend and Honourable Mr. Hill, once one of the Lords of the Treasury.

Seventh Fellow, The Reverend Dr. Sleech.

The present masters are,

Dr. Henry Bland, Head Master.
Mr. Francis Goode, Second Master.

N.B. The Provost has a noble house and garden, besides the use of the college gardens, at his pleasure.

And now being come to the edge of Middlesex, which is a county too full of cities, towns, and palaces, to be brought in at the close of a letter, and with which I purpose to begin my next travels; I conclude this letter, and am,

SIR,
Your most humble servant.

THE END OF THE FOURTH LETTER

LETTER V

CONTAINING A DESCRIPTION OF THE CITY OF LONDON, AS TAKING
IN THE CITY OF WESTMINSTER, BOROUGH OF SOUTHWARK,
AND THE BUILDINGS CIRCUMJACENT

SIR,—As I am now near the center of this work, so I am to
describe the great center of England, the city of London, and
parts adjacent. This great work is infinitely difficult in its
particulars, though not in itself; not that the city is so difficult
to be described, but to do it in the narrow compass of a letter,
which we see so fully takes up two large volumes in folio, and
which, yet, if I may venture to give an opinion of it, is done
but by halves neither.

However, be the task difficult, as it is, yet it must be done;
to be concise and short, is absolutely necessary; to be plain and
significant, as necessary; I shall observe both, as near as I can.

London, as a city only, and as its walls and liberties line it
out, might, indeed, be viewed in a small compass; but, when
I speak of London, now in the modern acceptation, you expect
I shall take in all that vast mass of buildings, reaching from
Black-Wall in the east, to Tot-Hill Fields in the west; and
extended in an unequal breadth, from the bridge, or river, in
the south, to Islington north; and from Peterburgh House on
the bank side in Westminster, to Cavendish Square, and all
the new buildings by, and beyond, Hannover Square, by which
the city of London, for so it is still to be called, is extended to
Hide Park Corner in the Brentford Road, and almost to Mari-
bone in the Acton Road, and how much farther it may spread,
who knows? New squares, and new streets rising up every day
to such a prodigy of buildings, that nothing in the world does,
or ever did, equal it, except old Rome in Trajan's time, when
the walls were fifty miles in compass, and the number of
inhabitants six million eight hundred thousand souls.

It is the disaster of London, as to the beauty of its figure, that
it is thus stretched out in buildings, just at the pleasure of every
builder, or undertaker of buildings, and as the convenience of
the people directs, whether for trade, or otherwise; and this

has spread the face of it in a most straggling, confus'd manner, out of all shape, uncompact, and unequal; neither long or broad, round or square; whereas the city of Rome, though a monster for its greatness, yet was, in a manner, round, with very few irregularities in its shape.

At London, including the buildings on both sides the water, one sees it, in some places, three miles broad, as from St. George's in Southwark, to Shoreditch in Middlesex; or two miles, as from Peterburgh House to Montague House; and in some places, not half a mile, as in Wapping; and much less, as in Redriff.

We see several villages, formerly standing, as it were, in the country, and at a great distance, now joyn'd to the streets by continued buildings, and more making haste to meet in the like manner; for example, 1. Deptford, This town was formerly reckoned, at least two miles off from Redriff, and that over the marshes too, a place unlikely ever to be inhabited; and yet now, by the encrease of buildings in that town itself, and the many streets erected at Redriff, and by the docks and building-yards on the river side, which stand between both, the town of Deptford, and the streets of Redriff, or Rotherhith (as they write it) are effectually joyn'd, and the buildings daily increasing; so that Deptford is no more a separated town, but is become a part of the great mass, and infinitely full of people also; Here they have, within the last two or three years, built a fine new church, and were the town of Deptford now separated, and rated by itself, I believe it contains more people, and stands upon more ground, than the city of Wells.

The town of Islington, on the north side of the city, is in like manner joyn'd to the streets of London, excepting one small field, and which is in itself so small, that there is no doubt, but in a very few years, they will be intirely joyn'd, and the same may be said of Mile-End, on the east end of the town.

Newington, called Newington-Butts, in Surrey, reaches out her hand north, and is so near joining to Southwark, that it cannot now be properly called a town by itself, but a suburb to the burrough, and if, as they now tell is us undertaken, St. George's Fields should be built into squares and streets, a very little time will shew us Newington, Lambeth, and the Burrough, all making but one Southwark.

That Westminster is in a fair way to shake hands with Chelsea, as St. Gyles's is with Marybone; and Great Russel Street by Montague House, with Tottenham-Court: all this is very evident, and yet all these put together, are still to be called London: Whither will this monstrous city then extend? and where must a circumvallation or communication line of it be placed?

I have, as near as I could, caused a measure to be taken of this mighty, I cannot say uniform, body; and for the satisfaction of the curious, I have here given as accurate a description of it, as I can do in so narrow a compass, as this of a letter, or as I could do without drawing a plan, or map of the places.

As I am forced, in many places, to take in some unbuilt ground, so I have, on the other hand, been obliged to leave a great many whole streets of buildings out of my line: So that I have really not stretched my calculations, to make it seem bigger than it is; nor is there any occasion of it.

A LINE OF MEASUREMENT, DRAWN ABOUT ALL THE CONTINUED BUILDINGS OF THE CITY OF LONDON, AND PARTS ADJACENT, INCLUDING WESTMINSTER AND SOUTHWARK, ETC.

The Line begins, for the Middlesex Side of the Buildings,

Miles Fur. Rods

1. At Peterborough House, the farthest house west upon the River Thames, and runs N.W. by W. by the marshes to Tutthill Fields, and passing by the Neat Houses, and Arnold's Brewhouse, ends at Chelsea Road, measured - - - 1 6 16

2. Then, allowing an interval from Buckingham House cross the park, about one furlong and half to the corner of my Lord Godolphin's garden wall, the line goes north behind the stable-yard buildings, and behind Park-Place, and on the park wall behind the buildings; on the west side of St. James's Street, to the corner in Soho, or Pickadilly, then crossing the road, and goes along the north side of the road west to Hide Park Gate 1 2 11

3. Then the line turns N.E. by E. and taking in the buildings and streets, called May-Fair, and holds on east till the new streets formed out of Hide House Garden, cause it to turn away north, a point west reaching to Tyburn-Road, a little to

Carried over - - - - 3 0 27

Miles Fur. Rods

Brought over   -   -   -   -   3   0   27

the east of the great mother conduit; then it goes
north, and crossing the road, takes in the west
side of Cavendish Square, and the streets adjoining,
and leaving Marybone, goes away east, 'till it
reaches to Hampstead-Road, near a little village
called Tottenham Court   -   -   -   -   2   5   20

4. From Tottenham Court, the line comes in
a little south, to meet the Bloomsbury buildings,
then turning east, runs behind Montague and
Southampton Houses, to the N.E. corner of
Southampton House, then crossing the path,
meets the buildings called Queen's Square, then
turning north, 'till it comes to the N.W. corner
of the square, thence it goes away east behind the
buildings on the north side of Ormond Street,
'till it comes to Lamb's Conduit   -   -   1   1   13

5. Here the line turns south, and indents to
the corner of Bedford Row, and leaving some few
houses, with the cock-pit, and bowling green,
goes on the back of Gray's Inn Wall, to Gray's
Inn Lane, then turns on the outside of the buildings, which are on the west side of Gray's Inn
Lane, going north to the stones end, when turning
east, it passes to the new river bridge without
Liquor-pond Street, so taking in the Cold Bath
and the Bear Garden; but leaving out Sir John
Old-Castle's and the Spaw, goes on east by the
Ducking-Pond to the end of New Bridewell, and
crossing the Fairfield, comes into the Islington Road
by the Distiller's House, formerly Justice Fuller's,   1   2   6

6. Here to take in all the buildings which
joyn Islington to the streets, the line goes north
on the east side of the road to the Turk's Head
ale-house; then turning north west, passes to the
New River House, but leaving it to the west, passes
by Sadler's Well, from thence to Bussby's House,
and keeping on the west side of Islington, 'till it

Carried over   -   -   -   -   8   1   26

Brought over   -   -   -   -   8   1   26

comes opposite to Cambray House-Lane, turns
into the road, and passes south almost to the lane
which turns east down to the lower street, but then
turns east without the houses, and goes to the
Cow-keeper's in the lower street crossing the road,
and through the Cow-keeper's Yard into Frog-
lane, then running west on the south side of the
town, just without the buildings, joyns again to
the buildings on the west side of Wood's-Close,
passing behind the Sheep-market wall   -   -   2   4   39

7. From Wood's-Close, the line goes due east to
Mount Mill, where, leaving several buildings to the
north, it passes on, crossing all the roads to Brick-
lane, to the north side of the great new square in
Old-street, and taking in the Pest-house wall, turns
south at the north-east corner of the said wall, to
Old-street Road; then going away east till it meets
the buildings near Hoxton Square, it turns north
to the north west corner of the wall of Ask's Hospital, then sloping north east, it passes by Pimlico,
the Cyder House, and the two walls to the north
end of Hoxton, when it turns east, and inclosing the
garden walls, comes into the Ware road, just at
the King's Head in the new buildings by the Land
of Promise   -   -   -   -   -   2   0   16

8. From the King's Head, the line turns south,
running to the stones end in Shoreditch, then turning east, it takes in a burying ground and some
buildings in the Hackney road, when sloping
south east by south, it goes away by the Virginia
House to a great brewhouse, and then still more
east to the back of Wheeler-street, and then east
by south, to Brick-lane, crossing which, it goes
away east towards Bethnal Green; but then turning short south, it goes towards White Chapel
Mount, but being intercepted by new streets, it
goes quite up to the south end of the Dog-Row at
Mile End   -   -   -   -   -   -   1   6   19

Carried over   -   -   -   -   14   5   20

Brought over   -   -   -   -   14   5   20

9. From the Dog-Row, the line crosses the road, and takes in a little hamlet of houses, called Stepney, tho' not properly so, and coming back west to the streets end at White Chapel Mill, goes away south by the Hog-houses into Church Lane, and to Rag Fair, when turning again east, it continues in a strait line on the north side of Ratcliff High-way, 'till it comes almost to the farther Glass-houses, then turning north, it surrounds all Stepney and Stepney causeway to Mile End Road, then turning east again, and afterwards south, comes back to the new streets on the north side of Lime-house, and joyning the marsh, comes down to the water side at the lower shipwright dock in Lime-house Hole   -   -   -   -   -   -   3   7   01

                                                                          18   4   21

N.B. This line leaves out all the north side of Mile End town, from the end of the Dog-Row, to the Jews Burying Ground, which is all built; also all the north part of the Dog-Row, and all Bethnal Green: Also all Poplar and Black-Wall, which are, indeed, contiguous, a trifle of ground excepted, and very populous.

For the Southwark Side of the Buildings, the Line is as follows ;

Having ended the circumference of the Middlesex buildings at Lime-house, and the street extending towards Poplar, the hamlets of Poplar and Blackwall, tho' very near contiguous in buildings, being excluded, I allow an interval of two miles, from Poplar, cross the Isle of Dogs, and over the Thames, to the lower water gate at Deptford, and tho' in measuring the circumference of all cities, the river, where any such runs through any part of the buildings, is always measured, yet; that I may not be said to stretch the extent of the buildings which I include in this account, I omit the river from Limehouse to Deptford (where, if included, it ought to begin) and begin my line as above.

Miles Fur. Rods

1. From the said upper water-gate at Deptford, the line goes east to the corner next the Thames, where the shipwright's yard now is, and where I find a continued range of buildings begins by the side of a little creek or river, which runs into the Thames there, and reaches quite up the said river, to the bridge in the great Kentish road, and over the street there, taking in the south side of the street, to the west corner of the buildings in that street, and then measuring down on the west side of the long street, which runs to the Thames side, 'till you come to the new street which passes from Deptford to Rederiff, then turning to the left, passing on the back side of the king's yard to Mr. Evelin's house, including the new church of Deptford, and all the new streets or buildings made on the fields side, which are very many, this amounts in the whole, to -   -   -   3   1   16

2. From Mr. Evelin's garden gate, the line goes north west, taking in all the new docks and yards, the Red-house, and several large streets of houses, which have been lately built, and by which the said town of Deptford is effectually joined to the buildings, reaching from Cuckold's Point, east-ward, and which are carried out, as if Rederiff stretch'd forth its arm to embrace Deptford; then for some length, the said street of Rederiff continues narrow 'till you come to Church-street, where several streets are also lately built south, and others parallel with the street, till gradually, the buildings thicken, and extend farther and farther to the south and south by east, 'till they cross over the east end of Horslydown to Bermondsey Church, and thence east to the sign of the World's End, over against the great fort, being the remains of the fortifications drawn round these parts of Southwark in the late civil wars. This extent is, by computation, four miles; but being measured, as the streets indented, the circuit prov'd -   -   5   6   12

Carried over   -   -   -   -   8   7   28

	Miles	Fur.	Rods
Brought over - - - -	8	7	28

3. From this fort, to the corner of Long Lane, and through Long Lane to the Lock, at the end of Kent-street, is - - - - -   1 7 02

4. From the corner of Kent-street to the town of Newington Butts, drawing the line behind all the buildings as they stand, and round the said village of Newington, to the Haberdashers Alms Houses, and thence by the road to the windmill, at the corner of Blackman-street, is - -   3 2 16

5. From the windmill crossing St. George's Fields, on the back of the Mint, to the Fighting Cocks, thence to the Restoration Gardens, and thence on the outside of all the buildings to Lambeth-Wells, and on to Faux-Hall Bridge, over against the other fort of the old fortifications, being just the same length that those old fortifications extended, tho' infinitely fuller of buildings; this last circuit measures - -   3 5 12

                                           17 6 18

Thus the extent or circumference of the continued buildings of the cities of London and Westminster, and borough of Southwark, all which, in the common acceptation, is called London, amounts to thirty six miles, two furlongs, thirty nine rods.

N.B. The town of Greenwich, which may, indeed, be said to be contiguous to Deptford, might be also called a part of this measurement; but I omit it, as I have the towns of Chelsea and Knights Bridge on the other side, tho' both may be said to joyn the town, and in a very few years will certainly do so.

Were it possible to reduce all these buildings to a compact situation, 'tis generally thought, that the whole body so put together, allowing the necessary ground, which they now employ for the several trades in the out-parts, such as the building yards by the river, for shipwrights, tanners yards, dyers, whitsters, &c. I say, 'tis believed the whole would take up twenty eight miles in circumference, very compactly built.
The guesses that are made at the number of inhabitants,

have been variously form'd; Sir William Petty, famous for his political arithmetick, supposed the city, at his last calculation, to contain a million of people, and this he judges from the number of births and burials; and by this rule, as well by what is well known of the increase of the said births and burials, as of the prodigious increase of buildings, it may be very reasonable to conclude, the present number of inhabitants within the circumference I have mentioned, to amount to, at least, fifteen hundred thousand, with this addition, that it is still prodigiously increasing.

Nor is it hard to account for this increase of people, as well as buildings in London; but the discourse seems too political to belong to this work, which, rather, relates to the fact than the reason of it, and is properly to describe the thing, not to shew why it is so, for which reason I omit entring into the enquiry.

The government of this great mass of building, and of such a vast collected body of people, though it consists of various parts, is, perhaps, the most regular and well-ordered government, that any city, of above half its magnitude, can boast of.

The government of the city of London in particular, and abstractedly considered, is, by the lord mayor, twenty four aldermen, two sheriffs, the recorder and common council; but the jurisdiction of these is confined to that part only, which they call the City and its Liberties, which are marked out, except the Borough, by the walls and the bars, as they are called, and which the particular maps of the city have exactly lin'd out, to which I refer.

Besides this, the lord mayor and aldermen of London have a right presidial, as above, in the borough of Southwark, as conservators of the bridge, and the bridge itself is their particular jurisdiction.

Also the lord mayor, &c. is conservator of the River Thames, from Stanes Bridge in Surrey and Middlesex, to the River Medway in Kent, and, as some insist, up the Medway to Rochester Bridge.

The government of the out parts, is by justices of the peace, and by the sheriffs of London, who are, likewise, sheriffs of Middlesex; and the government of Westminster is, by a high bailiff, constituted by the Dean and Chapter, to whom the civil administrations is so far committed.

The remaining part of Southwark side, when the city jurisdiction is considered, is govern'd, also by a Bench of Justices, and their proper substituted peace officers; excepting out of this the privileges of the Marshalseas, or of the Marshal's Court, the privilege of the Marshal of the King's Bench, the Mint, and the like.

To enter here, into a particular description of the city of London, its antiquities, monuments, &c. would be only to make an abridgment of Stow and his continuators, and would make a volume by itself; but while I write in manner of a letter, and in the person of an itinerant, and give a cursory view of its present state, and to the reader, who is supposed to be upon the spot, or near it, and who has the benefit of all the writers, who have already entered upon the description; it will, I believe, be allowed to be agreeable and sufficient to touch at those things principally, which no other authors have yet mentioned, concerning this great and monstrous thing, called London.

N.B. By this may be plainly understood, that I mean not the city only, for then I must discourse of it in several parts, and under several denominations and descriptions, as,

1. Of the city and liberties of London.
2. Of the city and liberties of Westminster.
3. Of the Tower and its hamlets.
4. Of the suburbs or buildings annex'd to these, and called Middlesex.
5. Of the borough of Southwark.
6. Of the Bishop of Winchester's reserv'd privileg'd part in Southwark, called the Park and Marshalsea.
7. Of Lambeth.
8. Of Deptford, and the king's and merchants yards for building.
9. Of the Bridge-house and its reserv'd limits, belonging to the city.
10. Of the buildings on Southwark side, not belonging to any of these.

But by London, as I shall discourse of it, I mean, all the buildings, places, hamlets, and villages contain'd in the line of circumvallation, if it be proper to call it so, by which I have computed the length of its circumference as above.

We ought, with respect to this great mass of buildings, to observe, in every proper place, what it is now, and what it was within the circumference of a few years past; and particularly, when other authors wrote, who have ventured upon the description of it.

It is, in the first place, to be observed, as a particular and remarkable crisis, singular to those who write in this age, and very much to our advantage in writing, that the great and more eminent increase of buildings, in, and about the city of London, and the vast extent of ground taken in, and now become streets and noble squares of houses, by which the mass, or body of the whole, is become so infinitely great, has been generally made in our time, not only within our memory, but even within a few years, and the description of these additions, cannot be improper to a description of the whole, as follows.

A BRIEF DESCRIPTION OF THE NEW BUILDINGS ERECTED IN AND ABOUT THE CITIES OF LONDON AND WESTMINSTER AND BOROUGH OF SOUTHWARK, SINCE THE YEAR 1666

This account of new buildings is to be understood,

1. Of houses re-built after the great fires in London and Southwark, &c.

2. New foundations, on ground where never any buildings were erected before.

Take, then, the city and its adjacent buildings to stand, as described by Mr. Stow, or by any other author, who wrote before the Fire of London, and the difference between what it was then, and what it is now, may be observed thus:

It is true, that before the Fire of London, the streets were narrow, and publick edifices, as well as private, were more crowded, and built closer to one another; for soon after the Fire, the king, by his proclamation, forbid all persons whatsoever, to go about to re-build for a certain time, viz. till the Parliament (which was soon to sit) might regulate and direct the manner of building, and establish rules for the adjusting every man's property, and yet might take order for a due inlarging of the streets, and appointing the manner of building, as well for the beauty as the conveniency of the city, and for safety, in case of any future accident; for though I shall not inquire, whether the city was burnt by accident, or by treachery, yet nothing was more certain, than that as the city stood before, it was strangely exposed to the disaster which happen'd, and the buildings look'd as if they had been form'd to make one general bonefire, whenever any wicked party of incendiaries should think fit.

The streets were not only narrow, and the houses all built

of timber, lath and plaister, or, as they were very properly call'd paper work, and one of the finest range of buildings in the Temple, are, to this day, called the Paper Buildings, from that usual expression.

But the manner of the building in those days, one story projecting out beyond another, was such, that in some narrow streets, the houses almost touch'd one another at the top, and it has been known, that men, in case of fire, have escaped on the tops of the houses, by leaping from one side of a street to another; this made it often, and almost always happen, that if a house was on fire, the opposite house was in more danger to be fired by it, according as the wind stood, than the houses next adjoining on either side.

How this has been regulated, how it was before, and how much better it now is, I leave to be judged, by comparing the old unburnt part of the city with the new.

But tho' by the new buildings after the fire, much ground was given up, and left unbuilt, to inlarge the streets, yet 'tis to be observed, that the old houses stood severally upon more ground, were much larger upon the flat, and in many places, gardens and large yards about them, all which, in the new buildings, are, at least, contracted, and the ground generally built up into other houses, so that notwithstanding all the ground given up for beautifying the streets, yet there are many more houses built than stood before upon the same ground; so that taking the whole city together, there are more inhabitants in the same compass, than there was before. To explain this more fully, I shall give some particular instances, to which I refer, which there are living witnesses able to confirm: For example,

1. Swithen's Alleys by the Royal Exchange, were all, before the Fire, taken up with one single merchant's house, and inhabited by one Mr. Swithin; whereas, upon the same ground where the house stood, stands now about twenty-two or twenty-four houses, which belong to his posterity to this day.

2. Copt-Hall-Court in Throckmorton-street, was, before the Fire, also a single house, inhabited by a Dutch merchant; also three more courts in the same streets, were single houses, two on the same side of the way, and one on the other.

The several alleys behind St. Christopher's Church, which are now vulgarly, but erroneously, call'd St. Christopher's-Churchyard, were, before the Fire, one great house, or, at least, a house and ware-houses belonging to it, in which the famous

Mr. Kendrick lived, whose monument now stands in St. Christopher's Church, and whose dwelling, also, took up almost all the ground, on which now a street of houses is erected, called Prince's-street, going through into Lothbury, no such street being known before the Fire.

Kings-Arms-Yard in Coleman-street, now built into fine large houses, and inhabited by principal merchants, was, before the fire, a stable-yard for horses and an inn, at the sign of the Kings Arms.

I might fill up my account with many such instances, but 'tis enough to explain the thing, viz. That so many great houses were converted into streets and courts, alleys and buildings, that there are, by estimation, almost 4000 houses now standing on the ground which the Fire left desolate, more than stood on the same ground before.

Another increase of buildings in the city, is to be taken from the inhabitants in the unburnt parts following the same example, of pulling down great old buildings, which took up large tracks of ground in some of the well inhabited places, and building on the same ground, not only several houses, but even whole streets of houses, which are since fully inhabited; for example;

Crosby-Square within Bishopsgate, formerly the house of Sir James Langham merchant.

Devonshire-Square and Street, with several back streets and passages into Petticoat-Lane one way, and Hounsditch another way, all built on the ground where the old Earl of Devonshire had a house and garden, and are all fully inhabited.

Bridgwater-Square, and several streets adjoyning all fully inhabited, built on the ground where the Earl of Bridgwater had a large house and garden in Barbican.

Billeter-Square, and several passages adjoyning, built upon the grounds of one great house, in which, before that, one merchant only lived.

All those palaces of the nobility, formerly making a most beautiful range of buildings fronting the Strand, with their gardens reaching to the Thames, where they had their particular water-gates and stairs, one of which remains still, viz. Somerset House, have had the same fate, such as Essex, Norfolk, Salisbury, Worcester, Exceter, Hungerford, and York Houses; in the place of which, are now so many noble streets and beautiful houses, erected, as are, in themselves, equal to a large city, and extend from the Temple to Northumberland-House; Somerset House and the Savoy, only intervening; and the latter of these may be said to be, not a house, but a little town, being parted into innumerable tenements and apartments.

Many other great houses have, by the example of these, been also built into streets, as Hatton-House in Holborn, and the old Earl of Bedford's great garden, called New Convent Garden; but those I omit, because built before the year 1666; but I may add the Lord Brook's house in Holborn; the Duke of Bedford's last remaining house and garden in the Strand, and many others.

These are prodigious enlargements to the city, even upon that which I call inhabited ground, and where infinite numbers of people now live, more than lived upon the same spot of ground before.

But all this is a small matter, compared to the new foundations raised within that time, in those which we justly call the out parts; and not to enter on a particular description of the buildings, I shall only take notice of the places where such enlargements are made; as, first, within the memory of the writer hereof, all those numberless ranges of building, called Spittle Fields, reaching from Spittle-yard, at Northern Fallgate, and from Artillery Lane in Bishopsgate-street, with all the new streets, beginning at Hoxton, and the back of Shoreditch Church, north, and reaching to Brick-Lane, and to the end of Hare-street, on the way to Bethnal Green, east; then sloping away quite to White Chapel Road, south east, containing, as some people say, who pretend to know, by good observation, above three hundred and twenty acres of ground, which are all now close built, and well inhabited with an infinite number of people, I say, all these have been built new from the ground, fince the year 1666.

The lanes were deep, dirty, and unfrequented, that part now called Spittlefields-Market, was a field of grass with cows feeding on it, since the year 1670. The Old Artillery Ground (where the Parliament listed their first soldiers against the King) took up all those long streets, leading out of Artillery Lane to Spittle-yard-back-Gate, and so on to the end of Wheeler-street.

Brick-Lane, which is now a long well-pav'd street, was a deep dirty road, frequented by carts fetching bricks that way into White-Chapel from Brick-Kilns in those fields, and had its name on that account; in a word, it is computed, that about two hundred thousand inhabitants dwell now in that part of London, where, within about fifty years past, there was not a house standing.

2. On the more eastern part, the same increase goes on in proportion, namely, all Goodman's Fields, the name gives evidence for it, and the many streets between White-Chapel and Rosemary Lane, all built since the year 1678. Well Close, now called Marine Square, was so remote from houses, that it used to be a very dangerous place to go over after it was dark, and many people have been robbed and abused in passing it; a well standing in the middle, just where the Danish church is now built, there the mischief was generally done; beyond this, all the hither or west end of Ratcliff-high-way, from the corner of Gravel-Lane, to the east end of East Smithfield, was a road over the fields; likewise those buildings, now called Virginia-street, and all the streets on the side of Ratcliff-high-way to Gravel-Lane above named.

3. To come to the north side of the town, and beginning at Shoreditch, west, and Hoxton-Square, and Charles's-Square adjoyning, and the streets intended for a market-place, those were all open fields, from Anniseed-clear to Hoxton Town, till the year 1689, or thereabouts; Pitfield-street was a bank, parting two pasture grounds, and Ask's Hospital was another open field: Farther west, the like addition of buildings begins at the foot way, by the Pest-house, and includes the French hospital, Old street two squares, and several streets, extending from Brick-Lane to Mount-Mill, and the road to Islington, and from the road, still west, to Wood's Close, and to St. John's, and Clerkenwell, all which streets and squares are built since the year 1688 and 1689, and were before that, and some for a long time after, open fields or gardens, and never built on till after that time.

From hence we go on still west, and beginning at Gray's-Inn, and going on to those formerly called Red Lyon Fields, and Lamb's Conduit Fields, we see there a prodigious pile of buildings; it begins at Gray's-Inn Wall towards Red-Lyon Street, from whence, in a strait line, 'tis built quite to Lamb's Conduit Fields, north, including a great range of buildings yet unfinish'd, reaching to Bedford Row and the Cockpit, east, and including Red Lyon Square, Ormond Street, and the great new square at the west end of it, and all the streets between that square and King's Gate in Holbourn, where it goes out; this pile of buildings is very great, the houses so magnificent and large, that abundance of persons of quality, and some of the nobility are found among them, particularly in Ormond Street, is the D—— of Powis's house, built at the expence of France, on account of the former house being burnt, while the Duke D'Aumont, the French Ambassador Extraordinary lived in it; it is now a very noble structure, tho' not large, built of free-stone, and in the most exact manner, according to the rules of architecture, and is said to be, next the Banquetting House, the most regular building in this part of England.

Here is also a very convenient church, built by the contribution of the gentry inhabitants of these buildings, tho' not yet made parochial, being called St. George's Chapel.

Farther west, in the same line, is Southampton great square, called Bloomsbury, with King-street on the east side of it, and all the numberless streets west of the square, to the market place, and through Great-Russel-street by Montague House, quite into the Hampstead road, all which buildings, except the old building of Southampton House and some of the square, has been form'd from the open fields, since the time above-mentioned, and must contain several thousands of houses; here is also a market, and a very handsome church new built.

From hence, let us view the two great parishes of St. Giles's and St. Martin's in the Fields, the last so increased, as to be above thirty years ago, formed into three parishes, and the other about now to be divided also.

The increase of the buildings here, is really a kind of prodigy; all the buildings north of Long Acre, up to the Seven Dials, all the streets, from Leicester-Fields and St. Martin's-Lane, both north and west, to the Hay-Market and Soho, and from the Hay-Market to St. James's-street inclusive, and to the park wall; then all the buildings on the north side of the street, called Picadilly, and the road to Knight's-Bridge, and between that and the south side of Tyburn Road, including Soho-Square, Golden-Square, and now Hanover-Square, and that new city on the north side of Tyburn Road, called Cavendish-Square, and all the streets about it.

This last addition, is, by calculation, more in bulk than the cities of Bristol, Exeter and York, if they were all put together; all which places were, within the time mentioned, meer fields of grass, and employ'd only to feed cattle as other fields are.

The many little additions that might be named besides these, tho' in themselves considerable, yet being too many to give room to here, I omit.

This is enough to give a view of the difference between the present and the past greatness of this mighty city, called London.

N.B. Three projects have been thought of, for the better regulating the form of this mighty building, which tho' not yet brought to perfection, may, perhaps, in time, be brought forwards, and if it should, would greatly add to the beauty.

1. Making another bridge over the Thames.
2. Making an Act of Parliament, abrogating the names as well as the jurisdictions of all the petty privileged places, and joyning or uniting the whole body, Southwark and all, into one city, and calling it by one name, London.
3. Forbidding the extent of the buildings in some particular places, where they too much run it out of shape, and letting the more indented parts swell out on the north and south side a little, to balance the length, and bring the form of the whole more near to that of a circle, as particularly stopping the running out of the buildings at the east and west ends, as at Ratcliff and Deptford, east, and at Tyburn and Kensington roads, west, and encouraging the building out at Moor-fields, Bunhil-fields, the west side of Shoreditch, and such places, and the north part of Gray's-Inn, and other adjacent parts, where the buildings are not equally filled out, as in other places, and the like in St. George's Fields and behind Redriff on the other side of the water.

But these are speculations only, and must be left to the wisdom of future ages. I return now, to some short description of the parts; hitherto I have been upon the figure and extent of the city and its out-parts; I come now to speak of the inside, the buildings, the inhabitants, the commerce, and the manner of its government, &c.

It should be observed, that the city being now re-built, has occasioned the building of some publick edifices, even in the place which was inhabited, which yet were not before, and the re-building others in a new and more magnificent manner than ever was done before.

1. That beautiful column, called the Monument, erected at the charge of the city, to perpetuate the fatal burning of the whole, cannot be mentioned but with some due respect to the building itself, as well as to the city; it is two hundred and two feet high, and in its kind, out does all the obelisks and pillars of the ancients, at least that I have seen, having a most stupendous stair-case in the middle to mount up to the balcony, which is about thirty feet short of the top, and whence there are other steps made even to look out at the top of the whole building; the top is fashioned like an urn.

2. The canal or river, called Fleet-ditch, was a work of great magnificence and expence; but not answering the design, and being now very much neglected, and out of repair, is not much spoken of, yet it has three fine bridges over it, and a fourth, not so fine, yet useful as the rest, and the tide flowing up to the last; the canal is very useful for bringing of coals and timber, and other heavy goods; but the warehouses intended under the streets, on either side, to lay up such goods in, are not made use of, and the wharfs in many places are decay'd and fallen in, which make it all look ruinous.

The Royal Exchange, the greatest and finest of the kind in the world, is the next publick work of the citizens, the beauty of which answers for itself, and needs no description here; 'tis observable, that tho' this Exchange cost the citizens an immense sum of money re-building, some authors say, eighty thousand pounds, being finished and embellished in so exquisite a manner, yet it was so appropriated to the grand affair of business, that the rent or income of it for many years, fully answered the interest of the money laid out in building it: Whether it does so still or not, I will not say, the trade for millenary goods, fine laces, &c. which was so great above stairs for many years, being since scattered and removed, and the shops, many of them, left empty; but those shops, of which there were eight double rows above, and the shops and offices round it below, with the vaults under the whole, did at first, yield a very great sum.

Among other publick edifices, that of the hospital of Bethlehem, or Bedlam, should not be forgot, which is at the very time of writing this, appointed to be inlarged with two new wings, and will then be the most magnificent thing of its kind in the world.

Likewise the Custom-House, an accidental fire having demolished part of it, and given the commissioners opportunity to take in more ground, will, when it is finished, out-shine all the custom-houses in Europe.

The churches in London are rather convenient than fine, not adorned with pomp and pageantry as in Popish countries; but, like the true Protestant plainness, they have made very little of ornament either within them or without, nor, excepting a few, are they famous for handsome steeples, a great many of them are very mean, and some that seem adorned, are rather deform'd than beautified by the heads that contrived, or by the hands that built them.

Some, however, hold up their heads with grandeur and magnificence, and are really ornaments to the whole, I mean by these, such as Bow, St. Brides, the new church in the Strand, Rood-Lane Church, or St. Margaret Pattons, St. Antholins, St. Clement Danes, and some others, and some of the fifty churches, now adding by the county and charity of the government, are like to be very well adorned.

Three or four Gothick towers have been rebuilt at the proper expences of the fund appointed, and are not the worst in all the city, namely St. Michael at Cornhill, St Dunstan in the East, St. Christophers, St. Mary Aldermary, and at St. Sepulchre's.

But the beauty of all the churches in the city, and of all the Protestant churches in the world, is the cathedral of St. Paul's; a building exceeding beautiful and magnificent; tho' some authors are pleased to expose their ignorance, by pretending to find fault with it: 'Tis easy to find fault with the works even of God Himself, when we view them in the gross, without regard to the particular beauties of every part separately considered, and without searching into the reason and nature of the particulars; but when these are maturely inquired into, viewed with a just reverence, and considered with judgment, then we fly out in due admirations of the wisdom of the Author from the excellency of His works.

The vast extent of the dome, that mighty arch, on which so great a weight is supported (meaning the upper towers or lanthorn of stone work seventy feet high) may well account for the strength of the pillars and butments below; yet those common observers of the superficial parts of the building, complain, that the columns are too gross, that the work looks heavy, and the lower figures near the eye are too large, as if the Dorick and the Attick were not each of them as beautiful in their place as the Corinthian.

The wise architect, like a compleat master of his business, had the satisfaction, in his lifetime, of hearing those ignorant reprovers of his work confuted, by the approbation of the best masters in Europe; and the church of St. Peter's in Rome, which is owned to be the most finished piece in the world, only exceeds St. Paul's in the magnificence of its inside work; the painting, the altars, the oratories, and the variety of its imagery; things, which, in a Protestant church, however ornamental, are not allowed of.

If all the square columns, the great pilasters, and the flat pannel work, as well within as without, which they now alledge are too heavy and look too gross, were filled with pictures, adorned with carved work and gilding, and crowded with adorable images of the saints and angels, the kneeling crowd would not complain of the grossness of the work; but 'tis the Protestant plainness, that divesting those columns, &c. of their ornaments, makes the work, which in itself is not so large and gross as that of St. Peter's, be called gross and heavy; whereas neither by the rules of order, or by the necessity of the building, to be proportioned and sufficient to the height and weight of the work, could they have been less, or any otherwise than they are.

Nay, as it was, those gentlemen who in Parliament opposed Sir Christopher Wren's request, of having the dome covered with copper, and who moved to have had the lanthorn on the top made shorter, and built of wood; I say, those gentlemen pretending skill in the art, and offering to reproach the judgment of the architect, alledged, That the copper and the stone lanthorn would be too heavy, and that the pillars below would not support it.

To which Sir Christopher answered, That he had sustained the building with such sufficient columns, and the buttment was every where so good, that he would answer for it with his head, that it should bear the copper covering and the stone lanthorn, and seven thousand ton weight laid upon it more than was proposed, and that nothing below should give way, no not one half quarter of an inch; but that, on the contrary, it should be all the firmer and stronger for the weight that should be laid on it; adding, That it was with this view that the work was brought up from its foundation, in such manner, as made common observers rather think the first range of the buildings too gross for its upper part; and that, if they pleased, he would undertake to raise a spire of stone upon the whole, a hundred foot higher than the cross now stands.

When all these things are considered complexly, no man that has the least judgment in building, that knows any thing of the rules of proportion, and will judge impartially, can find any fault in this church; on the contrary, those excellent lines of Mr. Dryden, which were too meanly applied in allegory to the praise of a paltry play, may be, with much more honour to the author, and justice to this work, applied here to St. Paul's Church.

> Strong Dorick pillars form the base,
> Corinthian fills the upper space;
> So all below is strength, and all above is grace.

Sir Christopher's design was, indeed, very unhappily baulked in several things at the beginning, as well in the situation as in the conclusion of this work, which, because very few may have heard of, I shall mention in publick, from the mouth of its author.

1. In the situation: He would have had the situation of the church removed a little to the north, that it should have stood just on the spot of ground which is taken up by the street called Pater-noster-Row, and the buildings on either side; so that the north side of the church should have stood open to the street now called Newgate-street, and the south side, to the ground on which the church now stands.

By this situation, the east end of the church, which is very beautiful, would have looked directly down the main street of the city, Cheapside; and for the west end, Ludgate having been removed a little north, the main street called Ludgate-street and Ludgate-Hill, would only have sloped a little W.S.W. as they do now irregularly two ways, one within, and the other without the gate, and all the street beyond Fleet-Bridge would have received no alteration at all.

By this situation, the common thorough-fare of the city would have been removed at a little farther distance from the work, and we should not then have been obliged to walk just under the very wall as we do now, which makes the work appear quite out of all perspective, and is the chief reason of the objections I speak of; whereas, had it been viewed at a little distance, the building would have been seen infinitely to more advantage.

Had Sir Christopher been allowed this situation, he would then, also, have had more room for the ornament of the west end, which, tho' it is a most beautiful work, as it now appears, would have been much more so then, and he would have added a circular piazza to it, after the model of that at Rome, but much more magnificent, and an obelisk of marble in the center of the circle, exceeding any thing that the world can now shew of its kind, I mean of modern work.

But the circumstance of things hindered this noble design, and the city being almost rebuilt before he obtained an order and provision for laying the foundation; he was prescribed to the narrow spot where we see it now stands, in which the building, however magnificent in itself, stands with infinite disadvantage as to the prospect of it; the inconveniencies of which was so apparent when the church was finished, that leave was at length, tho' not without difficulty, obtained, to pull down one whole row of houses on the north side of the body of the church, to make way for the ballister that surrounds the cimetry or church-yard, and, indeed, to admit the light into the church, as well as to preserve it from the danger of fire.

Another baulk which, as I said, Sir Christopher met with, was in the conclusion of the work, namely, the covering of the dome, which Sir Christopher would have had been of copper double gilded with gold; but he was over-ruled by Party, and the city thereby, deprived of the most glorious sight that the world ever saw, since the temple of Solomon.

Yet with all these disadvantages, the church is a most regular building, beautiful, magnificent, and beyond all the modern works of its kind in Europe, St. Peter's at Rome, as above, only excepted.

It is true, St. Peter's, besides its beauty in ornament and imagery, is beyond St. Paul's in its dimensions, is every way larger; but it is the only church in the world that is so; and it was a merry hyperbole of Sir Christopher Wren's, who, when some gentlemen in discourse compared the two churches, and in compliment to him, pretended to prefer St. Paul's, and when they came to speak of the dimensions, suggested, that St. Paul's was the biggest: I tell you, says Sir Christopher, you might set it in St. Peter's, and look for it a good while, before you could find it.

Having thus spoken of the city and adjacent buildings of London, and of the particulars which I find chiefly omitted by other writers, I have not room here to enter into all the articles needful to a full description: However, I shall touch a little at the things most deserving a stranger's observation.

Supposing now, the whole body of this vast building to be considered as one city, London, and not concerning myself or the reader with the distinction of its several jurisdictions; we shall then observe it only as divided into three, viz. the city, the Court, and the out-parts.

The city is the center of its commerce and wealth.

The Court of its gallantry and splendor.

The out-parts of its numbers and mechanicks; and in all these, no city in the world can equal it.

Between the Court and city, there is a constant communication of business to that degree, that nothing in the world can come up to it.

As the city is the center of business; there is the Custom-house, an article, which, as it brings in an immense revenue to the publick, so it cannot be removed from its place, all the vast import and export of goods being, of necessity, made there; nor can the merchants be removed, the river not admitting the ships to come any farther.

Here, also, is the Excise Office, the Navy Office, the Bank, and almost all the offices where those vast funds are fixed, in which so great a part of the nation are concerned, and on the security of which so many millions are advanced.

Here are the South Sea Company, the East India Company, the Bank, the African Company, &c. whose stocks support that prodigious paper commerce, called Stock-Jobbing; a trade, which once bewitched the nation almost to its ruin, and which, tho' reduced very much, and recover'd from that terrible infatuation which once overspread the whole body of the people, yet is still a negotiation, which is so vast in its extent, that almost all the men of substance in England are more or less concerned in it, and the property of which is so very often alienated, that even the tax upon the transfers of stock, tho' but five shillings for each transfer, brings many thousand pounds a year to the government; and some have said, that there is not less than a hundred millions of stock transferred forward or backward from one hand to another every year, and this is one thing which makes such a constant daily intercourse between the Court part of the town, and the city; and this is given as one of the principal causes of the prodigious conflux of the nobility and gentry from all parts of England to London, more than ever was known in former years, viz. That many thousands of families are so deeply concerned in those stocks, and find it so absolutely necessary to be at hand to take the advantage of buying and selling, as the sudden rise or fall of the price directs, and the loss they often sustain by their ignorance of things when absent, and the knavery of brokers and others, whom, in their absence, they are bound to trust, that they find themselves obliged to come up and live constantly here, or at least, most part of the year.

This is the reason why, notwithstanding the encrease of new buildings, and the addition of new cities, as they may be called, every year to the old, yet a house is no sooner built, but 'tis tenanted and inhabited, and every part is crouded with people, and that not only in the town, but in all the towns and villages round, as shall be taken notice of in its place.

But let the citizens and inhabitants of London know, and it

may be worth the reflection of some of the landlords, and builders especially, that if peace continues, and the publick affairs continue in honest and upright management, there is a time coming, at least the nation hopes for it, when the publick debts being reduced and paid off, the funds or taxes on which they are establish'd, may cease, and so fifty or sixty millions of the stocks, which are now the solid bottom of the South-Sea Company, East-India Company, Bank, &c. will cease, and be no more; by which the reason of this conflux of people being removed, they will of course, and by the nature of the thing, return again to their country seats, to avoid the expensive living at London, as they did come up hither to share the extravagant gain of their former business here.

What will be the condition of this overgrown city in such a case, I must leave to time; but all those who know the temporary constitution of our funds, know this, 1. That even, if they are to spin out their own length, all those funds which were given for thirty-two years, have already run out one third, and some of them almost half the time, and that the rest will soon be gone: 2. That as in two years more, the Government which receives six per cent. and pays but five, and will then pay but four per cent. interest, will be able every year to be paying off and lessening the publick debt, 'till, in time, 'tis to be hoped, all our taxes may cease, and the ordinary revenue may, as it always used to do, again supply the ordinary expence of the government.

Then, I say, will be a time to expect the vast concourse of people to London, will separate again and disperse as naturally, as they have now crouded hither: What will be the fate then of all the fine buildings in the out parts, in such a case, let any one judge.

There has formerly been a great emulation between the Court end of the town, and the city; and it was once seriously proposed in a certain reign, how the Court should humble the city; nor was it so impracticable a thing at that time, had the wicked scheme been carried on: Indeed, it was carried farther than consisted with the prudence of a good government, or of a wise people; for the Court envy'd the city's greatness, and the citizens were ever jealous of the Court's designs: The most fatal steps the Court took to humble the city, and which, as I say, did not consist with the prudence of a good government, were, 1. The shutting up the Exchequer, and, 2. The bringing a *quo warranto* against their Charter; but these things can but be touch'd at here; the city has outliv'd it all, and both the attempts turn'd to the discredit of the Court party, who pushed them on: But the city, I say, has gained the ascendant, and is now made so necessary to the Court (as before it was thought rather a grievance) that now we see the Court itself the daily instrument to encourage and increase the opulence of the city, and the city again, by its real grandeur, made not a glory only, but an assistance and support to the Court, on the greatest and most sudden emergencies.

Nor can a breach be now made on any terms, but the city will have the advantage; for while the stocks, and Bank, and trading companies remain in the city, the center of the money, as well as of the credit and trade of the kingdom, will be there.

Nor are these capital offices only necessarily kept in the city, but several offices belonging to the public oeconomy of the administration, such as the Post Office, the Navy, the Victualling, and the Pay Offices, including the Ordnance Office, which is kept in the Tower. In a word, the offices may, indeed, be said to be equally divided.

The city has all those above-mentioned, and the Court has the Admiralty, the Exchequer, and the Secretaries of State's Offices, with those of the Pay-Masters of the Army, &c.

Besides these, the Council, the Parliament, and the Courts of Justice, are all kept at the same part of the town; but as all suits among the citizens are, by virtue of their privileges, to be try'd within the liberty of the city, so the term is obliged to be (as it were) adjourned from Westminster-Hall to Guild-Hall, to try causes there; also criminal cases are in like manner tried monthly at the Old Baily, where a special commission is granted for that purpose to the judges; but the Lord Mayor always presides, and has the chair.

The equality, however, being thus preserved, and a perfect good understanding between the Court and city having so long flourished, this union contributes greatly to the flourishing circumstances of both, and the publick credit is greatly raised by it; for it was never known, that the city, on any occasion, was so assistant to the government, as it has been since this general good agreement. No sum is so great, but the Bank has been able to raise. Here the Exchequer bills are at all times circulated, money advanced upon the funds as soon as laid, and that at moderate interest, not incroaching on the government, or extorting large interest to eat up the nation, and disappoint the sovereign, and defeat his best designs, as in King William's time was too much the practice.

By this great article of publick credit, all the king's business is done with chearfulness. provisions are now bought to victual the fleets without difficulty, and at reasonable rates. The several yards where the ships are built and fitted out, are currently paid: The magazines of millitary and naval stores kept full: In a word, by this very article of publick credit, of which the Parliament is the foundation (and the city, are the architectures or builders) all those great things are now done with ease, which, in the former reigns, went on heavily, and were brought about with the utmost difficulty.

But, to return to the city; Besides the companies and publick offices, which are kept in the city, there are several particular offices and places, some built or repaired on purpose, and others hired and beautified for the particular business they carry on respectively: As,

Here are several great offices for several societies of ensurers; for here almost all hazards may be ensured; the four principal are called, 1. Royal Exchange Ensurance: 2. The London Ensurers: 3. The Hand in Hand Fire Office: 4. The Sun Fire Office.

In the two first of those, all hazards by sea are ensured, that is to say, of ships or goods, not lives; as also houses and goods are ensured from fire.

In the last, only houses and goods.

In all which offices, the *premio* is so small, and the recovery, in case of loss, so easy and certain, where no fraud is suspected, that nothing can be shewn like it in the whole world; especially that of ensuring houses from fire, which has now attained such an universal approbation, that I am told, there are above seventy thousand houses thus ensured in London, and the parts adjacent.

The East-India House is in Leadenhall-Street, an old, but spacious building; very convenient, though not beautiful, and I am told, it is under consultation to have it taken down, and rebuilt with additional buildings for warehouses and cellars for their goods, which at present are much wanted.

The African Company's house is in the same street, a very handsome, well-built, and convenient house, and which fully serves for all the offices their business requires.

The Bank is kept in Grocer's Hall, a very convenient place, and, considering its situation, so near the Exchange, a very spacious, commodious place.

Here business is dispatch'd with such exactness, and such expedition and so much of it too, that it is really prodigious; no confusion, nobody is either denied or delayed payment, the merchants who keep their cash there, are sure to have their bills always paid, and even advances made on easy terms, if they have occasion. No accounts in the world are more exactly kept, no place in the world has so much business done, with so much ease.

In the next street (the Old Jury) is the Excise Office, in a very large house, formerly the dwelling of Sir John Fredrick, and afterwards, of Sir Joseph Hern, very considerable merchants. In this one office is managed an immense weight of business, and they have in pay, as I am told, near four thousand officers: The whole kingdom is divided by them into proper districts, and to every district, a collector, a supervisor, and a certain number of gaugers, called, by the vulgar title excise men.

Nothing can be more regular, than the methods of this office, by which an account of the whole excise is transmitted from the remotest parts of the kingdom, once every six weeks, which is called a sitting, and the money received, or prosecutions commenced for it, in the next sitting.

Under the management of this office, are now brought, not only the excise upon beer, ale, and other liquors, as formerly, but also the duties on malt and candles, hops, soap, and leather, all which are managed in several and distinct classes, and the accounts kept in distinct books; but, in many places, are collected by the same officers, which makes the charge of the collection much easier to the government: Nor is the like duty collected in any part of the world, with so little charge, or so few officers.

The South-Sea House is situate in a large spot of ground, between Broad-Street and Threadneedle-Street, two large houses having been taken in, to form the whole office; but, as they were, notwithstanding, straighten'd for room, and were obliged to summon their general courts in another place, viz. at Merchant-Taylors Hall; so they have now resolved to erect a new and compleat building for the whole business, which is to be exceeding fine and large, and to this end, the company has purchased several adjacent buildings, so that the ground is inlarged towards Threadneedle-Street; but, it seems, they could not be accommodated to their minds on the side next Broad-Street, so we are told, they will not open a way that way, as before.

As the company are enlarging their trade to America, and

have also engaged in a new trade, namely, that of the Greenland whale fishing, they are like to have an occasion to enlarge their offices. This building, they assure us, will cost the company from ten to twenty thousand pounds, that is to say, a very great sum.

The Post Office, a branch of the revenue formerly not much valued, but now, by the additional penny upon the letters, and by the visible increase of business in the nation, is grown very considerable. This office maintains now, pacquet boats to Spain and Portugal, which never was done before: So the merchants letters for Cadiz or Lisbonne, which were before two and twenty days in going over France and Spain to Lisbonne, oftentimes arrive there now, in nine or ten days from Falmouth.

Likewise, they have a pacquet from Marseilles to Port Mahone, in the Mediterranean, for the constant communication of letters with his majesty's garrison and people in the island of Minorca.

They have also a pacquet from England to the West-Indies; but I am not of opinion, that they will keep it up for much time longer, if it be not already let fall.

This office is kept in Lombard-Street, in a large house, formerly Sir Robert Viner's, once a rich goldsmith; but ruined at the shutting up of the Exchequer, as above.

The penny post, a modern contrivance of a private person, one Mr. William Dockraw, is now made a branch of the general revenue by the Post Office; and though, for a time, it was subject to miscarriages and mistakes, yet now it is come also into so exquisite a management, that nothing can be more exact, and 'tis with the utmost safety and dispatch, that letters are delivered at the remotest corners of the town, almost as soon as they could be sent by a messenger, and that from four, five, six, to eight times a day, according as the distance of the place makes it practicable; and you may send a letter from Ratcliff or Limehouse in the East, to the farthest part of Westminster for a penny, and that several times in the same day.

Nor are you tied up to a single piece of paper, as in the General Post-Office, but any packet under a pound weight, goes at the same price.

I mention this the more particularly, because it is so manifest a testimony to the greatness of this city, and to the great extent of business and commerce in it, that this penny conveyance should raise so many thousand pounds in a year, and employ so many poor people in the diligence of it, as this office employs.

We see nothing of this at Paris, at Amsterdam, at Hamburgh, or any other city, that ever I have seen, or heard of.

The Custom House I have just mentioned before, but must take up a few lines to mention it again. The stateliness of the building, shewed the greatness of the business that is transacted there: The Long Room is like an Exchange every morning, and the croud of people who appear there, and the business they do, is not to be explained by words, nothing of that kind in Europe is like it.

Yet it has been found, that the business of export and import in this port of London, is so prodigiously increased, and the several new offices, which they are bound to erect for the managing the additional parts of the customs, are such, that the old building, though very spacious, is too little, and as the late Fire burnt or demolish'd some part of the west end of the Custom House, they have had the opportunity in rebuilding, to enlarge it very much, buying in the ground of some of the demolished houses, to add to the Custom House, which will be now a most glorious building.

The keys, or wharfs, next the river, fronting not the Custom House only, but the whole space from the Tower stairs, or dock, to the bridge, ought to be taken notice of as a publick building; nor are they less an ornament to the city, as they are a testimony of the vast trade carried on in it, than the Royal Exchange itself.

The revenue, or income, brought in by these wharfs, inclusive of the warehouses belonging to them, and the lighters they employ, is said to amount to a prodigious sum; and, as I am told, seldom so little as forty thousand pounds per annum: And abundance of porters, watchmen, wharfingers, and other officers, are maintained here by the business of the wharfs; in which, one thing is very remarkable, That here are porters, and poor working men, who, though themselves not worth, perhaps, twenty pounds in the world, are trusted with great quantities of valuable goods, sometimes to the value of several thousand pounds, and yet 'tis very rarely to be heard, that any loss or embezzlement is made. The number of these keys extending, as above, from the bridge to the Tower Dock, is seventeen.

From these publick places, I come next to the markets, which, in such a mass of building, and such a collection of people, and where such business is done, must be great, and very many. To take a view of them in particular;

First, Smithfield Market for living cattle, which is, without question, the greatest in the world; no description can be given of it, no calculation of the numbers of creatures sold there, can be made. This market is every Monday and Friday.

There is, indeed, a liberty taken by the butchers, to go up to Islington, and to Whitechapel, and buy of the country drovers, who bring cattle to town; but this is called forestalling the market, and is not allowed by law.

There is also a great market, or rather fair for horses, in Smithfield every Friday in the afternoon, where very great numbers of horses, and those of the highest price, are to be sold weekly.

The flesh markets are as follow.

Leaden-Hall, Honey-Lane, Newgate, Clare, Shadwell, Southwark, Westminster, Spittle Fields, Hoxton (forsaken) Brook, Bloomsbury, Newport, St. James's, Hungerford.

N.B. At all these markets, there is a part set by for a fish market, and a part for an herb market; so that when I say afterwards, there are fish markets, and herb markets, I am to be understood, such as are wholly for fish, or for herbs and fruit. For example,

Fish markets	Billingsgate, Fishstreet Hill, and Old Fishstreet.
Herb markets	Covent Garden, and Stocks Market.
N.B. Cherry market, and apple market - -	At the Three Cranes.
Corn markets	Bear Key, and Queen Hith.
Meal markets	Queen Hith, Hungerford, Ditch-Side, and Whitecross-Street.
Hay markets	Whitechapel, Smithfield, Southwark, the Hay-Market-Street, Westminster, and Bloomsbury.
Leather market	Leaden Hall.
Hides and skins	Leaden Hall, and Wood's Close.
Coal markets	Billingsgate, Room Land.
Bay market	Leaden Hall.
Broad cloth market -	Blackwell Hall.

N.B. The last three are, without doubt, the greatest in the world of those kinds.

Bubble market	Exchange Alley.

These markets are so considerable in themselves, that they will merit a longer and more particular description, than I have room for in this place. I shall, however, briefly mention them again in their order.

Of the fourteen flesh markets, or markets for provisions, seven of them are of antient standing, time out of mind: But the other seven are erected since the enlargement of buildings mentioned above. The old ones are, Leaden-Hall, Honey-Lane, Newgate Market, Southwark, Clare, St. James's, and Westminster; and these are so considerable, such numbers of buyers, and such an infinite quantity of provisions of all sorts, flesh, fish, and fowl, that, especially the first, no city in the world can equal them. 'Tis of the first of these markets, that a certain Spanish ambassador said, There was as much meat sold in it in one month, as would suffice all Spain for a year.

This great market, called, Leaden-Hall, though standing in the middle of the city, contains three large squares, every square having several outlets into divers streets, and all into one another. The first, and chief, is called, the Beef Market, which has two large gates, one into Leaden Hall Street, one into Grace-church Street, and two smaller, viz. One by a long pav'd passage leading into Limestreet, and one under a gateway from the second square. In this square, every Wednesday is kept a market for raw hides, tann'd leather, and shoemakers tools; and in the warehouses, up stairs on the east and south sides of the square, is the great market for Colechester bayes.

The second square is divided into two oblongs, in the first is the fish market, and in the other, a market for country higlers, who bring small things, such as pork, butter, eggs, pigs, country dress'd, with some fouls, and such like country fare.

The north part of the fish market, the place being too large for the fishmongers use, are the stalls of the town butchers for mutton and veal, the best and largest of which, that England can produce, is to be bought there, and the east part is a flesh market for country butchers.

The third, and last square, which is also very large, is divided into three parts: Round the circumference, is the butter market, with all sorts of higglary goods, as before: The south part is the poultry market, and the bacon market, and the center is an herb market.

All the other markets follow the same method in proportion to the room they have for it; and there is an herb market in every one; but the chief markets in the whole city for herbs and garden-stuff, are the Stocks and Covent Garden.

There are but two corn markets in the whole city and out parts; but they are monsters for magnitude, and not to be matched in the world. These are Bear Key, and Queen Hith: To the first comes all the vast quantity of corn that is brought into the city by sea, and here corn may be said, not to be sold by cart loads, or horse loads, but by ship loads, and, except the corn chambers and magazines in Holland, when the fleets come in from Dantzick and England, the whole world cannot equal the quantity bought and sold here.

This is the place whither all the corn is brought, which, as I have observed, is provided in all the counties of England, near the sea coast, and shipp'd for London, and no quantity can be wanted, either for home consumption, or for foreign exportation, but the corn factors, who are the managers of this market, are ready to supply it.

The other, which I call a corn market too, is at Queen Hith; but this market is chiefly, if not wholly, for malt; as to the whole corn, as the quantity of malt brought to this market is prodigious great, so I must observe too, that this place is the receiver of all the malt, the barley of which, takes up the ground of so many hundred thousand acres of land in the counties of Surrey, Bucks, Berks, Oxford, Southampton, and Wilts, and is called west country malt.

It is true, there is a very great quantity of malt, and of other corn too, brought to some other places on the river, and sold there, viz. To Milford Lane, above the bridge, and the Hermitage, below the bridge; but this is but, in general, a branch of the trade of the other places.

It must not be omitted, that Queen Hith is also a very great market for meal, as well as malt, and, perhaps, the greatest in England.

The vessels which bring this malt and meal to Queen Hith, are worth the observation of any stranger that understands such things. They are remarkable for the length of the vessel, and the burthen they carry, and yet the little water they draw; in a word, some of those barges carry above a thousand quarter of malt at a time, and yet do not draw two foot of water. N.B. A thousand quarter of malt must be granted to be, at least, a hundred tun burthen. Note also, Some of these large barges come as far as from Abbington, which is above one hundred and fifty miles from London, if we measure by the river.

The next market, which is more than ordinary remarkable, is the coal market at Billingsgate. This is kept every morning on the broad place just at the head of Billingsgate Dock, and the place is called Room Land; from what old forgotten original it has that name, history is silent. I need not, except for the sake of strangers, take notice, that the city of London, and parts adjacent, as also all the south of England, is supplied with coals, called therefore sea-coal, from Newcastle upon Tyne, and from the coast of Durham, and Northumberland. This trade is so considerable, that it is esteemed the great nursery of our best seamen, and of which I shall have occasion to say more in my account of the northern parts of England. The quantity of coals, which it is supposed are, *communibus annis*, burnt and consumed in and about this city, is supposed to be about five hundred thousand chalder, every chalder containing thirty-six bushels, and generally weighing about thirty hundred weight.

All these coals are bought and sold on this little spot of Room Land, and, though sometimes, especially in case of a war, or of contrary winds, a fleet of five hundred to seven hundred sail of ships, comes up the river at a time, yet they never want a market: The brokers, or buyers of these coals, are called crimps, for what reason, or original, is likewise a mystery peculiar to this trade; for these people are noted for giving such dark names to the several parts of their trade; so the vessels they load their ships with at New Castle, are called keels, and the ships that bring them, are called cats, and hags, or hag boats, and fly boats, and the like. But of that hereafter.

The increase of this consumption of coals, is another evidence of the great increase of the city of London; for, within a few years past, the import of coals was not, in the river of Thames, so great by very near half.

It must be observed, that as the city of London occasions the consumption of so great a quantity of corn and coals, so the measurement of them is under the inspection of the lord mayor and court of aldermen, and for the direction of which, there are allowed a certain number of corn meeters, and coal meeters, whose places are for life, and bring them in a very considerable income. These places are in the gift of the lord mayor for the time being, and are generally sold for three or four thousand pounds a piece, when they fall.

They have abundance of poor men employ'd under them, who are called, also, meeters, and are, or ought to be, freemen of the city.

This is, indeed, a rent-charge upon the buyer, and is a kind of gabel, as well upon the coals as the corn; but the buyer is abundantly recompensed, by being ascertained in his measure without any fraud; so that having bought his coals or corn, he is perfectly unconcerned about the measure, for the sworn meeters are so placed between the buyer and seller, that no injury can be offered, nor have I heard that any complaint of injustice is ever made against the meeters, who are generally men of good character, are sworn to do right, and cannot easily do wrong without being detected; so many eyes being about them, and so many several persons concerned in the work, who have no dependance one upon another.

There is one great work yet behind, which, however, seems necessary to a full description of the city of London, and that is the shipping and the Pool; but in what manner can any writer go about it, to bring it into any reasonable compass? The thing is a kind of infinite, and the parts to be separated from one another in such a description, are so many, that it is hard to know where to begin.

The whole river, in a word, from London-Bridge to Black Wall, is one great arsenal, nothing in the world can be like it: The great building-yards at Schedam near Amsterdam, are said to out-do them in the number of ships which are built there, and they tell us, that there are more ships generally seen at Amsterdam, than in the Thames.

As to the building part, I will not say, but that there may be more vessels built at Schedam, and the parts adjacent, than in the River Thames; but then it must be said;

1. That the English build for themselves only, the Dutch for all the world.

2. That almost all the ships the Dutch have, are built there, whereas, not one fifth part of our shipping is built in the Thames; but abundance of ships are built at all the sea-ports in England, such as at New-Castle, Sunderland, Stockton, Whitby, Hull, Gainsborough, Grimsby, Lynn, Yarmouth, Alborough, Walderswick, Ipswich and Harwich, upon the east coast; and at Shoram, Arundel, Brighthelmston, Portsmouth, Southampton, Pool, Weymouth, Dartmouth, Plymouth, besides other places, on the south coast.

3. That we see more vessels in less room at Amsterdam; but the setting aside their hoys, bilanders and schoots, which are in great numbers always there, being vessels particular to their inland and coasting navigation; you do not see more

ships, nor near so many ships of force, at Amsterdam as at London.

4. That you see more ships there in less room, but, perhaps, not so many ships in the whole.

That part of the river of Thames which is properly the harbour, and where the ships usually deliver or unload their cargoes, is called the Pool, and begins at the turning of the river out of Lime-house Reach, and extends to the Custom-house-Keys: In this compass I have had the curiosity to count the ships as well as I could, *en passant*, and have found above two thousand sail of all sorts, not reckoning barges, lighters or pleasure-boats, and yatchs; but of vessels that really go to sea.

It is true, the river or Pool, seem'd, at that time, to be pretty full of ships; it is true also, that I included the ships which lay in Deptford and Black-Wall reaches, and in the wet docks, whereof, there are no less than three; but 'tis as true, that we did not include the men of war at the king's yard and in the wet dock there at Deptford, which were not a very few.

In the river, as I have observed, there are from Battle-Bridge on the Southwark side, and the Hermitage-Bridge on the city-side, reckoning to Black-Wall, inclusive,

> Three wet docks for laying up
> Twenty two dry docks for repairing } merchants ships.
> Thirty three yards for building

This is inclusive of the builders of lighters, hoys, &c. but exclusive of all boat-builders, wherry-builders, and above-bridge barge-builders.

To enter into any description of the great magazines of all manner of naval stores, for the furnishing those builders, would be endless, and I shall not attempt it; 'tis sufficient to add, That England, as I have said elsewhere, is an inexhaustible store-house of timber, and all the oak timber, and generally the plank also, used in the building these ships, is found in England only, nay, and which is more, it is not fetched from the remoter parts of England, but these southern counties near us are the places where 'tis generally found; as particularly the counties of Berks and Bucks, Surrey, Kent, Sussex, Essex and Suffolk, and very little is brought farther, nor can all the ship-building the whole kingdom are able to build, ever exhaust those counties, tho' they were to build much more than they do.

But I must land, lest this part of the account seems to smell of the tarr, and I should tire the gentlemen with leading them out of their knowledge.

I should mention, for the information of strangers, &c. that the buildings of this great city are chiefly of brick, as many ways found to be the safest, the cheapest, and the most commodious of all other materials; by safe, I mean from fire, and as by Act of Parliament, every builder is bound to have a partition wall of brick also, one brick and half thick between every house, it is found to be, indeed, very helpful in case of fire.

And as I am speaking of fire and burning of houses, it cannot be omitted, That no where in the world is so good care taken to quench fires as in London; I will not say the like care is taken to prevent them; for I must say, That I think the servants, nay, and masters too in London, are the most careless people in the world about fire, and this, no doubt, is the reason why there are frequently more fires in London and in the out-parts, than there are in all the cities of Europe put them together; nor are they the more careful, as I can learn, either from observation or report, I say, they are not made more cautious, by the innumerable fires which continually happen among them.

And this leads me back to what I just now said, That no city in the world is so well furnished for the extinguishing fires when they happen.

1. By the great convenience of water which being every where laid in the streets in large timber pipes, as well from the Thames as the New-River, those pipes are furnished with a fire plug, which the parish officers have the key of, and when opened, let out not a pipe, but a river of water into the streets, so that making but a dam in the kennel, the whole street is immediately under water to supply the engines.

2. By the great number of admirable engines, of which, almost, every parish has one, and some halls also, and some private citizens have them of their own, so that no sooner does a fire break out, but the house is surrounded with engines, and a flood of water poured upon it, 'till the fire is, as it were, not extinguished only, but drowned.

3. The several ensurance offices, of which I have spoken above, have each of them a certain sett of men, who they keep in constant pay, and who they furnish with tools proper for the work, and to whom they give jack-caps of leather, able to keep them from hurt, if brick or timber, or any thing not of too great a bulk, should fall upon them; these men make it their business to be ready at call, all hours, and night or day, to

assist in case of fire; and it must be acknowledged, they are very dextrous, bold, diligent, and successful. These they call fire-men, but with an odd kind of contradiction in the title, for they are really most of them water-men.

Having mentioned, that the city is so well furnished with water, it cannot be omitted, that there are two great engines for the raising the Thames water, one at the bridge, and the other near Broken Wharf; these raise so great a quantity of water, that, as they tell us, they are able to supply the whole city in its utmost extent, and to supply every house also, with a running pipe of water up to the uppermost story.

However, the New-River, which is brought by an aqueduct or artificial stream from Ware, continues to supply the greater part of the city with water, only with this addition by the way, that they have been obliged to dig a new head or basin at Islington on a higher ground than that which the natural stream of the river supplies, and this higher basin they fill from the lower, by a great engine worked formerly with six sails, now by many horses constantly working; so from that new elevation of the water, they supply the higher part of the town with the same advantage, and more ease than the Thames engines do it.

There was a very likely proposal set on foot by some gentle-men, whose genius seem'd equal to the work, for drawing another river, rather larger than that now running, and bringing it to a head on some rising grounds beyond Mary le Bonne.

This water was proposed to be brought from the little Coln or Cole near St. Albans, and the river, called Two Waters, near Rickmansworth, and as I have seen the course of the water, and the several supplies it was to have, and how the water-level was drawn for containing the current, I must acknowledge it was a very practical undertaking, and merited encouragement; but it was opposed in Parliament, and dropt for the present: This design was particularly calculated for supplying those prodigious additions of buildings, which I have already describ'd at the west end of the town.

However, tho' this be laid aside, as also several water-houses in other parts, particularly one at Wapping, one near Battle-Bridge in Southwark, and the famous one at York-Buildings, yet it cannot be denied, that the city of London is the best supplied with water of any great city in the world, and upon as easy terms to its inhabitants.

There were formerly several beautiful conduits of running-water in London, which water was very sweet and good, and was brought at an infinite expence, from several distant springs, in large leaden pipes to those conduits, and this was so lately, that several of those conduits were re-built since the Fire, as one on Snow-Hill and one at Stocks-Market, which serves as a pedestal for the great equestrian statue of King Charles II. erected there at the charge of Sir Robert Viner, then Lord Mayor, and who was then an eminent banker in Lombard-street; but his loyalty could not preserve him from being ruined by the common calamity, when the king shut up the Exchequer.

They tell us a merry story of this statue, how true it may be, let those testify who saw it, if any such witnesses remain, viz. That a certain famous Court lady, I do not say it was the D——ss of Portsmouth, being brought to bed of a son late in the night, the next morning this glorious equestrian statue had a pillion handsomely placed on it behind the body of the k——, with a paper pinned to the trapping of the pillion, with words at length, Gone for a midwife.

It is scarce worth while to give an account of the statues in this city, they are neither many, or are those which are, very valuable.

The statue of King Charles II. in marble, standing in the middle of the Royal Exchange, is the best beyond comparison; one of the same prince, and his father, standing in two large niches on the south front of the same building, and being bigger than the life, are coarse pieces compared to it.

The statues of the kings and queens, seventeen of which are already put up in the inside of the Royal Exchange, are tolerable, but all infinitely inferior to that in the middle.

There is a statue of Sir Thomas Gresham, the founder of the Royal Exchange, which outdoes many of those kings, only that it stands in a dark corner, and is little noticed; 'tis placed in a nitch under the piazza, in the north west angle of the Exchange, just regarding the Turky walk, and he has a bale of silk lying by him.

There is another equestrian statue, and but one, as I remember, within the city, and that is of King James the First on the north front of one of the gates of the city called Aldersgate: This was erected on the occasion of that king's entring the city at that gate when he arrived here from Scotland, to take the crown after the death of Queen Elizabeth; when that statue was finely painted and gilded, which is not usual, nor is the gilding yet worn off; there are some emblematick figures remaining, which were then suited to the occasion of his triumphal entry, and there was another arch form'd for the day at the bars, where the liberties of the city end, that way which is now called Goswell-street, but that was taken down soon after.

The gates of the city are seven, besides posterns, and the posterns that remain are four, besides others that are demolished.

The gates are all remaining, two of them which were demolished at the fire, being beautifully re-built: These are Ludgate and Newgate; the first a prison for debt for freemen of the city only, the other a prison for criminals, both for London and Middlesex, and for debtors also for Middlesex, being the county gaol.

Moregate is also re-built, and is a very beautiful gateway, the arch being near twenty foot high, which was done to give room for the city Train'd Bands to go through to the Artillery Ground, where they muster, and that they might march with their pikes advanc'd, for then they had pikemen in every regiment, as well in the army as in the militia, which since that, is quite left off; this makes the gate look a little out of shape, the occasion of it not being known. Cripplegate and Bishopsgate are very old, and make but a mean figure; Aldersgate is about one hundred and twenty years old, and yet being beautified, as I have said, on the occasion of King James's entry, looks very handsome.

Aldgate was very ancient and decay'd, so that As old as Aldgate, was a city proverb for many years; but this gate was re-built also, upon the triumphant entry of K. James I. and looks still very well; on the east side of this gate are two statues in stone, representing two men, from the waste upward, and in armour, throwing down two great stones, supposing it to be on an enemy assaulting the gate, which I mention, because some time ago, one of these men in armour, whether tired with holding it so long, or dreaming of enemies assaulting the gate, our authors do not inform us; but he threw down the stone, or rather let it fall, after having held it upwards of an hundred years; but, as it happened, it did no harm.

Most of these gates are given by the city to the chief of the officers of the city to live in, and the houses are very convenient dwellings.

Temple-Bar is the only gate which is erected at the extent of the city liberties, and this was occasioned by some needful ceremonies at the proclaiming any King or Queen of England, at which time the gates are shut; the Herald at Arms knocks hard at the door, the sheriffs of the city call back, asking who is there? Then the herald answers, "I come to proclaim," &c. according to the name of the prince who is to succeed to the crown, and repeating the titles of Great Britain, France and Ireland, &c. at which the sheriffs open, and bid them welcome, and so they go on to the Exchange, where they make the last proclamation.

This gate is adorned with the figures of kings below, and traytors above, the heads of several criminals executed for treason being set up there; the statues below are of Queen Elizabeth and King James I. King Charles I. and II. and this is the fourth statue of King Charles II. which is to be seen in the city of London, besides his picture nobly done at full length, which was set up formerly in the Guild-Hall.

There are in London, and the far extended bounds, which I now call so, notwithstanding we are a nation of liberty, more publick and private prisons, and houses of confinement, than any city in Europe, perhaps as many as in all the capital cities of Europe put together; for example:

Public GAOLS.

The Tower.
Newgate.
Ludgate.
King's Bench.
The Fleet.
Bridewell.
Marshalseas.
The Gatehouse.
Two Counters in the city.
One Counter in the Burrough.
St. Martin's le Grand.
The Clink, formerly the prison to the Stews.

Whitechapel.
Finsbury.
The Dutchy.
St. Katherines.
Bale-Dock.
Little-Ease.
New-Prison.
New-Bridewell.
Tottil-Fields Bridewell.
Five night prisons, called Round-houses, &c.

Tolerated PRISONS.

Bethlem or Bedlam.
One hundred and nineteen Spunging Houses.
Fifteen Private Mad-Houses.
The King's Messengers-Houses.
The Sergeant at Arms's Officers Houses.
The Black Rod Officers-Houses.

Cum aliis.

Three Pest-houses.
The Admiralty Officers-Houses.
Tip-staffs Houses.
Chancery Officers Houses.

N.B. All these private houses of confinement, are pretended to be little purgatories, between prison and liberty, places of advantage for the keeping prisoners at their own request, till they can get friends to deliver them, and so avoid going into publick prisons; tho' in some of them, the extortion is such, and the accommodation so bad, that men choose to be carried away directly.

This has often been complained of, and hopes had of redress; but the rudeness and avarice of the officers prevails, and the oppression is sometimes very great; but that by the way.

In a word; To sum up my description of London, take the following heads; There are in this great mass of buildings thus called London,

Two cathedrals.

Four choirs for musick-worship.

One hundred and thirty five parish churches.

Nine new churches unfinished, being part of fifty appointed to be built.

Sixty nine chapels where the Church of England service is perform'd.

Two churches at Deptford, taken into the limits now describ'd.

Twenty eight foreign churches.

Besides Dissenters meetings of all persuasions;

Popish chapels; and

One Jews synagogue.

There are also, thirteen hospitals, besides lesser charities, call'd Alms-houses, of which they reckon above a hundred, many of which have chapels for divine service.

Three colleges.

Twenty-seven publick prisons.

Eight publick schools, called Free Schools.

Eighty three Charity Schools.

Fourteen markets for flesh.

Two for live cattle, besides two herb-markets.

Twenty three other markets, as describ'd.

Fifteen Inns of Court.

Four fairs.

Twenty seven squares, besides those within any single building, as the Temple, Somerset House, &c

Five publick bridges.

One town-house, or Guild-Hall.

One Royal Exchange.

Two other Exchanges only for shops.

One Custom-house.

Three Artillery Grounds.

Four Pest-houses.

Two bishops palaces; and

Three royal palaces.

Having dwelt thus long in the city, I mean properly called so, I must be the shorter in my account of other things.

The Court end of the town, now so prodigiously increased, as is said before, would take up a volume by itself, and, indeed, whole volumes are written on the subject.

The king's palace, tho' the receptacle of all the pomp and glory of Great Britain, is really mean, in comparison of the rich furniture within, I mean the living furniture, the glorious Court of the King of Great Britain: The splendor of the nobility, the wealth and greatness of the attendants, the oeconomy of the house, and the real grandeur of the whole royal family, out-does all the Courts of Europe, even that of France itself, as it is now managed since the death of Lewis the Great.

But the palace of St. James's is, I say, too mean, and only seems to be honoured with the Court, while a more magnificent fabrick may be erected, where the King of England usually resided, I mean at White-Hall.

The ruins of that old palace, seem to predict, that the time will come, when that Phœnix shall revive, and when a building shall be erected there, suiting the majesty and magnificence of the British princes, and the riches of the British nation.

Many projects have been set on foot for the re-building the antient palace of White-hall; but most of them have related rather to a fund for raising the money, than a model for the building: But as I once saw a model for the palace itself, know its author, and when it was proposed, and that I still believe that scheme will, at last, be the ground-plot of the work itself, I believe it will not be disagreeable to give a brief account of the design.

A Scheme for a Royal Palace in the Place of White-Hall

First, it was proposed, That the whole building should be of Portland stone, and all the front be exactly after the model of the Banquetting House, with such alterations only, as the length and height of the building made necessary.

That the first floor of the building should be raised from the present surface, at least eight feet, as the present building of the Banquetting House now is.

That the whole building should make four fronts, one to the water-side and one to the canal in the park, a third to the north facing Charing-Cross, and the fourth to the south facing King-street in Westminster.

That every front should contain 400 yards, or 1200 feet, in length; that there should be four areas or squares in the inside of the building, the first from the north entrance to be oblong, taking up the whole length of the building from east to west, and that then a long building should cross the whole work, eighty feet broad, and from the east range one thousand feet broad to the west; and in the middle of which, should be a great arch or gate looking to the south gate of the palace: That the other side of the palace be divided into three squares, having two ranges of buildings to run cross them from south to north, and each range to joyn the great range of building which runs from east to west.

That the whole building be withdrawn from the river so far, at least, as where the statue of King James II. now stands, and a spacious terras to be carried on into the Thames twelve feet beyond low-water-mark, and over the river a handsome foot-bridge of twelve great arches only, with a causeway at the end over St. George's Fields; That the terras and space between the palace and the water, be made into a fine garden, with an orangery on the north side, reaching to the edge of the terras so effectually, as it may cover the garden from the view of any of the buildings on the Strand side, and a royal *bagnio* at the other end likewise, to cover the necessary buildings for the kitchins which are behind it.

For the extent north, 'tis proposed, That all the buildings be taken down to the wall of Northumberland House, on that side; and to the north side of the Spring Garden, opposite to Suffolk-street and the Hay-Market on the other side; so the front of the building that way, will extend from the hither part of Scotland-yard-Gate, to Prince Rupert's Garden, and the gate of the palace being in the center of the building, will open in that which is now called the Spring Garden.

One gate of the palace opening thus north, a ballustrade of iron, like that which surrounds St. Paul's Church, should take in a large parade, reaching to the Meuse-Gate, a space for the street only excepted, and in proportion the other way towards Pall-Mall; and here on the east side, and on the west side, two large guard-houses should be erected, fitted, the one for the horse guards, and the other for the foot, both within the ballustrade, but without the palace, and two smaller guard-houses for detachments of both, be likewise placed on the south side, all at a proper distance from the main building, and all low built.

The canal in the park would be necessarily filled up for about a hundred yards, for the extent of the building that way; the street that now is, must, at the same time, be turned, and a large street for communication with Westminster, be allowed to cross the park from the Pall-Mall south, towards Westminster, to come out at the new iron gate, now leading to Queen's-Square and Tottil-street; but no houses to be built in it, and four gates in the said street, to lead over the street, from the first floor of the palace, by galleries into the park; All buildings adjoining to the park to be taken down, nor any private doors or keys to be allowed; a stone wall of twenty feet high and eight feet thick, to be built round the park, and the park to be extended west, by taking in Buckingham House, with its gardens.

In this building, the proposer's scheme was, To have all the offices of the King's Exchequer, the Revenue, the Council, the Secretaries of State, the Admiralty, the Courts of Justice, and both Houses of Parliament, contain'd within the palace, as was the usage in former times.

To this purpose, the cross range of buildings, going from east to west, through the center of the palace, and looking into the great oblong court, which would contain a thousand feet, exclusive of the east and west fronts, and of the great arch or gate in the center, should be divided thus; That part on the east side of the gate to contain two spacious rooms, one for the House of Peers, the other for the House of Commons, with sufficient offices, galleries of communication, rooms of conference for committees, a court of requests, &c. for the use of the members, and rooms for all other occasions of Parliament business.

The west part of this great range of building to contain a hall, as Westminster-Hall now is, with proper separated courts for the King's Bench, Chancery, Common-Pleas, and Exchequer-Bars, and a distinct court fix'd, and suitably prepared, for tryals of peers or others, by the House of Lords, notwithstanding which, this court would be sufficiently large to celebrate the Coronation feast, with all its ceremonies, the building being from the middle arch to the west range of buildings, five hundred feet long at least, and one hundred feet broad.

Thus the king's Court of Justice, his High Court of Parliament, and all the affairs of the Administration, would be managed within his own house, as it anciently was; and as the two cross ranges of buildings, which form'd the three courts on the south side of the Parliament House and Hall of Justice, would be very large, they would afford room for the Lord Chamberlain's Office, the Admiralty, the War Office, the Green-Cloth, the Wardrobe Office, and all the other family offices, too many to name here.

Then the main range of building on the north side of the palace, should contain (because nearest the city) the Treasury Office, the Secretary's Offices, the Council Chambers, and the Exchequer Offices.

The apartments of the other three ranges to be wholly taken up with the king's houshold: for example;

1. For the royal apartments, being the king's lodgings, rooms of state and audience, the closet, the oratory, and all the rooms belonging to the apartment of a king; this to take up the east range, fronting the terras garden and the Thames, and looking directly towards the city.

2. The queen's lodgings to be in the east end of the south range, fronting the City of Westminster; but between the said city and the lodgings, the queen's garden to be extended from the terras garden mentioned before, to a wall joining a passage from Westminster to the south gate, which wall begins at the iron ballustrade and gate of the great parade before the south entrance of the palace, and ends at the outer stone wall, which surrounds the garden and park. The family for the royal children, to take up the west end of the said south range of buildings, with the like garden also, and a gate joyning the two walls in the middle of the passage, leading to the south gate of the palace, by which, with an easy ascent of steps, a communication should be made between the said two gardens.

The west range of buildings fronting the park, should be divided also into two parts, the first being the north end, to consist of royal apartments for the entertainment of foreign princes and foreign ambassadors, at the pleasure of the king, and the other half, or south end to be called the Prince's Lodgings, and to be for the Prince of Wales for the time being, and his family.

The great arch in the center of the whole, and in the middle of the long range of buildings, to support a large church or chapel royal, for the service of all the houshold, and for preaching before the Houses of Parliament on publick days, as is now at St. Margaret's and at the Abbey: over this church a large dome or cupola of stone, covered with copper and double gilded.

At the two angles of the building, fronting the river, two private chapels, the one for the queen and her houshold, and the other for the king and his houshold, and either of these to support a dome covered with copper and gilded, as before, tho' smaller than the other, with a large lanthorn on the top, and a small spire, all of stone.

The fronts to have pavilions and pediments in their proper places; the whole work to be built with the utmost regularity, in the Corinthian order of building, and with all possible beauty and ornament.

The galleries of the royal chapel to be supported with pillars of marble, of the finest and most beautiful workmanship also, the E. end of the building, the altar and balustrade of the same, also niches, with their columns, and pediments of the same, and two pillars of the finest marble, eighteen feet high, standing single, one on each side the steps to the communion table, and on them two statues of the apostles St. Paul and St. Peter, or as the king shall direct, the statues to be large as the life, the capitals of the columns gilded.

All the carv'd work in the walls, and round the cornish, and architrave within and without, double gilded; the ceiling of the chapel to contain one great oval, the rim of it of stone, carved as at St. Paul's, and gilded, and the middle painted by the best masters, with either a figure of the ascention or the resurrection, the device to be new.

All the carved work in wood, and mouldings, and cornish in the quire and over the stalls, to be double gilded, as likewise of the organ and organ loft.

All the gates and door cases in the out-sides of the work, with all the columns and carv'd work belonging to them, especially the north and south gates, and the two fronts of the great arch in the middle, to be of the finest marble.

All the chimneys and foot paces before them, to be of marble of divers colours, as well English as foreign: The steps, also, of the king and queen's great stair-cases to be of marble, all the other stair-cases to be of the finest free-stone, fetch'd from Stamford in Lincolnshire, where is the whitest stone in England, and to be built as the stair-case in that called the Queen's House at Greenwich; no wood to be allowed in any of the stair-cases, except for wainscotting up the side.

All the great stair-cases to be painted in the most curious manner possible, as also the ceilings of all the royal apartments, as well the queen's as the king's.

An equestrian statue of the king in the center of one half of the first great court, and the like of the late King William, in the other half.

Large fountains to be kept constantly playing in the smaller courts, and in the terras garden.

Buckingham-House to be bought, and taken in, to be made a royal lodge for the park, with an observatory, and a chamber of rarities: And Marlborough House to be bought, and be made a green-house for exotick plants, and all botannick rarities, and the old royal garden to be again restored, laid open to the park, and be a planted orangery; all the orange and lemon trees to be planted in the earth, so as not to be removed in the winter, but covered and secured separately, as at Beddington in Surrey.

A large building to be added under the wall in the park, next to Tottil-street, Westminster, with separate wards for keeping the lyons and other the strange and foreign bred brutes, which are now kept in the Tower, and care to be taken to furnish it with all the rarities of that kind that the world can procure, with fowls, also, of the like foreign kinds.

A royal bagnio annexed to the green-house in the terras garden, like that for the ladies in the queen's garden; but both distant from the palace.

A large alottment from the lodgings at the two ends of the N. and E. ranges, for the king's kitchens, which should have also an additional range of low buildings, separate from the palace, and running down to the water-side; this building would stand just between the terras garden wall, which should hide it, and the wall of Northumberland House: And here (a dock being made for that purpose) all heavy things, needful for the kitchens, and for the whole palace, should be brought in by water; as coals, and wood, and beer, and wine, &c. at the east end, and the prince's at the west end; the kitchens for the queen and the younger princes or childrens apartments, to be at the other extremes of their respective appartments.

Every range of building to have double rows on the same floor; but the royal apartments to have also a long gallery behind them, reaching the whole length, the one end to joyn to the Treasury Office and Council Chamber in the north range, and the other end to reach the queen's royal lodgings at the south range; on the east side of this gallery and in the peers, between the windows on the west side, should be placed, all the fine paintings that the Court are possess'd of, or that can be procur'd.

In the north west angle of the building, a large room or rooms for the royal library, with apartments for the library keeper; galleries in the great room to come at the books, and a cupola upon the top.

In the south west angle, a like repository for the records, as well of the Exchequer as of Parliament, with apartments for the record-keeper, or register, and a dome over it as at the other angle.

The north and south gates of the palace to be embellished in the most exquisite manner possible, and the statues of the king and prince over the arch wrought in marble, in the finest manner possible; the gates to rise twenty five feet above the building, with an attick, and such other work as shall be contriv'd for the utmost beauty and ornament.

The great stair-cases to be in the angles of the building, built projecting into the squares, that of the king's apartment, to open into the first court, and into the garden also, and in the like manner the queen's stair-case, at the other side, to open into the little square and into the privy gardens.

The stair-cases to land upon the galleries, before they enter the apartments, and for that reason, to be in the inside of the building, and to be distinct from it, to prevent taking up any of the apartments of the angles, which are appointed for other purposes; in the middle of the king's great gallery, doors should be made, leading into the great middle range of buildings; by one of which, his majesty may enter a gallery leading to the House of Lords, and by the other, enter thro' another gallery to the chapel royal: In the great gallery and in the hall, sixteen large bouffetts or cupboards of gold and gilt plate of all kinds, to be set open on publick days.

Likewise by these doors, the king will have ready access to all the offices, to all the lodgings, and through the gates formerly mention'd, crossing the great New Street, which have steps to pass over their arches, and descend into the park.

This, indeed, is but an embryo; but it must be confess'd, it would be a magnificent building, and would very well suit the grandeur of the British Court: Here a King of Great Britain would live like himself, and half the world would run over to see and wonder at it.

This whole building, the person projecting it, offered to finish, that is to say, all the out-side work, masonry and bricklayers work, with plaisterers, glasiers, plumbers, carpenters and joyners work, carvers, stone-cutters, copper work, iron work, and lead, including ballustrade and fine gates, and, in a word, the whole palace, except painting, gilding, gardening and waterworks, for two million three hundred thousand pounds, the king giving timber, but the undertaker to cut it down, and bring it to the place, the king giving the Portland stone also, and bringing it by water to the place.

Also the king to lay in four thousand blocks of Italian marble of the usual dimensions, the builder to make all the imagery that are to be made of stone; but the king to be at the charge of the equestrian statues in brass; the builder to form all the fountains and basins for the water-works; but all the pipes, vasa, busts, and statues in the gardens, to be at the king's expence.

But I return to the description of things which really exist, and are not imaginary: As the court is now stated, all the offices and places for business are scatter'd about.

The Parliament meets, as they ever did, while the Court was at Westminster, in the king's old palace, and there are the courts of justice also, and the officers of the Exchequer, nor can it be said, however convenient the place is made for them; but that it has a little an air of venerable, tho' ruin'd antiquity: What is the Court of Requests, the Court of Wards, and the Painted Chamber, tho' lately repair'd, but the corps of the old English Grandeur laid in state?

The whole, it is true, was anciently the king's palace or royal house, and it takes up full as much ground as the new palace, which I have given a scheme of, would do, except only the gardens and parks, the space before it, which is still called Palace-yard, is much greater than that which would be at the north gate of the palace of White-hall, as proposed. The gardens, indeed, were not large, but not despicable neither, being the same where my Lord Hallifax's house and gardens now are, and took up all the ground which we see now built upon between the river and the old palace, where the tellers of the Exchequer, as well as the auditor, have handsome dwellings and gardens also.

But, alas! as I say, tho' they seem now even in their ruins, great; yet compared to the beauty and elegancy of modern living, and of royal buildings in this age, what are they!

The royal apartments, the prince's lodgings, the great officers apartments, what are they now, but little offices for clerks, rooms for coffee-houses, auctions of pictures, pamphlet and toy-shops?

Even St. Stephen's Chapel, formerly the royal chapel of the palace, but till lately beautify'd for the convenience of the House of Commons, was a very indifferent place, old and decay'd: The House of Lords is a venerable old place, indeed; but how mean, how incoherent, and how straitned are the several avenues to it, and rooms about it? the matted gallery, the lobby, the back ways the king goes to it, how short are they all of the dignity of the place, and the glory of a King of Great Britain, with the Lords and Commons, that so often meet there?

Some attempts were made lately, to have restored the decrepid circumstances of this part of the building, and orders were given to Mr. Benson, then surveyor of the king's buildings, to do his part towards it; but it was directed so ill, or understood so little, that some thought he was more likely to throw the old fabrick down, than to set it to rights, for which ignorance and vanity, 'tis said, some have not fared as they deserv'd.

It is true, the sitting of the Parliament is by the order of the Houses themselves, accommodated as well as the place will admit; but how much more beautiful it would be in such a building, as is above contrived, I leave to the contriver to describe and to other people to judge.

Come we next to Westminster-Hall; 'tis true, it is a very noble Gothick building, ancient, vastly large, and the finest roof of its kind in England, being one hundred feet wide; but what a wretched figure does it make without doors; the front, a vast pinacle or pedement, after the most ancient and almost forgotten part of the Gothick way of working; the building itself, resembles nothing so much as a great barn of three hundred feet long, and really looks like a barn at a distance.

Nay, if we view the whole building from without doors, 'tis like a great pile of something, but a stranger would be much at a loss to know what; and whether it was a house, or a church, or, indeed, a heap of churches; being huddled all together, with differing and distant roofs, some higher, some lower, some standing east and west, some north and south, and some one way, and some another.

The Abbey, or Collegiate Church of Westminster, stands next to this; a venerable old pile of building, it is indeed, but so old and weak, that had it not been taken in hand some years ago, and great cost bestowed in upholding and repairing it, we might, by this time, have called it a heap, not a pile, and not a church, but the ruins of a church.

But it begins to stand upon new legs now, and as they continue to work upon the repairs of it, the face of the whole building will, in a short while, be intirely new.

This is the repository of the British kings and nobility, and very fine monuments are here seen over the graves of our ancient monarchs; the particulars are too long to enter into here, and are so many times described by several authors, that it would be a vain repetition to enter upon it here; besides, we have by no means any room for it.

The monarchs of Great Britain are always crown'd here, even King James II. submitted to it, and to have it perform'd by a Protestant bishop. It is observable, that our kings and queens make always two solemn visits to this church, and very rarely, if ever, come here any more, viz. to be crown'd and to be buried.

Two things I must observe here, and with that I close the

account of it. 1. 'Tis very remarkable, that the royal vault, in which the English royal family was laid, was filled up with Queen Ann; so that just as the family was extinct above, there was no room to have buried any more below. 2. It is become such a piece of honour to be buried in Westminster-Abbey, that the body of the church begins to be crowded with the bodies of citizens, poets, seamen, and parsons, nay, even with very mean persons, if they have but any way made themselves known in the world; so that in time, the royal ashes will be thus mingled with common dust, that it will leave no room either for king or common people, or at least not for their monuments, some of which also are rather pompously foolish, than solid and to the purpose.

Near to this church is the Royal Free-School, the best of its kind in England, not out-done either by Winchester or Eaton, for a number of eminent scholars.

The antiquities of this church, for it is very ancient, are published by two or three several authors; but are particularly to be seen in Dugdale's *Monasticon*. The revenues of it were very great, and the abbot sat as a spiritual peer in the House of Lords. The revenues are still very large, and the dean is generally Bishop of Rochester; the fate of the late bishop I desire to bury with him, who is gone to oblivion. The Dean and Chapter have still great privileges as well as revenues, and particularly the civil government, or temporal jurisdiction of the city of Westminster, is so far in them, that the High-Steward and the High-Bailiff are named by them absolutely, without any reserve either to king or people. Their present High-Steward is the Earl of Arran, brother to the late Duke of Ormond, and their High-Bailiff, is William Norris, Esq.

Being got into this part of Westminster, I shall finish it as I go, that I may not return; 'Tis remarkable, that the whole city, called properly, Westminster, and standing on the S. side of the park, is but one parish, and is the only city of one parish in England. There is now another great church erected, or rather erecting, by the commissioners for building fifty new churches; but they have been strangely mistaken in the situation, which is a fenny marshy ground, and it is not found so able to support the weight as, perhaps, they were told it would; I say no more. The building was very curious, especially the roof; but the towers are not so beautiful as it is thought was intended, the foundation not being to be trusted.

The Earl of Peterborough's house stands at the extremity of

the buildings, and is the point of measurement for the length of London, which from that house to Lime-house, is reckoned seven miles and a quarter, and some rods: This house might have been a monitor for the builders of the new church, for they tell us it has sunk several yards, since it was first built, tho' this I do not affirm.

There are three chapels of ease to St. Margaret's in this part of Westminster, besides that, great numbers of people go to the Abbey, so that there is no want of churches. There is but one meeting-house in this whole part, which is called Calamy's Meeting, and was formerly supplied by Mr. Stephen Lobb, who, tho' a Dissenter, lived and died a Jacobite.

The Cottonian Library is kept here in an ancient building, near Westminster-Hall gate; we were told it would be removed to the royal library, and then, that it would be removed to a house to be built on purpose; but we see neither yet in hand. This is one of the most valuable collections in Britain, and, the Bodleian Library excepted, is, perhaps, the best: It has in it some books and manuscripts invaluable for their antiquity; but I have not room so much as to enter upon giving an account of the particulars.

This part of Westminster has but one street, which gives it a communication with London, and this is called King-street, a long, dark, dirty and very inconvenient passage; but there seems to be no remedy for it, for most passengers get out of it through the Privy Garden, and some by private passages into the park, as at Locket's, at the Cock-Pit, and the new gate from Queen's-Square; but these are all upon sufferance.

From hence we come through two very handsome, tho' ancient gates, into the open palace before White-Hall and the Banqueting-house.

Having mentioned White-Hall already, I have nothing more to say of it, but that it was, and is not, but may revive. There is, doubtless, a noble situation, fit to contain a royal palace, equal to Versailles; but I have given you my thoughts on that subject at large.

Nor can I dwell here upon a description of his majesty's Court, or an account of the politicks managed there; it does not relate to this work; let it suffice to say, his majesty resides, especially all the winter, at St. James's; but the business of the government, is chiefly carried on at the Cock-pit: This is a royal building, was once part of White-hall, first the Duke of Monmouth lived in it, then Prince George of Denmark and his princess, afterwards Queen Ann, and since the fire at White-Hall, the Treasury, the Secretary's office, the Council Chamber, the Board of Trade, and the Lord Chamberlain, hold all their particular offices here; and here there is also, a by-way out of Duke-street into the park.

From thence we come to the Horse Guards, a building commodious enough, built on purpose, as a barrack for a large detachment of the Horse-Guards, who keep their post here, while attending on duty; over it are offices for payment of the troops, and a large court of judicature, for holding councils of war, for tryal of deserters and others, according to the articles of war.

In the same range of buildings, stood the Admiralty Office, built by the late King William; but tho' in itself a spacious building, is found so much too narrow now the business is so much increased, and as there is a sufficient piece of spare ground behind it, to inlarge the building, we find a new and spacious office is now building in the same place, which shall be sufficient to all the uses required.

This office is, perhaps, of the most importance of any of the publick parts of the administration, the royal navy being the sinews of our strength, and the whole direction of it being in the hands of the commissioners for executing this office. The Navy and the Victualling Offices, are but branches of this administration, and receive their orders from hence, as likewise the docks and yards receive their orders from the navy: the whole being carried on with the most exquisite order and dispatch. The Admiralty has been in commission ever since the death of Prince George; the present commissioners are,

Right Honourable James Earl of Berkeley.
Sir John Jennings.
John Cockburn, Esq;
William Chetwynd, Esq;
Sir John Norris.
Sir Charles Wager.
Daniel Pultney, Esq;

From this part of the town, we come into the publick streets, where nothing is more remarkable than the hurries of the people; Charing-Cross is a mixture of Court and city; Man's Coffee-house is the Exchange Alley of this part of the town, and 'tis perpetually throng'd with men of business, as the others are with men of play and pleasure.

From hence advancing a little, we see the great equestrian statue of King Charles the First in brass, a costly, but a curious piece; however, it serves sufficiently, to let us know who it is, and why erected there. The circumstances are two, he faces the place where his enemies [1] triumph'd over him, and triumphs, that is, tramples in the place where his murtherers were hang'd.[2]

From this place due north, are the king's stables, called the Meuse, where the king's horses, especially his coach-horses, are kept, and the coaches of state are set up; it is a very large place, and takes up a great deal of ground, more than is made use of: It contains two large squares, besides an out-let east, where is the managerie for teaching young gentlemen to ride the great saddle; in the middle of the first court is a smith or farryer's house and shop, a pump and horse-pond, and I see little else remarkable, but old scatter'd buildings; and, indeed, this place standing where a noble square of good buildings might be erected, I do not wonder that they talk of pulling it down, contracting the stables into less room, and building a square of good houses there, which would, indeed, be a very great improvement, and I doubt not will be done.

On the right side of the street, coming from White-Hall, is Northumberland-House, so called, because belonging to the Northumberland family for some ages; but descending to the Duke of Somerset in right of marriage, from the late dutchess, heiress of the house of Piercy.

'Tis an ancient, but a very good house, the only misfortune of its situation is, its standing too near the street; the back part of the house is more modern and beautiful than the front, and when you enter the first gate, you come into a noble square fronting the fine lodgings: 'Tis a large and very well design'd building, and fit to receive a retinue of one hundred in family; nor does the duke's family come so far short of the number, as not very handsomely to fill the house.

The present duke having married the greatest heiress in Britain, and enjoy'd her and the estate for above forty years, and besides, having been master of the horse many years also, he is immensely rich, and very well merits the good fortune he has met with.

Advancing thence to the Hay-Market, we see, first, the great new theatre, a very magnificent building, and perfectly accom-

---

[1] The statue faces the broad place before White-Hall, where the king was beheaded.

[2] The gibet, where the regicides were executed, stood just where the statue now stands.

modated for the end for which it was built, tho' the entertainment there of late, has been chiefly operas and balls.

These meetings are called BALLS, the word *masquerade* not being so well relished by the English, who, tho' at first fond of the novelty, began to be sick of the thing on many accounts; However, as I cannot in justice say any thing to recommend them, and am by no means, to make this work be a satyr upon any thing; I choose to say no more; but go on.

From hence westward and northward, lie those vastly extended buildings, which add so exceedingly to the magnitude of the whole body, and of which I have already said so much: It would be a task too great for this work, to enter into a description of all the fine houses, or rather palaces of the nobility in these parts: To touch them superficially, and by halves, is too much to imitate what I complain of in others, and as I design a particular account of all the houses of the nobility and men of quality in London, and the country fifteen miles round, in a work by itself; I bespeak my readers patience, and go on.

The hospitals in and about the city of London, deserve a little further observation, especially those more remarkable for their magnitude, as,

I. Bethlem or Bedlam: This and Bridewell, indeed, go together, for though they are two several houses, yet they are incorporated together, and have the same governors; also the president, treasurer, clerk, physician and apothecary are the same; but the stewards and the revenue are different, and so are the benefactions; but to both very great.

The orders for the government of the hospital of Bethlem are exceeding good, and a remarkable instance of the good disposition of the gentlemen concerned in it, especially these that follow;

1. That no person, except the proper officers who tend them, be allowed to see the lunaticks of a Sunday.

2. That no person be allowed to give the lunaticks strong drink, wine, tobacco or spirits, or to sell any such thing in the hospital.

3. That no servant of the house shall take any money given to any of the lunaticks to their own use; but that it shall be carefully kept for them till they are recovered, or laid out for them in such things as the committee approves.

4. That no officer or servant shall beat or abuse, or offer any force to any lunatick; but on absolute necessity. The rest of the orders are for the good government of the house.

*N 820

This hospital was formerly in the street now called Old Bedlam, and was very ancient and ruinous: The new building was erected at the charge of the city in 1676, and is the most beautiful structure for such a use that is in the world, and was finished from its foundation in fifteen months; it was said to be taken ill at the Court of France, that it was built after the fashion of one of the King of France's palaces.

The number of people who are generally under cure in this hospital, is from 130 to 150 at a time.

There are great additions now making to this hospital, particularly for the relief and subsistence of incurables, of which no full account can be given, because they are not yet finished, or the full revenue ascertained: The first benefactor and author of this design itself, was Sir William Withers late alderman, and who had been lord mayor, who left 500l. to begin it with.

II. The hospital of Bridewell, as it is an hospital, so it is also a house of correction. The house was formerly the king's city palace; but granted to the city to be in the nature of what is now called a work-house, and has been so employed, ever since the year 1555.

As idle persons, vagrants, &c. are committed to this house for correction, so there are every year, several poor lads brought up to handicraft trades, as apprentices, and of these the care is in the governors, who maintain them out of the standing revenues of the house.

There are two other Bridewells, properly so called, that is to say, houses of correction; one at Clarkenwell, called New Prison, being the particular Bridewell for the county of Middlesex, and another in Tuttle-fields, for the city of Westminster.

The other city hospitals, are the Blue-coat Hospital for poor freemens orphan children, and the two hospitals for sick and maimed people, as St. Bartholomew's and St. Thomas's: These three are so well known by all people that have seen the city of London, and so universally mention'd by all who have written of it, that little can be needful to add; however I shall say something as an abridgment.

III. Christ's Hospital was originally constituted by King Edward VI. who has the honour of being the founder of it, as also of Bridewell; but the original design was, and is owing to the lord mayor and aldermen of London, and the Christian endeavours of that glorious martyr, Dr. Ridley then Bishop of London, who never ceased moving his charitable master, the king, till he brought him to join in the foundation. The design is for entertaining, educating, nourishing and bringing up the poor children of the citizens, such as, their parents being dead, or fathers, at least, have no way to be supported, but are reduced to poverty.

Of these, the hospital is now so far increased in substance, by the benefactions of worthy gentlemen contributors, they now maintain near a thousand, who have food, cloathing and instruction, useful and sufficient learning, and exceeding good discipline; and at the proper times they are put out to trades, suitable to their several genius's and capacities, and near five thousand pounds a year are expended on this charity.

IV. St. Bartholomew's Hospital adjoyns to Christ Church, and St. Thomas's is in Southwark, both which, however, being the same in kind, their description may come under one head, tho' they are, indeed, two foundations, and differently incorporated: The first founder is esteem'd to be King Henry VIII. whose statue in stone and very well done, is, for that very reason, lately erected in the new front, over the entrance to the Cloyster in West-Smithfield: The king gave 500 marks a year, towards the support of the house, which was then founded for an hundred poor sick, and the city was obliged to add 500 marks a year more to it.

From this small beginning, this hospital rose to the greatness we now see it arrived at, of which take the following account for one year, viz. 1718;

Cur'd and discharg'd, of sick, maimed and wounded, from all parts	3088
Buried at the expence of the house	198
Remaining under cure	513

V. St. Thomas's Hospital in Southwark, has a different foundation, but to the same purpose; it is under the same government, viz. the lord mayor, aldermen and commonalty of the city of London, and had a revenue of about 2000*l*. per annum, about 100 years ago.

This hospital has received greater benefactions than St. Bartholomew's; but then 'tis also said to have suffered greater losses, especially by several great fires in Southwark and elsewhere, as by the necessity of expensive buildings, which, notwithstanding the charitable gifts of divers great benefactors, has cost the hospital great sums. The state of this hospital is so advanced at this time, that in the same year as above, viz. 1718, the state of the house was as follows;

Cur'd and discharged of sick, wounded and maimed, from all parts	} 3608
Buried at the expence of the house	216
Remaining under cure	566

Adjoining to this of St. Thomas's, is lately laid a noble foundation of a new hospital, by the charitable gift and single endowment of one person, and, perhaps, the greatest of its kind, next to that of Sutton's Hospital, that ever was founded in this nation by one person, whether private or publick, not excepting the kings themselves.

This will, I suppose, be called Guy's Hospital, being to be built and endowed at the sole charge of one Mr. Thomas Guy, formerly a bookseller in Lombard Street, who lived to see the said hospital not only design'd, the ground purchased and cleared, but the building begun, and a considerable progress made in it, and died while these sheets were in the press.

It was not till this gentleman died, that the world were told it was to be a separate hospital; but it was generally understood to have been intended for a ward, or an addition to the old hospital of St. Thomas's, for the reception of such as were accounted incurable.

But when Mr. Guy died, his will being made publick, it appeared, that it was really a separate, independent and distinct hospital, under distinct governors, and for a separate purpose, to wit, for receiving such poor persons as have been dismissed from other hospitals as incurable.

Nor are these restrained to the patients of the adjoining hospital of St. Thomas only; but they are allowed to receive such from St. Bartholomew's also, and also from Bethlehem, only with this restriction as to the latter, That the number of incurable lunaticks shall never exceed twenty at a time.

This hospital is, by Mr. Guy's will, to consist of two great squares of buildings, in which, besides the offices and accommodation for necessary servants and overseers, who must be lodg'd in the house, such as stewards, treasurer, masters, matrons, nurses, &c. are to be beds and appartments furnished for four hundred patients, who are all to be supplied with lodging and attendance, food and physick.

What the revenue, when settled, will be; what the building will amount to when finished; what the purchase of the land, and what the expence of finishing and furnishing it, cannot be estimated, 'till it be further look'd into; but we are told without doors, that besides all the expence of purchase, building, furnishing and finishing as above; there will be left more than two hundred thousand pounds for endowing the hospital with a settled revenue, for maintaining the said poor, and yet the charitable founder was so immensely rich, that besides leaving four hundred pounds a year to the Blue-coat Hospital of London, and besides building an hospital for fourteen poor people at Tamworth in Staffordshire, where he was chosen representative; and besides several considerable charities which he had given in his life-time; He also gave away, in legacies, to his relations and others, above a hundred thousand pound more, among which 'tis observable, That there is a thousand pounds a piece given to near eighty several persons, most of them of his own relations; so that he cannot, as has been said by some, be said to give a great charity to the poor, and forget his own family.

How Mr. Guy amass'd all this wealth, having been himself in no publick employment or office of trust, or profit, and only carrying on the trade of a bookseller, till within a few years of his death, that is not the business of this book; 'tis enough to say, he was a thriving, frugal man, who God was pleased exceedingly to bless, in whatever he set his hand to, knowing to what good purposes he laid up his gains: He was never married, and lived to be above eighty years old; so that the natural improvements of this money, by common interest, after it was first grown to a considerable bulk, greatly increased the sum.

This hospital is left to the immediate direction of his executors, and the governors, named in his will, who are at present most of them, if not all, governors of St. Thomas's Hospital, and he has appointed them to apply to his majesty and the Parliament to have them incorporated. The executors are as follows;

Sir Gregory Page, Bart. appointed also to be first president of the corporation, when obtained.
Charles Joy, Esq; appointed also treasurer of the house.
William Clayton, Esq;
Mr. Thomas Hollis Sen.
John Kenrick, Esq;
John Lade, Esq;
Dr. Richard Mead
Moses Raper, Esq;
Mr. John Sprint.

Also he desires, That when the corporation shall be obtained as above, either by Letters Patent or Act of Parliament, all the nine persons named as above, to be his executors, with the fourteen following, may be the first committee for managing the said charity, viz.

Mr. Benj. Braine, Sen.	Mr. Matthew Howard
Mr. Thomas Clarke	Mr. Samuel Lessingham
William Cole, Esq;	Mr. Henry Lovell
Dr. William Crow	Mr. Samuel Monk
Dr. Francis Fanquier	Mr. Joseph Price
Dr. Edward Hulse	Mr. Daniel Powell
Mr. Joshua Gee	Mr. Thomas Stiles.

Next to these hospitals, whose foundations are so great and magnificent, is the work-house, or city work-house, properly so called, which being a late foundation, and founded upon meer charity, without any settled endowment, is the more remarkable, for here are a very great number of poor children taken in, and supported and maintained, fed, cloath'd, taught, and put out to trades, and that at an exceeding expence, and all this without one penny revenue.

It is establish'd, or rather the establishment of it, is supported by an old Act of Parliament, 13, 14. Car. II. impowering the citizens to raise contributions for the charge of employing the poor, and suppressing vagrants and beggars, and it is now, by the voluntary assistance and bounty of benefactors, become so considerable, that in the year 1715 they gave the following state of the house, viz.

Vagabonds, beggars, &c. taken into the house, including fifty-five which remained at the end of the preceding year - - - - - - - - - 418

Discharged, including such as were put out to trades - - - - - - - - - - - - - - 356

Remaining in the house 62

Not one buried that whole year.

But the supplies and charities to this commendable work, have not of late come in so readily as they used to do, which has put the governors to some difficulties; upon which, anno 1614, the Common Council, by virtue of the powers above-mentioned, agreed to raise five thousand pounds upon the whole city, for the support of the house; but we do not find that any new demand has been made since that.

There are three considerable charities given by private persons in the city of Westminster, viz.

1. The Gray-coat Hospital, founded by a generous subscription or contribution; but chiefly by the charity of one —— Sands, Esq; It maintains 70 boys and 40 girls, cloathed, fed, and taught, and in some measure provided for, by being put out to trades.

2. The Green-coat Hospital, in the same Fields, founded by King Charles I. for poor fatherless children of St. Margaret's parish; and next to this hospital is the house of correction, or the Westminster Bridewell.

3. The Emanuel Hospital, founded by the Lady Ann Dacres, for ten poor men, and ten poor women, in the forty-third year of Queen Elizabeth. Near this, are seven several setts of alms-houses; but not of any magnitude to be called hospitals.

There has been, also, a very noble hospital erected by contribution of the French refugees, for the maintenance of their poor: It stands near the Pest-house, in the foot-way to Islington in the parish of Cripplegate, and two ranges of new alms-houses in Kingsland Road beyond Shoreditch Church.

The hospital call'd the Charter House, or Sutton's Hospital, is not by this supposed to be forgot, or the honour of it lessen'd. On the other hand, it must be recorded for ever, to be the greatest and noblest gift that ever was given for charity, by any one man, publick or private, in this nation, since history gives us any account of things; even not the great Bishop of Norwich excepted, who built the great church of Yarmouth, the cathedral at Norwich, and the church of St. Mary's at Lynn; The revenue of Mr. Sutton's hospital being, besides the purchase of the place, and the building of the house, and other expences, little less than 6000l. per annum revenue.

The Royal Hospitals at Greenwich and Chelsea, are also not mentioned in this account, as not being within the reach of the most extended bounds of the city of London.

These are the principal hospitals, the rest of smaller note are touch'd before; but it will not be a useless observation, nor altogether improper to take notice of it here, That this age has produced some of the most eminent acts of publick charity, and of the greatest value, I mean from private persons, that can be found in any age within the reach of our English history, excepting only that of Sutton's Hospital; and yet they tell us, that even that of Mr. Sutton's is exceeded in this of Mr. Guy's, considering that this gentleman gave a very noble gift to this same hospital before; besides that as before, he had left an hundred thousand pounds in private gifts among his own relations; as to children he had none, for he never was married.

The other benefactions, I speak of which this age had produced, are already touch'd at in this work, and may be referred to in the reading, such as Dr. Ratcliff's Gift, amounting to above forty thousand pounds to the university of Oxford: The gift of ten thousand pounds to Magdalen College in the same university, by their late representative; the several charities of Sir Robert Clayton, Alderman Ask, Sir Stephen Fox, Dr. Busby, Sir John Morden and others.

These, added to the innumerable number of alms-houses which are to be seen in almost every part of the city, make it certain, that there is no city in the world can shew the like number of charities from private hands, there being, as I am told, not less than twenty thousand people maintained of charity, besides the charities of schooling for children, and besides the collections yearly at the annual feasts of several kinds, where money is given for putting out children apprentices, &c. so that the Papists have no reason to boast, that there were greater benefactions and acts of charity to the poor given in their times, than in our Protestant times; and this is indeed, one of the principal reasons for my making mention of it in this place; for let any particular age be singled out, and let the charities of this age, that is to say, for about fifteen or twenty years past, and the sums of money bestowed by protestants in this nation on meer acts of charity to the poor, not reckoning gifts to the church, be cast up, it will appear they are greater by far, than would be found in England in any the like number of years, take the time when we will.

Nor do I conclude in this, the money collected by briefs all over England, upon casualties by fire, though that is an eminent act of charity as any can be; nor the money given either in publick or private, for re-building St. Paul's and other churches demolished by the Fire of London, or the augmentation of poor benefices by the bounty of Queen Ann, and many other such gifts.

I come now to an account of new edifices and publick buildings, erected or erecting in and about London, since the writing the foregoing account; and with this I conclude.

1. The fine new church of St. Martin's in the Fields, with a very fine steeple, which they tell us is 215 feet high, all wholly built by the contribution of that great parish, and finished with the utmost expedition.

2. The new Admiralty Office near White-hall, being on the same ground where the old office stood; but much larger, being both longer in front and deeper backward, not yet finished.

3. Mr. Guy's new hospital for incurables, mentioned above, situated on ground purchased for that purpose, adjoyning to St. Thomas's Hospital in Southwark, being a most magnificent building not yet quite finished.

4. Two large wings to the hospital of Bedlam, appointed also for incurables; proposed first by the charitable disposition of Sir William Withers deceased; this also not yet finished.

5. A large new meeting-house in Spittle-fields, for the sect of Dissenters, call'd Baptists, or Antepædo Baptists.

6. The South-Sea House in Threadneedle-street, the old house being intirely pulled down, and several other houses adjoyning being purchased, the whole building will be new from the foundation; this not finished.

7. Several very fine new churches, being part of the fifty churches appointed by Act of Parliament, viz. One in Spittle-fields, one in Radcliff-High-way, one in Old-street, one at Lime-house, with a very beautiful tower, and one in Bloomsbury, and five more not finished.

8. The parish church of St. Botolph without Bishopsgate, pulled down and re-building, by the contribution of the inhabitants, not as one of the fifty churches.

N.B. In removing the corpses buried in this church, they found the body of Sir Paul Pindar, buried there about eighty years before, which was taken up and deposited again; and we are told, a new monument will be set up for him by the parish, to which he was a good benefactor.

9. The Custom-house, which since the late fire in Thames-street, is ordered to be inlarged; but is not yet finished.

All these buildings are yet in building, and will all, in their several places, be very great ornaments to the city.

10. A new street or range of houses taken out of the south side of the Artillery Ground near Morefields, also an enlarge-ment to the new burying ground as it was formerly called, on the north side of the same ground.

11. The iron ballustrade, or as others call it, balcony, on the lanthorn upon the cupola of St. Paul's Church, gilded. It was done at the cost and as the gift of an Irish nobleman, who scarce lived to see it finished.

12. A new bear-garden, called Figg's Theater, being a stage

for the gladiators or prize-fighters, and is built on the Tyburn Road.

N.B. The gentlemen of the science, taking offence at its being called Tyburn Road, though it really is so, will have it called the Oxford Road; this publick edifice is fully finished, and in use.

I conclude this account of London, with mentioning something of the Account of Mortality, that is to say, the births and burials, from whence Sir William Petty thought he might make some calculations of the numbers of the inhabitants, and I shall only take notice, that whereas, the general number of the burials in the year 1666, and farther back, were from 17000 to 19000 in a year, the last yearly bill for the year 1723, amounted as follows,

Christenings 19203.   Burials 29197.

Here is to be observed, that the number of burials exceeding so much the number of births, is, because as it is not the number born, but the number christened that are set down, which is taken from the parish register; so all the children of Dissenters of every sort, Protestant, Popish and Jewish are omitted, also all the children of foreigners, French, Dutch, &c. which are baptized in their own churches, and all the children of those who are so poor, that they cannot get them registred: So that if a due estimate be made, the births may be very well supposed to exceed the burials one year with another by many thousands.

It is not that I have no more to say of London, that I break off here; but that I have no room to say it, and tho' some things may be taken notice of by others, which I have pass'd over; yet I have also taken notice of so many things which others have omitted, that I claim the ballance in my favour.

I am, SIR,

Yours, &c.

THE END OF THE FIFTH LETTER

END OF VOL. I

BIOGRAPHY

CLASSICAL

ESSAYS AND BELLES-LETTRES

4

ORATORY

POETRY AND DRAMA

REFERENCE

ROMANCE

SCIENCE

THEOLOGY AND PHILOSOPHY

TRAVEL AND TOPOGRAPHY

EVERYMAN'S LIBRARY was founded in 1906, and the series stands without rival today as the world's most comprehensive low-priced collection of books of classic measure. It was conceived as a library covering the whole field of English literature, including translations of the ancient classics and outstanding foreign works; a series to make widely available those great books which appeal to every kind of reader, and which in essence form the basis of western culture. The aim and scope of the series was crystallized in the title Everyman's Library, justified by world sales totalling (by 1960) some forty-four millions.

There were, of course, already in being in 1906 other popular series of reprints, but none on the scale proposed for Everyman. One hundred and fifty-five volumes were published in three batches in the Library's first year; they comprised a balanced selection from many branches of literature and set the standard on which the Library has been built up. By the outbreak of the First World War the Library was moving towards its 750th volume; and, in spite of the interruptions of two world wars, the aim of the founder-publisher, a library of a thousand volumes, was achieved by the jubilee in 1956, with Aristotle's *Metaphysics* translated by John Warrington.

In March 1953 a fresh development of the Library began: new volumes and all new issues of established volumes in Everyman's Library were now made in a larger size. The larger volumes have new title-pages, bindings and wrappers, and the text pages have generous margins. Four hundred and twenty-two volumes in this improved format had been issued by 1960. In that year new pictorial wrappers appeared and they have provided the volumes with a surprisingly contemporary 'look'.

Editorially the Library is under constant survey; volumes are examined and brought up to date, with new introductions, annotations and additional matter; often a completely new translation or a newly edited text is substituted when transferring an old volume to the new format. New editions of Pepys's *Diary*, Caesar's *War Commentaries*, *The Anglo-Saxon Chronicle* and Professor T. M. Raysor's reorganization of Coleridge's *Shakespearean Criticism* are examples of this type of revision.

The new larger volumes are in keeping with the original 'home-library' plan but are also in a suitable size for the shelves of all institutional libraries, more so since many important works in Everyman's Library are unobtainable in any other edition. This development entails no break in the continuity of the Library; and fresh titles and verified editions are being constantly added.

A Classified Annotated Catalogue of the library is available free, the annotations giving the year of birth and death of the author, the date of first publication of the work and in many instances descriptive notes on the contents of the last revised Everyman's Library edition. Also available (as a volume in the Library, No. 889) is A. J. Hoppe's *The Reader's Guide to Everyman's Library*, revised and reissued in 1961. It gives in one alphabetical sequence references and cross-references of a comprehensive kind, including all authors and all works, even works included in anthologies, and a factual annotation of each work. Running to more than 400 pages, and referring to 1,260 authors, it is virtually a guide to all books of classic standing in the English language.